Out of the Ivory Tower:
Feminist Research for Social Change

Out of the Ivory Tower:

Feminist Research for Social Change

Edited by

ANDREA MARTINEZ

&

MERYN STUART

SUMACH
PRESS

WOMEN'S ISSUES PUBLISHING PROGRAM

SERIES EDITOR BETH MCAULEY

NATIONAL LIBRARY OF CANADA CATALOGUING IN PUBLICATION DATA

Out of the ivory tower: feminist research for social change/
edited by Andrea Martinez and Meryn Stuart.

Includes bibliographical references.
ISBN 1-894549-24-4

1. Women — Social conditions. 2. Women — Canada —
Social conditions. 3. Feminism. I. Martinez, Andrea, 1955-
II. Stuart, Meryn Elisabeth

HQ1206.O88 2003   305.42   C2003-904869-1

Edited by Beth McAuley
Design by Liz Martin

*Sumach Press acknowledges the support of the Canada Council for the Arts
and the Ontario Arts Council for our publishing program.
We acknowledge the Government of Ontario through the
Ontario Media Development Corporation's Ontario Book Initiative.*

ONTARIO ARTS COUNCIL
CONSEIL DES ARTS DE L'ONTARIO

Printed and bound in Canada

Published by

SUMACH PRESS
1415 Bathurst Street #202
Toronto, Canada
M5R 3H8

sumachpress@on.aibn.com
www.sumachpress.com

CONTENTS

Acknowledgements

We would like to thank, first of all, Margot Charbonneau, who has been our most constant and generous administrative assistant and supporter at the Institute of Women's Studies at the University of Ottawa. Kathleen O'Grady, the Bank of Montreal Visiting Scholar in 2000–2001, worked hard to co-ordinate the beginning of this book. Beth McAuley, Series Editor of the Women's Issues Publishing Program at Sumach Press, gave us encouragement and advice from the beginning to the end of this project. We also wish to thank the peer review panel who responded on time and with diligence. Our families also deserve our appreciation for their belief in us and our efforts. We hope that the contributors are as proud of this book as we are.

Bodies, Spaces and Technologies

Meryn Stuart & Andrea Martinez

THIS COLLECTION OF INNOVATIVE WORK by scholars who are primarily associated with the University of Ottawa's Institute of Women's Studies (IWS)[1] began in the fall of 2000 when the Worldwide March for Women was energizing the women's movement and feminist studies globally. The executive committee of the IWS wanted to take advantage of this momentum to build new links to our colleagues on campus and in the community in order to consolidate feminist research at the University of Ottawa and to promote the dissemination of feminist knowledge to a wider audience outside our walls. While the newly created IWS inspired us to search for more opportunities to work together, we believed that most of us were not aware of the feminist work being done within our university nor how this work could be linked to the wider political agendas we wished to support. Thus, the idea of an anthology that could capture these two important aspects was born.

We opted for an open and rather unusual method of collecting essays and put out a general call for research papers without setting any specific boundaries on what authors should write about. In our attempt to move beyond a fixed approach with rigid thematic demarcations, we did not overlook the fact that we could possibly receive either disparate or conflicted material. The preliminary phase of this project was co-ordinated by Kathleen O'Grady, the Bank of Montreal Visiting Scholar in 2000–2001 at the IWS. Thanks to her hard work and dedication, we received a wide range of contributions that revealed unexpected paths for collaboration between sites of academic production that are traditionally isolated from one another: arts, health sciences, medicine and social sciences. After an insightful reading of the manuscripts, we agreed, indeed, that they all conveyed a complex but dynamic interconnection of feminist voices, and sent them out to be peer-reviewed by external Women's Studies scholars. *Out of the Ivory Tower* evolved as a result of Canadian, multi-disciplinary work that features a diversity of approaches and scholars on the broad topic of women's relationships to their bodies, history, public and private spaces and new technologies. These essays are meant for Women's Studies faculty and students in Canada and elsewhere as well as for social and political activists, policy-makers and educators in the broader feminist community.

As with any discipline, research in Women's Studies, gender studies and feminist studies is replete with endless possibilities and excitement over new insights. And, it goes without saying, that a common set of approaches, experiences and feelings does not drive the feminist community today, nor characterize women in general. Since the late 1980s, essentialist attitudes and thoughts have been challenged by younger feminists, Black feminists, First Nations women, post-structuralists and post-modernists, among others. Along with the recognition that feminist discourses provide renewed analyses and strategies for improving women's lives, *Out of the Ivory Tower* brings to the fore a constellation of issues and concerns relevant to women's political, social and personal lives.

We have ordered the essays in four sections that are built around the following research themes: (1) recovering histories and meanings through the analysis of older (nursing) and newer (science and engineering) professions for women, as well as through the histories of lesbian community activism in a comparative, international focus; (2) "negotiating" the female body as a site of both control and resistance in the family, in cities, in prisons and in the globalized world; (3) shaping equity for women in employment, education and leadership positions; and (4) negotiating the "new" technologies in cyberspace. In contrast to a monolithic feminist approach, each of these themes interfaces with issues of gender, race, ethnicity, social class, language, age and sexual orientation. More specifically, our collection explores the social construction of binary opposites or categories such as victim and perpetrator; uncontrolled woman and suburban housewife; docile and resistant body; masculinity and femininity; public and private space; women's work and men's work; heterosexual and lesbian/bisexual; equity and inequity; and sexual and asexual identities. The chapters in this book deconstruct and re-conceptualize these differences and tensions.

Section I: Recovering Histories and Meanings

One of the basic questions in this book is: How do we understand our relationship to others, to culture and to the world? Many feminists argue that women do this through our bodies, namely, through the ways our bodies are so often "on the line" in situations such as abortion, murder, "coming out" as a lesbian, being racialized or being incarcerated in prison. As feminist scholar Sherene Razack put it recently, anti-racist encounters have to be explained "up close" — through the accelerating heart rate, for example, or at the level of the material body.[2] We are also conscious that women's bodies must be tamed, purified and mediated through human effort, often with painful consequences, as in, for example, the ancient cultural "fashion" of foot binding in China, through female genital mutilation or through cosmetics and plastic surgery.[3]

We need to look back in time to help us see how women's bodies were shaped (and, indeed, damaged) by the dominant discourses around sexuality, femininity and the appropriate behaviour for women when they occupied previously male-dominated space. How did women resist? How did they acquiesce? What is unspoken? In the first chapter, Sharon Cook explores the "many silences" surrounding young women and the smoking of cigarettes. She examines Canadian educational texts of the early to late twentieth century and, surprisingly, finds that Canadian health textbooks have never addressed smoking as a gendered behaviour. Only in the past two decades has public health begun to include girls and women in discussions of the dangers of smoking. Cook also examines film and television as a source for her analysis and finds that these media sources encourage smoking by girls because smoking is so frequent and because it is often associated with an actress's "ideal" body type.

In chapter 2, Ruby Heap looks at the history of women in science and engineering in Canada, beginning her historical account with the Montreal Massacre of 1989, when female students in engineering school were murdered because they were women. Her historical account then traces the spaces created for middle-class white women in science in the early twentieth century and those that were narrowed dramatically after the Second World War when women were encouraged to retreat from their scientific careers and into full-time marriages. She emphasizes why it is important to study women and their relationship to science and technology and highlights the gender-specific experiences of many female scientists and engineers.

In chapter 3, literary critic Tina O'Toole explores the history of lesbians organizing for their own space in society and in the women's movement in Ireland and in Canada. The reader sees how women's bodies (and feminism itself) were literally "on the line" with issues such as abortion, divorce, "coming out" and lesbian parenting and custody in the 1970s and 1980s. Lesbians endured personal violence, rape, ostracism, losing jobs and even death in this period, as they organized to clear spaces for differences *among* women and finally began using the Internet in order to bring women together over wide geographical areas. Irish lesbian and Canadian lesbian experiences were remarkably similar, although mobilization began about a decade earlier in Canada.

In the last chapter of this section, Cynthia Toman examines the second generation of military nurses in Canada, known by rank and title as Nursing Sisters, as they negotiated relationships with men and experienced the sexualization of their bodies within the hegemonic male military hierarchy. The nurses' "relative" rank meant that they inhabited the space between male military authority and female powerlessness over male soldiers, unless the soldiers were hospital orderlies. The signs and signifiers of the use of nurses' bodies in the medical technologies of war are surprising, and Toman's analysis reveals the dominant discourse of war-time femininity and masculinity.

Section II: The Language of Sexuality: "Negotiating" the Female Body

The appropriation of women's bodies by the penal system, by the medical system or by male familial domination is a focus of much of feminist research. The essays in this section are no exception, focusing on the idea that patriarchal power in all its forms and theoretical analyses must be grounded historically and culturally, as must resistance, agency and autonomy.[4]

In chapter 5, Aoua LY-Tall explores the ways in which female genital mutilation (FGM) has been brought to North America from Africa, and how it continues to damage the lives of girls and women. Globalization and the transnational characteristic of the treatment of women's bodies are powerfully examined. Although LY-Tall reminds us that European (white) societies, and others, have also practised FGM in the past, in sub-Saharan Africa today, six thousand young girls a day are subjected to this procedure. She concludes with a discussion of the strategies developed by the African women's movement whose hope is that FGM will be eliminated by 2015.

Sylvie Frigon's essay in chapter 6 gives us a comprehensive analysis of the "simultaneous construction of the bodies of incarcerated women as *sites of control* and as *sites of resistance,* as well as the notions of the *dangerous body* and *the body in danger* in order to uncover how the (re)production of the 'docile body' operates." How does confinement mark the body? How are penal laws imprinted on it? How is governance achieved through it? Frigon's investigation of the management of the "dangerous" body uses the case of the Emergency Response Team's intervention at the Kingston Penitentiary for Women in April 1994. During the raid, women inmates were strip searched and segregated by male guards in a brutal and gendered fashion that "marked" their bodies in the process. Her poignant exploration of women's lived experiences in prison challenges our interpretation of how their sufferings, their desires, their alienation and their pleasures are engraved on their bodies and mediated through their creative works.

In chapter 7, Michelle Mullen looks at empirical research in bioethics, drawing on research in the practice of using electively aborted fetal tissue (FTT) for medical treatment of a variety of debilitating or fatal medical conditions. She argues that "a concern with the maldistribution of power and opportunity within society is central to a feminist bioethics as it seeks to evaluate the ethical and human impact of new healthcare practices and their impact on marginalized groups." Mullen also examines what it means to undertake empirical, feminist bioethics research from a methodological point of view. Her analysis of the different ways in which (male and female) medical practitioners who perform elective abortions and female counsellors in abortion clinics view the ethics of both informed consent and women's right to know is both surprising and disturbing. Her findings speak to how FTT practices and debate evolved with very little attention paid to how it reflected prevalent attitudes towards women or to women's voices in the matter.

Chapter 8, the final chapter in this section, by Agatha Schwartz explores the idea of women as both *victims and perpetrators* and the related question of female aggression. Using the literary fiction of two contemporary Austrian women writers, Elfriede Jelinek *(Lust)* and Lilian Faschinger

(Magdalena the Sinner), Schwartz examines the theme of the woman as victim who becomes perpetrator — the murder-infanticide of a male child in *Lust* and the murder of seven lovers in *Magdalena the Sinner.* In analyzing the narratives of these two novels, and in discussing media and societal reactions to each, Schwartz turns on its head the idea that these two concepts as applied to women (victim and perpetrator) are binary opposites. In fact, these protagonists have stepped out of the frame of the female victim's expected behaviour and exposed acts of resistance to brutality within marriage (in *Lust*) and to abuse and patriarchy in personal sexual relationships (in *Magdalena the Sinner*).

Section III: Shaping Equity for Women in Public Spaces

Inequity has been defined by the 1984 Royal Commission on Equality of Employment "as a systemic condition that intentionally or accidentally limit[s] an individual's or a group's right to opportunities generally available." The Commission designated four groups as disproportionately disadvantaged: Aboriginal peoples, visible minorities, persons with disabilities and women.[5] This section analyzes the equity/inequity issues that continue to pervade women's lives, particularly racialized, working-class and other marginalized groups of women in the public sphere.

In chapter 9, Caroline Andrew looks at "gender as a constitutive element in the analysis of Canadian urban space." She asks: What are women doing in urban landscapes, who are they and what roles do they play in the structuring and restructuring of this landscape? In answering these questions, Andrew critically examines the urban work of women (paid and volunteer), the discourses on women and cities and current feminist urban policies. Especially interesting are the initiatives around urban safety for women. Raising issues about women's fears of the urban environment (such as walking alone at night) brings up questions about the unequal power of women, and of particular groups of women, and how their bodies are subjected to potential violence and the fear-responses that limit women's security and confidence in themselves.

From the macro-level, we move to the micro-level. In chapter 10, Christabelle Sethna and Donatille Mujawamariya evaluate employment and educational equity at the University of Ottawa since 1988, at which time the university made twenty recommendations in its equity study. In particular, they explore what progress has been made by women at the undergraduate, graduate and professorial levels, especially in the traditionally male faculties of engineering, science and medicine. Race and disability as factors in the hiring of professors are also discussed. Despite the Royal Commission on Equality of Education in the 1980s, they find that, although women have gained some ground at the undergraduate and professorial levels, the percentages of women in the traditionally male and more technological fields are stagnant and that women earn only 93.5 percent of what men do.

Cora Voyageur examines the experiences of fifty-four First Nations female chiefs as they negotiate their multiple roles as women, mothers, administrators, mediators, liaisons, community representatives and decision-makers. She raises the questions: How did they obtain leadership, how do they maintain it, and what are the costs and rewards? Only 15 percent of more than six hundred chiefs in Canada are women, and many of these women have been elected since 1990. Equity with men in First Nations communities has been slow in coming, but the findings support the claim that First Nations women are becoming more politically active and are seeking decision-making roles within their communities. Their public profiles and expectations have meant that their private spaces are disrupted: the community "owns" them as one chief described it. As Voyageur points out, women who are elected to the position of chief emphasize community healing in addition to economic ventures and have developed political savvy in the public arena.

Section IV: The Intersection of Gender, Class, Language and Ethnicity in Cyberspace

The last three chapters of the book look at new and emerging technologies and the ways in which they affect women. They also look at how women are shaping their relationships with new technologies from the margins of the technological epicentres. In chapter 12, Ann Denis and Michèle Ollivier analyze data from the most recent Canadian General Social Survey in order to see how women have fared in the "knowledge-based, networked society." As well, they use data from a survey carried out with senior francophone high-school students in different regions of Ontario. They found that women experience unequal access to the Internet as a result of their lower household incomes and lack of control over their time. In addition, they found that race and language inequities have widened the accessibility gap between women and men and between the French-speaking and English-speaking. Women are labelled as somehow deficient when it comes to technology, by both feminists and others, and "this may inadvertently contribute to the reproduction of a binary conception of the world ... in which the Internet is seen as a threatening and unsafe space for them."

Andrea Martinez and Elizabeth Turcotte offer complementary reflections on the contributions that Aboriginal women of the Americas have made to opening democratic spaces of action through the Internet. In chapter 13, the authors explore selective Web sites in order "to better understand the role that the Internet plays in their ability to ... weave a 'rhizomatic' (horizontal and underground) new, gender-based fabric of struggle." They reiterate that the Internet has played a critical role in the development of a "global sense of proximity," but that old patterns of cultural domination continue to be reinforced. In this context, Aboriginal women in North, Central and South America are elaborating new kinds of electronic grassroots communication that are very gradually making inroads into developing women's worlds. By looking at the political meanings and opportunities of their democratic electronic connections, the authors reveal the potential of counterhegemonic engagements, despite the uncertainty of outcomes.

In sharp contrast to the historical consciousness that drives political alliances and coalitions among Aboriginal women, the closing chapter by Leslie Regan Shade focuses on the gendering of a recent communication technology, 3Com's Audrey™, an Internet "appliance" rooted in what Nancy Miller calls "the dominant social text."[6] Structured by and experienced as a Western marketing narrative, Audrey™ was meant to be used in a woman's domestic space — in her kitchen and in the private sphere of her world. It was advertised explicitly to upper-class white women who were pictured as the ideal users of this appliance, which would keep track of the whole family through a household calendar. Audrey™ also featured an Internet browser and e-mail capabilities. It was meant to be a "part of the family" and made to look like other appliances in the kitchen. Another new communication technology being developed (which opens like a makeup compact) reflects the woman's body back to her through a "biorhythm calculator" that keeps track of calories and menstrual cycles. In all of these new designs, gender is assumed to involve homogenous characteristics as a state of nature.

Activism and Feminist Research: The Priorities

Our outreach to the wider community, and to activists in particular, is very important to us. The women's movement of the last thirty years has broadened the feminist consciousness in Western society, such that, as American historian Marilyn Boxer points out, "[e]ven women and men who reject the designation 'feminist,' express, as their own, ideas that derive from this women's movement."[7] But there are problems. The growing conservatism in politics and academia, the stress on supporting programs that pay their own way (or reap a profit), as well as the backlash against affirmative action and teaching about gender and race mean that hard choices have been made about who will teach and what will be taught in Women's Studies programs in today's universities.[8]

Younger scholars have criticized Women's Studies departments and individuals for not valuing or rewarding activism in the everyday world. Students are coming to academia with anger about the racism, heterosexism and classism they have experienced in their lives and want to work towards changing that reality. However, these aspirations are often not valued, nor even recognized. As Canadian graduate student Meera Sethi wrote recently:

> To learn just about disengaged theory that has no ties to on-ground activist politics seems to me to be the sort of graduate work that interests only those whose motivations for entering graduate school in the first place did not involve a desire for social change.[9]

We have tried to be sensitive to these issues and have attempted in this collection to address questions of global social change and activism that are being brought to us by our students and by community members. For example, Aoua Boucar LY-Tall's chapter on the global nature of female genital mutilation is directed at action, and describes plans that have been put into place by African and Québécoise women's associations to change this practice. Andrea Martinez and Elizabeth Turcotte's piece is focused on analyzing and sharing Aboriginal women's use of technology so that new ways can be found to elaborate electronic grassroots communication. We also feel that the inclusion of two pieces specifically exploring First Nations women's experiences is an important step in an anti-racist agenda that we wish to actively promote.

However, there is an area that we would have liked to include in order to represent the everyday reality of women's lives. We did not elicit research by, nor about, women with disabilities, nor any papers with a specific "disability" analysis. We regret this, although there are a few very good Canadian collections available in this regard, including those with a women's health focus, and those hard-to-find chapters with an anti-racist/anti-ableist analysis.[10]

Women's exclusion and alienation on the basis of race, ethnicity, disability, language and class are important foci of research in Women's Studies today, although it hasn't always been so. As Somer Brodribb wrote in 1987: "A simple add-women-and-stir approach could not have revealed these biases, or elaborated new conceptual models to grasp these realities."[11] We need new applied theories and analyses to account for racialized constructions of women and for the systematic subordination of, for example, working-class and disabled women. We need the application of post-colonial theory and studies of diaspora and feminisms in global contexts. There is a burgeoning literature in all these fields — some of which is Canadian — that we need to read, discuss and internalize.[12] As Canada becomes increasingly preoccupied with policing borders in the post–September 11 era, we especially need to hear first-person accounts about the effects of post-colonialism and racism on women's lives today and their exclusion from the acclaimed advantages of global capitalism and technology.[13] We need to hear about citizenship and what that means for refugees and immigrants coming to Canada, and how gender, race, class and disability affect women's and men's experiences.

*

We are buoyed up by the vitality and freshness of the new research in this collection. Psychologist Jill Morawski has written:

> To occupy a liminal social zone is not necessarily to be stuck in or stuck by something, but rather to be not so encumbered or detained. Likewise the paradoxes of that position need not be read as debilitating contradictions.[14]

Thus, we have the possibility to transform the way feminist knowledge is produced and read and also how that knowledge connects to the political and social world around us so that change can take place. We hope that the essays in *Out of the Ivory Tower* will stimulate the writing and production of more feminist research in the future.

NOTES

1. The IWS was founded in 1999, replacing the Women's Studies Program, which was first approved in 1983 as an undergraduate program. Courses in Women's Studies have been given in the faculties of social sciences and arts since 1970. The fully bilingual, collaborative master's level program was approved in 1995.

2. Sherene Razack, keynote address at the Body Talk Symposium, University of Ottawa, November 23, 2002. See also her work on gender, race and colonialism, *Looking White People in the Eye: Gender, Race and Culture in Courtrooms and Classrooms* (Toronto: University of Toronto Press, 1999). Two of many recent books on making sense of embodiment in a feminist context are Joan Cassell, *The Woman in the Surgeon's Body* (Cambridge: Harvard University Press, 1998) and Janine Marchessault and Kim Sawchuk, eds., *Wild Science: Reading Feminism, Medicine and the Media* (New York: Routledge, 2000).

3. For a fascinating feminist analysis of footbinding, see Wang Ping, *Aching for Beauty: Footbinding in China* (Minneapolis: University of Minnesota Press, 2000). On the American cosmetic industry, including an analysis of its effect on African-American women, see Kathy Peiss, *Hope in a Jar: The Making of America's Beauty Culture* (New York: Henry Holt, 1998).

4. With thanks to Margaret Lock and Patricia Kaufert's edited book on the medicalization of bodies, *Pragmatic Women and Body Politics* (Cambridge: Cambridge University Press, 1998), for helping us formulate these ideas.

5. Abigail B. Bakan and Audrey Kobayashi, *Employment Equity Policy in Canada: An Interprovincial Comparison* (Ottawa: Status of Women Canada, March 2000), 13–14.

6. Nancy Miller, *Subject to Change: Reading Feminist Writing* (New York: Columbia University Press, 1988), 112.

7. Marilyn Jacoby Boxer, *When Women Ask the Questions: Creating Women's Studies in America* (Baltimore: The Johns Hopkins University Press, 1998), 242.

8. For a cogent discussion of these issues, see the Editorial in *Signs: Journal of Women in Culture and Society,* Special Issue, *Feminisms at a Millennium* 25, no. 4 (Summer 2000), xxiii–xxvi.

9. Meera Sethi, "Out in the Cold: Surviving Graduate School as a Woman of Colour," *Resources for Feminist Research* 29 (2001/2002), 138.

10. See, for example, Baukje Miedema, Janet M. Stoppard and Vivienne Anderson, *Women's Bodies/Women's Lives: Health, Well-Being and Body Image* (Toronto: Sumach Press, 2000), and Razack, *Looking White People in the Eye.*

11. Somer Brodribb, "Women's Studies in Canada: A Discussion," *Resources for Feminist Research* (1987), 1. This is the first published historical and analytic overview of the field in Canada.

12. Two of the many recent American books that provocatively question the progress that racialized women have made are Gloria E. Anzaldúa and AnaLouise Keating, eds., *This Bridge We Call Home: Radical Visions for Transformation* (New York:

Routledge, 2002); The Social Justice Group at the Center for Advanced Feminist Studies, University of Minnesota, eds., *Is Academic Feminism Dead? Theory in Practice* (New York: New York University Press, 2000). See also *The Women's Review of Books,* Special Issue on "Women Writing the Asian Diaspora" (July 2002). For Canada, see Njoki Nathani Wane, Kathy Deliovsky and Erica Lawson, *Back to the Drawing Board: African-Canadian Feminisms* (Toronto: Sumach Press, 2002).

13. Two accounts are by Canadian academics and they are convincing and disturbing. There are undoubtedly many others. See Nuzat Amin, "South Englishes, North Englishes," *Canadian Woman Studies/les cahiers de la femme* 17, no. 2 (1997), 139–141, for an account of the oppressive effects of having an "accent" in Canada when one immigrates from a South Asian country; and Run P. Mukherjee, "In But Not at Home: Women of Colour in the Academy," *Resources for Feminist Research* 29 (2001/2002), 125–133.

14. Jill Morawski, *Practicing Feminism, Reconstructing Psychology: Notes on a Liminal Science* (Ann Arbour: University of Michigan Press, 1994), 55, quoted in P. McCallum and L. Radtke, "Break-throughs, Break-ins and Break-ups: The Impact of Gender Studies across the Disciplines," *Resources for Feminist Research* 29 (2001/2002), 12.

I

RECOVERING

HISTORIES

AND

MEANINGS

CHAPTER 1

"Smokin' in the Boys' Room": Girls' Absence in Anti-Smoking Educational Literature

Sharon Anne Cook

... CIGARETTE-SMOKING GIRLS lose the peculiar characteristics of young womanhood which are its charm ... cigarettes STRIKE A BLOW AT EVERY VITAL ORGAN ... cigarettes UNBALANCE THE MIND. "Many of the most pitiable cases of insanity in our asylums are cigarette fiends"... cigarettes STEAL THE BRAINS. High School testimony is, "memory impaired; clearness of thought hindered; application made more difficult; ambition deadened; the power of will broken" ... cigarettes GRADUALLY KILL THE POWER OF DECISION. The ability to say "no" is lost. THE VERDICT IS: "CIGARETTE-SMOKERS ARE COMMIT-ING SUICIDE ON THE INSTALLMENT PLAN."
— Mrs. Stella B. Irvine, "Sound the Alarm!"[1]

STELLA IRVINE'S APPROPRIATELY titled handbill, "Sound the Alarm!," was produced around 1922 for the Woman's Christian Temperance Union. Directed at both young women and men, it signalled a level of panic, which was not reflected in the health and hygiene textbooks of the day, over the increasing popular pastime of smoking among girls.[2] Fears about young male smokers, however, were copiously documented in health textbooks from the 1880s onwards, demonstrating a persistent but more measured rhetoric than that in Stella Irvine's document. This failure to recognize the young female smoker — as well as failing to understand her reasons for taking up smoking, her continuing the habit in the face of health dangers and fashioning effective arguments to convince her to quit — is understandable in those eras when the specter of a girl smoking was contrary to conventional norms of female behaviour, as it was, for example, in the 1920s with the dawn of the girl smoker. However, this excuse cannot be accepted once the smoking girl became the smoking woman and had been integrated into popular culture, which dates at least from the 1950s or even earlier, with the advent of popular films.

Even more disturbing is the fact that by the 1990s, more adolescent women than men had taken up smoking (30 percent versus 27 percent, respectively),[3] with young women doing so earlier than young men.[4] The most recent figures indicate that adolescent women smoke more than their male peers by 24 percent to 21 percent,[5] so the preponderance of female adolescent smokers is more, not less, of a problem. Canadian health textbooks[6] have never addressed smoking as a gendered behaviour, however, and have only begun to include young women in discussions about the dangers of smoking within the past two decades.

This essay explores the power of and the many silences surrounding young women and cigarettes presented in official educational texts, teaching resources and curriculum documents of the twentieth century. "Young women" refers to both school-age girls and women for whom these educational texts were intended. The essay considers the implications of this absence of young women and alternative sites for girls' education about the performative uses of smoking. Contrary to Irvine's contention that smoking robbed girls of their most charming qualities, images of women smokers in popular culture throughout most of the twentieth century offered young women smokers the means to visualize assertions of independence, even countercultural norms, as well as feminized refinement, beauty and authority in ways that would otherwise have been difficult to demonstrate.

The notion of "performance" has been developed by Judith Butler in her fascinating studies on gender construction.[7] She argues that identities are moulded and refined through the expression of performative speech and behaviour in a kind of improvisational theatre. "Transgressive performances" occur when social conventions (such as smoking being "unladylike") are contested and appropriated by the actor for different uses than is currently expected. Props are often employed in this "theatrical remaking of the body" and the interplay of repetitive posturing with these props provides a window into their symbolic meanings by people who either are unwilling or unable to verbally articulate their significance. The act of smoking for girls would seem to be one example of this unexpected use for performative purposes.

Despite Stella Irvine's overheated prose and her sometimes creative claims, the fundamental sentiment expressed in her handbill found support when it was published and continues to this day to reflect worries about cigarette-smoking youths. Given our own era's ongoing preoccupation with this social problem, it is striking that so little attention is paid to girls smoking. Yet the popularity of boys smoking in modern youth culture was accurately portrayed in the 1974 hit song *Smokin' in the Boys' Room*.[8] In this adolescent male's celebration of rebellion, the singer includes not listening to teachers, whose instructions "just ain't my bag," a school regimen aiming to "fill me up with your rules" and a hard-won escape for a quick smoke in the boys' room. Needless to say, while no comparable smoking song exists for rebellious girls, any female teacher will attest to the many pre-adolescent and adolescent girls who have used school time for "smokin' in the girls' room." Yet this is not a form of female adolescent expression which is memorialized in song. The same gap appears in the historical literature.

Studies of Smoking

Nothing approaching a balanced analysis of tobacco's importance in society, and especially its allure for youths, was published before the 1980s, although several studies of temperance work with youths date from this period, with which tobacco is traditionally associated.[9] The focus of the few historical studies undertaken during the 1980s was placed almost exclusively on the history of the North American tobacco industry itself, its specious health arguments and its unrelenting efforts to market its product in the developed and developing worlds.[10] The 1990s mirrored these concerns with heavy newspaper, periodical and film[11] coverage of the chicanery and manipulation of powerful tobacco executives in their unrelenting campaign to dupe smokers and draw more unsuspecting victims into their net. These included accounts of enormous lawsuits levelled against the tobacco giants by North American federal and state or provincial governments.[12]

Absent from the standard narrative has been any sustained consideration of tobacco as a moral issue or of its powerful allure for young people, especially girls.[13] This absence is the more striking since tobacco has traditionally been and currently is grouped with alcohol, drugs and other risky behaviours by historians, addiction professionals and popular essayists.[14] Adult women have been better served in studies by Lorraine Greaves and Cheryll Krasnick Warsh. Warsh has demonstrated that during the 1920s, when cigarettes appealed to many women as a symbol of their general enfranchisement, sophistication and consumerism, women were also engaging in their own campaign to extend their provincial civic rights through the vote.[15]

If the popular cultural, educational and historical communities have sidestepped any sustained analysis of smoking in adolescent female culture, it could be questioned whether resource materials are available on which to base textbook treatments. However, a number of impressive resources have been developed, especially since 1994.[16] Yet despite the escalating numbers of girls over boys choosing to smoke, school textbooks are still silent about the greater predilection of girls to smoke. This is indefensible. While girl smokers first entered the health and biology textbooks in the 1970s, the distinctive motives, "performative" uses and dangers faced by girls who make this choice have been and continue to be ignored. The only way these issues are addressed is through the old assumption that in speaking to boys, they are speaking to girls too.

Smoking and Texts

Anti-smoking messages have been delivered to both girls and boys throughout the twentieth century, primarily through a range of authoritative texts, including, most prominently, the classroom textbook. Educational texts do more than simply impart information to receptive subjects; they are also directly implicated in the process of cultural transmission, including gendered behaviours. As "subjects," administrators, teachers and students in the educational enterprise are presented with ideals and purported facts through the textbook. These facts are thought to be so important for the students' welfare that they are generally taught through "direct instruction," that is, through methods that do not invite debate or minority opinions. Furthermore, the message is structured in a "spiral" so that students at various levels receive similar messages, which become increasingly more complicated as they mature. In Ontario for example, the dangers of cigarettes are first presented to children in fourth-grade health classes, but each year afterwards, the message is reinforced, using illustrations and examples in keeping with the adolescent and youth stages of life. Since the 1970s, curricula such as these have been designed to take into account a variety of different learning styles and ability levels. Considering all of this, the absence of a gender variable is the more striking and troubling.

The knowledge that is received through formal education constitutes one of the prime means by which the hegemonic order shapes public perceptions. The field of Cultural Studies has made us aware of how invisible the authoritative stance is to those within and outside the privileged culture and how powerful the rules set by this group are. As Stuart Hall notes:

> [T]he circle of dominant ideas does accumulate the symbolic power to map or classify the world for others; its classifications do acquire not only the constraining power of dominance over other modes of thought but also the initial authority of habit and instinct. It becomes the horizon of the taken-for-granted: what the world is and how it works, for all practical purposes.[17]

A good deal, perhaps most, of the taken-for-granted knowledge that must be transmitted to schoolchildren is defined through the medium of the aptly termed textbook, one of many "texts" underlying the educational enterprise. It has been estimated that primary and elementary students spend a great deal of time working with texts — 75 percent of their time in classrooms and 90 percent of their time while doing homework.[18] Today, as in the past, text materials are the fundamental way in which dominant groups' "cultural capital" — or the cultural vision resulting from complex intersections of class, gender and race relations — is reproduced economically and culturally in the next generation.[19] One example of this is the assumption that the only anti-smoking arguments that need to be presented coherently and regularly are to boys, the only smokers in youth culture, and that these arguments need only be shaped around male concerns.

At the same time, it must not be assumed that a particular textbook's knowledge is uncontested or unmediated. Instead, cultural incorporation is a dynamic process in which participants continuously remake and religitimize the culture's "plausibility system."[20] The fluid process of cultural incorporation assumes an active and often subversive role for those who are marginalized, unwittingly or intentionally. Thus, girls who do not see themselves represented in textbooks as smokers, or who recognize the structure of the anti-smoking arguments as applying only to males, will look elsewhere to educate themselves about the uses to which they can put this practice to serve their own purposes of cultural and personal authority. Of course, this is not a new process: young people have always supplemented and tested their didactic lessons against the societal messages they receive through popular culture.

A text taught is not a text learned or, it might be admitted, even received. If we grant that students are their own active agents and, as such, actively manipulate and construct knowledge for their own purposes, we must grant too that a text will be read in any number of ways by those students.[21] Sometimes the intervention of a teacher will mediate the text's meaning; sometimes, physical surroundings and peer reception will fundamentally alter its reception. Very importantly, and perhaps most importantly, a text's reception by the reader will be influenced by its situation in relation to other competing or supportive messages. As an example of this, texts presenting a given reality on, say, gender prescriptions in a society are likely to be less convincing to readers who find this received truth contested by knowledge and values as they are represented in their families, on the street, in the playground, in magazines, on television and in movies.

A text that idealizes social relations — or anything else — in a manner inconsistent with the lived experience of a learner is not likely to be absorbed by that learner in the uncritical fashion anticipated by the author. However, a message that is compelling and consistent — even in its absence, as in the case of anti-smoking messages for girls — and that is supported by other messages in popular culture and with lived experience will strike a deeper resonance in its readers and result in more fundamental learning. Hence, any didactic message presented in the textbook must be "read" in the context of the surrounding culture of which it is a part, but *only* a part.

A History of Anti-smoking Texts

As a discrete area of the curriculum, anti-tobacco education formally entered the syllabus through the study of temperance. Hygiene curricula were introduced in most provinces during the 1880s, with courses in "Scientific Temperance Instruction" (STI) culminating in popularity during the 1890s and in the first decade of the 1900s. Originally preoccupied with questions relating to "purity" in thought, word, deed and bodily action — with special interest devoted to those substances like alcohol, narcotics and foul language that polluted the body — STI courses and concerns diversified after 1910 and took up such issues as pure food and beverage, exercise regimes that included callisthenics, school design to encourage healthful ventilation and access to natural light and non-alcoholic purgatives and medicines.[22] STI courses evolved into "hygiene" and then "physiology" courses, and are now known as "health" curricula. Separate curricula for girls and boys first emerged in "purity" topics and were commonplace whenever gendered needs were recognized, as, for example, in sex education.

Textbooks produced during this period owe a great deal to the early temperance primers; the movement away from an essentially moral justification towards a more sharply focused scientific rationale was gradual. However, by the First World War, textbooks directed to Canadian public schoolchildren were reorganized: instead of fitting the vicissitudes of tobacco use into a treatise mainly devoted to alcohol temperance, the focus of these books was physiological balance and health. Rather than underlining tobacco's poisonous nature, its function as a narcotic on the circulatory, respiratory and nervous systems was emphasized. "Wellness" replaced the disease model.[23] A.P. Knight's *Hygiene for Young People*, which was widely used after 1909 in Ontario and in the West, adopted a breezy tone that could easily have replaced the teacher's Socratic presentation.[24]

The changing focus and content of health textbooks throughout this period reflect a change in the authors. Nineteenth-century texts were often written by clergy or other moral leaders. For instance, a text entitled *First Lessons in Christian Morals for Canadian Families and Schools,* which discussed tobacco use, was written by Egerton Ryerson, Minister of Education for Ontario and a Methodist minister.[25] However, as the temperance rationale gave way to a health-based argument against smoking, drinking and drugs, the authors were more likely to be medical authorities. The most popular late nineteenth- and early-twentieth-century textbook used in Ontario was by Benjamin Ward Richardson, a Fellow of the Royal College of Physicians. In Manitoba, the authorized textbook for this period was by H.W. Conn, a professor of biology at Wesleyan University.[26] A.P. Knight, noted above, was a professor of physiology at Queen's University in Kingston. However, as the twentieth century progressed, an increasing number of authors of health textbooks were teachers or school administrators with a specialty in physiology. One of the most popular textbooks of the mid-century was co-authored by the team of J.T. Phair, who had been a deputy minister of health for Ontario, and N.R. Speirs, a director of physical education for the Toronto region.[27]

In all of these textbooks, the smoker is by definition male, with girls and women cast in supportive or enabling roles:

Many girls and women will say, "Why, our fathers and brothers have smoked ever since they were boys, and it does not appear to have done them much harm." This is no doubt very true … but it is nevertheless true that the habit of smoking tobacco is bad for all young people.[28]

More positively, some anti-smoking advocates regarded women as "gate-keepers" who prohibited smoking in their presence and thereby prevented the negative example of mature and successful men smoking in the presence of boys. The Woman's Christian Temperance Union called for women to enforce "rigorous exclusion, for the sake of their young sons, of smoking from their own presence and from the society which they control."[29]

Even in textbooks from this period that ostensibly addressed both boys and girls by using the collective noun "children," the reasons put forward to discourage smoking suggest that the subjects were exclusively male. For example, the teachers' manual to *The Golden Rule Books*, dating from 1916 and widely used in Ontario, suggests that

> there is a general consensus of opinion on the part of students of hygiene in regard to the effects of cigarette smoking on children. It appears to have been established that the poison of the nicotine in cigarettes weakens the action of the heart, irritates the nerves, and retards physical development. Many school principals attribute to it the mental inefficiency which in many cases leads to truancy, and from truancy to crime. Even if there were a doubt on this subject, there is no gain from the practice, and abstinence from cigarette smoking on the part of boys should, accordingly, be taught as a virtue.[30]

Thus, the argument that teachers presented to (male) students was clearly defined: tobacco induced physical and mental inefficiency which could lead to truancy and crime. It could injure and weaken the physical system, create trembling so that the smoker would be a poor marksman and stunt intellectual growth by sabotaging concentration. In a throwback to Victorian worries, many textbook authors pointed to a smoker's lack of ambition as the greatest threat — this failure of the soul overcast all other features. All of these negative effects, many of which are admittedly unconvincing, were associated with males in the literature of the era. Had the concern also extended to girls, there would undoubtedly have been some mention of girls' moral sensibilities being compromised or their reproductive abilities being reduced.

The 1920s was the first decade in which many women began to experiment with smoking. When many women took up smoking as a rebellious act with the intention to shock, anti-smoking forces took notice. But still girls' attraction to cigarettes went unmentioned in the textbooks of the time. During the 1920s up until the post–Second World War, textbook advice adopted arguments whose dominant message was that cigarettes paved the route to self-abasement rather than self-improvement.[31] Pedagogically, these hygiene studies were made more attractive by extending the range of issues of nutrition and health to exercise, healthful rest, nature study, ventilation and even first aid.[32] This line of reasoning had the potential for equal application of anti-smoking education to both boys and girls, but this remained unexplored in textbooks.

The link between tobacco and pathogenesis raised even more possibilities for anti-smoking education.[33] Tobacco's carcinogenic properties continued to be contested within both the science and medical communities (and would be contested until after the tabling of the American Surgeon General's Report in 1964), although anti-tobacco campaigners had no trouble finding doctors who would testify to the damage it wreaked on individuals, most of whom were male.[34] The result of the disagreements over linking smoking with any particular disease, including cancer, meant that anti-smoking educators fell back almost exclusively on hygienic arguments, and particularly on the negative effects of tobacco on athletic and academic performance, both of which were regarded at the time as primarily male concerns.

Hence, the quality which most captured public attention between 1920 and 1950 was nicotine's classification as a narcotic rather than its association with disease. Almost all textbooks of the interwar period grouped tobacco with the other feared drugs of hashish, cocaine, opium and alcohol. Students of the time were alerted that some of these drugs acted as stimulants on the body, while others, like nicotine, were narcotics that "deaden the nervous system and weaken its action; they slacken the muscles and lessen their strength."[35] One Saskatchewan textbook from 1923 recommended that a "boy who wishes to become large and strong should let cigarettes alone during his growing years, for there is every reason to believe that young smokers fail to reach their full development either of body or of mind."[36] As a relaxant, nicotine presented an alluring but insidious threat to the young man on the rise; nicotine could easily lull him into accepting his present circumstances rather than striving towards greater self-improvement.

The determinedly male orientation in textbooks was reinforced when all of the images and examples were of boys and their concerns. Donald Fraser and George Porter's *Ontario Public School Health Book* dating from

1925, for example, takes the line that tobacco contains poisons which can make a boy listless, stupid, forgetful and unable to concentrate. These were not presented as life-threatening but as destructive to a young man's attainment of fortune and responsibility. To appeal directly to the male reader, the authors invoke the horrifying image of a schoolboy losing interest in sports: "Now one of the most important things for success in games is staying power, and one cannot have that if his 'wind,' as it is called, is not good." Next, he loses his appetite: "A boy smoker, with his stained fingers, his pale face, and general listless manner, is far from being at his best."[37] Despite educational authorities' identification of girls as endangered by cigarettes and as requiring special physiology and hygiene courses,[38] texts continued to ignore them as imagined readers.[39] That girls were not considered to be a client group in this period, during which young women began to take up the habit, is especially notable, since so many other concerns were exhaustively discussed under the general heading of the "girl problem."[40]

By the 1950s health textbooks were promoting an alternative message for children and adolescents. The experience of the war had clearly influenced notions about smoking: the new textbooks portrayed tobacco as a socially accepted relaxant and as a natural accessory of vigorous men, many of whom were barely out of adolescence. One popular text, published in 1951, soothed young men with the happy news that "only a small fraction of the nicotine that tobacco contains is absorbed in smoking, and after many trials the nerve cells become accustomed" to it. Furthermore, while "tobacco does have a harmful effect on young people during the period of growth," only "some people are more subject to injury from tobacco than others." In fact, "smoking is a social custom that makes for friendliness and comradeship.... It is fairly universal ... No one likes to be different from his friends."[41] Even better, in a 1955 publication entitled *You're Growing Up*, the authors point out that once a smoker has grown up, any real danger seems to pass: "Some doctors and research workers think that smoking is fairly harmless to most *healthy adults* who smoke *moderately. But all authorities agree that smoking is harmful to growing boys and girls.*"[42]

Should a young man acquire this unfortunate "habit," how is he to stop? Thankfully, this requires nothing more than will power, for smoking is presented as a harmless male diversion. Much is made of authority figures who protested that young men should not smoke yet they themselves indulged in this pleasure. It is repeatedly argued that smoking is one of the harmless social activities in which young men engage. Rather than isolating the sinner, as anti-smoking advocates earlier in the century had posited, textbook writers of the 1950s saw smoking as binding together the social order through an easy male camaraderie. As if to support this benign message, tobacco discussion was no longer grouped with hard drugs, such as opium and cocaine, but was increasingly included with discussions of alcohol[43] and defined as an agent "used as a result of custom and tradition"[44] yet not required by the body.

Teachers' guides from this period also stress the commonplace nature of smoking among adolescents and encourage educators to seek the underlying reasons for "acts of defiance," including drinking and smoking:

> Health education programs should take account of these practices, with due regard to their health and social aspects. It is particularly important that ... students be exposed to facts, not prejudices, as they formulate opinions concerning personal behaviour with regard to smoking and drinking. Direct prohibition is not education and it contains the seeds of failure.[45]

At the same time, the assumption that smoking and drinking constituted strategies used by teenagers to promote their social integration during a trying period of personal development was inconsistently applied in the pedagogical literature of the period. The topic of smoking was as often ignored for both genders as it was excused.[46] The popular literature indicates that during the 1950s, almost 50 percent of the Canadian population smoked.[47]

But much remained consistent between post-war texts and those of the earlier period. The most striking similarities of all were that the smokers remained male and smoking was shown as serving male purposes and societal functions. In addition, all examples and images continued to feature only males, and teachers' guidebooks provided exercises and classroom strategies that showed only males.

However, with the publication of the American Surgeon General's bombshell report in 1964 everything changed. The evidence considered by the ten members of the Surgeon General's Advisory Committee included animal experiments, clinical or autopsy studies and population studies. Their conclusion, that "[c]igarette smoking is a health hazard of sufficient importance in the United States to warrant appropriate remedial action," emerged from the causal relationships between cigarette smoking and cancer of the lungs, the larynx, the esophagus and the urinary bladder as found in studies *of men*. It also established a relationship between cigarette smoking, pulmonary emphysema, chronic bronchitis and coronary heart disease, all in trials of males.[48] The link between smoking and disease etiology was now incontrovertible, and the presumed application was also made to women, although without a clear sense of the particular dangers for them. The old battles within the scientific and medical communities were a thing of the past and a new spirit of public condemnation of cigarette smoking became evident through a range of publications.

Not surprisingly, the anti-smoking impulse was not immediately reflected in textbooks. By the early 1970s, however, textbooks had caught up with the new research. They devoted much more space to the dangers of cigarettes and extended their arguments in an effort to appeal to Canadian youth. One outstanding textbook published in 1971 was entitled *Tomorrow Is Now: Today's Psychology and Your Health*.[49] It devoted a complete chapter of thirty pages to a careful examination of smoking, its causes and multiple deleterious effects on the body's physical and emotional well-being. However, even in this extensive and impressive example of health education that presents smoking as a serious topic for adolescents (again grouping tobacco in all its forms with other drugs), girls are addressed only peripherally. Nonetheless, they do make a welcome appearance.

During the 1980s and 1990s, students were presented with a formulaic anti-smoking discussion that emphasized the danger of smoking to the cardio-respiratory system. More positively, students were encouraged to increase their levels of exercise, eat healthily and control stress. The treatment of smoking was notable for its gender-blindness and, until 1994, for arguments that persistently pointed to concerns of the middle-aged authors but not to adolescents. For example, smoking was cited as contributing to hypertension or high blood pressure, to emphysema or heart attacks. Although women's issues began to appear in the literature of the 1970s, they were presented in a way that was not likely to resonate with pre-adolescent and adolescent girls. For example, the danger to the fetus of smoking mothers was consistently noted as a reason to avoid smoking.[50] But what adolescent girl believes that she is likely to become pregnant? To the charge that no adolescent with a history of reasonable health believes that he or she is a candidate for degenerative diseases like heart disease, the texts noted that autopsies of young people "killed in accidents or war have found that many 20-year-olds have blood vessels already up to 50% closed by atherosclerosis."[51]

Clearly, part of the explanation for so little in the way of adolescent-centred arguments is the same for the paucity of female interests reflected in these texts: the research base was itself androcentric and therefore blind to the kinds of issues that might have convinced adolescents of smoking's many dangers. It was only in 1994, after the passage of the *Tobacco Sales to Young Persons Act* the previous year and the prohibition of smoking in all Ontario high schools that adolescent-directed anti-smoking resources became more available.

Although girls were first addressed as imagined readers of these textbooks in the 1970s, modern textbooks continue to ignore the particular concerns of girls who are deciding whether or not to smoke. Not a single textbook from the 1980s and 1990s offers a gendered approach to discourage smoking. It is notable as well that teacher-prepared resources for classroom instruction often disregard girls' particular reasons for smoking. The major resource guide for Ontario health teachers, produced in 2000 by the Ontario Health and Physical Education Association in accordance with the new guidelines, presents no strategies or resources of particular interest to girls; it also includes a single case study that explores reasons adolescents begin smoking — the adolescents are two boys.[52] The mandated curriculum guideline for Ontario makes no suggestions for the inclusion of gendered views of smoking.

Motivations for Smoking

Research into reasons adolescents and youths choose to start smoking has been developing since the 1970s and shows a number of causal forces common to both males and females. Among these are a desire to cover up social insecurities by using the cigarette as a prop, the need to share activities and be accepted by peers, a desire to demonstrate maturity in mimicry of "adult" behaviour and the need to reduce stress. It has been recently established that reasons for starting to smoke are different than reasons for continuing to smoke. Clearly, once a youth begins to see smoking as a useful function in her or his life, it is much more difficult to interrupt the habit. Almost all the reasons offered by youth for continuing to smoke are related to self-esteem.[53]

At the same time, some motivating factors have been shown to be distinct to girls or expressed in distinctive ways by them.[54] Girls seem to be drawn to smoking because of their empathetic responses to female role models who smoke. This helps to explain the much stronger influence on girls than boys, for example, of a mother who smokes. In addition, certain advertising messages strike a stronger chord with girls than boys. Rather than appealing to young men's desire for greater personal control (which seems to be a prime motivator for working-class males, in particular), young women have been shown to be especially vulnerable to advertising that suggests that smoking makes a woman more attractive, refined and successful in a career. The reality is quite the opposite — women with little education and lower incomes are much more likely to smoke.[55] But because these facts are not addressed in textbooks, how are the myths to be dispelled?

A prime reason young women begin and continue to smoke is to control weight gain, which is a direct link to their self-esteem. This important factor does not appear in any of the health or biology textbooks up to the year 2000, although it is reflected in the research. The rise of the aesthetic of thinness, which dates from the 1970s, has resulted in new norms for women's body shape and body weight. Smoking has long been seen by young women as one way to suppress the appetite without the need to take additional substances. The scourge of anorexia nervosa in the adolescent female population is one expression of this aesthetic run wild. It might be hypothesized that the appearance of anorexia in health textbooks would parallel the admission that many young women smoke to reduce their cravings for food. But this silence too is striking. While textbooks directed to adolescents began to first treat the problem of anorexia in the 1980s,[56] there is virtually no comment in either textbooks or teacher education materials[57] about the restrictive aesthetic of thinness for women or the link between smoking and weight control.[58] Even more troubling is the fact that discussions of smoking's dangers continued to cite appetite depressant as a *problem* (for the male athletic who bulks up for "battle") well into the late 1980s. To a female reader, this would read as an advertisement in favour of smoking, not a warning against it. It was not until the early 1990s that the problem of weight gain after quitting smoking was addressed in textbooks for adolescents, often with attendant tips to reduce this undesirable result.[59] But in no textbook produced before 2000 is the connection made between smoking and body shape for female students. It is possible that the combination of easy access to cigarettes and the pressure on women to achieve thinness have contributed to the accelerated rate of female smokers in the 1990s.

The Performance of Women Smoking

Girls who do not find themselves in the curriculum will seek messages elsewhere, just as they have always done: from their peers and families, from role models and the media. And advertisers, including those employed by the tobacco industry, have been keen to offer direction to young women since the 1920s. For example, in a 1922 advertisement, two fearless young women in avant-garde smoking suits flaunt more than their cigarettes (which are emphasized by decorative cigarette holders): both women strike provocative poses of exaggerated and masculinized repose.[60] One stands tall, leaning against a fireplace with her legs wide apart, while the other balances a foot on a chair — striking poses that men often assume in the "smoking room." The message to girls would be unmistakable: smokers are liberated. Perhaps Stella Irvine had this duo in mind as she penned her handbill.

A 1940s ad for Chesterfield cigarettes picks up the theme of independence and evokes the 1940s belle who announces her priorities. The woman's back is facing the viewer; her dress is cut low, exposing her skin; her head turned to look over her left shoulder; she's holding a package of Chesterfields in her left hand. The caption reads: "After a man's heart ... Nothing else will do ... when smokers find out the good things Chesterfields give them."[61] The first of her "good things" is a man's heart, and thereafter, her Chesterfield cigarettes. This woman is pretty and stylish, with rolled hair, rouged cheeks and carefully plucked and pencilled eyebrows. She smiles demurely but confidently. Like her sisters in the 1920s image, she is prosperous and in a position to choose what and how she will smoke.

Just as in the earlier images, women in the advertisements of the 1970s continued to represent the values of their era. In a Salem cigarette ad entitled "Salem refreshes naturally," which appeared on the May 1974 back cover of *Ms.* magazine, two young women are drawn to the "natural" life of the outdoors; they relax with two handsome male companions with whom they share the pleasure of "naturally grown menthol," presumably in contrast to artificially induced nicotine addictions. Both young women are very thin, but buxom; the women stand or sit in attendance to the men who stand on either side of a raft, guiding it along a river. Despite the studied raggy appearances (all are wearing cut-off shorts and halter tops), these women and men portray comfort and confidence, not poverty. The slenderness of all four characters would not be lost on girls seeking "performative" uses for smoking and fashion.

By the 1980s, the images of women in cigarette ads had begun to change. In a June 1981 ad for More cigarettes, which also appeared on the back cover of the June issue of *Ms.* magazine, a tall, slender woman in a form-fitting shirt and slacks and impossibly high heels exclaims, "I'm More satisfied," telegraphing much more about the sources from which she demands satisfaction than simply her cigarettes. Part of an overtly sexualized series of advertisements directed at young women, the extra-long cigarette suggests that sexual satisfaction — "that extra measure of satisfaction" — is a legitimate claim to be made by a young woman of her partner. Along with gendered presentations of smoking, this is a lesson she is not likely to find in her health textbook, but one she is undoubtedly interested in learning.

In a 1987 ad for the same cigarette brand, sophistication takes over where vampishness left off. In this ad, an authoritative women asserts: "I looked for something different. And found myself with More. More cigarette. More pleasure. Adventure has its rewards."[62] Her advice to demand "More. Never settle for less," harkens back to the 1920s women in their avant-garde smoking suits: the 1980s woman is wearing a dramatic hat, gigantic earrings, couturier-produced clothing and perches on a designer's chair. She holds her cigarette aloft in one hand, the package of cigarettes in the other, and smiles seductively for the camera. She is of indeterminate age, but trumpets her demands very much as an adolescent might. Ultimately, the message is one of hedonism: the quest she describes begins in seeking "something different" and ends with pleasure. This is every teenager's dream.

Since 1988, advertising cigarettes in Canadian magazines, especially those images directed at youths, has been curtailed by two federal statutes: Bill C-204, the *Non-Smoker's Health Act,* and Bill C-51, the *Tobacco Products Control Act,* both of which prohibit tobacco advertising. This legislation was followed in 1993 by the *Tobacco Sales to Young Persons Act,* which sought to control sales to youths by setting eighteen as the minimum age for tobacco purchases and by prohibiting cigarette-vending machines in public places, except in bars. The tobacco industry fought the 1988 legislation through the courts up to the Supreme Court of Canada, which eventually ruled that the ban on advertising infringed rights under the Canadian Charter of Rights and Freedoms. In 1996, limited advertising resumed, but this was presumably aimed only at the adult population.[63] It should not be assumed from this, however, that Canadian adolescent girls were protected from "performative" displays of the uses to which young women can put cigarettes — those American magazines distributed widely in Canada continued running advertisements;[64] the tobacco industry maintained its sponsorship of high-visibility sports and cultural events of interest to young people, for example auto racing and rock festivals; and billboard advertising, including that within walking distance of schools, was limited only by the industry's own code of ethics.

Beyond the print media, displays of women smoking in film have been common since the 1930s[65] and have been used as a dramatic prop since the 1970s. A research project entitled "Smoke Free Movies" conducted by the Public Media Center in the U.S. demonstrated that two out of three tobacco shots in the Top 50 American movies (between April 2000 and March 2001) were in child-rated films, many of which were rapidly converted to video for even wider distribution. *The Perfect Storm*, for example, clocked in at thirty-three "shots" or references to tobacco products per hour of film.[66] Interactive Web sites which log the ways in which women's smoking appears in films that are popular with adolescents offer a glimpse of how youths (it is not clear whether these refer to male or female adolescents) see the performative possibilities of smoking by women in "acted" situations. Documenting Jennifer Rubin's smoking performance in the 1987 film *Nightmare on Elm Street 3: Dream Warriors*, a contributor notes: "Rubin: one 30 sec. scene, shows pull [on cigarette] then [the visual] cuts away, then shows puff and talk-nose-exhale."[67] Another contribution for the 1996 film *Kiss and Tell* underlines the desirable gauntness which smoking promotes in women: "Caught by her anti-smoking husband in mid-exhale, [Cheryl Ladd] smiles impishly and her cheeks sink in as she takes another hard drag, opening her mouth wide to inhale. There is a voluminous side-on-talk-and-nasal exhale against a dark background as she explains that it is 'just one.'" Well into the 1990s, television situation comedies also provided many examples of *how and why* young women should smoke.[68]

*

Young women who are ignored in official school textbooks and burdened by an idealized body image that emphasizes impossible thinness will find ways to learn and mature by using other means. Most often, these means are produced to convince girls of their power as consumers, not as self-directed and confident young women with marketable skills that will provide them with a satisfying lifestyle and a reasonable set of goals. Furthermore, young women and men attempting to alter their lifestyles, including quitting smoking, are most easily influenced early in their smoking practices, particularly before the age of nineteen.[69] If school textbooks continue to deny the interests and needs of this growing group of smokers, including their efforts to stop smoking, we will abrogate one of education's primary functions: to support young people by providing them with knowledge and awareness that can empower them.

NOTES

I wish to thank Dr. Terry Cook for his insights and perceptive questions on an earlier draft of this chapter.

1. Mrs. Stella B. Irvine, "Sound the Alarm!," handbill, c. 1922, OA, WCTU Collection, MU 8396, Archives of Ontario.

2. I would like to thank Ken Montgomery who generously provided outstanding research support for this and other tobacco-related articles.

3. Health Canada, *Survey on Smoking in Canada, Cycle 2* (November 1994.) Retrieved from <http://www.hc-sc.gc.ca/hecs/sesc/tobacco/prof/cessation_program/improving_trends.html>. August 29, 2002. The figures for 1999 continue to show that 29 percent of adolescent girls smoked as compared with 28 percent of teenage boys.

4. A 1992 study indicated that by age fifteen, 55 percent of males and 62 percent of females will have tried smoking at least once. It is estimated that about 30 percent of this group will continue to smoke throughout their lives. See A.J.C. King and B. Coles, *The Health of Canada's Youth* (Ottawa: Health and Welfare Canada, 1992). The Canadian Tobacco Use Monitoring Survey for 1999 (Wave 2) indicates that 41 percent of girls aged fifteen to seventeen who define themselves as smokers had their first cigarette before age thirteen; the comparable figure for boys is 29 per-cent. See Health Canada, *Survey on Smoking in Canada*. Smoking rates for thirteen- and fourteen-year-old youths are dramatically reduced according to the Health Canada Web site (September 2002), yet still with girls outdistancing boys (14 percent to 12 percent). See <http://www.hc-sc.gc.ca/main/hppb/tobaccoreduction/publications/youth/ssbs/ ssbsos.htm#4a>.

5. For 2001 Canadian figures, see the Canadian Tobacco Use Monitoring Survey for 2001. Available from <http://www.hc-sc.gc.ca/hecs-sesc/tobacco/research/ctums/2001/summary.html>. By the late teens, it appears that more young males than females smoke, however with males smoking more cigarettes per day than girls. Nevertheless, the balance does not change until age eighteen.

6. This statement applies also to the latest textbooks used in middle- and high-school Canadian classrooms. See for example, Jerrold Greenberg and Robert Gold, *Holt Health* (Toronto: Holt, Rinehart and Winston, Harcourt Brace, 1999), 285–297, or Mary Bronson Merki, Don Merki and Gale Cornelia Flynn, *Glencoe Health: A Guide to Wellness,* 6th ed. (Toronto: Glencoe McGraw-Hill, 1999), 528–547.

7. See Judith Butler, *Gender Trouble: Feminism and the Subversion of Identity* (London: Routledge, 1990), and "Performativity's Social Magic," in Theodore R. Schatzki and Wolfgang Natter, eds., *The Social and Political Body* (New York: The Guilford Press, 1996).

8. *Smokin' in the Boys' Room*, words and music by Lutz-Coda, published by Big Leaf Music (adm. by Walden Music, Inc.).

9. See Sharon Anne Cook, "'Earnest Christian Women, Bent on Saving our Canadian Youth': The Ontario Woman's Christian Temperance Union and Scientific Temperance Instruction, 1881–1930," *Ontario History* 86, no. 3 (1994), 249–267; Sharon Anne Cook, "Do Not ... Do Anything that You Cannot Unblushingly Tell Your Mother: Gender and Social Purity in Canada," *Histoire sociale/Social History* 30, no. 60 (November 1997), 215–238; and Sharon Anne Cook, "Educating for Temperance: The Woman's Christian Temperance Union and Ontario Children, 1880–1916," *Historical Studies in Education/Revue d'histoire de l'éducation* 5 (Fall 1991) 251–277. See also Lillian Lewis Shiman, "The Band of Hope Movement: Respectable Recreation for Working-Class Children," *Victorian Studies* 17 (September 1973), 49–74; and John Welshman, "Images of Youth: The Issue of Juvenile Smoking, 1880–1914," *Addiction* 91 (1996), 990, 1379–1386.

10. For the United States, see Larry C. White, *Merchants of Death: The American Tobacco Industry* (New York: William Morrow, Beech Tree Books, 1988); Howard Cox, "Growth and Ownership in the International Tobacco Industry: BAT 1902–27," *Business History* 31, no. 11 (1989), 44–67. For Canada, see Timothy Dewhirst, "The Federal Government and Sport Sponsorship in Canada" (PhD diss., University of British Columbia, 1999), and Rob Cunningham, *Smoke & Mirrors: The Canadian Tobacco War* (Ottawa: International Development Research Centre, 1996). For the "specious health arguments," see Edith Efron, *The Apocalyptics: Cancer and the Big Lie* (New York: Simon and Schuster, 1984), and Robert H. Miles, *Coffin Nails and Corporate Strategies* (Englewood Cliffs, NJ: Prentice Hall, 1982). For developing nations, see, for example, Peter Taylor, "The Smoke Ring: Politics and Tobacco in the Third World," *Southern Exposure* 12, no. 5 (1984), 37–48.

11. See, for example, the acclaimed film *The Insider,* which depicts a morality play between a "whistle-blowing" scientist following the dictates of his conscience and the depraved tobacco industry executives out to silence him.

12. See Cassandra Tate, *Cigarette Wars: The Triumph of 'The Little White Slaver'* (Oxford: Oxford University Press, 1999), and Richard Kruger, *Ashes to Ashes: America's Hundred-Year Cigarette War, the Public Health and the Unabashed Triumph of Philip Morris* (New York: Alfred A. Knopf, 1996).

13. See Joseph Gusfield, "The Social Symbolism of Smoking," in S. Sugarman and R. Rabin, eds. *Smoking Policy: Law, Politics and Culture* (New York: Oxford University Press, 1993), and Joseph Gusfield, *Contested Meanings: The Construction of Alcohol Problems* (Madison: University of Wisconsin Press, 1996).

14. See Ian Tyrrell, *Deadly Enemies: Tobacco and Its Antagonists in Australian History* (Kensington, New South Wales: University of New South Wales Press, 1999); and

Ian Tyrrell, "The Temperance Movement and Smoking in Australia: Themes and Implications for the Study of Drugs and Social Reform Movements," *The Social History of Alcohol Review* 38/39 (1999), 28–34. In the Canadian context, see Sharon Anne Cook, *"Through Sunshine and Shadow": The Woman's Christian Temperance Union, Evangelicalism and Reform in Ontario, 1874–1939* (Montreal: McGill-Queen's University Press, 1995); Sharon Anne Cook, "Evangelical Moral Reform: Women and the War against Tobacco, 1874–1900," in Marguerite Van Die, ed., *Religion and Public Life in Canada* (Toronto: University of Toronto Press, 2001), 177–195; Jarrett Rudy, "'Unmaking Manly Smokes': Church, State Governance and the First Anti-Smoking Campaigns in Montreal, 1892–1914" (paper presented to the Annual Meeting of the Canadian Historical Association, Laval University, Quebec City, 2001); Peter Pope, "Fish into Wine: The Historical Anthropology of Demand for Alcohol in Seventeenth-Century Newfoundland," *Histoire sociale/Social History* 27 (November 1994), 270–276.

15. Lorraine Greaves, *Smoke Screen: Women's Smoking and Social Control* (Halifax and London: Fernwood Publishing and Scarlet Press, 1996); Cheryl Krasnick Warsh, "Smoke and Mirrors: Gender Representation in North American Tobacco and Alcohol Advertisements Before 1950," *Histoire sociale/Social History* 31 (November 1998), 183–222.

16. Health Canada, *Improving the Odds* (Ottawa: Health Canada, 1994), and the Ontario Physical and Health Education Association, "You Can Make a Difference: Helping Young Women Choose a Tobacco-Free Lifestyle" (North York: OPHEA, 1996).

17. Stuart Hall, "The Toad in the Garden: Thatcherism Among the Theorists," in Cary Nelson and Lawrence Grossberg, eds., *Marxism and the Interpretation of Culture* (Urbana: University of Illinois Press, 1988), 44.

18. Paul Goldstein, *Changing the American Schoolbook* (Lexington, MA: D.C. Heath, 1978), 1.

19. Michael W. Apple, "The Culture and Commerce of the Textbook," in Michael W. Apple and Linda K. Christian-Smith, eds., *The Politics of the Textbook* (New York: Routledge, 1991), 23.

20 Allan Luke, *Literacy, Textbooks and Ideology* (Philadelphia: Falmer Press, 1988), 27–29.

21. See Michael W. Apple and Linda K. Christian-Smith, "The Politics of the Textbook," in Apple and Christian-Smith, eds. *The Politics of the Textbook,* 13–14.

22. Cook, *"Through Sunshine and Shadow,"* 116–117.

23. See, for example, H.W. Conn, *An Elementary Physiology and Hygiene for Use in Schools, Authorized by the Advisory Board for Manitoba* (Toronto: Copp, Clark Company, 1903), 182–184, and Chalmers Watson, M.D., F.R.C.P.E., *The Story of the Human Body: A Reader in Hygiene for Pupils in Form III of the Public Schools, Recommended by the Minister of Education for use in School Libraries in Ontario* (Toronto: Thomas Nelson and Sons, 1910).

24. A.P. Knight, *Hygiene for Young People: A Reader for Pupils in Form III of the Public Schools Recommended by the Minister of Education for Use in School Libraries in Ontario* (Toronto: Copp, Clark Company, 1909). Also his *The Ontario Public*

School Hygiene, Authorized by the Minister of Education for Ontario for Use in Forms IV and V of the Public Schools (Toronto: Copp, Clark Company, 1910), 224–225; the Rev. J.O. Millar, *Short Studies in Ethics: An Elementary Text-Book for Schools* (Toronto: The Bryant Press, 1895); and Charles H. Stowell, *The Essentials of Health: A Text Book on Anatomy, Physiology and Hygiene, Adapted for Canadian Schools with an article on the prevention and treatment of tuberculosis* by C.J. Fagan, M.D., Secretary of the Provincial Board of Health, Victoria, BC, Prescribed for Use in the Public and High Schools of British Columbia (Toronto: The Educational Book Co., 1912), 239–265.

25. Egerton Ryerson, *First Lessons in Christian Morals for Canadian Families and Schools* (Toronto: Copp, Clark and Co., 1871). Similarly, Gage Company's *Temperance Text, The Temperance Primer: An Elementary Lesson Book on the Nature and Effects of Alcohol,* dating from 1883, was written by G.D. Platt, Inspector of Schools for Prince Edward County.

26. See, for example, Benjamin Ward Richardson, *Public School Temperance* (Toronto: The Grip Printing and Publishing Company, 1887); and Conn, *An Elementary Physiology and Hygiene for Use in Schools.*

27. See J.T. Phair and N.R. Speirs, *Good Health* (Toronto: Ginn and Company, 1951).

28. Knight, *Hygiene for Young People,* 41–42.

29. Edith Smith Davis, "Graded Scientific Temperance Lessons for the Use of Teachers," in Edith Smith Davis, ed., *The Temperance Educational Quarterly* (Evanston, IL: National Woman's Christian Temperance Union, 1913), 90.

30. Ibid., 13–14. See also A.P. Knight, *The Ontario Public School Hygiene Revised Edition, Authorized by the Minister of Education for Ontario for Use in Forms IV and V of the Public Schools* (Toronto: Copp, Clark Company, 1919).

31. See Pierre Schrumpf-Pierron, *Tobacco and Physical Efficiency: A Digest of Clinical Data* (New York: Paul B. Hoeber, 1927).

32. See, for example, National Archives of Canada, *Reports of Public Schools of British Columbia (1917),* A30. The province of British Columbia called its course "Nature Lessons and Hygiene."

33. "The Time to Smoke," *The Canadian Lancet* 52, no. 9 (May 1919), 436; and "Men Need Tobacco," *The Canadian Lancet* 56, no. 6 (February 1921), 336–337.

34. See, for example, William M. Goldsmith, *Human Poisons: Individual and Racial Effects* (Winfield, KS: William M. Goldsmith, 1929). See especially "Medical Men Speak," 47–53.

35. John W. Ritchie, Revised by George G. Nasmith and Jean E. Brown, *Primer of Physiology* (Toronto: W.J. Gage and Co., 1923), 155.

36. Ibid., 157.

37. Donald T. Fraser and George D. Porter, *Ontario Public School Health Book* (Toronto: Copp, Clark Company, 1925), esp. 107.

38. National Archives of Canada, *Twenty-Fifth Annual Report of the Department of Education of the Province of Alberta* (Edmonton: NAC, 1930).

39. Donald Y. Solandt, *Highways to Health* (Toronto: The Ryerson Press, 1933), 84–85,

offers almost precisely the same arguments as in the previous decade.

40. See, for example, Carolyn Strange, *Toronto's Girl Problem: The Perils and Pleasures of the City, 1880–1930* (Toronto: University of Toronto Press, 1995).

41. Phair and Spears, *Good Health,* 318–322.

42. Helen Shacter, Harold Johns and Archibald McKie, *You're Growing Up* (Toronto: W.J. Gage and Company, 1955), 214. Italics in original.

43. As in all cases, however, there are exceptions to this rule. The popular American textbook by Edwina Jones, Edna Morgan and Paul E. Landis, *For Healthful Living* (River Forest, IL: Laidlaw Brothers, 1957), continued with the old grouping with such narcotics as heroin, marijuana and opium, and allows two paragraphs to tobacco on pages 44–45. A second textbook by the same authors, intended for the pre-adolescent student, groups tobacco with other drugs and is so careful in its claims that it is patently unconvincing to either boys or girls. For example, "It may make the heart beat faster and over-work. It may have a bad effect on the throat and lungs. It may affect the nerves of young people. Tobacco may take away a person's appetite for proper foods. Then the person would lose weight and strength." Edwina Jones, Edna Morgan and Paul E. Landis, *Your Health and You* (River Forest, IL: Laidlaw Brothers, 1957).

44. Phair and Speirs, *Good Health,* 318. See also J.T. Phair and N.R. Spiers, *Good Health Today* (Toronto: Ginn and Company, 1958), 334–339. For an almost identical message, see James S. Nicoll, Julia Foster and William W. Bolton, *Your Health Today and Tomorrow* (River Forest, IL: Laidlaw Brothers, 1958), 177–178.

45. Helen Shacter, Gladys Gardner Jenkins and W.W. Bauer, *Guidebook for the Health and Personal Development,* Book 7: *You're Growing Up* (Toronto: W.J. Gage and Company, 1951), 123.

46. See Helen Shacter, Gladys Gardner Jenkins and W.W. Bauer, *Guidebook for the Health and Personal Development,* Book 8: *Into Your Teens* (Toronto: W.J. Gage and Company, 1952); and Helen Shacter and W. W. Bauer, *You and Others* (Toronto: W.J. Gage and Company, 1955).

47. Bud Getchell, *Physical Fitness: A Way of Life,* 3d ed. (Toronto: John Wiley and Sons, 1983), 178.

48. John Sinacore, *Health: A Quality of Life,* 2d ed. (New York: Macmillan Publishing Co., 1974), 341–342.

49. H. Silverman, E. Chant Robertson, W.A. Hawke and G.I. Heintz, *Tomorrow Is Now: Today's Psychology and Your Health* (Toronto: Holt, Rinehart and Winston of Canada, 1971).

50. It is interesting to note that where the topic of smoking and pregnancy are addressed in classroom resources, teaching strategies emphasize women's guilt. One pedagogical source encourages high-school students to discuss this case study: "You are married and you have just learned your wife is pregnant. She is a pack-a-day smoker and she has no intention of quitting. As the father, you are concerned about the implications for your child. Describe three strategies you would employ to have your wife quit smoking. Come up with a master list from your class of strategies that can be used to encourage a pregnant woman to stop smoking. Which do you

feel would be most effective and why?" Linda Brower Meeks, Philip Heit and Sharon Mitchell Pottebaum, *Teaching Health Science* (Dubuque: Wm. C. Brown Company Publishers, 1981), 283. For a much superior treatment of smoking and pregnancy, see Gordon Berry and David Lynn, *Biology of Ourselves,* 2d ed. (Toronto: John Wiley and Sons, 1990), 205, and Merki, Merki and Flynn, *Glencoe Health*, 541.

51. Alan Robertson, Gordon Mutter, Jean Saunders and Ronald Wakelin, *Health Canada Series: Decisions for Health* (Scarborough: Nelson Canada Limited, 1981), 50.

52. Ontario Physical and Health Education Association, *Health and Physical Education Curriculum Support Document, Grade 4* (Toronto: OPHEA, 2000), 178. See also the otherwise useful support documents for Grades 5, 6, 7 and 8, all of which group tobacco with other drugs.

53. Health Canada, *Survey on Smoking in Canada.*

54. Health Canada, *Improving the Odds* (Ottawa: Health Canada 1994), see esp. page 19.

55. About 14 percent of university-educated women smoke, while 28 percent of women with some high school smoke, and 47 percent of unemployed women smoke. Health Canada, *Survey on Smoking in Canada.*

56. Here too the treatment is spotty. Anorexia nervosa was ignored in a number of otherwise commendable health textbooks well into the 1990s. See, for example, Grant Ellis, Vicki O'Brien and Cameron Young, *Young Canada Health* (Scarborough: Nelson Canada Ltd., 1990). Its treatment in pedagogical literature is likewise uneven. Most often, it is considered a neurotic response to societal messages but with the implications for healthy women or girls unmentioned. See, for example, Myron H. Dembo, *Applying Educational Psychology in the Classroom,* 3d ed. (New York: Longman, 1988), 92–93. It appears much earlier, however, in university-level textbooks in abnormal psychology. See for example, James C. Coleman, *Abnormal Psychology and Modern Life,* 5th ed. (Glenview, IL: Scott, Foresman and Company, 1976), 287.

57. Fourteen sample pedagogical textbooks for educational psychology and health education were surveyed between 1970 and 1995; not one commented on the issue.

58. See, for example, Merita Lee Thompson, Ruth Ann Althaus, Charles Corbin, Gerald E. Gray, Stephen R. Sroka and Kelly G. Thompson, *Choosing Good Health* (Toronto: Gage Educational Publishing Company, 1985). Texts of this era began to first picture female smokers.

59. See, for example, Mary Bronson Merki and Don Merki, *Health: A Guide to Wellness,* 3d ed. (New York: Macmillan McGraw-Hill, 1993), 450–452.

60. The ad I am referring to is entitled "Smoking Suits, 1922" and is reproduced in Alan Jenkins, *The Twenties* (New York: Universe Books, 1974), 62. Cigarette advertisement in the period under discussion generally targeted middle-class women of European descent.

61. A reproduction of the advertisement can be found in the *New York State Journal of Medicine* 83, no. 13 (December 1983), 1243.

62. The ad appeared on the back cover of *Ms.* (June 1987).

63. Cunningham, *Smoke and Mirrors,* esp. chap. 7.

64. These advertisements too were becoming more focused through then president Bill Clinton's final revisions to regulations of the United States' Food and Drug Administration. See Cunningham, *Smoke and Mirrors,* 300.

65. Stars like Rosalind Russell, Katharine Hepburn and Bette Davis incorporated the "long drag" into carefully timed dramatic sequences where cigarettes underlined their independence, sexual assertiveness and strength of character. In the 1938 film *Bringing Up Baby,* Katharine Hepburn directs a group of men who have surround- ed her with the command, "Cigarette me." Public Media Center. <www.Public MediaCenter.org>. August 30, 2002.

66. Other ratings included *What Women Want,* twenty-five shots; *Charlie's Angels,* twen- ty-three; *The Family Man,* nineteen; *X-Men,* nineteen; *Vertical Limit,* fourteen; *102 Dalmations,* thirteen; *Save the Last Dance,* twelve; *Road to El Dorado,* eleven; *Shanghai Noon,* ten. Public Media Center. <www.PublicMediaCenter.org>. August 30, 2002.

67. "Female Celebrity Smoking List." *Smoking from All Sides.* <http:// smokingsides. com >. June 26, 2003.

68. Sit-coms such as *Married ... with Children* or *Third Rock from the Sun* as well as soap operas seem to have been especially fertile.

69. Health Canada, *Survey on Smoking in Canada.* Of smokers aged ten to fourteen, 83 percent reported that they were considering quitting, while of the fifteen to nine- teen age group, it was 55 percent; for smokers twenty to twenty-four years old, it was 45 percent.

CHAPTER 2

Writing Them Into History:
Canadian Women in Science and Engineering since the 1980s

Ruby Heap

Feminism, Science and Engineering:
A Largely Uncharted Territory

ON WEDNESDAY, DECEMBER 6, 1989, Marc Lépine enters classrooms in Montreal's École Polytechnique armed with a shotgun. Before turning the gun on himself, he kills fourteen young women engineering students and injures thirteen others. His victims, he proclaimed, were all feminists ("Vous êtes des féministes"). Indeed, a suicide note found on his body blamed women, and specifically feminists, for ruining his life. One of the victims who pleaded with Lépine protested, "We are not feminists. We are just women who want to study" (On n'est pas des féministes. On est juste des femmes qui veulent étudier).[1]

For the feminist historian interested in Canadian women in science and engineering, what is commonly referred to as the "Montreal Massacre" is rich in meanings. On the one hand, Lépine's extreme act brutally reminds us that, in 1989, engineering was still a male stronghold within universities and that the presence of a minority of women in this historically male-dominated field could be viewed as something strange by many and as something highly disturbing by some. On the other hand, the female student's anguished outburst denied any links between herself, her classmates and feminism. While Lépine did not hesitate to identify his victims as feminists who threatened the patriarchal order, one of them, as well as other female students interviewed after the massacre, was eager to dissociate herself from feminists.

In a tragic way, this scenario reminds the feminist historian of the complex relationship that exists between contemporary feminism and the world of science and, to an even greater extent, the world of engineering, where the under-representation of women has been severe.[2] In Canada, this relationship has played out in various ways, all of which feminist historians need to explore. For example, we need to measure the impact of second-wave feminism on women's entry into and participation in science and engineering. American feminist scholars Sue Rosser and Londa Schiebinger, who have examined the various policies and strategies adopted across the border to improve women's status in these fields, have associated these strategies with the goals of liberal feminism. They point out, however, that these types of initiatives have rarely been formerly linked with feminism, even its liberal stand, either because of a lack of knowledge of feminist theories or, more fundamentally, because of a general distrust of feminism.[3]

Can we discern similar patterns in Canada? The research I have conducted so far suggests that, up until recently, the greatest influence of the contemporary women's movement in Canada has been in the area of affirmative action and equity. In 1970, the Report of the Royal Commission on the Status of Women in Canada, which set the foundation for liberal feminism in this country, articulated the rhetoric of equal access and equal opportunity for women in all spheres of public life, more specifically in the "masculine professions." Significantly, one of the Commission's strongest voices for women's equal rights in these male-dominated fields was Elsie Gregory MacGill, whose celebrated career as an aeronautical engineer both at home and abroad made her a pioneering figure in the history of women in the profession.[4]

During the 1970s and 1980s, the Canadian women's movement pursued various strategies aimed at fighting discrimination and at providing equal opportunities for women in the paid labour force. Equal-rights feminism began to record significant victories with the creation, in 1972, of the National Action Committee on the Status of Women (NAC). The creation of NAC spurred the establishment of several advisory councils, status of women committees and other women's organizations committed to equality politics,[5] and with the inclusion ten years later of a sex-equality clause in the Canadian Charter of Human Rights and Freedoms, the door to affirmative action programs and policies was opened. This led many activists within the women's movement to seek state-supported initiatives aimed at increasing the numbers of girls studying mathematics, science and engineering, on the grounds that women could excel in "non-traditional careers" as much as men if they were given the same opportunities.[6]

Meanwhile, many Canadian women scientists and engineers began to express a growing concern about those barriers preventing their full access and participation in their respective fields. As a result, they created alternative support networks to offset their exclusion from the established male-dominated associations and organizations; to engage in various strategies designed, mainly, to increase the participation of girls and women in science, technology and engineering; to promote equal opportunities for women scientists and engineers; and to counteract gender stereotyping.[7]

The Montreal Massacre was a catalytic event that precipitated the adoption of a new series of programs and policies with similar goals. These were initiated and sponsored by the federal and provincial governments, industry, universities and professional organizations, as well as by national funding agencies such as the National Science and Engineering Research Council of Canada (NSERC). One major initiative in 1997 was the funding of five regional chairs in Women in Science and Engineering that were awarded to female faculty.[8] Significantly, these initiatives occurred at a time when organized feminism had begun to lose considerable support from the state, which was becoming increasingly neo-conservative and implementing severe budget cuts.[9] In fact, in Canada, as in the United States, these programs and policies have not been officially linked with feminism. But over the years, feminism has certainly influenced individual women scientists and engineers, especially those working in universities where Women's Studies programs are located and where feminist scholarship is produced. In the 1980s, for example, Ursula Franklin, Margaret Benston and other Canadian female scientists involved in "the women's movement in science" published feminist critiques of science and technology.[10] In the late 1970s, Karen Messing, a professor of genetics at the Université du Québec in Montreal and one of the founders of Women's Studies of that institution, began to conduct groundbreaking feminist-oriented research on women's occupational health. In the 1990s, women scientists and engineers actively promoting women's participation in these fields raised issues and expressed concerns that go beyond the boundaries of liberal feminism.[11] During the past thirty years, then, different and opposing feminist views of science have been developed in Canada. To borrow the terms used by American scholar Sandra Harding, while some feminists critique "bad science" by focusing on its androcentric, classist and racial bias, others take the "science-as-usual" approach believing that the essential task at hand is to enable more women to become scientists by attacking the formal and informal barriers that prevent them from gaining the opportunities in science that are available to men.[12]

To unravel the interrelationship between feminism, science and engineering is thus a complex matter. In fact, before we can effectively measure the impact of feminism on these fields, we must examine the evolution of feminist scholarship that is concerned with the place and role of women in these fields and with the relationship between gender and science. In what particular settings has this scholarship evolved? What disciplines have been the most active in its development? Did the institutionalization of Women's Studies foster research in this field? What are the main approaches developed by this scholarship? So far, there aren't any studies that can give us clear answers to these questions. One reason for this is that, unlike in the United States, Canada has not yet witnessed the growth of what is referred to as "feminist science studies." As Sue Rosser recently explained, this area of scholarship has emerged in the United States after twenty-five years of "cross-fertilization" between Women's Studies scholars in such disciplines as history, philosophy and sociology and scholars in the natural and physical sciences.[13] The increasing number of publications in the United States over the last few years illustrates the outburst of scholarship in this interdisciplinary field, and illustrates as well that feminists in science and engineering are connecting with their sisters from the humanities and social sciences and that feminist scientists and engineers are making more formal links with Women's Studies.[14]

The history of women in science has played a critical role in the development of feminist science studies in the United States, as have other areas of scholarship that discuss the current status of women in science, the teaching of science and engineering, the development of a feminist critique of science and the potential of a feminist theory of science.[15] In this chapter, I examine the major developments and trends in the history of women in science and engineering in Canada. A preliminary overview of the American scholarship produced in these fields provides a useful comparative lens through which we can view the state of scholarship in Canada. I hope the following inspires further discussion among feminists working in science and engineering in this country.

The History of American Women in Science and Engineering

In the United States, the history of women in science took off during the 1970s and 1980s as a result of the increasing number of women entering history on the one hand and those entering sciences on the other. Up until then, historians of science had neglected women both as subjects and objects of science, and they had discounted gender as a critical category of analysis. Even the revisionist scholarship produced by the new "science studies," which took off in the 1970s in the wake of such influential works as Thomas S. Kuhn's *The Structure of Scientific Revolutions,* suffered from this neglect. Science was no longer considered a value-free and objective activity but was scrutinized as a social activity and as a historically contingent feature of society. Still, the relationship between gender and the nature and practice of science was not addressed. It would be up to feminist scholars in the U.S. to integrate women and gender into the mainstream scholarly work devoted to the scientific enterprise.[16]

Women historians took up this challenge in several ways. Following in the footsteps of the early practitioners who had retrieved women "hidden from history," they began to identify women who had worked in science in America, to document their access to the scientific world and to record their achievements. This approach led to the publication of biographical studies devoted to "great women scientists." It soon came under criticism because it took the dominant male standards of performance and success in science as its main reference and because it paid no significant attention to the gendering of science.[17] Nevertheless, by identifying past women scientists and by making them visible, this literature called for the inclusion of women in the history of science and raised several questions concerning women's place and role within the scientific community. The same can be said of the biographical studies produced by women working in science who were eager to "right the record" by discussing the scientific contributions of their predecessors.[18]

Meanwhile, feminist historians began to move beyond the discovery of "exceptional" women scientists; they sought, rather, to depict and explore those factors, both personal and external, both empowering and inhibiting, that shaped women's experiences in science. Margaret Rossiter's seminal study on American women scientists thus discussed the two dominant gender barriers — one territorial and the other hierarchical — that confined women to the less-prestigious and less-rewarded jobs and activities. But Rossiter also broke important ground by showing that despite barriers there still were many women working in science and by examining the various survival strategies they had developed to overcome these barriers.[19] In the meantime, other historians closely explored the intersections of the private and public in the lives of women scientists; as they discovered, spousal and family support was in many cases a determining factor in these women's pursuit of a career in science.[20]

Finally, in addition to focusing on women practitioners of science, feminist historians, along with feminist philosophers of science, located gender as a critical variable in the history of science and of the scientific community. Overall, the field of "gender and science" encompasses three different areas of scholarship: women's experiences in science, the scientific constructions of gender and the influence of gender in historical constructions of science. Feminist historians in the U.S., especially those engaged in the history of science, have been involved in all three areas and have made a major contribution to the critical re-evaluation of science as a gender-neutral activity.[21] Some scholars conducted pioneering work by investigating the evolution of gender representations within science,[22] while others have located the critical importance of scientific discourses in the construction of the female body, and by extension, of gender roles.[23] Still others have examined the role of gender in the shaping of the contents, methods and practices of science.[24] Evelyn Fox Keller, a biophysicist and a leading scholar in the area of "gender and science," recently observed that over the years the field has become a "gargantuan entity — not only huge, but amorphous and ever changing."[25] Indeed, it is moving in all kinds of directions and is raising an array of questions, which makes it difficult to identify clear trends in the existing scholarship. As Keller puts it, however, it is no longer sufficient to examine the impact of gender on "women in science"; we must now answer the question "Which women?" by exploring how race, class, ethnicity and sexual orientation shape women's experiences.[26]

Despite the rapid growth of research on women and gender in science, there are still areas that await investigation. The presence and role of women in physics and mathematics, the "hardest" of the sciences, is slowly attracting attention.[27] The history of women in engineering is also in its early phase.[28] A highly male-dominated profession that has fostered a strong masculinist ideology, engineering has had a tenuous relationship with feminism both within and outside academia — which might explain the paucity of historical research on the minority of women who have entered the field.[29]

The History of Canadian Women in Science and Engineering

In Canada, the history of women in science has clearly not experienced the same growth as its American counterpart. One cannot find a historical study on Canadian women scientists, let alone engineers, before the 1980s.[30] As I suggest above, feminist scholarship in this field as a whole has not expanded to the same extent as it has in the U.S, which might explain the paucity of historical materials. In the 1980s, special issues were devoted to women in science by the two leading feminist journals in Canada: *Canadian Woman Studies/les cahiers de la femme* in 1984 and *Resources for Feminist Research/ Documentation sur la recherche féministe* in 1986. Articles in both issues focused mainly on contemporary matters, but in *Resources for Feminist Research,* some historical material was provided by Marianne Gosztonyi Ainley who has, without a doubt, opened the field in Canada. She explained the difficulties she had in finding materials about early Canadian women scientists, whose lives and achievements have been overlooked by historians of science, despite the fact that quite a few of the women had received recognition from the scientific community in their time. Since most of these women had not left any public record of their careers, Ainley sent a plea to retired women scientists urging them not to throw away their personal papers.[31]

Trained as an industrial chemist in Hungary, Ainley worked some twenty years as an "invisible" chemist in Hungary, Sweden and Canada. Deciding to recycle herself as a historian, she completed a doctorate in the history and philosophy of science at McGill University in 1985.[32] She soon developed a strong interest in the history of Canadian women in science, teaching and researching extensively on this subject at Concordia University, where she was director of the Women's Studies Program and principal of the Simone de Beauvoir Institute. Since 1995, she has been teaching in the Women's Studies Program at the University of Northern British Columbia. In 1990, she published the landmark anthology *Despite the Odds: Essays on Canadian Women and Science.* This multidisciplinary collection includes contributions from historians, social scientists and several practising scientists. An ambitious undertaking, *Despite the Odds* explores the relationship of Canadian women to science in its various dimensions by including essays on women scientists and on women who are users of science. It further includes studies on the attitudes of girls towards science classes and discussions on the relationship between gender and science and technology. In her introduction, Ainley explains how the history of women scientists in Canada was given "short shrift" both by women historians, who focused more on other groups like female teachers and immigrants in their efforts to reconstruct the social history of Canada, and from historians of Canadian science, who were few in number and who were more concerned with the task of establishing the field.[33]

The collection illustrates some of the main approaches to studying the history of women in science. Its biographical essays "right the record" by recovering the lives and experiences of Canadian women scientists, most of whom have been overlooked in the mainstream historical record. Some articles use the "great women" approach and focus on better-known women scientists like botanist Carrie Derrick, geologist Alice Wilson and nuclear physicist Harriet Brooks. But other contributors follow in the footsteps of Margaret Rossiter by looking at different groups of women who participated in various ways in the scientific enterprise: as amateurs, popularizers of scientific knowledge and consumers; as the "invisible" graduate students, assistants and technicians working in the shadows of male supervisors; and as partners in a "two-person single career."

Despite the Odds highlights many of the themes that characterize the historical scholarship at the time, including Marianne Ainley's numerous articles.[34] The most important of these are the growing access to scientific education in the late nineteenth and early twentieth centuries; the multidimensional and gender-specific "careers" of Canadian women in various scientific fields and in diverse institutional settings like high schools, colleges and universities, museums, government agencies and organizations; and the significant contribution of women "amateurs" in the production and dissemination of scientific knowledge. Essays also touch on the themes of formal and informal exclusion, marginalization, sex-segregation and a lack of recognition and advancement, and on the conflict between marriage and the pursuit of a professional scientific career. Many early women scientists did not marry; for those who did, employment opportunities declined and the potential for a successful career was greatly reduced.

This was the case of Canadian nuclear physicist Harriet Brooks, who is the subject of a biography published in 1992 by Marelene F. Rayner-

Canham and Geoffrey Rayner-Canham, two Memorial University academics trained in physics and chemistry, respectively.[35] Their study illustrates many of the possibilities enjoyed by women interested in scientific activities in the late nineteenth and early twentieth centuries, as well as the barriers and difficulties they encountered along the way. Brooks thus benefited from the increasing number of opportunities offered to middle-class white women in higher education during this period and from the employment opportunities generated, as Margaret Rossiter has shown, by rapidly growing areas like physics, where qualified women were hired in large numbers as support staff. The authors also credit the importance of a supportive graduate supervisor, Ernest Rutherford, for Brooks's early success. However, Brooks's partnership with Rutherford obscured her contribution to the field. She suffered from considerable self-doubt and eventually opted for the security of marriage, which terminated her professional career. Like most other women scientists of the time, Brooks never succeeded in reaching the upper echelons of the scientific hierarchy. While many, like herself, opted for marriage and the end of their professional life, others became teachers or occupied second-class positions as "assistants."

More recently, Marianne G. Ainley has re-examined the interconnections between women scientists' personal and professional lives. Along with other American historians, she explores in detail the many facets of the relationships constructed and reconstructed by some "creative couples in the sciences." She concludes that, in Canada as in the United States, most married women scientists worked in the shadows of their husbands as unpaid researchers and assistants; however, some enjoyed successful collaborative relationships because of the support they enjoyed from their spouses. Her research also demonstrates how the male model of the "ideal linear and uninterrupted career" in science does not fit with the experiences of many married women scientists who, like those studied by Ainley, enjoyed success later in their lives, following years devoted to marriage and motherhood. Indeed, the ebb and flow of both single and married women's scientific activities is another major theme that appears in the Canadian and American literature.[36]

What about the contribution of Canadian feminist historians to the field? During the 1990s, a growing number began to conduct research in this area. Alison Prentice stands out as a leading figure in this group because of her seminal work on the history of Canadian women in physics. A prominent scholar in the field of women's history and educational history,

Prentice began researching the history of Canadian women academics in the late 1980s, a route that led her to investigate the lives and experiences of Canadian women working in physics. As Prentice herself admits, she became interested in these women as the wife of a retired member of a university physics department.[37] She knew personally the subject of one of her biographical studies, Elizabeth Allin, who was the first woman to be appointed full professor in the University of Toronto's physics department.[38]

Prentice's articles provide important insights into many of the major themes related to the history of women in science — the barrier of marriage; the support or lack of support from family and relatives; the gender-based obstacles to entering science and pursuing a career in the field. They also depict the resilience of women and the strategies they adopted to survive and thrive in "men's professions." As the existing literature demonstrates, some women openly confronted the situation, while many others chose to bury their gender identity in the hope of being accepted. Still others were able to adapt their private lives to their situation and to rely on family support. Some, like Clara Benson, who was the first Canadian woman to obtain a doctorate in chemistry at the University of Toronto, opted for territorial segregation by pursuing an academic career at the university in the female-dominated Faculty of Household Science.[39]

Alison Prentice's work also makes an important contribution to the study of the relationship between gender and the professionalization of science. She demonstrates the damage that the increasing professionalization of physics did to women's careers and argues convincingly that women's work was a major contribution to the early development of Canadian physics. Indeed, she posits that there were more university jobs for women in physics than there were in the humanities and social sciences during the first decades of the twentieth century. However, women lost considerable ground in the post–Second World War era, a pattern identified by Margaret Rossiter in the U.S. and by Marianne G. Ainley in Canada.

Prentice keenly reflects on the methodological challenges and pitfalls facing historians trying to retrieve and reconstruct the lives of women scientists who turn to oral history and to the more traditional documentary records as their sources. In the case of oral history, for example, the critical issue is whether or not to identify the women who are interviewed, each option bearing advantages and disadvantages. In the case of documentary records, information may not always be reliable. As Prentice recently admitted, she wrongly identified Vivian Pound as the first woman to receive a doctorate in physics from the University of Toronto in 1913 (when, in fact, Vivian Pound was a man), since the sources she had used provided only the names of the graduates and no further clues about their gender. This is both a fascinating and instructive tale that should be read by all historians of women in science.[40]

The increasing use of oral history has strongly fostered a feminist biographical approach in the field.[41] As Prentice explains, "It seems useful to balance a record biased by countless biographies of men; for another, we need women's stories as well as men's if we hope to develop a full picture of how science works."[42] In addition, feminist historians are paying more attention to the life course of women scientists instead of focusing exclusively on their professional work. Such is the case of Ainley who, in a recent article, explains how she is now studying women scientists through a different lens. While her earlier work compared women's and men's careers in science, she is now focusing on women's life-course changes. This has enabled her to see these women as agents rather than as mere victims of the male-dominated scientific establishment. While not totally abandoning her first lens, Ainley's shift in focus has convinced her of the necessity of problematizing the prevailing notions of "career" and "success," since they do not account for the gender-specific experiences of many women scientists.[43]

In the past few years, groups of women performing scientific work have been examined by graduate students in history. Inspired by Margaret Rossiter, they have produced solid and innovative dissertations that explore the participation, contribution and experiences of the less visible and less public female figures in science, such as women working in the federal Department of Agriculture in the late nineteenth and early twentieth centuries, and women geoscientists in Alberta in more recent times.[44] For my part, I have been studying the professional education of women engineers in Canada since 1920. There are very few published historical works on Canadian women engineers and during my search for materials, Ainley's and Prentice's observations about the difficulty in finding and collecting material from a scattered and diverse body of primary sources came vividly to mind. Women engineers are even more invisible than women scientists because of their minuscule numbers and because of engineering's masculinist culture, and they have been even less likely to leave public records of their lives and experiences than women scientists.

However, my findings support Ruth Schwartz Cowan's observations on the importance of rescuing women engineers from obscurity. Their scarcity, she argues, "is itself both interesting and instructive." Indeed, in her view, "the effort to study people who are non-conformists, mold-breakers and gender-benders, requires that we stretch our imagination and reconstruct the categories into which we usually pigeon-hole our knowledge."[45] My investigations, which are based on a combination of printed sources, archival material and oral history, have so far revealed the complexity and diversity of women engineers' lives and professional experiences. Class, ethnicity, religion and sexuality have to be considered as seriously as gender in the exploration of their career paths. To reconstruct the history of engineering in Canada by considering these different variables will provide significant insight into the factors that led these mould-breakers into engineering as well as the factors that were detrimental to their full participation in the profession. For example, at the University of Toronto's Faculty of Applied Science and Engineering, the small number of female students enrolled in the first part of the twentieth century belonged to the white Protestant middle and upper classes, which was not the case for their male counterparts. Most of these women pioneers had supportive parents, and some had fathers or brothers who were engineers. After the Second World War, the FASE admitted female students from China and Eastern Europe; according to these women's testimonies, women engineers were not perceived as "oddities" in their home country, hence the shock many felt when pursuing their studies in Canada where women were not so easily accepted.

The state of the economy, critical events such as the two world wars and, of course, the women's movement are other factors that need to be considered when studying the history of women engineers. Finally, to depict the specific "culture of engineering" that prevails in the institutional settings of faculties and schools of engineering and in the subdisciplines of engineering is an essential dimension to include. So far, this approach has produced significant results. For instance, the experiences of the young women enrolled in Montreal's École Polytechnique have proven to be different in many ways from those female students enrolled at the University of Toronto or at Queen's University, a situation that may well be attributed to the institution's Catholic and francophone background, to the status of francophone male engineers in Canada and to Quebec's social and economic context. I have also established comparisons between students at the FASE and those enrolled in other professional schools at the University of Toronto, another approach that has proven fruitful when trying to capture the specific profiles of female engineering students.

The history of women engineers also reveals the many strategies and survival techniques they have adopted during their years at university, one of the most common being "acting like one of the boys." Paradoxically, local newspapers and professional publications reporting on female engineering students focused mainly on their femininity and their desire to eventually marry and raise a family. These narratives indicate the extent to which the history of women engineers can provide precious insights into the dominant forms of masculinity and femininity at any given time. But above all, my ongoing research confirms that it is essential to specify the location of women engineers not only in time but also in their particular institutional and cultural settings.[46]

Where Do We Go From Here?

Despite the important inroads it has witnessed since the 1990s, the history of women in science in Canada is still in its early stages. For example, we lack comprehensive studies on the historical relationship between gender and science in this country, and we have not really begun to systematically explore issues of race, ethnicity and sexual orientation. The experiences of Native women, of minority women and of most francophone women in science still await investigation, as Marianne Ainley recently observed.[47]

Where, then, do we go from here? This question brings me back to my earlier concern about the almost non-existent state of feminist science studies in Canada. As a feminist historian, I am convinced of the urgent need to measure the impact of feminism, or feminisms, on Canadian women practising science and engineering within academia as well as in other professional settings. Did the feminisms that were institutionalized in Canadian Women's Studies prove to be less appealing to these women than the liberal feminism that has informed the affirmative action policies largely conducted outside Women's Studies? How are historians and other feminist scholars engaged in Women's Studies — most of whom have been trained in the humanities and social sciences — currently attempting to work with their colleagues in science and engineering to develop feminist science studies in Canada? Or do science and engineering remain at the margins of Women's Studies in this country?

We can hope that a closer and more open collaboration between the two groups will foster an expansion of the field in this country as it has in the U.S. during the past decade, when such a meeting of the minds led to the creation of a "critical mass" of scholars with interest and training in both feminism and science.[48] The co-editors of a recent American anthology have defined feminist science studies as "a body of work that applies feminist analyses to scientific ideas and practices to explore the relationship between feminism and science and what each can learn from the other," and that also "explores the intersections between race, class, gender and science and technology."[49] The social relations of science, as well as its epistemologies and methodologies, are major areas of focus, since one of the field's main goals is to expand the basis of what constitutes "science" and "scientific inquiry."[50] This definition provides an important agenda for Canadian scholars working in the field.

The coming together of scholars from Women's Studies and from science and engineering will certainly not be achieved overnight. Many women scientists and engineers are still not familiar with nor interested in the work produced by scholars in Women's Studies or in the humanities and social sciences. Many others fear or are hostile to those feminist critiques of science and engineering that question the scientific method itself, especially its claim to objectivity and neutrality. While some do agree that the male domination of science and engineering has led to the exclusion and/or marginalization of women and to an androcentric bias in research, others are reluctant to see themselves as the "victims of the patriarchal order."[51] For my part, there is no doubt that feminist historians have a role to play in the creation of a critical mass of scholars who will pursue this agenda in Canada. Down the road, Women's Studies scholars and women scientists and engineers might well realize that feminism can take various forms and be practised in different ways, and they may come to understand that feminism has had a greater impact on science and engineering than we tend to believe.

NOTES

The research conducted for this essay has been funded by a grant from SSHRC for a project entitled "The Professional Education of Women Engineers in Quebec and Ontario Universities, 1920–1990." I wish to thank Monique Frize, the co-investigator for this project, for her useful insights, as well as my research assistants, Amber Lloydlangston, Stéphane Lang and Zoi Coucopoulos for their assistance and support.

1. For the feminist viewpoint on the Montreal Massacre see Louise Malette and Marie Chalouh, eds., *Polytechnique, 6 décembre* (Montréal: Les Éditions du remue-ménage, 1990).

2. I will use the term "science" to refer to the natural and physical sciences (mathematics, physics, chemistry, biology) and to engineering, all of which do not deal with human beings; I am thus excluding those disciplines that are part of the humanities, social sciences and health sciences.

3. See Londa Schiebinger, *Has Feminism Changed Science?* (Cambridge, MA: Harvard University Press, 1999), 3–4; and Sue Rosser, "Interdisciplinarity and Identity: Women's Studies and Women in Science Programs," in Kate Conway-Turner, Suzanne Cherrin, Jessica Schiffman and Kathleen Doherty Turkel, eds., *Women's Studies in Transition: The Pursuit of Interdisciplinarity* (Newark: University of Delaware Press, 1994), 255–258.

4. For a recent biography of MacGill, see Pamela Wakewich, "'The Queen of the Hurricanes': Elsie Gregory MacGill, Aeronautical Engineer and Women's Advocate," in Sharon Cook, Lorna R. McLean and Kate O'Rourke, eds., *Framing Our Past: Canadian Women's History in the Twentieth Century* (Montreal: McGill-Queen's University Press, 2001), 396–401. On the Royal Commission on the Status of Women and its ties with liberal feminism, see Monique Bégin, "The Royal Commission on the Status of Women in Canada: Twenty Years Later," in Constance Backhouse and David E. Flaherty, eds., *Challenging Times: The Women's Movement in Canada and the United States* (Montreal: McGill-Queen's University Press, 1992), 21–38. Bégin, who served as executive secretary on the Commission, states that MacGill was "already a feminist" when she was selected as a member.

5. On NAC, see Jill Vickers, Pauline Rankin and Christine Appelle, *Politics as if Women Mattered* (Toronto: University of Toronto Press, 1993).

6. See Karen Whyte, "'Can We Learn This? We're Just Girls!'" *Resources for Feminist Research* 17 (June 1988), 6–9.

7. These networks took the form of separate women's organizations such as SCWIST (Society for Canadian Women in Science and Technology) and WISE (Women in Science and Engineering), which were both established in 1982, or of Standing Committees on the Status of Women in already-established professional societies. On these developments, see Rose Sheinin, "Women in Science: Issues and Actions," *Canadian Woman Studies/les cahiers de la femme* 5 (Summer 1984), 70–77.

8. On the creation and goals of the five regional chairs, see Monique Frize et al., "A Unique National Project to Increase the Participation of Women in Science and Engineering." NSERC/Nortel Joint-Chair for Women in Science and Engineering in Ontario. Retrieved from <http://www.carleton.ca/cwse-on/engfound.htm>. June 2003. The chairholders were expected to act as role models through their teaching, research and mentoring activities, and to scrutinize the various factors that limited the participation of women in these fields.

9. See Barbara A. Crow and Lise Gotell, eds., *Open Boundaries: A Canadian Women's Studies Reader* (Toronto: Prentice-Hall Canada, 2000).

10. See Ursula M. Franklin, *Will Women Change Technology?* (Ottawa: Canadian Research Institute for the Advancement of Women, 1985) and *The Real World of*

Technology (Toronto: CBC Enterprises, 1990); Margaret Benston, "Feminism and the Critique of the Scientific Method," in Geraldine Finn and Angela Miles, eds., *Feminism in Canada: From Pressure to Politics* (Montreal: Black Rose Books, 1982), 47–66; Anne Innis Dagg, *Harems and Other Horrors: Sexual Bias in Behavioral Biology* (Waterloo: Otter Press, 1983); Roberta Mura, *Searching for Subjectivity in the World of Sciences: Feminist Viewpoints* (Ottawa: CRIAW, 1991). For a discussion of the "women's movement in science" in Canada, see Linda Christiansen-Ruffman, "Community Base and Feminist Vision: The Essential Grounding of Science in Women's Community," *Canadian Woman Studies/les cahiers de la femme* (Winter 1993), 16–20. This article is part of the journal's special issue on "Women in Science and Technology" which was dedicated to Margaret Benston, following her death in 1991.

11. See, for example, the Canadian Committee on Women in Engineering (CCWE), *More than Just Numbers* (Fredericton: University of New Brunswick, 1992); Peggy Tripp-Knowles, "Androcentric Bias in Science: An Exploration of the Discipline of Forest Genetics," *Women's Studies International Forum* 17 (1994), 1–8; Monique Frize, "Féminiser le domaine de l'ingénierie, pourquoi pas?" in Lucie Dumais and Véronique Boudreau, eds., *Femmes et sciences: Au coeur des débats institutionnels et épistémologiques* (Ottawa: ACFAS-Outaouais, 1996), 53–60; Claire Deschênes, "Les femmes, la science, l'ingénierie et la technologie," *Recherches féministes* 15, no. 1 (2002), 1–6. Claire Deschênes holds the NSERC/Alcan Chair for Women in Science and Engineering in Quebec. She is the guest editor of the special issue of *Recherches féministes*, "Sciences, ingénierie et technologie."

12. See Sandra Harding, *Whose Knowledge? Whose Science? Thinking from Women's Lives* (Ithaca, NY: Cornell University Press, 1991), 53–54.

13. Sue Rosser, "Editorial: Building Inclusive Science: Connecting Women's Studies and Women in Science and Engineering," *Women's Studies Quarterly* 28, nos. 1/2 (Spring/Summer 2000), 6.

14. Recent collections include Maralee Mayberry, Banu Subramaniam and Lisa H. Weasel, eds., *Feminist Science Studies: A New Generation* (New York: Routledge, 2001); Angela N. H. Creager, Elizabeth Lunbeck and Londa Schiebinger, eds., *Feminism in Twentieth-Century Science, Technology, and Medicine* (Chicago: University of Chicago Press, 2001).

15. For a discussion of these various categories, see Sue Rosser, "Feminist Scholarship in the Sciences: Where Are We Now and When Can We Expect a Theoretical Breakthrough?" in Nancy Tuana, ed., *Feminism and Science* (Bloomington: Indiana University Press, 1989), 3–14.

16. See the comments made by historian of science David A. Hollinger in his foreword to Evelyn Fox Keller's tenth anniversary edition of *Reflections on Gender and Science* (New Haven: Yale University Press, 1995), x–xii.

17. For reviews and critiques of this approach, see Londa Schiebinger, "The History and Philosophy of Women in Science: A Review Essay," *Signs: Journal of Women in Culture and Society* 12 (1987), 312–315; Marina Benjamin, ed., *Science and Sensibility: Gender and Scientific Inquiry, 1780–1945* (Oxford, UK: Basil Blackwell, 1991), 10–11.

18. A good example of this kind of work is G. Kass-Simon and Patricia Farnes, eds., *Women of Science: Righting the Record* (Bloomington: Indiana University Press, 1990).

19. Margaret W. Rossiter, *Women Scientists in America: Struggles and Strategies to 1940* (Baltimore: The Johns Hopkins University Press, 1982), and *Women Scientists in America: Before Affirmative Action, 1940–1972* (Baltimore: The Johns Hopkins University Press, 1995).

20. Helena M. Pycior, Nancy G. Slack and Pnina Abir-Am, eds., *Creative Couples in the Sciences* (New Brunswick, NJ: Rutgers University Press, 1996).

21. For a good discussion of the feminist scholarship in this area, see Marina Benjamin's introduction to her *Science and Sensibility*, 2–13. See also Sally Gregory Kohlstedt and Helen Longino, "The Women, Gender and Science Question: What Do Research on Women in Science and Research on Women in Science Have to Do with Each Other?" in Sally Gregory Kohlstedt and Helen Longino, eds., *Women, Gender and Science: New Directions*, Special Issue of *Osiris* 1, no. 12 (1997), 3–15.

22. Carolyn Merchant, for example, demonstrates how the historical association between women and nature and between men and science resulted in the domination and exploitation of both nature and women. See Carolyn Merchant, *The Death of Nature: Women, Ecology, and the Scientific Revolution* (San Francisco: Harper and Row, 1980).

23. See, for example, Londa Schiebinger, *Nature's Body: Gender in the Making of Modern Science* (Boston: Beacon Press, 1993), and Ludmilla Jordanova, *Sexual Visions: Images of Gender in Science and Medicine between the Eighteenth and Twentieth Centuries* (Madison: University of Wisconsin Press, 1989).

24. See, for example, Schiebinger, *Has Feminism Changed Science?*

25. Evelyn Fox Keller, "Making a Difference: Feminist Movement and Feminist Critique of Science," in Creager, Lunbeck and Schiebinger, eds., *Feminism in Twentieth-Century Science, Technology, and Medicine*, 100.

26. Ibid.

27. On feminist studies in physics, see Schiebinger, *Has Feminism Changed Science*, chap. 9. Margaret M. Murray, who teaches mathematics at Virginia Polytechnic Institute and State University, has recently published an excellent study on women in this discipline in the 1940s and 1950s. See *Women Becoming Mathematicians: Creating a Professional Identity in Post–World War II America* (Cambridge, MA: The MIT Press, 2000).

28. Recent studies include Ruth Oldenziel, *Making Technology Masculine: Men, Women and Modern Machines in America, 1870–1945* (Amsterdam: Amsterdam University Press, 1999); Annie Canel, Ruth Oldenziel and Karin Zachmann, eds., *Crossing Boundaries, Building Bridges: Comparing the History of Women Engineers, 1870s–1990s* (Amsterdam: Harwood Academic Publishers, 2001); and Amy Sue Bix, "Feminism Where Men Predominate: The History of Women's Science and Engineering Education at MIT," *Building Inclusive Science*, Special Issue of *Women's Studies Quarterly* 28, nos. 1/2 (Spring/Summer 2000), 24–45.

29. For a recent discussion on this issue, see Pamela Mack, "What Difference Has

Feminism Made to Engineering in the Twentieth Century?" in Creager, Lunbeck and Schiebinger, eds., *Feminism in Twentieth-Century Science, Technology, and Medicine*, 149–168.

30. One such study, devoted to "Canada's first woman geologist" Alice Wilson, was published by Anne Montagnes in Mary Quayle Innis, ed., *The Clear Spirit: Twenty Canadian Women and Their Times* (Toronto: University of Toronto Press, 1966), 260–270. Brief sketches on women natural scientists were written in 1976 by Lorraine G. Smith. See "Canadian Women Natural Scientists — Why Not?" *The Canadian Field-Naturalist* 90, no. 1 (1976), 1–4.

31. Marianne Gosztonyi Ainley, "Women Scientists in Canada: The Need for Documentation," *Resources for Feminist Research/Documentation sur la recherche féministe* 15 (November 1986), 7–8.

32. Marianne Gosztonyi Ainley, ed., *Despite the Odds: Essays on Canadian Women and Science* (Montreal: Véhicule Press, 1990), 375.

33. Ibid., 17–21.

34. These include Marianne G. Ainley and Catherine Millar, "A Select Few: Women and the National Research Council of Canada, 1916–1991," in Richard Jarell and Yves Gingras, eds., *Building Canadian Science: The Role of the National Research Council*, Special Issue of *Scientia Canadensis* 15, no. 2 (1991), 105–116; Marianne G. Ainley and Tina Crossfield, "Canadian Women's Contributions to Chemistry, 1900–1970," *Canadian Chemical News* (April 1994), 16–18; Marianne G. Ainley, "Women's Work in Geology: A Historical Perspective on Gender Division in Canadian Science," *Geoscience Canada* 21, no. 3 (1994), 140–142; Marianne G. Ainley, "Soaring to New Heights: Changes in the Life Course of Mabel McInstosh," in Elspeth Cameron and Janice Dickin, eds., *Great Dames* (Toronto: University of Toronto Press, 1997), 206–223.

35. Marelene F. Rayner-Canham and Geoffrey W. Rayner-Canham, *Harriet Brooks: Pioneer Nuclear Scientist* (Montreal: McGill-Queen's University Press, 1992).

36. See Marianne G. Ainley, "Marriage and Scientific Work in Twentieth-Century Canada: The Berkeleys in Marine Biology and the Hoggs in Astronomy," in Pycior, Slack and Abir-Am, eds., *Creative Couples in the Sciences*, 143–155. For comments on the American literature, see Sally Gregory Kohlstedt, ed., *History of Women in the Sciences: Readings from Isis* (Chicago: The University of Chicago Press, 1999), 7.

37. Alison Prentice, "Vivian Pound Was a Man?" *Historical Studies in Education/Revue d'histoire de l'éducation* 13, no. 2 (2001), 103.

38. Alison Prentice, "Elizabeth Allin: Physicist," in Cameron and Dickin, eds., *Great Dames*, 264–287, and "Three Women in Physics," in Elizabeth Smyth, Sandra Acker, Paula Bourne and Alison Prentice, eds., *Challenging Professions* (Toronto: University of Toronto Press, 1999), 119–140.

39. Ruby Heap, "From the Science of Housekeeping to the Science of Nutrition: Pioneers in Canadian Nutrition and Dietetics," in Smyth et al., eds., *Challenging Professions*, 141–170.

40. Prentice, "Vivian Pound Was a Man?"

41. Recent examples include Marianne G. Ainley, "Norah Toole: Scientist and Social

Activist," in Cook et al., eds., *Framing Our Past*, 308–310, and, in the same volume, E. Tina Crossfield, "Alice V. Payne, Mining Geologist: A Lifetime of 'Small Difficult Things,'" 311–313.

42. Prentice, "Three Women in Physics," 120.

43. Marianne G. Ainley, "Une nouvelle optique concernant la recherche sur l'histoire des femmes canadiennes et les sciences," *Recherches féministes* 15, no. 2 (2002), 93–11.

44. See Amber Lloydlangston, "'Seminal Women': Women in Science in the Canadian Federal Department of Agriculture" (PhD diss., University of Ottawa, 2002), and Cynthia Nelles O' Donnell, "Alberta Women in the Field: Geoscientists in the Resource Industry, Government Research and Academia, 1914-1999" (PhD diss., OISE/UT, 2000).

45. Ruth Schwartz Cowan, "Foreword: Musings about The Woman Engineer as Muse," in Canel, Oldenziel and Zachmann, eds., *Crossing Boundaries, Building Bridges*, xiii, xvi.

46. See, for example, Ruby Heap, "Female Students at the University of Toronto's Faculty of Applied Science and Engineering, 1910–1950," *Historical Studies in Education/Revue d'histoire de l'éducation* (forthcoming 2004); Ruby Heap and Ellen Scheinberg, "'They're Just One of the Gang': Women at the University of Toronto's Faculty of Applied Science and Engineering," in Ruby Heap, Wyn Millar and Elizabeth Smyth, eds., *Becoming Professionals? Professional Education in Historical and Contemporary Perspectives* (Ottawa: University of Ottawa Press, forthcoming 2004), and Wyn Millar, Ruby Heap and Robert Gidney, "Degrees of Difference: The Students of Three Professional Schools at the University of Toronto, 1910 to 1950s," in *Becoming Professionals?*

47. Ainley, "Une nouvelle optique ...," 108–109.

48. Rosser, "Editorial: Building Inclusive Science," 6.

49. Mayberry, Subramaniam and Weasel, eds., *Feminist Science Studies*, 9, 5.

50. Ibid., 6.

51. For a discussion on the similar views held by women scientists in the U.S., see Sue V. Rosser, *Women, Science and Society: The Crucial Union* (New York: Teachers College, Columbia University, 2000), 112–113.

CHAPTER 3

Moving into the Spaces Cleared by Our Sisters:
Lesbian Community Activism in Ireland and Canada

Tina O'Toole

IN HER INTRODUCTION TO *The House that Jill Built,* a history of the Lesbian Organization of Toronto (LOOT) and its influence in Canada, Becki Ross describes a scenario that is as familiar to lesbians in Ireland as it is to lesbians here:

> Among those of us privileged to be out and to have access to [communi-ty] resources, there is little collective knowledge of how they came to exist, who was responsible for their genesis, and how fragile they contin-ue to be. When I came out, even the immediate lesbian past seemed remote; I joined a collective state of unknowing that is both personally disabling and politically dangerous.[1]

Ross goes on to emphasize the importance of a sense of collective and indi-vidual memory as a basis for future activism and political change. An awareness of the movement's history enables activists to recognize past achievements, to critically evaluate earlier strategies and to avoid reinvent-ing the wheel. This work is as important for scholars as it is for feminist activists and community workers. Historically, in many fields of scholarly inquiry, there has tended to be a dichotomy between theory and practice.

The arrival of "new" disciplines such as Women's Studies in the academy heralded a new approach to practice — deriving from an activist movement, it would maintain links between "community" and "academy." However, as time has passed and as Women's Studies has become a core subject in the modular degrees of many universities, students may no longer have links with feminist activism nor a personal investment in feminist politics. One way to invigorate feminist studies and to make students (and teachers) aware of the challenges that feminist research and activism pose to patriarchal and heterosexist norms is to go back to primary sources. Oral history projects and archival work are just two of the ways that this might be achieved.

This chapter, whose title is taken from the poetry collection by the Irish lesbian poet, writer and activist Mary Dorcey,[2] outlines some aspects of lesbian feminist activism in Ireland and Canada, and examines the ways in which lesbian activists in the 1970s and 1980s worked to clear political, social and cultural spaces for themselves as well as for their bisexual and heterosexual sisters. My research is rooted in an archival study of the Irish Women's Movement (IWM), and my interest (and involvement) in lesbian activism in Ireland prompted my investigation of lesbian activism in the 1970s and 1980s at the Canadian Women's Movement Archives (CWMA).[3] Thus, my work underscores the importance of recovery projects and the preservation of archival resources for feminist research and theory.

In examining the origins of lesbian activism in the 1970s and 1980s, I refer to national organizations but more specifically I am concerned with lesbian communities in the cities of Cork[4] and Dublin, Toronto and Montreal.[5] My research is based principally on primary documents, first-hand accounts of lesbian experience, and published research in this field. Although this is not a comparative study, it is informed by a knowledge and understanding of the Irish feminist context and does make some comparative connections with Canadian lesbian feminist activism in the same period. As with any term, the use of "Irish feminist context" in the singular is a highly contested one, begging the question, *Which* Irish feminists are under discussion? Definitions of Irishness are problematized not only by the division of Ireland into two different states,[6] and the various ways in which the label "Irish" is used both within the country and abroad, but also by factors of class and location and the frequent occlusion of Irish emigrant women, as Linda Connolly reminds us.[7] For the most part, I refer to the

Republic of Ireland and, unless otherwise stated, specifically to Cork- and Dublin-based feminist activism.

I begin by delineating aspects of Irish feminist history, which may be more unfamiliar to Canadian readers, before going on to describe the early days of lesbian community-building. Considering the strategic deployment of identity politics in this period, I trace the development of these discourses by interrogating some of the issues currently being raised in lesbian, bisexual and transgender (LBT)[8] communities, and the ways in which community resources are being redefined today.

Irish and Canadian Feminisms: Contrasts and Dissonances

Drawing parallels between social change in Ireland and Canada is not to compare like with like. It is by now almost a cliché to point out that Irish society has changed rapidly over the past twenty years and that the women's movement has played a major role in these changes.[9] But more important, perhaps, is that these changes in the moral, political and social order have come about some twenty or thirty years *after* corresponding revolutions in countries such as Canada. The reasons for this time lag are varied — Ireland came to independence less than a century ago, and the early years of the Irish state were marked by economic and moral protectionism. As Chrystel Hug points out, the new state was shaped by the joint forces of the Catholic church and the rule of majoritarianism, that is, the law of the highest number.[10] This meant that discourses outside the mainstream of white Catholic family values — such as feminisms, socialism or, indeed, any political or social philosophy which differed from the dominant culture — were seen as voices of dissent, with the capability of destroying the moral (and by implication the national) order, and they were dealt with accordingly.[11] Thus, in the early days of the second-wave Irish women's movement, feminists in Ireland faced stiff opposition.

Discussing the impact of feminist politics in the Canadian national referendum in 1992, Marjorie Cohen writes: "In Canada, the women's movement is now an established political force and in all the major political debates in this country, a feminist perspective is aired."[12] Although in the intervening ten years the effects of the backlash against feminism have become apparent in Canada, the achievements of the feminist movement are evident here in areas such as childcare, healthcare and employment equality legislation. The same situation does not pertain in Ireland, where we are now in the predicament of experiencing the backlash against feminism without having had gains in terms of social policy and legislation on anything like the same scale as our Western neighbours.

Another difference between Irish and Canadian feminisms is in the size of the two countries. As an Irish woman in Canada, I am continually struck by Canadians' surprise at how small Ireland actually is. For those Canadians who are not of Irish descent — and even for some of those who are — it is as if Ireland has been reflected at several times its natural size, perhaps because of the legacy of Irish immigration to Canada and the influence of Irish-Americans in the neighbouring U.S.A. Laura Sabia's threat to march two million women to Parliament Hill if the government refused a Commission on the Status of Women[13] is astonishing when set against the Irish context — such a march would require the participation of half of Ireland's population.

One Canadian lesbian feminist activist I interviewed was intrigued by this difference and questioned me closely about the lack of anonymity in such a small country — how could one separate from one's family, she asked, or have any privacy? In Ireland, it is not possible to lead a double life. It would be next to impossible, for example, to move from a small town in New Brunswick to Toronto, come out, become part of a lesbian feminist group and write policy documents for the revolution without everyone in your hometown knowing all about it. To be in the vanguard of feminist politics in Ireland in the 1970s was not only to strike against the social order but also to have to do so in the full glare of one's family and local community. Lesbian mothers with children, needless to say, had even more reason to be circumspect, up until 1992 they automatically lost the right to custody of their children before the courts by reason of their sexuality.[14]

Writings about what it is to be lesbian, how this changes over time and place, and the struggles lesbians have faced in a variety of international contexts have been available to Irish women in a range of published documents since the late 1960s. One example I found in the collection at the Irish Women's Movement archives is an undated copy of the New York Radicalesbians manifesto "The Woman-Identified Woman," which suggests that American lesbian theory and politics influenced Irish lesbian groups in the 1970s and 1980s. This document was reproduced throughout English Canada in 1972, appearing in feminist publications such as *The Pedestal* (Vancouver) and *The Other Woman* (Toronto). Unlike Canadian lesbian social history, which has been explored in recent years by Becki Ross, Line Chamberland and Miriam Smith,[15] among others, research and publications on lesbian experience(s) in Ireland are few. Íde O'Carroll and Eoin

Collins's 1995 study, *Lesbian and Gay Visions of Ireland*, is one of the few texts relating to Irish GLBTQ social history, and it is now almost ten years old.

Recovery work on this history is just beginning to emerge in the articles and papers from Women's Studies centres around Ireland, ably supported by the annual Lesbian Lives Conference, the Queeries seminar series, and Lesbian and Queer Studies courses run by the Women's Education Research and Resource Centre (WERRC) at University College Dublin. Such work, both practical and theoretical, provides a series of support structures to the ongoing activism in GLBTQ communities in various parts of Ireland and internationally. Furthermore, some of the more recent material being produced by younger scholars indicates a transition from early lesbian feminist activism, which prioritized writing from the standpoint of experience, to analyzing and problematizing versions of lesbian experiences and identities that have been passed down through written records.

Lesbians and the Women's Movement

Despite the active participation of lesbians in the women's movements in both Canada and Ireland, lesbian issues were not on the early feminist agenda. In both countries, solidarity between women was a feature of the early feminist years (i.e., the late 1960s and 1970s); but instead of investing in the diversity of women's experiences, this solidarity was based on finding common cause. In order to present a unified opposition to the dominant culture, differences between women such as class, sexuality, politics (and especially Republican politics in Ireland) were perceived as problematic elements that had the power to distract from the main focus of the movement or even destroy it from within. It was felt that these subjects could not be openly discussed in feminist groups during the period without causing controversy and internal strife. Lesbian identity was regarded as a political liability by the leaders of the feminist movement for a variety of different reasons, which ranged from overt homophobia within feminist organizations to a recognition of the ways in which lesbian identity would be used by opponents of the feminist movement.

Identifying all feminists as lesbians is a charge that has been very effectively deployed by a variety of anti-feminist organizations down through the years, usually as a way of censoring heterosexual women and disrupting solidarity between women (and, in fact, this ploy recently resurfaced during the 2002 abortion referendum in Ireland). One of the arguments made by women within second-wave feminist organizations was that women outside the movement would refuse to join for fear of being identified as lesbian. Ross discusses the debates raging in Canadian feminist organizations as to whether or not to identify with lesbianism and at what cost.[16] Much to the chagrin of their lesbian members, the Toronto New Feminists, founded in 1969, publicly denied the presence of lesbians in their organization. Sixteen years later, not much had changed for some Canadian lesbians. In the 1985 article "Lesbian Witch Hunt," the unnamed writer reveals some of the consequences for a group of lesbians who were publicly outed following a conference at a local women's centre in Charlottetown, PEI:

> Their credibility as workers, the Centre's ability to serve the women's community and their funding was called into question. The reputation of other women's groups attending the conference came under attack, as they were viewed as being pro-lesbian. As an invited speaker, I was publicly identified as a lesbian. Articles I had written on incest from a feminist perspective were taken to my employer as evidence to fire me.[17]

This was followed by an appeal by REAL Women,[18] in which they alleged that lesbian groups were the primary recipients of government funding, and their letter-writing campaign calling on the Secretary of State to investigate the funding of groups which supported and/or hired lesbians. Likewise, lesbian issues were not openly on the Irish feminist agenda. Feminists who became involved in the first feminist organization in the south of Ireland, the Irish Women's Liberation Movement (IWLM), tacitly agreed to leave their "difference(s)" at the door, or at least, not to publicly own them.

Like their Canadian contemporaries, Irish lesbian activists have been a part of every movement for social and political liberation, including campaigns for access to contraception (legalized following feminist campaigns in Ireland in 1979), social housing, the provision of rape crisis services, divorce (made available in 1996), Traveller rights,[19] disability issues, abortion rights[20] and the decriminalization of (male) homosexuality in 1993. As well, they have been involved with trade unions, environmental groups and socialist and nationalist platforms. Yet, as both Connolly and Ross point out, there is a dearth of research on lesbian involvement in feminist organizations in both Ireland and Canada.[21] In a conference address in 1988, Nell McCafferty (one of the founders of the IWLM) reflected on the question of lesbian involvement in early Irish feminist groups:

> There was another undercurrent, called sexual self-determination, we didn't give a name [to] ... lesbianism, where women who loved women

were given a certain freedom ... it didn't matter, there was no separatism then ... There came a stage in 1975 when practically every woman in the movement was, (pause) not really ... pretending to be gay — it actually got boring, you longed to see a heterosexual restored [sic], for a little bit of diversity and plurality and tolerance.[22]

Despite this very positive, tongue-in-cheek account of co-operation between women in the early 1970s, it is clear even from this statement, which points out that lesbianism wasn't explicitly *named* by members of the Irish women's movement, that there were unresolved tensions on a variety of different fronts between members of the IWLM, who had come to feminism from a range of different subject positions. The IWLM charter of "seven minimum demands" called for equal pay, legal rights and educational opportunities for women, raised the subjects of contraception and divorce and addressed the contemporary housing crisis by calling for "one family, one house." Sexuality, or more specifically, lesbian sexuality, was not referred to either within this document or informally within the IWLM. Here, Mary Dorcey recalls the early days of IWLM: "I came back to Ireland [from Paris]. I went to the Women's Movement (then in its second year). I met wonderful women. I was enchanted by the exhilaration, the self-confidence, energy, wit, anger, vision but, to my surprise, no one declaring themselves lesbians or speaking about it."[23]

The first Irish group to specifically address lesbian and gay issues was set up following an open meeting in Dublin. Dorcey describes seeing the poster for that meeting in 1973:

"The Sexual Liberation Movement Meets Tonight at Eight O'Clock." Bewildering and ludicrous as it seems from this vantage point, that night twenty-two years ago was the first time I think the word "sexual" was written anywhere in public. The Women's Movement had been in action for one year, the Pill train[24] had taken place, and I had seen some of the group on the Late Late Show, but while they demanded the right to legal contraception, I don't remember that anyone talked about sex.[25]

As a result of this meeting, lesbians involved in the women's movement began to discuss their sexuality more openly. Following the dissolution of the IWLM, Irishwomen United (IWU) was set up in 1975 to act as an umbrella organization for all of the new feminist groups that had sprung up in the early 1970s. IWU was more radical than its forerunner, best-known for its publication of the feminist newspaper *Banshee*.[26] Lesbian feminists made up at least one-third of its membership, which may have been why lesbian experience was finally referred to, albeit somewhat obliquely, in the IWU charter (based on the earlier IWLM "seven minimum demands"). IWU called for "the right of all women to our own self-defined sexuality," and as a part of other "issues," addressed lesbian sexuality at consciousness-raising sessions. Little co-operative work was done between Irish lesbians and gay men during this period (a point I return to later). Most lesbian feminist activists were members of Irishwomen United rather than of the Irish Gay Rights Movement (IGRM), which they regarded as a gay men's group.

Clearing the Spaces: Constructing Lesbian Communities

In this section, I describe the factors that contributed to the construction of distinct lesbian groups and organizations in both Canada and Ireland before outlining the kinds of groups and centres established during this period, the naming of lesbian organizations and the development of these communities over time. First of all, in order to understand the formation of lesbian communities in Canada and Ireland, I suggest that it is more useful to replace our perception of "the" lesbian feminist movement with a more fluid concept of interacting groups and social scenes in different geographical locations. This problematizes efforts to depict the "gay movement" as a single social movement, with common goals and a shared vision, which frequently obliterates the politics, actions and experiences of the women involved. During the 1970s and 1980s, some lesbians chose to work with gay men, some continued to work within the wider feminist movement and others still went it alone, setting up women-only or lesbian-only groups.

Canadian Lesbian Organizations

One of the early contributing factors to the establishment of distinct lesbian groups and communities was the growing disaffection among lesbians with the wider feminist movement. Despite the obvious cultural differences between the two countries, and the fact that lesbian activism mobilized earlier in Canada than in Ireland, there are broad similarities here between the experiences of lesbians in the wider feminist movement. Difficulties in Canada began in the early 1970s, as one Toronto lesbian describes:

> One of the first things we were told is that making the gay–straight distinction was being divisive, cutting ourselves off from other women, "alienating the new women." On a personal level, some women often say sexual distinctions are irrelevant to them, "people are just people." Why would there be a need for a women's liberation movement at all if it were

so easy to transcend the sexism conditioned in all of us and relate to "people as people"? I feel that women who say this to me are telling me that my sexuality is irrelevant to straight women or is somehow not a factor in the meeting situation.[27]

Similarly, Irish lesbians who continued to work on political campaigns in tandem with their heterosexual sisters (and brothers) frequently found a lack of support when it came to organizing on issues directly related to lesbian lives and experiences. The first Irish lesbian conference was held in Dublin in May 1978, and the flyer announcing the conference touches on some of these issues:

Lesbianism has not been explored by public debate or within the women's movement here. Lesbians have been in the vanguard of the fight for radical change — the struggle for an autonomous lifestyle for women will not be complete while lesbians are oppressed, therefore we should not be disclaimed publicly or in the context of women's liberation. We feel this conference will break down the barriers of silence and ignorance surrounding lesbian sexuality. We invite all women to participate in a sharing of lesbian experience and sensibilities, rather than in defence of your own sexuality — whatever it is![28]

Despite the progress made by lesbians within the feminist movement, several women began to realize that their issues and experiences were being ignored or sidelined by the wider movement. Joni Sheerin put this forcefully in a review of a Kate Millett lecture in Dublin in 1980, asking,

Why has it taken ten years before the word "lesbian" could be uttered at an Irish feminist meeting? Why, even in the most radical group yet — Irishwomen United — was the existence of lesbians ignored? ... Veiled references and tokenism after years of activism is just not good enough. For ten years we have struggled alongside our sisters for contraception, divorce, justice for deserted and battered wives, equal pay, and every legal and social issue that has arisen. We've given a large degree of energy and ideas, time and commitment. Most of the time these issues have not been central to the lives of lesbians.[29]

There were positive response from heterosexual feminists to this challenge which, as Sheerin comments, "indicates the degree of support and solidarity which is present just below the surface but still not articulated." However, for some lesbians this was cold comfort, and their response was to turn away from mainstream feminist organizing and work on projects within their own communities, sometimes in collaboration with gay men.

However, lesbian/gay alliances proved just as difficult — sometimes even more difficult — than working within the wider feminist movement. In an article in 1973, one Montreal lesbian writer comments on this strained solidarity: "But there is a problem, and that problem is this: sexism makes it difficult for women to work with men."[30] By the mid-1970s, it seems as if many Canadian lesbian feminists had given up on their efforts at co-operation with gay men. Pat Smith spells out this position in "Why I Didn't Go to the Gay Pride Rally":

> I have this sneaky suspicion that what is meant by "common oppression" is in fact male homosexual oppression ... For even if we did end harassment of homosexual bars and restaurants it would not end my harassment in such places. I would still be elbowed off the dance floor ... And we could fight for an amendment to the Human Rights Code together which would end discrimination in employment by sexual preference. Homosexual men could then keep their $650 a month manager trainee position and I could keep my $400 a month clerk job doing exactly the same work for the same employer ... Homosexual men have a lot more in common with straight men than they do with lesbian women ... even if a gay man doesn't extend his male privilege over a woman in bed, he uses and benefits from that privilege every time he walks down the street, applies for credit, finds a job, takes his shirt off in public — and I've met few men who are concerned by that. But I have a lot in common with straight women — a lot more than with gay men ... All the "Gay Pride Week" rallies in the world aren't going to change that.[31]

Women began to leave "gay" organizations in the latter part of the 1970s. Montreal lesbians split from GAY to form the Montreal Gay Women Association, which first established a women's centre and then a designated lesbian centre where they published the first lesbian magazine in Canada, *Long Time Coming*. In 1976, the women who began discussing "lesbian community" at the Community Homophile Association of Toronto (CHAT) left to set up their own organization, the Lesbian Organization of Toronto (LOOT):

> At first we talked of another women's centre. However, many feminist groups and services were available for our straight sisters and we as lesbians seldom feel comfortable in these settings. There were homosexual/lesbian organizations. But what we really needed was an organization and a place that centred on our own concerns and was open to a variety of activities. So we talked and in November 1976 the Lesbian Organization of Toronto emerged.[32]

LOOT shared a home with the Three of Cups Collective, which ran a feminist coffee house and other social events (nominally open to all women, but mostly attended by lesbians) and established *The Other Woman* newspaper collective. They operated a phone line, provided drop-ins twice weekly and distributed a monthly newsletter (which reached four hundred women per issue by the time the organization folded in 1980). LOOT was also a focal point for a variety of groups and political campaigns.

Irish Lesbian Organizations

The beginning of the 1980s is the point where we see the emergence of specific lesbian communities in Ireland. The organizations and groups they started and belonged to were mainly urban-based during this period. In terms of the LBT "scene" in the early 1970s, there were no equivalents of the Three of Cups coffee house, which can be attributed in part to the relatively small scale of the Irish lesbian scene. Early efforts to organize a lesbian social scene relied on the attendance of a very small number of women. An advertisement in the second issue of *Wicca*, the Irish feminist newspaper, promoted the idea of holding a women's camp and advertised for women to join the collective organizing it. The Irish Women's Camp, originally the Galway Women's Camp, continues to be held each July. In the back pages of a 1978 issue of *Sapphire*, Ireland's first gay publication that was produced by gay men in Cork, there is a notice that reads:

> Since the formation of the Cork Branch of the IGRM the gay women in this city have been considering setting up a social scene for themselves ... The first women's meeting will take place on Monday 30th Jan '78 at 8.00 pm and hopefully will continue on each subsequent Monday at the same time.[33]

This is the first documentary evidence we can find of a lesbian scene in Cork. Cork lesbians contributed to many new radical organizations and created a variety of new spaces in the city in that decade, some of which are now well-established parts of the local landscape — some examples being the annual Cork Women's Fun Weekend, the Quay Co-Op, Walleroo Daycare Centre and the Cork Rape Crisis Centre. In Cork, the first focal point of emerging gay and lesbian communities was the Quay Co-Op, set up by a diverse co-operative group as an alternative community centre in the city, which housed a bookstore, whole-food co-op, vegetarian café, a women-only space and a resource centre with meeting areas for lesbian, gay and other groups. This space, which continues to function as a health-food store and café, has had a checkered history from the perspective of Cork lesbians, who eventually left the Co-Op to set up their own community space, the Women's Place on McCurtain Street.

However, in contrast to activists in Toronto and Montreal, Irish lesbians on the whole continued to coalesce with gay men's groups throughout the 1980s and into the early 1990s, despite privately acknowledging the difficulties of such co-operative work. Possibly because of the size of Ireland and close family ties, but also because of the coalitions that had sprung up earlier between individuals in a wide range of "radical" organizations, Irish lesbian feminism was not characterized by the separatism of, for example, lesbian communities in the U.S.A. This tendency to maintain co-operation with other groups, among them gay men's groups, may have resulted from scare resources, money and community space all of which could be accessed by them as part of wider gay and lesbian organizations. Similarly, in the early stages of Montreal's GLBTQ community activism, lesbians recognized the difficulties in operating independently of gay men:

> It's often very difficult for gay women to leave men and set up their own organization. Even in large cities there are usually not that many women coming out to meetings and getting actively involved in gay liberation groups. In smaller cities there may only be a handful of women who feel that they want to have a separate group and don't feel that there are enough of them to make it work.[34]

Despite maintaining such links, it is possible to see a discernible lesbian presence growing in strength and visibility within the lesbian, gay and feminist movements, with some of the new groups consisting almost entirely of lesbian feminists. They were involved at the grassroots level, forming groups, exploring ideas, finding and redecorating premises, devising policies and organizing events. The atmosphere of this period is captured here by Deirdre Walsh:

> Discussion groups, action groups, sprung up all over around issues affecting women's lives: contraception, abortion, divorce, sexual freedoms including lesbianism. It was the first time it felt safe for me to march under a Lesbian banner with other straight women's groups in an International Women's Day march down Patrick Street in Cork ... There was, for a time, an incredible feeling of, dare I say it, "sisterhood." It was the first time for me, and also for many other women involved, of solidarity based on our gender, and it was as powerful as it was idealistic.[35]

Walsh's account of the early days, complete with lesbians marching down Cork's main thoroughfare, gives a flavour of lesbian life in Cork in the

1980s. She goes on to describe the first lesbian political meeting in November 1984 that gave rise to the both the Lesbian Line and the Cork Women's Fun Weekend, which I discuss below.

Second-wave feminism drew attention to the importance of language in power dynamics, and lesbian feminists devoted much time and energy to discussing the names for their new groups and organizations. Ross points out that Canadian groups formed during this period were "officially open to all women, and were not referred to as *lesbian spaces*; the word lesbian did not appear in their names" even where the entire membership and direction of an organization was based on lesbian energies.[36] This suggests an ideological motivation to label an event or space a "women-only" rather than a "lesbian-only" area. In contrast to this, the difficulties for Irish lesbians in being publicly "out," particularly in the early days of lesbian feminist activism, were the primary motivations behind a more open designation. Joni Crone, one of the first Irish lesbian activists to come out publicly, describes the Irish lesbian community of the 1970s and 1980s as "an underground minority, a subculture whose members [had] been unwilling or unable to court publicity, because to do so may have invited violence, rape or even death." She goes on to discuss the difficulties of being identified as lesbian in the late 1970s, when she was involved in organizing the first lesbian conference in Ireland:

> It was only quite late in the proceedings that we realized that if we called the event a "lesbian conference" most of the organizing collective would be unable to attend because "walking through the door would be a public statement" … it was sobering to discover that most of the lesbian women we knew were leading double lives. At home, at work, and even within the Women's Movement, they were open about their feminism, but they disguised their sexual identity. Our compromise solution was to call the weekend a "Women's Conference on Lesbianism." This meant that women of every sexual persuasion were free to attend.[37]

Albeit based on such motives of self-protection, as Ross suggests, defining a space or event as a "women's space" opened it to the participation of all women, irrespective of their sexual orientation. The Women's Place, a resource centre on McCurtain St. in Cork, and the Galway Women's Camp chose to define their space in this way, rejecting the boundaries imposed on lesbians by heteronormative categories. The Cork Women's Fun Weekend continues to name itself after this fashion, although it is primarily aimed at a lesbian audience.

By focusing almost entirely on the atmosphere *within* lesbian feminist communities, it is possible to lose sight of the fact that the cogs of societal opposition were slowly grinding into action to combat this challenge to heteronormativity. As Joni Crone's comments indicate above, the wider Irish society wasn't quite ready for the revolution. In 1985, when two lesbian nuns from the U.S.A. appeared on the Irish television chat show *The Late Late Show*, there was a storm of controversy. The women, Rosemary Curb and Nancy Manahan, were on a book tour to promote their just-published *Breaking Silence: Lesbian Nuns on Convent Sexuality*.[38] Buswell's Hotel refused to provide their accommodation, the host of the show received death threats and a police escort had to be arranged to and from the television studio. This puts into context the bravery of local lesbian activists who were willing to come out. Chris Bearchell, a member of the political caucus of LOOT in the 1970s, suggests that problems lesbians faced when they came out were not specific to Ireland:

> As women, we have so much to lose if we come out. We may have children. We usually have lower paying jobs. And we almost always have less chance for advancement and financial stability than do men, regardless of their sexual orientation ... These facts are part of our oppression. Lesbian invisibility and lesbian isolation are mutually reinforcing.[39]

For every lesbian able to come out in Ireland, there were many more keeping their heads down. It is possible to compare the experiences of some of these women with those described in the first Canadian lesbian magazine *Long Time Coming*, based in Montreal:

> Isolation makes coming out hard. So does a strong religious belief, since most organized religions equate being gay with sinning ... Coming out when there's a husband and children around can be traumatic; people get hurt. Your husband doesn't understand and is threatened. He and society can take your children away.[40]

Many Irish lesbians solved this problem by emigrating and coming out in their adopted communities. One such woman was a Cork lesbian who rang the Samaritans Helpline for advice in the late 1970s only to be told that her sexuality was just a phase that would pass. Like many others, she left for England when she was eighteen. As a result of these migrations, there were a lot of cross-currents between, for example, British and Irish feminist communities. The 1970s and 1980s in Ireland were years of economic recession, and large numbers of Irish people, mostly in their twenties and thirties, emigrated to Britain or the U.S.A. Many lesbians who left became involved in a variety of political groups abroad, and the exchanges between individuals there and their friends "back home" gave much-needed support, literature, and theoretical perspectives to those who stayed in Ireland. Other women lived abroad for several years and then returned to Ireland, where they became involved in feminist and lesbian politics. Here, Nikki Keeling talks about coming out in Brighton in the early 1980s before moving to Cork:

> I used to hang around the women's centre in Brighton — there was a lot
> of politics but also a lot of socialising and I was there for the *craic*.[41] The
> lesbians kind of scared me, they seemed so sure of their identity. I didn't
> know how I should be as a lesbian. Soon after that I came to Cork and
> ... I felt I met other dykes equally and I didn't feel that I had to prove
> anything.[42]

There were rapid changes in Irish society during the 1980s, and those women who emigrated and later returned were in a position to compare the Ireland they had left with the one they returned to. This is curious when set against the context of the wider feminist community, which tended to remember the 1980s in Ireland as a demoralizing period, partly because of the 1983 Pro-Life Constitutional Amendment and ensuing court cases taken by the pro-life movement against groups providing abortion information[43] and partly because of high unemployment and emigration from the country. That lesbians tend to regard this as a period of optimism and of things changing for the better is indicative that for them the 1970s was not a period of liberation but a period when their experiences were not included in the wider feminist agenda. Keeling describes the development of lesbian politics in the 1980s:

> It was good to be a part of the lesbian presence and to be there when
> women went away and for those that came back expecting Ireland to have
> nothing for lesbians. I was proud of the scene and the progress we'd made.
> I travelled to Belfast and Galway and through meeting all these other dif-
> ferent "types" of lesbians that I broadened my definition of what a lesbian
> was.[44]

Contrasting this with the invisibility and repression of lesbians in the not-too-distant past made these changes all the more striking. Although this seems to coincide with the rise of "difference feminism(s)" on the international scene in the 1980s, in fact what we see here is the very early stirrings of lesbian groups in Ireland. This can be directly compared with ten years earlier in Toronto, the first lesbian conference held in June 1973 was described as having "provided a platform for women to get together out of their isolation and to learn from each other's experiences and politics. It was also the organizing point for at least two, possibly three, groups of lesbians."[45] It would be another ten years in Ireland before mainstream feminism would begin to address areas of difference(s).One of the principal and longest-running groups that emerged in the early 1980s was the national Lesbian Line telephone support network. In 1984, *Women's News* in Belfast received a grant from Co-Operation North to facilitate cross-border initiatives and this facilitated an exchange between the Lesbian Lines in the North and South of Ireland. This kind of North–South co-operation was rare during this period, so it is all the more to the credit of Irish lesbian communities that they refused to allow state politics to dictate who their allies might be. These links were built on in the course of the 1980s, and the success of this dialogue can still be seen today in the networking between lesbian groups and individuals throughout Ireland.

The Cork Women's Fun Weekend is now heading into its twentieth year and continues to be one of the highlights of the lesbian social calendar. As mentioned above, it began in response to the serious and somewhat earnest political atmosphere in feminist groups in the 1980s. The Women's Weekend became a focal point for many lesbians living abroad to "come home" for the weekend. Reviewing the 1990 Women's Weekend, one woman described it as "a stamp of encouragement for women all over Ireland, and [for] those who have emigrated abroad to keep in touch and establish a network."[46] Commenting on political divisions among Toronto lesbians in the late 1980s, Lorna Weir argues that it is "small wonder that lesbian politics has as a rule taken the form of a festival — an outpouring of spontaneous musical solidarity."[47] Despite the falling-away of many of the more political activities in the intervening period, events such as the Women's Weekend continue to thrive, which might be an indication of the secondary status of political discussion and activism in many GLBTQ communities in both countries today.[48]

Ideological Spaces: Deploying Identity Politics

LOOT's very existence is a political act in itself. Two years ago, we defined ourselves as lesbians. Without this definition, without this house, both the gay movement and the women's movement in this city would lack strength.[49]

In the first Lesbian Group meeting in the Women's Place in the Quay Co-Op, a group of women turned up and it was the first time just sitting down talking about ourselves and our sexuality and from there really I took on the label or identity.[50]

A central part of community-building projects in 1970s Toronto and 1980s Cork was the investment in identity politics — the deployment of categories such as "women" and "lesbians" during this period was a call to arms to those who self-identified as feminist or lesbian. As Gayatri Spivak and others have pointed out, this kind of essentialism is used frequently by marginalized groups as a way to raise consciousness and gather political momentum.[51]

Shane Phelan describes this understanding of the power of language as "a matter not only of ontology, but also of strategy," pointing out that such use of language by lesbian feminists is conscious: "Arguments and definitions are proposed less with an eye to eternal truth than with a view toward their concrete implications for community membership and political strategy."[52] Texts such as Rita Mae Brown's widely circulated "The Woman-Identified Woman" gave a theoretical perspective to this work, suggesting that lesbians use the terms of their oppression to redefine the world rather than themselves. In a similar vein, Toronto activist Pat Leslie writes: "If hostility to men causes Lesbianism, then in a male-dominated society Lesbianism is a sign of mental health, for hostility towards your oppressor is healthy."[53] Thus, coming out, self-identifying as lesbian and redefining the terms of engagement were all ways in which lesbian feminists revolutionized the known social world. This process of redefinition/coming out is described in an article in *Long Time Coming*:

> You learn to fight. Maybe the first person you fought was yourself. You fought against what society told you. You tried to develop healthy feelings about yourself. You learned to respect your strengths and to understand your weaknesses. You began to understand that society, wanting us to obey, forbidding us to be gay, encourages us to be sick. In fact, society wants us to be unhealthy. It doesn't want uppity gays.[54]

Rejecting the charge made by queer theorists that activists in this period were "unreflective essentialists," Linda Garber points out that lesbian-feminist politics highlighted the social construction of identities by inviting all feminists to become lesbians, thus rejecting biological predisposition or sexual behaviour as the root of lesbian identity.[55] During the same period, gay men generally adhered to the biological model as a definition of gay and lesbian identities — this was one of the tensions between lesbians and gay men in the 1970s and 1980s in Canada. Nonetheless, in their efforts to construct a new political and social movement, lesbian feminists, just as their straight sisters before them, downplayed or ignored the differences within their communities. Thus, exclusion and the silencing of "other" voices are not only charges that can be levelled at the heteronormative environment "outside" our communities, but must be acknowledged within our communities as well. As Phelan points out, "Any sense of the plurality of lesbian lives was lost in the construction of 'the' lesbian — the unified epistemological and volitional agent ... The political lesson we may learn from this, then, is that the real danger facing us is not one of doctrine, nor of behaviour, but more fundamentally of the impulse to totalization."[56]

Irish lesbian communities are only now beginning to look at the ways we have organized in the past, who we included and who we excluded in our groups. Although there was never the same level of difficulty between Irish lesbians and bisexual women (which again may relate to the small size of feminist groups and communities), they have experienced ideological differences. (A full discussion of this issue, which is beyond the scope of this article, has been addressed by many scholars.[57]) Recent initiatives such as workshops on racism facilitated by WERRC in LBT communities and the efforts of L.Inc, a Cork-based group and resource centre, to include the transgender community in its activities suggest that communities are coming of age and beginning to address exclusionary practices. L.Inc's policy states that their resource centre "is primarily for women who identify as lesbian or bisexual, which may include transgender people (or those in transition) who identify as lesbian or bisexual." They have facilitated the participation of transgender people in their groups by inviting transgender communities to contribute to their policy-formation and by hosting individuals from the transgender communities to speak at seminars for the Cork LBT communities.

After the Revolution: Coming Out in Public

Although lesbians in Toronto and Cork began to construct an identity politics and activist movement around the same time and by using the same tools, the trajectory of the two movements is not identical. One difference is the ease with which women were able to come out in the two cultures. The public face of activism in the GLBTQ communities in Ireland in the 1980s and 1990s focused mainly on service provision during the

HIV/AIDS crisis and on rights-based activism (specifically on the decriminalization of male homosexuality).

Many lesbians participated in this work, but the lack of a political focus and of media attention meant that they did not have the same kind of public profile as did their gay male counterparts. Hug suggests one explanation for this: "Irish lesbians commanded less of our attention since no laws and no papal pronouncements have attacked them."[58] In an interesting parallel, Smith points out that in Quebec as early as 1977, the gay liberation movement had secured sexual orientation as one of the grounds of discrimination in the *Charte des droits*, this had the effect of cutting off the process of social movement mobilization. In the rest of Canada, however, the exclusion of lesbian and gay rights in the 1980 Charter of Rights and Freedoms presented groups with a political opportunity to mobilize.[59]

Unlike Canadian lesbian activists, most Irish women involved in community activism tended to take a back seat in terms of the public eye. This relates to the difficulties Irish lesbians had in being publicly "out," which is still prevalent today and which is rooted in gendered societal attitudes towards Irish women and sexuality. For example, it has always been quite difficult to find lesbians willing to participate in Irish television documentaries and chat shows. Research recently carried out by LASI (Lesbian Advocacy Services Initiative) on the needs of lesbians and bisexual women in the North, involved interviews with young women just coming out into GLBTQ spaces in Belfast. Marie Quiery, one of the researchers, talks about her disquiet at seeing the same invisibility and obstacles faced by these women as were faced by an earlier generation:

> These were women who are not part of any organisation and have no ambitions to join an organisation. To describe them as apathetic does them an injustice — I was shocked by how closeted their lives are and by the enormity of the obstacles facing them in "coming out." In the North it would appear that the main obstacle is still the reaction of families, straight friends and employers — I suspect that there is little difference in the experience of lesbians in other parts of Ireland. It is hardly surprising then that we have difficulty in persuading women to organise collectively when they have to prepare themselves for the hostility, shock or hurt of their other or "birth" communities when they become more visible.[60]

This suggests that, despite the huge strides made by lesbian feminist activists in Ireland over the past twenty-five years, much work remains to be done. For example, although recent equality legislation in Ireland guarantees protection against discrimination on the grounds of sexual orientation,[61] only a few cases made so far involve lesbians. To make such a case involves taking a public stand, and clearly few lesbians are ready to take this step. In an apparent contrast, in Canada, many lesbians have taken forward several important cases. However, in one of the best-known "gay rights" cases, *M v. H* (a spousal-support case between lesbians), the parties were not publicly known. This suggests that there is still a need for anonymity, even when lesbians are engaged in a struggle for civil rights.

Despite the introduction of equality legislation, lesbians in Irish society still do not enjoy the privileges of other citizens, especially those of married couples. This point was noted by the recent Mee and Ronayne report, *Partnership Rights of Same-Sex Couples.*[62] Furthermore, in a country where a woman's position in the family is constitutionally enshrined, lesbian parenting is just one of the challenges posed by our redefinitions of "family." Angela O'Connell writes about the difficulties Irish lesbian couples experience in obtaining information about donor insemination:

> Anyone who has spent time in Ireland will be aware that much of what goes on in the corridors of power is unregulated by law, and unavailable to the general public for debate and scrutiny. Decisions are made without reference to the wishes of the majority, or to the laws and constitution of the country, and this is allowed to happen because the institutions operate under their own authority.[63]

In Ireland, we have not made the shift from service provision to equality-seeking in quite the same way as in anglophone Canada, as described by Smith.[64] The inclusion of GLBTQ rights in the *Equal Status Act* was due to a combination of rights-seeking and grassroots activism in Ireland throughout the 1990s (and perhaps has more in common with the contemporary Quebec LBT model). When we consider both the achievements and the work remaining to be done by GLBTQ activists, it is important that we do not fall into the trap of seeing development as a Darwinian process with an end-result of higher status or transcendence and, for that matter, that we remain fully cognizant of the cultural specificity of GLBTQ communities in different social contexts. For example, I would question the assumptions behind statements like the one made by Becki Ross: "Considering the international scene, it is striking that lesbian and gay organizing largely remains specific to white, Western, industrialized countries, and, in particular, to large cities. There are, however, signs of change."[65] This suggests that there is only one model of GLBTQ activism and that its application to (or colonization of?) all societies is a mark of their enlightenment. Deconstructing this kind of worldview enables us to fully understand the interaction of different social discourses in specific locations and enables the fruitful exchange of learning between GLBTQ communities both in Canada (for example, exploring the differences between anglophone and francophone activism and ways of working) and internationally.

Redefining Community Spaces in the Twenty-first Century

How are Irish lesbians today redefining the social world? How does this compare with the current situation in Canada? In recent times, and despite the obstacles mentioned above by O'Connell, Ireland, like Canada, has seen a veritable "baby boom" in lesbian communities. This affects lesbian family structures, the way lesbian communities perceive themselves and, more crucially, the ways in which we are "read" by mainstream society. As Keeling points out, "Being lesbian is incorporated into who I am, and being a mother will mean I'll be visible in another world in the same way that being in a relationship made my lesbianism more visible in the world."[66] Definitions are more difficult to pin down if the lesbian body can also be the pregnant body — or when lesbians take on the traditionally sacrosanct role of Irish motherhood. She goes on to describe some of these shifting identities:

> Well, I think you never just come out and that's the end of it. Even what it means to be a lesbian changes all the time. Right now I'm living with my lover in a rural community, I'm part of her family and I'm soon to be a mother. As a pregnant woman and a mother I am and will become more visible to the straight community. This is more challenging for me as a lesbian in terms of self-protection and my own homophobia. I could be so invisible or intimidated and this is my challenge. It's something I took up when I moved out of the protection of the "lesbian world" ... I'm finding a new language to speak to my world now; the world of work and the world of a small community ... I'll be facing the straighter world of schools etc. with my baby and that'll be a challenge. But I find that I'm trying for myself not to judge people and to challenge myself about my attitude to others, just letting others be themselves.[67]

The transition of lesbian feminist activists such as Keeling, from activist political work in their communities to a different kind of life/activism in more mixed community settings, suggests a shift in the ways in which "lesbian community" can be understood.

Another recent feature that distinguishes the Irish lesbian landscape from the Canadian one is the growing number of returning migrants and non-Irish lesbians who are choosing to make their homes in Ireland. This makes a statement about the kind of LBT communities that have been developed over the past twenty-five years — Ireland is now perceived as a place where lesbians can live relatively openly. Part of this phenomenon, as touched on by Keeling above, is that more and more women are moving to rural parts of the country, making a firm commitment to the creation of "lesbian community" wherever they find themselves, thus overturning the Irish social stereotypes of urban-based "radicalism" versus rural "conservatism." These "newcomers" bring with them a variety of ways of working and of understanding the world, which can only serve to deepen our own understanding of the contexts we work within in Ireland. They also contribute to more diverse socio-political agendas and ways of life by choosing to live and work in more mixed settings, rather than in the urban ghettos previously seen as the only "safe space" for the LGBT communities to exist in. Most of the urban-based lesbians I interviewed in Canada spoke of having moved from rural communities to live in the city, which suggests perhaps a sharper distinction between the rural and urban experience of being lesbian or gay here (or perhaps this was merely the experience of my interviewees).

"'Networking' is both a feminist practice and a multinational corporate strategy — weaving is for oppositional cyborgs."[68] I invoke Donna Haraway's "A Manifesto for Cyborgs" as a preface to discussing the third way in which LBT communities in cyberspace are in the process of redefining spaces, community resources and coalition-building at the beginning of the twenty-first century. On-line communities here in Canada and in Ireland are now augmenting, sometimes even taking the place of, the resource centres set up by lesbian feminists twenty years ago. The home pages of GLBTQ sites provide information about services, facilities, accommodation and events in local communities; community counselling services are increasingly using chat rooms and e-mail to provide support, particularly to GLBTQ youth; while contemporary discussion groups and consciousness-raising sessions are ongoing in chat rooms and on message boards in a variety of social contexts. One of the strengths of cyber-communities is that participation is not contingent on being in any particular geographical location. Regulars posting on the L.Inc message board,[69] for example, are based in Belfast, London, Sydney and Ottawa, as well as a variety of rural areas throughout Ireland and in Cork itself, where the resource centre is located. This enables information exchanges and coali-tion-building across a wide range of social contexts and political groupings.

*

> We want a feminist revolution. This means we want to create a non-patriarchal, communal, pan-sexual world. (By pan-sexual we mean a world where sexuality is a free expression of love and is not restricted by gender or age. In this world terms like homosexual, heterosexual, bisex-ual, male, and female would become irrelevant in all walks of life.)[70]

The lesbian feminist project of the 1970–80s sought to explode the binaries of sex and gender and to disrupt the workings of the heteronormative econ-omy. Although the revolution as envisaged was never quite realized, the activism of this period was crucial. This is particularly apparent if we com-pare it with the experience of the generation just preceding lesbian feminist activism, a period marked by the "almost complete invisibility of lesbians in social and public life," as Smith points out.[71] The only notable exceptions to this were the bar cultures of large cities such as Montreal, documented by scholars like Line Chamberland.[72]

In other contexts, older lesbians tell us about the high rates of suicide among single women whose sexual identities were impossible to reconcile with the heteronormative environment they inhabited in the 1940s and 1950s. In Ireland, we see for ourselves the damage done by addictions among the older generation of women — some of whom were in a position to come out in later life, some of whom were not. A marked difference between contemporary LBTQ communities in Ireland and Canada can be discerned in terms of the age profile of both groups. Unlike Canada, in Ireland there is no visible presence of "out" lesbians or bisexual women over the age of sixty, which is telling. The pioneers who set up groups, resource centres, committees within other organizations and ran workshops focusing on lesbian issues made space for several generations of women where we could accept our own sexual identities. The range of resources and the growing body of legal and civil rights available to the GLBTQ communi-ties in Canada today are also a legacy of this period.

Remembering the past — or indeed, even the awareness that there *is* a continuum of lesbian activism in Ireland and Canada that began in the 1970s — is crucial to our development. Knowing our histories enables us to read contemporary struggles in the context of the politics and activism of earlier periods. It is also crucial that scholars and activists alike engage in "joined-up thinking" when it comes to analyzing the strategies and actions of political activism and social movements both in the present and the past. Interrogating the ways in which discourses were prised open, and an analysis of how activists deployed identity politics and engaged in theoretical struggles in the early days of the movement(s) may become strategies for redefining future activism.

Using archival material for recovery work, or using interviews with lesbians who were active in their communities in different ways, helps us to disprove the sanctioned ignorance of critics who point to the lack of sources as evidence of lesbian absences in a particular era. In appraising the current state of feminism, Sandra Gilbert has said, "So much of women's history involves 'a sleep and a forgetting' that I fear the same consciousness-raising revolutions may have to happen over and over again before truly definitive changes are implanted."[73] The lesbian-feminist "consciousness-raising revolution" of the 1970s is an integral part of feminist history and remains a vital element for the development of future feminist thought.

NOTES

My thanks to everyone who agreed to be interviewed for or to discuss this research with me, particularly Line Chamberland, Irène Demczuk, Joan McCarthy, Eileen Murphy and Kathy Sansom, Íde O'Carroll, Miriam Smith and Deirdre Walsh.

1. *The House that Jill Built* (Toronto: University of Toronto Press, 1995), 4.

2. Mary Dorcey, *Moving Into the Space Cleared by Our Mothers* (Galway: Salmon Press, 1991).

3. This research is part of a wider thematic study of the archives of the Irish Women's Movement at University College Cork as part of the three-year Women in Irish Society Project sponsored by the Irish Higher Education Authority. My research at the Canadian Women's Movement Archives was funded by a three-month Bank of Montreal Visiting Scholarship in Women's Studies at the University of Ottawa. Some research was also carried out at the Queer Archive in Dublin.

4. Cork is located on the southwestern seaboard of Ireland, and has a population of 180,000, making it the third largest city in Ireland after Dublin and Belfast.

5. Much of the material at the Canadian Women's Movement Archives at the University of Ottawa, where I carried out my research, relates to anglophone feminist groups and, more specifically, to Toronto-based groups. There are some holdings relating to Montreal feminist groups, such the group which produced the newspaper *Long Time Coming*.

6. The twenty-six-county Republic of Ireland tends to be referred to as "the South," while the six-county province in the north of Ireland (variously termed "the North" or "Ulster" depending on the ideological standpoint) remains a part of the United Kingdom.

7. Linda Connolly, *The Irish Women's Movement: From Revolution to Devolution* (London: Palgrave, 2002), 27.

8. Throughout this chapter, I use the acronym LBT or GLBTQ to refer to the gay/ lesbian/bisexual/transgender/queer communities.

9. For a feminist analysis of this period, see, for example, Connolly, *The Irish Women's Movement*; Pat O'Connor, *Emerging Voices: Women in Contemporary Irish Society* (Dublin: Institute of Public Administration, 1998); Chrystel Hug, *The Politics of Sexual Morality in Ireland* (London: Macmillan, 1999).

10. Hug, *The Politics of Sexual Morality in Ireland*, 3.

11. A good example of this was Noel Browne's efforts to introduce the "Mother and Child Scheme" to Ireland in the early 1950s. Browne, a member of a moderately left-wing Republican party, was the minister for health in a coalition government, and wanted to make healthcare freely available to mothers with small children in a country whose infant death rate at the time was the worst in Europe. This move was seen by the Church as encroaching on its territory, and it denounced it as "socialist medicine." Directly interfering in matters of state, the Church called upon the prime minister to reverse this policy as a matter of Catholic conscience, which he duly did, sacking his minister for health into the bargain.

12. Marjorie Griffin Cohen, "The Canadian Women's Movement," in Ruth Roach Pierson, Marjorie Griffin Cohen, Paula Bourne and Philinda Masters, eds., *Canadian Women's Issues*, Vol. 1, *Strong Visions* (Toronto: James Lorimer, 1993), 1.

13. Laura Sabia was the president of the Canadian Federation of University Women, who in 1996 became leader of the newly formed Committee for the Equality of Women (CEWC). One of the first actions taken by this group was to lobby the federal government to set-up a Royal Commission on the Status of Women, to enquire into women's experiences in the employment sector as a first step towards achieving equality for women in the workplace. Initially, the demands of the liberal feminist CEWC were ignored in government circles, until Sabia threatened to march two million women to Ottawa to ensure that they were taken seriously. Her threat hit the headlines in *The Globe and Mail* in January 1967, at which time Prime Minister Lester B. Pearson agreed to give the group a hearing, and the Royal Commission on the Status of Women was established in February 1967. Its groundbreaking report, launched three years later, established the basis of equality for women in Canada. For further reading on this, see Cerise Morris, "'Determination and Thoroughness': The Movement for the Royal Commission on the Status of Women in Canada," *Atlantis* 5 (Spring 1980), 1-21.

14. In May 1992, for the first time, the Irish courts awarded full custody to a Cork mother who was openly lesbian.

15. See Ross, *The House that Jill Built;* Line Chamberland, "Mixed Messages: Gays and Lesbians in Montreal Yellow Papers in the 1950s," in Ian McKay, ed., *The Challenge of Modernity: A Reader on Post-Confederation Canada* (Toronto: McGraw-Hill Ryerson, 1992), 422–431; "Remembering Lesbian Bars, Montreal, 1955–1975," *Journal of Homosexuality* 25, no. 3 (1993), 231–269; *Mémoires lesbiennes* (Montréal: Éditions du remue-ménage, 1996); and Miriam Smith, *Lesbian and Gay Rights in Canada: Social Movements and Equality-Seeking, 1971–1995* (Toronto: University of Toronto Press, 1999).

16. Ross, *The House that Jill Built,* 26.

17. "Lesbian Witch Hunt," *Breaking the Silence* 5, no. 1 (1986), 18–19.

18. Real and Active for Life (REAL) Women was part of the anti-feminist backlash of the late 1980s in Canada. The group appealed to women working in the family home for their support base, and it took an anti-abortion and homophobic stance on women's issues. Although the group did not last, and never gathered mainstream support, the frequency with which their statements were published by the media gave significant exposure to their anti-feminist position.

19. Travellers have been minority groups within Irish society for several centuries. They are nomadic groups with a separate language, identity, culture and history. Although they are ethnically Irish, racism against Travellers has long been a problem in Ireland.

20. Abortion in Ireland is still constitutionally prohibited unless the mother's life or health is at risk. The 2002 referendum was not a vote to provide abortion in Ireland, but rather to facilitate easy access to information on abortion and the freedom to travel to Britain for an abortion.

21. Ross, *The House that Jill Built;* Connolly, *The Irish Women's Movement.*

22. This was part of a paper on the Irish Women's Movement delivered at the Voices and Visions Conference in San Francisco in 1988. Tapes of this conference are in the Irish Women's Movement Archive, housed at the Boole Library, University College Cork.

23. Interview with Mary Dorcey in Íde O'Carroll and Eoin Collins, eds., *Lesbian and Gay Visions of Ireland* (London: Cassell, 1995), 35.

24. This was one of the best-publicized actions of the IWLM. Feminist activists took the train across the border to Belfast, where contraception was legal, bought contraceptive pills and condoms in breach of Irish law and, on re-entering the Irish Republic, declared openly their "smuggled goods" to the customs officials.

25. Dorcey, *Moving Into the Space Cleared by Our Mothers,* 35.

26. Sets of this periodical are held at the Irish Women's Movement Archive in UCC and in the library at Trinity College Dublin.

27. *The Other Woman* 1, no. 1 (May/June 1972), n.p.

28. In the Irish Women's Movement Archive, Boole Library, University College Cork.

29. "Lesbians in the Irish Feminist Movement," *Elektra* (November 1980). *Elektra* was the Trinity College Dublin Women's Group magazine.

30. "Changes Coming Down," *Long Time Coming* 1, no. 1 (1973), 5.

31. *Long Time Coming* 1, no. 9 (May/June 1974), 20–21.

32. *LOOT Newsletter* (September 1977), 4.

33. *Sapphire* (January 1978). In the Irish Lesbian and Gay Archives.

34. "Some of the Ways," *Long Time Coming* 1, no. 3 (Oct./Nov. 1973), 4.

35. Deirdre Walsh, "My Personal History of Cork," *LINC* 1, no. 1 (2000), 6.

36. Ross, *The House that Jill Built*, 55.

37. Joni Crone, "Lesbians: The Lavendar Women of Ireland," in O'Carroll and Collins, eds., *Lesbian and Gay Visions of Ireland*, 60–70.

38. Rosemary Curb and Nancy Manahan, eds., *Breaking Silence: Lesbian Nuns on Convent Sexuality* (London: Columbus, 1985).

39. "Images of Lesbians in the Media, Part II," *The Body Politic* (December/January 1977), 35.

40. "Coming Out," *Long Time Coming* 1, no. 1 (1973), 2.

41. An Irish word which means to enjoy yourself in good company, good conversation, and so on.

42. Interview with Nikki Keeling, conducted by Deirdre Walsh as part of the "Herstory" series devised in collaboration with the author, in *LINC* 2 (2001), 2.

43. Connolly, *The Irish Women's Movement*, 155–184.

44. Keeling, Interview, 3.

45. *Long Time Coming* 1, no. 2 (August 1973), 9–10.

46. Review of the Cork Women's Fun Weekend, *Gay Community News* (July 1990), n.p.

47. Quoted in Ross, *The House that Jill Built*, 10.

48. In contrast to this, ongoing grassroots political activism of francophone lesbians in Quebec suggests that this is not perhaps a universal situation in Canada.

49. *LOOT Newsletter* (May 1980).

50. Keeling, Interview, 3.

51. Donna Landry and Gerald MacLean, eds., *The Spivak Reader* (London: Routledge, 1996), 214.

52. Shane Phelan, *Identity Politics: Lesbian Feminism and the Limits of Community* (Philadelphia: Temple University Press, 1989), 136.

53. "Sisterhood," *The Other Woman* 1, no. 2 (September 1972), 3.

54. "Coming Out," *Long Time Coming* 1, no. 1 (1973), 2.

55. Linda Garber, *Identity Poetics: Race, Class and the Lesbian-Feminist Roots of Queer Theory* (New York: Columbia University Press, 2001), 18.

56. Phelan, *Identity Politics*, 138.

57. See, for example, Merl Storr, ed., *Bisexuality: A Critical Reader* (London: Routledge, 1999); and Paula C. Rust, *Bisexuality and the Challenge to Lesbian Politics: Sex,*

Loyalty, and Revolution (New York: New York University Press, 1995).

58. Hug, *The Politics of Sexual Morality in Ireland*, 238.

59. Smith, *Lesbian and Gay Rights in Canada*, 42.

60. "Dykes, Community and Change," *LINC* 1, no. 2 (2001), 2–3.

61. The *Employment Equality Act, 1998* and the *Equal Status Act, 2000* outlaw discrimination in employment, vocational training, advertising, collective agreements, the provision of goods and services and other opportunities to which the public have access on nine distinct grounds: gender, marital status, family status, age, disability, race, sexual orientation, religious belief and membership of the Traveller community.

62. John Mee and Kaye Ronayne, *Partnership Rights of Same-Sex Couples* (Dublin: The Equality Authority, 2001).

63. Angela O'Connell, "Rails, Jet-trails and E-mails: Routes to Pregnancy for Irish Lesbians" (MA thesis, University College Cork, 2000), 26.

64. Smith, *Lesbian and Gay Rights in Canada*, 35.

65. Ross, *The House that Jill Built*, 223.

66. Keeling, Interview, 3.

67. Ibid.

68. Donna Haraway, "A Manifesto for Cyborgs," in Linda Nicholson, ed., *Feminism/Postmodernism* (London: Routledge, 1990), 212.

69. Available through the L.Inc Web site at <http://www.linc.ie>. *LINC* magazine can also be downloaded from this site.

70. "On a Queer Day ... We Can See Forever: Lesbian Feminist Statement," *The Other Woman*, "The Lesbian Issue" (Sept./Oct. 1973).

71. Smith, *Lesbian and Gay Rights in Canada*, 28.

72. Chamberland, "Remembering Lesbian Bars."

73. Quoted by Susan Gubar in *Critical Condition: Feminism at the Turn of the Century* (New York: Columbia University Press, 2000), 26.

CHAPTER 4

"An Officer and a Lady":
Shaping the Canadian Military Nurse, 1939–1945

Cynthia Toman

WHEN NURSING SISTER Kathleen Rowntree arrived in England with No. 23 Canadian General Hospital (CGH), she drilled, went for route marches and spent the evenings in a "neat little pub" that had a dance hall. "One morning I got called into the matron's office and told that 'jitterbugging' was not becoming to an officer," she said. "That was the first of a few trips to the matron's office, but I survived."[1] Nursing Sister Jean Wheeler served with the South African Military Nursing Service (SAMNS) and, on arrival in South Africa, Matron Gladys Sharpe warned her group they were "not to disgrace themselves" through the use of alcohol — that one port or one sherry was the limit.[2] Nursing Sister Margaret Van Scoyoc served in England and in Europe with No. 12 CGH for almost three years. As she said, "We certainly didn't want to be sent home! Conduct was a very important factor!"[3]

Military nursing was an attractive, highly desirable option for Canadian nurses during the 1930s, but there were very few positions available.[4] The Royal Canadian Army Medical Corps (RCAMC) Permanent Force consisted of only five to fourteen nurses during the interwar years. They enjoyed working conditions that surpassed most civilian nursing jobs during the Depression: full-time employment, food, housing, medical and dental care, and a salary triple the average nurse's pay.[5] Several hundred nurses enrolled in the reserve force, positioning themselves for extremely rare vacancies in the Permanent Force. It became increasingly clear, however, that another war was likely and the RCAMC would need civilian nurses to fill the ranks beside the small cadre of permanent military nurses. When the order came to mobilize medical units on September 1, 1939, the large number of nursing applicants led to a moratorium on enlistment only ten days later.[6] Nurses readily filled every allotted position. Thousands put their names on waiting lists, which grew steadily during the war, while others responded enthusiastically to the need for nurses in allied forces such as South Africa and the United States.[7] As Nursing Sister Mary Bower said, "We all were trying to get in the army or air force or anything. We tried to go to Africa! Anything to get in the Armed Forces."[8]

These women made up the second generation of Canadian military nurses known by rank and title as Nursing Sisters. They were civilian nurses who were graduates of hospital training programs for the most part, and not members of a religious order. They were also the first and only women in the Canadian Forces until the formation of Women's Divisions in the respective branches took place between 1941 and 1942.[9] They inherited a commendable reputation as professional nurses, professional soldiers and quintessential women from their foremothers of the First World War (1914–1918),[10] who had clearly demonstrated that professional nursing made a significant difference — both in the care of soldiers and in the release for combat of non-commissioned men, who had been seconded for medical service.

The military expressed little doubt about the value of nurses as professionals. Medical officer T.S. Wilson quantified their value this way, "Of especial importance in a surgical centre are the attached nursing sisters, whose services like that of a Thomas Splint in compound fractures of the femur, are often worth five to ten bottles of blood or plasma in the eventual outcome of a case."[11] The military was, however, ambivalent about their presence in theatres of war. Some anxieties emerged from logistical issues when two sexes lived and worked together in close proximity twenty-four hours a day (such as plumbing, sex and "messing," that is, activities taking place in the Mess Hall). Other anxieties concerned issues of power that could arise if nurses held command over men of lower rank (potentially including medical officers), as well as the loss of public support for war should nurses be placed at risk for injury or death by enemy action.[12]

This chapter explores the incorporation of nurses into the military and the incorporation of the military into nurses during the Second World War. I have used oral history interviews, professional literature and archival records to examine who became Nursing Sisters and how the Armed Forces consciously moulded them as officers and ladies according to gender and class-based criteria. The military enlisted "the right kind" of nurse, and then shaped her into a "military" nurse. Although admonished to behave as officers and ladies, some nurses pushed the boundaries, aware that the Forces could "turn a blind eye" to them whenever their skills were needed.[13]

A Diversity of Settings

Nursing Sisters served with the RCAMC, the Royal Canadian Navy (RCN), the Royal Canadian Air Force (RCAF), and the SAMNS in England, France, Belgium, Holland, Germany, North Africa, Sicily, Italy, South Africa, Hong Kong, Newfoundland, the United States and in military hospitals throughout Canada. One-third had already volunteered for the Pacific campaign by the time the atomic bombs were dropped on Hiroshima and Nagasaki in August 1945.[14] Two nurses were prisoners of war in Hong Kong for twenty-one months. Nurses served in isolated stations across the Prairies and in northern Canada, at experimental stations for chemical and biological warfare, at internment camps, on hospital trains and ships and in rehabilitation hospitals.

Changes in the technologies of destruction, transportation and communication during the Second World War influenced the type of medical care available and where it was provided. In addition to treatments for the usual communicable and venereal diseases, there were invasive surgical interventions; a massive use of blood, blood products and intravenous fluids; the introduction of penicillin; and significantly different treatment of psychiatric problems than during the First World War. Expanded nursing care and expertise was required in each of these treatment areas, while large-scale campaigns involving the rapid movement of troops over long distances required that this care be delivered ever closer to the front lines. For example, blood and plasma transfusion in forward areas increased the number of soldiers surviving their initial wounds and requiring subsequent surgery in the field prior to evacuation. As the war progressed, military and medical policies changed to position nurses in small mobile field units that closely followed the troops — sometimes under enemy observation and enemy fire.

The type and size of medical units also varied as medical services adapted to changing needs. There were large Canadian general hospitals in England (600–1,200 beds), many of which converted into field hospitals of equal size, moving to the Mediterranean in 1943–44 and to Europe in 1944. There were smaller (200–600 beds) Casualty Clearing Stations (CCS) whose mandate was to stabilize and evacuate critically injured patients. By 1943, the RCAMC developed a system of "leap-frogging" paired CCSs so that one was moving forward to a new site while the other unit operated on and evacuated their patients. These mobile units moved with the troops and adapted to available facilities: schools, convents, barns, bombed-out factories, châteaux or canvas tents. Nursing Sister Evelyn Pepper was one of eight nurses in No. 5 CCS that leap-frogged with No. 4 CCS at least eighteen times in Italy.[15] Field Surgical Units and Field Dressing Stations were smaller yet, consisting typically of two nurses plus medical and support staff. They operated in assembly-line fashion (sometimes receiving patients within twenty minutes of being wounded), leaving the follow-up care for larger units.

These different nursing contexts were contingent on the course of military campaigns as medical officers and nurses accompanied the troops and provided medical and surgical care wherever needed. Changes in medical technology and a need to deliver care closer to the front led to expanded roles, responsibilities and closer living conditions that required careful selection of personnel for these units. The typical nurses' training had emphasized discipline, obedience, hard work and endurance. It also provided nurses with the necessary skills to cope with most of the various contexts they would encounter during the war.

Enlisting the "Right Kind" of Nurse

There has been little demographic analysis of Canadian military nurses. The reported number of Second World War Nursing Sisters varies between 3,600–4,800 while the most commonly cited source indicates the number as 4,480 Nursing Sisters and 300 SAMNS.[16] My research analyzed thirty-four demographic variables extracted from a 24 percent sample of RCAMC, RCAF, RCN and SAMNS Nursing Sisters (1,145 files).[17] The analysis reveals that only 91.8 percent (or 1,052) of the sampled files belong to nurses, and that some nurses enlisted more than once as a result of family illnesses, limited-term contracts or changes in marriage policies. Other professional women such as dieticians, physiotherapy aides, occupational therapists, lab technologists and "home sisters" (a type of housemother for co-ordinating living arrangements) made up the remaining 8.2 percent of the rank. Once adjustments are made for redundancy, it is highly probable that there were only 4,381 nurses among at least 4,748 Nursing Sisters who enlisted in one of the four nursing services. If the South African contingent is excluded, only 4,079 nurses actually served as members of the Canadian Forces.

The military relied on the civilian nursing profession to train and accredit a pool of nurses from which it could recruit. The primary, non-negotiable eligibility criteria were graduation from a school of nursing recognized by the Canadian Nurses Association (CNA) and membership in a provincial nurses' association.[18] Nursing was stereotyped as women's work and most schools of nursing in Canadian hospitals only admitted women. Although some psychiatric hospitals trained a few male nurses during the 1940s and the census reported 153 male nurses, military policy explicitly excluded male nurses until 1967.[19] As far as the Armed Forces were concerned, military nursing was gendered female and combat was gendered male. The construction of masculinity denied professional nursing status to fully qualified men, especially as "manpower" shortages developed during the war and conscription expanded to all eligible men. Admission requirements established by nursing programs also effectively eliminated women who were Asian, First Nations or Black, and discriminated against Jewish women.[20] Thus, the demographic profile of military nurses reflected the demographic profile of civilian nurses, with the exception of French-Canadian nurses who were under-represented in comparison with the civilian workforce.[21] My data reveal that these military nurses were a relatively homogeneous group. They were overwhelmingly white, Protestant, English-speaking, single women who came from working- and middle-class families with strong British roots.

After verification of the professional credentials, the military required employer and clergy references, rigorous interviews with district commanding officers and physical fitness tests. The RCAF even investigated the applicant's family background and home setting. Finally, the initial military training period screened out women perceived to be difficult to manage. Nurses discharged within the first six months (1.5 percent) were typically described as "not suited" to the military, "didn't fit in" or were labelled "unable to adjust to discipline."[22]

The King's Regulations and Orders for the Canadian Militia required Nursing Sisters to be "unmarried or widowed without children."[23] Nurses signed an "undertaking" on enlistment to remain single and to refrain from requesting "permission to marry" within their first year of service. They acknowledged that, if they did marry overseas, they would relinquish all claims for return transportation to Canada and would have to resign their commission. This marriage policy was consistent with the civilian social expectation that married women resign from the workforce. There were two resignations in 1939, twenty-five in 1940, fifty in 1941, and seventy-four in 1942.

Obligatory resignation became unenforceable by 1943, however, partly because nurses would marry and not reveal their changed status until pregnancy forced them to do so, and partly because the military could not afford to lose an increasing number of experienced military nurses during the buildup for two major campaigns. Changed regulations in January 1943 permitted married nurses to remain in the military until they were "unable to meet physical requirements," at which time they would be discharged "on compassionate grounds." Marriage became a career-limiting move because Nursing Sisters had to remain in England when the rest of their unit left for active theatres, and those who married while posted to active theatres were sent back to England.[24] Overall, 83.4 percent of the nurses remained single; 1.0 percent were widowed; 0.1 percent were divorced; and 15.1 percent married during the war.[25] No such constraints were placed on married male officers.

Initial age limits for enlistment were twenty-five to forty-five years old. By September 1943, in anticipation of a second front and an invasion, the minimum age was lowered to twenty-one and the maximum raised to fifty-five.[26] On average, nurses were twenty-eight years old, while 9.0 percent were over thirty-five and one woman was fifty-four at enlistment. They were significantly older than their patients and most other military women, because of the age and educational criteria required by nursing schools[27] and because the military preferred that nurses have at least two years of experience prior to enlistment. The combined effect of training and experience positioned nurses as "older sisters" in relation to the soldiers who were their patients and whom they fondly referred to as "our boys."[28] Age and experience became a liability at the end of 1944, when the RCAMC recalled nurses who were over forty years old from active theatres. Popularly known as WOOFs or "women of over forty,"[29] these Nursing Sisters were deeply angry at their forced departures which were based solely on their age and not their ability.

The majority of military nurses (97.3 percent) were either British immigrants or born in Canada of British ancestry. Thirty-one percent were from Ontario; 11 percent from Quebec; and 10.4 percent from Saskatchewan. They were predominantly Protestant (77.9 percent) and Catholic (20.8 percent), with a small minority who were Jewish (0.4 percent). Most of the Nursing Sisters from Quebec were graduates of the Montreal General and Royal Victoria Hospitals, which were anlgophone institutions. Only 0.3 percent of the Nursing Sisters were unilingual francophones, and they were typically posted to Kingston for English-language training.[30] The remaining nurses (99.7 percent) spoke English as either their first or second language. NS Gaëtane LaBonté was a French-Canadian nurse who said, "We thought the worst was over, as we had been transplanted very suddenly from our cozy French milieu to a completely different world in English … I was soon called 'All Wet' because [the Matron] would order me to sing that thing of a song that my generation never sang: Allouette."[31]

My analysis of these 1,052 nurses indicates that their fathers worked in farming (32.2 percent), in middle-class occupations (40.6 percent), or in skilled, semi-skilled and unskilled occupations (24.2 percent).[32] Just over 40 percent of the women were born during the First World War, trained as nurses during the Depression and began to work as professionals between 1936 and 1940. High unemployment and the lack of social-welfare programs frequently left nurses struggling with social expectations to provide support for needy family members while also trying to support themselves. More than 30 percent of the Nursing Sisters reported the death of one or both parents and 8.5 percent claimed either full or partial responsibility for the support of dependent parents, siblings or other relatives who had raised them.

Working conditions during the 1930s were extremely difficult for the majority of Canadian nurses who (like other women) experienced the Depression in particularly gendered ways.[33] Nursing was frequently the second or even third occupational change in a woman's search for economic security. As historian Kathryn McPherson writes, "While their brothers rode the rails looking for work and handouts, rural women went to nursing school" where hospitals provided room, board and skilled training for three years.[34] This strategy exacerbated the situation of oversupply and underemployment on graduation because hospitals hired very few nurses who were the supervisors, educators and "specials" for privately paying patients. The majority worked as private-duty nurses, who were paid by the patient or patient's family; and when work became increasingly scarce, nurses joined the unemployed.[35] One private-duty nurse combined construction work with nursing, finding that laying steel reinforcements for concrete and reading blueprints was easier and her wages were higher.[36]

A combination of devastating civilian working conditions and extremely good military working conditions shaped war as a relatively "happy" event for nurses, and it saved them from dire circumstances.[37] Nurses found work as well as opportunities for patriotism, travel, adventure and proximity to men. Clearly, the military would have no difficulty recruiting the right kind of nurse and expected relatively few difficulties turning them into officers and ladies. There were plenty of replacements for those who could not or would not fit into military life.

Shaping the Military Nurse

Most nurses had experienced a militaristic style of training as students and were not particularly eager to return to a system of regimentation that had an additional layer of military subordination. But once enlisted, the military set about incorporating nurses into the military and incorporating the military into the nurses. Military discipline became the price they had to pay to get what they wanted. Two of the mechanisms for militarizing nurses were relative rank and uniforms — and both were highly visible, symbolic representations of the prevailing gender and class ideology of women's roles and male privilege.

Canadian nurses had been an integral part of the militia with the relative rank and pay of a lieutenant since 1904, thereby being the first nurses (and women) of any modern armed forces to achieve officer rank.[38] Relative rank was not full officer status, however, because it excluded the power of command and, although it meant better pay and benefits for nurses, gender and class shaped it unequally in relation to male officers. Gender structured relative rank into a lesser status by assuring that women did not exercise authority over men. At the same time, it reserved nurses for social activities with male officers and prohibited their association with non-commissioned soldiers. Some nurses recalled having to "volunteer" or being assigned to attend dances in the Officers' Mess.[39] As Nursing Sister Mary Bray wrote, "[O]ne day one of the officers came in to our Major and said: 'I would like to have six of your assortment!'"[40]

Class structured relative rank by imposing strict middle-class standards on their activities, behaviours and appearance as a strategy to exert control

over the small number of women serving within a dominantly male domain
while assuring their public respectability. Paradoxically, relative rank placed
nurses in closer contact with physicians than was typical in civilian practice.
Nursing Sister Van Scoyoc said,

> We were a minority and these were our first experiences ... outside the
> medical profession ... It did change our ideas of our relationships with
> doctors in that we had always looked up to them as "gods." But they
> didn't spoil us ... [T]he officers from the other units really spoiled us ...
> [The doctors] were left without female company ... We benefited by hav-
> ing other male officers around and the doctors were sort of left out
> socially.[41]

In 1942, commissions were granted to Nursing Sisters and the power
of command over women was added to those in positions of authority with-
in the nursing service.[42] Nurses were accountable to the Director of Medical
Services through Matrons, Principal-Matrons and Matrons-in-Chief. They
enlisted as Lieutenants rising through the ranks to Captain, Major and
Lieutenant-Colonel, but their rank was always qualified by the addition of
"Nursing Sister" or "Matron." In February 1944, RCAMC Matron-in-
Chief Elizabeth Smellie became the first woman to become a full colonel.
RCN and RCAF nurses followed similar patterns but with different rank
titles. After the formation of the RCAF Women's Division (WD), there was
a concerted effort to move Nursing Sisters into the WD. Nurses resisted,
arguing that the change would reduce their wages by one-third and place
them outside the medical services administration. One male officer argued
that "if full membership was granted to Nursing Sisters, they would be eligible to act on the Mess committee and vote on all matters raised at Mess
meetings ... and that would not be desirable."[43] A prolonged and bitter
controversy eventually involved a Brigadier, the Canadian Nurses
Association and the Minister of Defence (Air) before the issue was settled.
Rank and power of command was confirmed for RCAF Nursing Sisters
within medical settings. Non-nurse RCAF female medical personnel (dieticians and physiotherapists) enlisted as members of the WD.[44]

Officer status permeated all spheres: the hospital, the military unit, and
civilian settings. As Nursing Sister Betty Nicolson said, "When you were in
the army (and especially overseas), you were in the army all the time."[45]
Rank worked in both directions and nurses could be the pride or the despair
of drill sergeants during training and "toughening up" exercises. Nursing
Sister Margaret Mills recalled, "A sergeant used to take us out on route

marches which was pretty strenuous for us and the sergeant was very nervous because we were all commissioned officers ... little did he know we were
more scared of him (I think) than he was of us."[46] Like other soldiers, nurses went where they were posted. When Nursing Sister Doris Carter
explained that her posting was incorrect, she learned "there were 'no mis-
takes' as such made in the Army" and when reprimanded for having liquor,
Carter also learned that "all my thinking would be done for me."[47] Nursing
Sister Bower struggled with rank throughout her army career and was
paraded by her matron. She said,

> There was the military protocol, you know ... I didn't really fit into that
> ever, I think, which was probably a problem to everybody ... I think they
> would have loved to cut my pips off ... [T]he sergeant-major came for
> me and he paraded me down to this room. I had no idea that I was going
> to be chastised or anything else. And I went in this room and the matron
> was there and my equals were sitting around in a circle ... the [com-
> manding officer] of the hospital was sitting behind a desk and the guy
> marches me up and salutes, you know, and stands there: "Prisoner at the
> bar." Me. And it was so stupid. He said I was ... inciting the soldiers to
> riot.[48]

For Nursing Sister Kay Christie, obedience meant becoming a POW.
She had volunteered for a semi-tropical posting (thinking of Jamaica) and
said, "[M]y heart just dropped when they said Vancouver. I thought, you
don't go to England (or Jamaica) by way of Vancouver. But I had said I
would go and it was too late."[49] She only learned on board ship that she was
headed to Hong Kong as one of two Canadian nurses serving with the
troops there. Three weeks after her arrival, Japanese troops attacked Hong
Kong and, on Boxing Day 1941, Christie began twenty-one months as a
prisoner of war. The Japanese army refused to recognize women as officers
or grant them officer rights to minimal pay, which could have been useful
on the black market to supplement meagre food rations. Christie and her
nursing colleague May Waters survived on eight ounces of cooked rice,
three ounces of flour, three-quarter ounces of meat or fish and some fairly
indigestible "greens" per day — suffering weight loss, vitamin deficiency
and visual impairment as a result. Although they were not tortured, they
witnessed brutal torture and killings as punishment for disobedience. Some
of their British nursing colleagues were raped and three were beheaded.

All officers had responsibilities and privileges, but for nurses class inter-
sected with rank to impose middle-class standards of conduct as "ladies."

Nurses already understood the expectations regarding professional deportment with physicians and patients, but military training lectures now admonished that they had a "twenty-four-hour" responsibility to represent the medical services in all military and civilian settings. Nurses were not to abuse their privilege in the mess, which was "primarily man's domain," nor wear out their welcome by "aimless sitting around ... drinking and chatting." They were to avoid fraternizing with the "other ranks" and complaining in public, and to remember that "no lady ever drinks too much." There were regulations about smoking, makeup, nail polish, jewelry, gum chewing, hair style, loud talking, cleanliness, travel, uniforms and shoes and more — but the guiding principle was, "Our actions should be dictated by the laws governing the conduct of a lady."[50]

Supposedly, ladylike conduct also covered appropriate sexual relationships, enforced by disciplinary processes such as "boarding out" (dismissal or forced resignation) and loss of entitlement benefits (for example, medals, war service gratuities, return transportation and education credits). Unlike male officers, nurses were expected to be celibate "for the duration" and, if they were not, they bore the primary consequences of pregnancy. One nurse described her situation as "a female paradise [where] there were all kinds of men. And even the most unattractive person was really 'rushed.'"[51] Another nurse called it "an abnormal way of life. You were over there mixing with married men and single men, and all of them were lonely, but the married men were perhaps the loneliest of all. There were a lot of affairs going on. If nurses got pregnant, they were sent home."[52]

Analysis of my data indicates that at least 6.5 percent of the nurses, including both married and single women, were pregnant at discharge. Pregnancy was sufficiently problematic that the army decided to test women prior to embarkation. Prior to embarkation from Debert, Nova Scotia, for England, Nursing Sister Jean Ciceri said, "One morning, throughout the two huts, you could see long lines of specimen bottles. A few nurses didn't get to go overseas."[53] Meanwhile in London, a department memo dated June 26, 1944, noted, "Rabbits are scarse [sic] and expensive" for Friedman pregnancy tests, and the military should "avoid excessive number of tests."[54] One nurse concealed her pregnancy until the eighth month, at which time it was considered unsafe for her to travel and she could not return to Canada. A civilian physician delivered her baby who was placed for adoption, and the nurse was discharged as "not well adapted to military service."[55]

The more visible symbol of gendered rank, however, was the Nursing Sisters' uniform. As the senior service, the RCAMC uniform became the model for all three services. Nursing Sister Carter described it this way:

> There were three types [versions] of uniforms, each with an Alice-blue two-piece suit with two rows of small brass Medical Corps buttons down the jacket, a peplum, white stiff collar and cuffs, a leather two-inch belt with a lion's head brass buckle ... and a slim, slightly-flaired [sic] skirt. One uniform was wool for winter dress affairs, one was silk for such events in summer, and one was cotton for work. Over the cotton uniform we wore a white cotton apron with a bib and straps, and the belt over the apron ... A white veil was worn with all these uniforms. A navy blue suit for "walking out" was worn with a light blue shirt from Morgan's Boys' Department ... with [a] navy blue tie, either wool or silk. We wore very smart navy blue brimmed felt hats by Stetson, with a ribbon band and the Medical Corps badge up front.[56]

Brown leather gloves, brown "sensible" walking shoes, black "pumps" for social affairs, navy blue raincoats and greatcoats, a purse, a lace handkerchief for the pocket, rank designations and the Canada shoulder badge completed the outfit. RCN nurses wore the darker colour of the Navy, a maroon distinction cloth with the gold lace and RCN insignia. RCAF nurses wore white uniforms and veils (with embroidered RCAF wings on it) for patient care, but adopted an Air Force blue uniform based on the RCAMC model for dress.[57]

Wearing the uniform properly was a matter of pride and discipline. Nursing Sister Elizabeth Dean contrasted her uniforms with the starkness of the 1930s, noting that she loved wearing them "because I'd grown up in Depression years and now I had all these uniforms."[58] The dress uniform served for all public functions from parades to weddings and dances.[59] Nursing Sister Dorothy Maddock recalled that RCN nurses were expected to be present when battleships came into port, whereupon they were "treated like queens" at the Captain's table. "You were somebody special ... You also dressed accordingly. I mean your uniforms had to be right too. I mean you had an image to keep up."[60] Ironically, these were almost the only occasions when the RCN permitted nurses on ships.

Admonished not to "disgrace" the uniform yet regulated to wear it, nurses were constantly reminded of the embedded behavioural expectations attached to it. At the HMCS *Stadacona*[61] in Halifax, a policy permitting women to wear "civvies" on Sundays quickly changed when civvies proved too provocative. NS Maddock stated, "In those days, you wore a white blouse usually and a sweater. And it was fairly tight-fitting. I think we had about a month-and-a-half of Sunday dinners with the admiralty house when we got a message that we were not to wear civvies anymore on Sundays. The sweaters were too tight! We had to wear our uniforms."[62]

Nursing Sisters wore bibbed aprons and veils with the cotton duty uniform. Beyond any utilitarian function, the aprons were reminiscent of student training days as well as the profession's subservient, domestic roots while the veils were reminiscent of the profession's association with religious sisterhoods and the care of strangers as a charitable duty performed by middle-class ladies. Nurses had long been portrayed as angels and sacrificial mothers. These symbols and metaphors constituted important tools for the social construction of nurses as respectable women, in contrast to disrespectable "camp followers."[63] One male officer escorting nurses at night under London's blackout conditions is reported to have remarked, "You know I'm not protecting you, you're protecting me [from prostitutes]."[64]

The veil was a particularly evocative symbol. Nurses took great care to starch, iron and wear it properly. Nursing Sister Van Scoyoc told how "the officers liked to play a trick, to try to take our veils off. We were not properly dressed if the veil was pulled off or askew. It was considered a great misdemeanour."[65] The veil remained a powerful post-war symbol of their military participation — of shared experiences forbidden to other women. Demobilized military nurses who worked at Department of Veterans Affairs' hospitals after the war wore civilian uniforms but they chose to retain the veil. As Nursing Sister Pauline Lamont explained, "We wore our veils you know ... We were so proud to have been in [the war]."[66]

When posted to active theatres, however, nurses stored their "blues" in England and adopted British-issued khaki battle dress. Nursing Sister Hallie Sloan wrote, "We packed our blue uniforms and white veils, donned khaki uniforms, berets, and high leather boots, and headed for Yorkshire for a toughening up period prior to D day." She continued, "[But] when the rains came ... everyone worked in gas capes, tin hats, and gumboots, completely shattering the illusion of 'ministering angels.'"[67] The transition from blues to khaki signified becoming "one of the boys," although there were still concessions to femininity. While bandanas and berets replaced the veil, khaki included skirts as well as pants. Long pants provided necessary protection after sundown against malaria-carrying mosquitoes, but skirts were usually worn during the day. Battle dress was practical given the living and working conditions, although it became a liability to dance in pants and heavy boots, according to Nursing Sister Nicolson.[68] Water was severely rationed and cleanliness became a challenge with some nurses surviving for months without a bath. Nursing Sister Jean MacBain, who served in France and Belgium just after the Normandy Invasion, wrote, "Khaki turbans kept our hair well hidden. Our shirts were also khaki so that solved our dirty shirt problem ... We had only three shirts and not enough water to wash them so we rotated daily, hung them up to air and sprinkled them with Chanel No. 5. We had more of that than water."[69]

The shift to wearing khaki and becoming "one of the boys" took on new meaning when the SS *Santa Elena* was torpedoed in the Mediterranean during November 1943 with ninety-five Nursing Sisters aboard. Although a troopship and a destroyer rescued them from their lifeboats, the nurses lost all of their personal belongings.[70] Replacement clothing consisted of men's khaki uniforms, but they discovered that small sizes were available in very limited quantities and the army didn't carry women's underwear. Nursing Sister Marjorie MacLean was one of those who lost all her clothing with the ship. She wrote to her brother in England asking for an assortment of bras because there were none in army stores.[71] Nursing Sister Pauline Cox grieved because she had "big feet" and her "nice new shoes" had gone down with the ship. Only one woman had abandoned ship carrying her lipstick (the only makeup that survived among the group).[72]

Trousers, cleanliness, underwear and makeup presented a number of challenges to the expectations for comportment as ladies. But for the nurses who were prisoners of war in Hong Kong, their uniforms became an essential resource from which they made other clothing. Nursing Sisters Waters and Christie cut up their uniforms and aprons to make shorts and "sun tops," which were more appropriate for the climate and living conditions. Christie described making "clogs" out of slabs of flooring for the soles, tying them to her feet with strips of blue uniform. When they were finally repatriated in a prisoner exchange, Christie said, "The Canadians were so raggedy that we were called down first to the store. Everyone else could have either a dress or a skirt and sweater but because we were so poor, we could have more."[73]

Relative rank and the Nursing Sisters' uniform constituted two strategies by which the Armed Forces incorporated military discipline into nurses. Both reminded nurses of their proper relationships to the men with whom they served while visibly reinforcing gender- and class-based expectations. Rank and uniforms also served to establish zones of safety within which the Armed Forces were obligated to provide respectability as well as protection.

*

There was a substantial pool of civilian nurses available for recruitment into the Armed Forces at the end of the Great Depression. Nurses responded overwhelmingly to the call for mobilization and served throughout the Second World War in almost every setting, enabling the delivery of medical and nursing care to the front lines. The military relied on the civilian profession to screen, train and accredit professional nurses, and then incorporated these civilian nurses into the forces as officers and ladies, assuring their respectability while maintaining societal approval for women's involvement in war. The military reinforced gendered status through relative rank, restrictions on nurses' power of command and denial of professional status and rank to male nurses. The Nursing Sister uniform constituted a visible symbol of embedded gender- and class-based behaviours as nurses learned to perform the different roles expected of them as soldiers, nurses and women. They learned when to become "one of the boys" and when to capitalize on "being one of the girls." When Nursing Sisters did resist policies, regulations or codes of behaviours, the military tolerated their indiscretions as long as their nursing skills were needed. But nurses who were considered "unable to adjust" to military discipline were typically screened out very early, and the acceptance of discipline was the price women paid for access to work, decent wages and benefits, status, adventure and access to men socially.

NOTES

1. Kathleen (Rowntree) Bowman, in E. A. Landells, ed., *The Military Nurses of Canada: Recollections of Canadian Military Nurses*, Volume I (White Rock, BC: Co-Publishing, 1995), 79. Hereafter referred to as *Military Nurses of Canada*.

2. Ellen Jean (Wheeler) Keays, audio-taped interview with Sheila Zerr at White Rock, British Columbia, 16 August 1994. Oral history collection, Registered Nurses Association of British Columbia Library (hereafter referred to as RNABC).

3. Margaret Van Scoyoc, audio-taped interview with author at Kingston, Ontario, 13 June 2001.

4. G.W.L. Nicholson, *Canada's Nursing Sisters* (Toronto: Samuel Stevens Hakkert and Company, 1975), 102–103; M. Leslie Newell, "'Led by the Spirit of Humanity': Canadian Military Nursing, 1914–1929" (MA thesis, University of Ottawa, 1996); W.R. Feasby, *Official History of the Canadian Medical Services, 1939–1945,* Volume 1, *Organization and Campaigns* (Ottawa: Queen's Printer, 1956), 12, 37.

5. Frances Ferguson Sutherland, audio-taped interview with author, 10 October 2001, Edmonton, Alberta; Ethel Johns, "A Background of Experience," *Canadian Nurse* 36, no. 2 (February 1940), 75.

6. C.P. Stacey, *Official History of the Canadian Army in the Second World War: Six Years of War: The Army in Canada, Britain and the Pacific,* Vol. 1 (Ottawa: Queen's Printer, 1955), 3, 43; G. W. L Nicholson, *Seventy Years of Service: A History of the RCAMC* (Ottawa: Borealis Press, 1977), 138.

7. Canadian nurse Betty Riddell saw the sign Uncle Sam Needs You! every day when she crossed the river to work in Detroit. She joined the United States Army Nurse Corps because the Canadian waiting list was too long. Audio-taped interview with author, 26 November 2001, Ottawa, Ontario.

8. Mary M. Bower White, audio-taped interview with author, 20 October 2001, Surrey, British Columbia.

9. *Equal to the Challenge: An Anthology of Women's Experiences during World War II,* prepared by Lisa Bannister for the Department of National Defence (Ottawa 2001), x.

10. Nicholson, *Canada's Nursing Sisters*; Meryn Stuart, "War and Peace: Professional Identities and Nurses' Training, 1914–1930," in Elizabeth Smyth, Sandra Acker, Paula Bourne and Alison Prentice, eds., *Challenging Professions: Historical and Contemporary Perspectives on Women's Professional Work* (Toronto: University of Toronto Press, 1999).

11. T.S. Wilson, "Resuscitation in Battle Casualties," *Journal of the Canadian Medical Services* 2, no. 5 (1945), 520.

12. Cynthia Enloe, *Maneuvers: The International Politics of Militarizing Women's Lives* (Berkeley: University of California Press, 2000), 223; Ruth Roach Pierson, "Wartime Jitters Over Femininity," in J.L. Granatstein and Peter Neary, eds., *The Good Fight: Canadians and World War II* (Mississauga, ON: Copp Clark, 1995), and *"They're Still Women after All": The Second World War and Canadian Womanhood* (Toronto: McClelland and Stewart, 1986).

13. Jean (MacBain) MacAulay, in *Military Nurses of Canada,* 111.

14. Statistics for this research are based on Department of National Defence records on the Nursing Sisters held at the National Archives of Canada (hereafter referred to as NAC). These files are restricted and not available to the general public.

15. Evelyn Pepper, in *Nursing Sisters Association of Canada: Commemorative Issue and Membership Directory* (Edmonton: Nursing Sisters Association of Canada, 1994), 34–35.

16. Most authors typically cite Nicholson's *Canada's Nursing Sisters,* 174–178, 208, or John Murray Gibbon and Mary S. Mathewson, *Three Centuries of Canadian Nursing* (Toronto: Macmillan Company of Canada, 1947), 456–458. Much of the variation between sources is based on four issues: who was included/excluded;

which dates were used; whether reported figures are accrued or taken from nominal lists; and if adjustments were made for multiple enlistments by the same persons.

17. I used RCAMC statistics and the actual nominal list of SAMNS nurses to corroborate my analysis of 1,145 Nursing Sister personnel records. I extrapolated the proportion of nurses to the most commonly accepted figures for RCAF and RCN Nursing Sisters while adjusting for multiple enlistments in the same service and remusters to different service branches. The RCAF files are especially contested due to an unsuccessful attempt to transfer nurses to the Women's Division. At least sixty-nine Nursing Sisters served in both the SAMNS and RCAMC and there were at least eighty-three fewer Nursing Sisters than is commonly reported. See "Appointment Statistics — Nursing Sisters, Physiotherapy Aides, Occupational Therapists, Dieticians and Home Sisters," 000.8 (D93), Directorate of History and Heritage, DND, Ottawa; "Numbers of Nurses Serving as Nursing Sisters in RCAF as at April 12, 1943," RCAF Nominal List, file HQ400-1-1, RG24, Series E-1b, v. 3365, NAC; memos of 23 October 1944, "Requirement for Nursing Sisters," and 22 November 1944 from J. E. Porteous, HQ 400-2-1, RG24, Series E-1b, v. 3365, NAC.

18. Jean S. Wilson, "Military Service," *Canadian Nurse* 35, no. 10 (October 1939), 562.

19. "District #4 Report for March 1940," Nursing Education Section, Minutes and Reports (1928–41) and CNA Annual Report for 1940, RNAO file 96B-1-09, Archives of Ontario; *Eighth Census of Canada, 1941,* Volume 7 (Ottawa: King's Printer, 1946), 328; Dean Care, David Gregory, John English and Peri Venkatesh, "A Struggle for Equality: Resistance to Commissioning of Male Nurses in the Canadian Military, 1952–1967," *Canadian Journal of Nursing Research* 28, no. 1 (1996), 103–117.

20. Kathryn McPherson, *Bedside Matters: The Transformation of Canadian Nursing, 1900–1990* (Toronto: Oxford University Press, 1996), 17, 118.

21. This is partially understandable given the controversy over conscription and the prevailing French-Canadian perspective that the Second World War was a British war.

22. These statistics are from my database of military files.

23. *King's Regulations and Orders for the Canadian Militia (1939)* (Ottawa: King's Printer, 1939), paragraphs 158 and 263.

24. Lenore Lancaster Menard, audio-taped interview with Terina Rindal, 14 March 1995, Lethbridge, Alberta. Alberta Association of Registered Nurses Library and Museum.

25. "Appointment Statistics." See also Pearl Lundgren Swift, in *The Military Nurses of Canada,* Volume II, 159–160; and Gaëtane (Labonté) Kerr, audio-taped interview with Lisa Weintraub, 11 April 1985. ISN 167796, NAC.

26. Feasby, *Official History of the Canadian Medical Services,* Volume I, 325.

27. McPherson, *Bedside Matters,* 117.

28. Grace Patterson, audio-taped interview with Joan Williams,18 November 1975. ISN 196088, NAC.

29. RCAF memo 8 June 1944, HQ54-27-93-15 FD15 (Personnel 1B), RG24, E-1-b, v. 3365, file 400-2-1, part II, NAC; Evelyn Pepper, in *Military Nurses of Canada*, Volume I, 51, 57; Elizabeth L. (Burnham) Lowe, in *Military Nurses of Canada*, Volume I, 158; and Jessie Morrison, in *Military Nurses of Canada*, Volume I, 241; Dorothy A. Macham interview with Norma Fieldhouse, 10 February 1988, Toronto, Ontario, MMA; and Nicholson, *Canada's Nursing Sisters*, 124, 140–141.

30. Bannister, *Equal to the Challenge*, xiii–xv.

31. Gaëtane (Labonté) Kerr, in *Military Nurses of Canada*, Volume I, 338.

32. These results support McPherson's findings that working-class women comprised 30 percent of student nurses and 20 percent of graduate nurses. See *Bedside Matters*, 121.

33. Veronica Strong-Boag, *The New Day Recalled: Lives of Girls and Women in English Canada, 1919–1939* (Toronto: Copp Clark Pitman, 1988).

34. McPherson, *Bedside Matters*, 124.

35. Barbara A. Keddy, "Private Duty Nursing: Days of the 1920s and 1930s in Canada," *Canadian Woman Studies/les cahiers de la femme* 7, no. 3 (Fall 1986), 100.

36. Dorothy M. (Grainger) Anderson, in *Military Nurses of Canada*, Volume I, 411.

37. Margaret Van Scoyoc, audio-taped interview with Lisa Weintraub, 4 June 1984. ISN 167825, NAC.

38. "Report of the Department of Militia and Defence for the Dominion of Canada for the year ending March 31, 1921," as cited in Newell, "'Led by the Spirit of Humanity,'" 28.

39. Doris V. Carter, *Never Leave Your Head Uncovered: A Canadian Nursing Sister in World War Two* (Waterdown, ON: Potlatch Publications, 1999), 103–104.

40. Mary Bray Hutton in Jean E. Portugal, ed., *We Were There: The Navy, the Army, and the RCAF: A Record for Canada*, Volume 5 (Shelburne, ON: The Battered Silicon Dispatch Box, 1998), 2243.

41. Van Scoyoc interview, NAC.

42. Feasby, *Official History of the Canadian Medical Services*, Volume I, 324.

43. Letter from #2 RCAF Training Command at Winnipeg, to National Defence (Air), 16 March 1942, E-1-b, v. 3365, file HQ400-1-1, NAC.

44. P. Wetzel, "Draft Narrative for the History of the RCAF (WDs) re. Women Medical Officers, Nursing Sisters, Physiotherapists, Orthopists, and Opthalmical Assistants," 181.003 (D1467), DHH; Letters from H.A. Peacock to Commodore R.W. Ryan, 29 May 1942 RG 24, E-1-b, v. 3365, part 1, and from Marion Lindeburgh to C.G. Power, 20 November 1942, RG24, series E-1-b, v. 3365, file 400-2-1, part 1, NAC.

45. Constance Betty Nicolson Brown, audio-taped interview with author, 3 June 2001, Ottawa, Ontario.

46. Margaret H. Mills, interview with Margaret M. Allemang, 5 April 1991, MMA.

47. Carter, *Never Leave Your Head Uncovered*, 4, 12.

48. White interview.

49. Kathleen G. Christie, "Experiences as a Prisoner-of-War, World War 2," interview with Charles G. Roland, 8 December 1982, HCM 28-82, McMaster University, Hamilton, Ontario.

50. "Responsibilities of Members of Nursing Sisters Service, Course in Aviation Nursing, Course No. 12 — August 23rd–Septmber 14, 1944," Royal Canadian Military Institute Library, Toronto.

51. Patterson interview.

52. Anne Farries, "War Nurse Recalls Second World War Experiences," *Cranbrook Daily Townsman* (Cranbrook, BC), 10 November 1992.

53. Jean Mary Ciceri, audio-taped interview with Nina Rumen, 13 January 1987, Victoria, British Columbia, RNABC.

54. London County Council Public Health Department memo, 26 June 1944, NAC.

55. I have preserved the nurse's anonymity on request.

56. Carter, *Never Leave Your Head Uncovered,* 6–7.

57. "The RCAF Nursing Service," *Canadian Nurse* 40, no. 3 (March 1944), 164–166; "The Royal Canadian Naval Nursing Service," *Canadian Nurse* 40, no. 2 (February 1944), 96–98; and Nicholson, *Canada's Nursing Sisters,* 183.

58. Elizabeth Dean Doe, audio-taped interview with author, 30 June 2001, Ottawa, Ontario.

59. Carter interview.

60. Dorothy Maddock, audio-taped interview with author, 26 June 2001, Ottawa, Ontario.

61. The RCN had nine land-based hospitals where Nursing Sisters served. These buildings were named and treated as ships although they were actually buildings and "never went to sea," which is why women were allowed on this "ship" but never on the sea-going vessels. It's very interesting that all naval terms applied. For example, when they had leave from the hospital, they were "permitted ashore," and they referred to the parts of the ship as fore, aft, port, starboard, heads and so on.

62. Maddock inteview.

63. Enloe, *Maneuvers,* 199.

64. Margaret H. Kellough, interview with Margaret M. Allemang, April and May 1987, MMA.

65. Van Scoyoc interview, NAC.

66. Pauline Lamont Flynn, audio-taped interview with author, 3 April 2001, Ottawa, Ontario.

67. Evelyn A. Pepper, Gaëtane (LaBonté) Kerr, Harriet J.T. Sloan and Margaret D. McLean, "'Over There' in World War II," *Canadian Nurse* 62, no. 11 (November 1966), 26 and 28.

68. Nicholson interview.

69. MacAulay, in *Military Nurses of Canada,* Volume II, 115.

70. There are many accounts of the attack on the SS *Santa Helena.* See "A Salute to Our Nursing Sisters," *Canadian Nurse* 39, no. 12 (December 1943), 795–799;

"Courage and Discipline," *Canadian Nurse* 40, no. 1 (January 1944), 21; Nicholson, *Canada's Nursing Sisters,* 139–140; and Feasby, *Official History of the Canadian Medical Services,* 313.

71. Marjorie MacLean Root, audio-taped interview with author, 15 June 2001, Ottawa, Ontario.

72. Pauline Cox Walker, audio-taped interview with author, 13 June 2001, Kingston, Ontario.

73. Kay Christie, audio-taped interview with Joan Williams, 20 November 1975. ISN 196090, NAC. See also Kay Christie interview with Margaret M. Allemang, 5 April and 3 June 1992, MMA; and Kay Christie, "Behind Japanese Barbed Wire — A Canadian Nursing Sister in Hong Kong," *Royal Canadian Military Institute Year Book* (Toronto: RCMI, 1979), 11–13.

II

The Language of Sexuality: "Negotiating" the Female Body

CHAPTER 5

Female Genital Mutilation and Its Migration from Africa to North America

Aoua Bocar LY-Tall

IN 1994, THE INTERNATIONAL FEDERATION OF GYNECOLOGY CONGRESS held in Montreal rang the alarm bells to alert the world that between 84 and 114 million women were suffering from health problems related to female genital mutilation (FGM).[1] Also known as female circumcision, FGM occurs in three forms. The first is the incision or *sunna*, which appears to leave the female genital organs intact. It consists of removing a small piece of the clitoris or alternatively of *pricking* or *piercing* the clitoris. The two other forms are *excision* and *infibulation*. The *excision* entails severing the prepuce from the clitoris and/or ablating the clitoris and a part or all of the labia minora; the *infibulation* entails entirely cutting off the labia minora and the clitoris and sewing the labia majora together, leaving only a minute opening for the passage of urine and the menstrual flow. Excision accounts for 85 percent of female genital mutilations, while infibulation represents 15 percent.[2]

The consequences of FGM on women's physical and mental health make it one of the extreme forms of violence against women. Its multiple effects may be immediate, short-term or long-term. Psychologically, the girl's state of shock due to bleeding, acute pain and fear may endure and may bring on behavioural problems that range from a lack of confidence in loved ones to neuroses or even psychoses.[3]

Certain physical complications (hemorrhage, infection, tetanus, death) may ensue immediately after the operation. Injury to adjacent organs (uterus, vagina, perineum or rectum) is frequent. Among the long-term complications are recurrent bleeding, chronic obstruction and infection of the urinary and genital passages, the formation of keloid scars, cysts, neuromas, calculi and vesico-vaginal fistulas. Painful sexual relations and reduced sensitivity may bring on sexual dysfunction. Penetration may be difficult or impossible and sometimes the scar must be re-opened. Menstrual disorders such as dysmenorrhea are frequent. These different complications may lead to incontinence and to sterility for women and place them in a critical social situation.[4] Problems related to pregnancy and childbirth are also numerous: the consequences of prolonged or obstructed labour are dangerous for mother and child, who may suffer neonatal cerebral lesions. Deinfibulation is sometimes necessary to allow the baby to be born. Repeated deinfibulation and reinfibulation render the scar tissue fragile. Transmission of HIV is also an increased risk for sexually mutilated women.

Female Genital Mutilation: A Universal Practice

Even though the origins of the practices of excision and infibulation remain poorly understood, we know that they are ancient. Paul Corréa maintains that the Greek historian Herodotus mentions them in the fifth century B.C., in Pharaonic times.[5] The origins appear to precede Islam, even though many observers appear convinced that FGM is an Islamic requirement and that this religion is the source of the practices. In contrast with male circumcision, which is practised mainly by Jews and Muslims, excision is anchored in the cultural foundations of many people separated by distance, ethnicity, race and religion (Muslims, Catholics, Protestants, Copts, animists, Jews and non-believers).

European societies are among those that have practised FGM at different moments in their histories. One Russian Christian sect, the Skoptzis, cite Christ as having required that his male faithful castrate themselves, women being constrained to excise themselves and to mutilate their breasts.[6] The French doctor Michel Erlich, who practised in East Africa for over ten years, confirms this: "Exotic peoples do not have a monopoly on bloody practices: a European centre for religiously-inspired male and female genital mutilation developed over two centuries in Russia."[7]

According to C. Brisset, an 1864 report stated that excision was practised in psychiatric hospitals in Great Britain and in France as a means of
combating masturbation among young girls.[8] The same held true in North
America. Karim Belal and Phillip Blanchot report another example of the
practice of excision in the West: 'In the twentieth century in the United
States, the Orificial Surgery Society took on the task of propagandizing for
ablation of the organs that were 'the devil's abode.'"[9] All of these historical
facts demonstrate the universal character of the practice of FGM. Today, as
we enter the twenty-first century, our most precise data come from sub-
Saharan Africa.

At the FIGO Congress, Dr. Nahid Toubia noted that every year at least
two million girls the world over are victims of female genital mutilation
(FGM), that is, six thousand per day or five every minute. Between 85 and
114 million women around the world today are thus affected, 5 percent of
whom are in the West.[10] But this number represents only the tip of the ice-
berg, since it includes only affected women from sub-Saharan Africa, who
are found in twenty-seven countries located in a band running from the east
to the west and the length of the Nile Valley. Beyond the African continent,
however, silence blankets the practice of FGM. We know very little and
have few details as to which forms of FGM are practised, nor how many
women are affected. We do know, though, that FGM is practised in certain
parts of the Middle East, in South and East Asia, for a total of forty countries worldwide, according to Dr. Nafis Sadik, executive director of the
United Nations Population Fund (UNFPA). All of these facts led the
Annual General Assembly of the WHO in 1994 to deplore the rise in the
practice of FGM: "[T]his figure has increased by 19 million compared with
the figures published in 1993. 'But I think it's a lot more,' said Dr. Tomris
Turmen, the WHO Director of Family and Reproductive Health, in a statement to the press."[11]

An Analytical Framework

A number of different disciplines are involved in analyzing the custom of
FGM. We need to clarify its origins and development (history); its cultural
foundations and related social representations (sociology/anthropology); its
effects on physical health (medicine) on psychic health (psychology/psy-
choanalysis); and its effects on the social life of a mutilated woman. As well,
since it affects the physical integrity of women's and girls' bodies, the act of
FGM falls within the purview of the law. In a Western context, FGM also

belongs in the field of ethnic studies. Hence, a multidisciplinary approach is essential if we want to define and analyze the phenomenon of FGM. Further, as it touches on many dimensions of women's lives, the question of female genital mutilation has become one of the new subjects on the curriculum of Women's Studies. The complete eradication of the practice will require both attention and activism from the feminist movement.

The scope of the FGM phenomenon must surely trouble our consciences: over 120 million women are affected and so many of these women experience disastrous consequences that range from sudden death (during the operation) to longer-term effects during childbirth. Given these statistics, we must ask ourselves the following question: "Is the custom of FGM a cultural value or does it constitute the most highly developed form of female sexual repression?" As well, the universality of the practice of FGM can lead us to the hypothesis that it is an integral part of the patriarchal system, where unequal power relations allow men to appropriate and control women.

The practice of FGM fits within the framework of the physical appropriation of women by men, as introduced by Collette Guillaumin. Mutilation of the female genital organs is the most highly developed form of control over women's sexuality, worse even than appropriating their "work," their "time," the "products of their bodies" and imposing sexual obligation or "physical use" upon them. Guillaumin exhorts women to repossess themselves as individuals and as a class: "To take back the ownership of ourselves supposes that our entire class re-takes possession of itself, socially, materially."[12] But the victims of FGM cannot fight back, they have been irreversibly "dispossessed," since the act of FGM is practically irreversible. All justifications of the custom fade away from this perspective and FGM appears as nothing but sexual repression.

FGM: A Way to Control Women's Sexuality

Many reasons are invoked to justify the practice of FGM. Some reasons are aesthetic and some are hygienic. According to one widespread opinion, the unexcised clitoris is "voluminous" and "horrible." Soramus, a Greek physician, considered a woman's sexual organs to be "a dreadful deformity" that made her resemble a man.[13] Where hygiene is concerned, many women believe that excision reduces vaginal secretions that can cause irritations around the vulva.

Moral reasons are also invoked. Nearly all enthusiasts of FGM remain profoundly convinced that it helps reduce women's sexual impulses. Excision is supposed to protect women from all excess and will thus help the young girl to keep her virginity. These beliefs are predominantly anchored in societies where virginity and feminine chastity are an obsession, which is the case for many traditional or conservative societies, whether in Africa, Asia or the West. Thus, "[m]utilations are often motivated by a desire to contain women's sexual appetites, to preserve virginity, chastity, faithfulness and the honour of the family."[14] In the West, even in the twentieth century, some patients suffering from hysteria or "nymphomania" were "treated" by excision: "[A] woman was considered cured when she renounced sexual pleasure, in particular the orgasm, in order to take up her normal role as mother and servant of the household."[15]

FGM is part of an ensemble of practices aiming to control women's bodies. It is one way for men to manage women's sexuality through the worldwide patriarchal system. It is the counterpart of the chastity belt imposed on women in medieval Europe, or of the persecution of "witches," which led to the massacre of 70,000 to 100,000 women because they sought to experience their sexuality freely. In the same vein, one might point to the number of cases of incest or rape of young girls by their own fathers or their mothers' partners in contemporary Western society; or to the torture of foot binding imposed on Chinese women or the obligation that Indian women rejoice in being burned alive along with their deceased husbands. These facts show that in every society there are different forms of control or abuse of girls' and women's physical integrity.

Migration of FGM Practices from Africa to North America

While continental Europe has encountered problems of FGM since the 1980s,[16] North America only began encountering FGM in the 1990s, with the arrival of many African immigrants from countries where excision was the custom. It was then that people began to realize the practice of FGM had become a reality. Experience from Europe has shown that those who leave "excising" countries perpetuate FGM in the host countries, the more so since some medical clinics agree to carry out these operations clandestinely and thus medicalize them.[17]

In 1993, Quebec registered 42,179 francophone immigrants from Africa of whom over 50 percent were women.[18] The majority of these women are of childbearing age, and they have or will have "exciseable" daughters. Since the educational level of these women is relatively low, there is a greater likelihood that they will maintain traditional practices and customs.[19] According to a consultative study sponsored by the federal government and carried out by Marian Shermarke and Marie-Claude Manga — both founding members of the African women's network Réseau Femmes Africaines, Horizon 2015 (FAH 2015) — immigrants from "excising" countries living in Quebec admit that elders back home continue to exert pressure on them to have young girls excised. Further, many whisper that FGM is practised on the quiet in Quebec.[20] In Ontario, home to immigrants from countries (Somalia, Ethiopia, Sudan) where the majority practise the extreme form of excision known as infibulation, the situation is similar, if not worse. It seems that, as in Europe, some medical clinics will agree to carry out an excision/infibulation procedure in return for large sums of money. Further, there are traditional practitioners who work within these communities. Recently, the newspaper *La Presse* exposed the case of a thirteen-year-old girl in Ontario who was excised in her own home by a member of the Canadian medical profession. The case is the subject of an ongoing police investigation.[21]

The Conseil du statut de la femme du Québec, the Canadian Advisory Council on the Status of Women, the Commission des droits de la personne du Québec and many feminist researchers agree that FGM has become a health problem in Canada, and that it is one of concern to all sectors (health, education, social services, justice, research and so on).[22] Beyond the risk of perpetuating these practices on young new-Canadian girls, there is the fact that the majority of adult females from "excising" countries have already undergone the operation before their arrival. Their state of health requires medical and psychological follow-up, above all during pregnancy or childbirth (for example, the need to deinfibulate to allow a baby to be born, the patient's request for reinfibulation after birth). However, by contrast with the situation in Europe where this problem has existed for the past twenty years at least, in North America, health professionals are not prepared for this kind of situation, neither technically nor psychologically.

In the United States in 1994, according to the Centers for Disease Control, there were 130,000 African girls and women from countries in which FGM is practised; in New York City in June 1997, there were 20,000 girls and women.[23] It seems that in the United States, FGM is being carried out quietly as well. Hence many states, including California, Delaware,

Minnesota, North Dakota, Rhode Island, Tennessee and Wisconsin, and the federal government promulgated laws in 1996 forbidding the practice of sexual mutilation.

Actions and Strategies

The persistence over time and across borders of a cultural practice that entails so many harmful effects might seem incomprehensible. Nonetheless, for the past forty years, international organizations have turned their attention to female genital mutilation with the intention of eradicating it. The United Nations Economic and Social Council addressed the question in 1958; the World Health Organization's Regional Office for the Eastern Mediterranean in 1979; the Organization for African Unity in 1981; the WHO and the UN Commission on Human Rights in 1982. The leadership of these international bodies concluded that the practice of FGM formed a part of African customs and traditions and that, out of respect, they should not interfere. In the cases where recommendations to governments were made, they were not acted upon. It should be noted that the recommending bodies consisted almost entirely of men.

Only in the period following International Women's Year (1975) did women become involved in the fight against female sexual mutilation. In 1977, a working group on female circumcision was created in Geneva. It was given the mandate of studying this practice and of identifying possibilities for collaboration with African states and organizations. In 1994, after seven years of discussion and work in the field through missions to Africa, this working group organized a seminar on the question of FGM in Dakar, Senegal, in collaboration with the Senegalese minister of public health and with support from the World Health Organization, the United Nations Children's Fund, the United Nations Population Fund and other funding agencies. The seminar was given the mandate to fight against harmful traditional practices (FGM, tube feeding, nutritional taboos) and to promote positive traditional African practices (breast-feeding, mother and baby massage). This meeting, which brought together women delegates from twenty-two African countries, led to the creation of the Inter-African Committee (IAC), whose mandate is to fight against harmful traditional practices. The involvement of African women in the issue of FGM marked a decisive turning point in the struggle to end FGM in Africa and around the world.

In fulfillment of its mission, the IAC supports the creation of national committees in each country. The Committee's responsibilities include following through on the implementation of FGM-related legislation, ensuring that education about hygiene sensitizes the public to the dangers of FGM and developing programs to dissuade health agents and traditional medical practitioners from the practice of FGM. Today, there are twenty-seven IAC-affiliated national committees working in each of the African countries where there is a tradition of excision or infibulation, as well as in many of the countries to which Africans immigrate.[24] Through these committees, the African women (in collaboration with their Western sisters and with the support of non-governmental organizations and international co-operative organizations like the Organization for African Unity or United Nations agencies) develop different strategies and actively work towards eliminating FGM from their cultures. Ever since Beijing and its follow-up conference, thanks to sustained lobbying from the IAC and anti-FGM activists in different countries, we have noted a significant change in attitudes towards abolishing the custom of FGM.[25]

Thanks to a sensitization campaign about the harm caused by FGM and to the IAC's lobbying efforts at the grassroots level as well as with African heads of state and international organizations, many African and Western governments have promulgated laws forbidding FGM. At the international level, in particular, the recommendations to governments and communities adopted following the World Conference on Women in Nairobi in 1985 included measures and strategies for the elimination of FGM and for assisting girls and women who are victims of FGM. These recommendations can be found in the *Convention on the Elimination of All Forms of Discrimination against Women*, the *Convention on the Rights of the Child*, the *Declaration on the Elimination of Violence against Women*, the *Beijing Declaration*, and in such documents as *Female Genital Mutilation: Common, Controversial and Bad for Women's Health* published following the 1994 International Conference on Population and Development in Cairo.

In Canada, the Criminal Code protects citizens against illicit attacks on their physical and mental integrity. In 1997, the government added two paragraphs to Article 268 of the Criminal Code that forbid genital mutilation of females. In Quebec, it is the Charter of Human Rights and Freedoms that forbids FGM. These laws include criminal penalties for people who practice FGM or who incite such practices, including parents who request an excision. In 1994, the Commission des droits de la personne du Québec released is document *Les mutilations sexuelles*, in which it states:

It is self-evident that the sexual mutilation of women constitutes an illicit attack on the integrity of the person, and that all those who participate in such practices are to be held responsible. If shaving prisoners without their consent violates their integrity, the violation of the law is more flagrant and more serious when it is a question of the permanent mutilation of a woman's genitals.[26]

It appears, therefore, that there are sufficient legal measures in force today to protect girls and women in their countries of origin and in their host countries against FGM. At the same time, however, it is clear that these laws can only act as supportive measures in the fight to eliminate FGM. It is primarily through educating and sensitizing mothers, community opinion leaders, traditional practitioners, men (above all the younger ones) and members of the medical profession that we will succeed in eliminating FGM. The IAC has taken stock of its actions over the past eighteen years of intensive education and public engagement. In the preparatory documents for its international conference in February 2003 in Addis Ababa, Ethiopia, the Inter-African Committee claimed some impressive results:

- The involvement of twenty-seven countries in the IAC network
- Breaking taboos and demystifying FGM
- Legislation against FGM adopted in fourteen African countries
- Support from the African Union (OAU)
- Mobilization of youth and religious leaders
- Recognition by the UN of the IAC's work (1995 Population Award)
- Public renunciation and "laying down of their knives" by hundreds of traditional practitioners who were offered alternative employment opportunities
- Care provided to women suffering the consequences of FGM

Better still, thanks to lobbying by the IAC, the World Health Organization developed a 1996–2015 Regional Action Plan aimed at accelerating the elimination of FGM and improving health and quality of life for women and girls in the "excising" countries.[27] The action plan is supported by other United Nations agencies such as UNICEF and many NGOs.

*

Eradicating the custom of female genital mutilation that has existed for thousands of years, dating from Pharaonic Egypt, is a long-term job. But, after two decades of disseminating information, promoting education and sensitization under the leadership of African women and with the implementation of national and international legislation considerable advances have been made. Nonetheless, much remains to be done to achieve definitive eradication of the practice of FGM. Both action and research are required. New research areas will have to be developed in order to increase understanding of the phenomenon of FGM and strategies tailored to the world context will need to be formulated in order to eliminate the practice. All of this opens up new fields of investigation for feminist studies.

NOTES

This chapter was translated from the French by Sharon Gubbay Helfer.

1. Nahid Toubia, "Female Genital Mutilation and the Responsibility of Reproductive Health Professionals," *International Journal of Gynecology and Obstetrics (FIGO)* 46, no. 2 (1994), 127–135.

2. Ibid.

3. World Health Organization (Division of Family Health), *Mutilations sexuelles féminines: Dossier d'information* (Geneva: WHO, 1994).

4. Ibid.

5. Paul Corréa, "L'excision," in *Rapport du séminaire sur les pratiques traditionnelles ayant effet sur la santé des femmes et des enfants en Afrique* (Dakar, Sénégal: Comité-Inter-Africain 1984), 50–71.

6. C. Brisset, "Trente millions de mutilées," *Le Monde*, 1 March 1979, 22.

7. Michel Erlich, *La femme blessée: Essai sur les FGM* (Paris: L'Harmattan, 1986).

8. Brisset, "Trente millions de mutilées."

9. Karim Belal and Phillip Blanchot, "L'excision entre crime et tradition," *Afrique Magazine* (April 1999), 54.

10. Toubia, "Female Genital Mutilation and the Responsibility of Reproductive Health Professionals."

11. Associated Press, "L'WHO s'inquiète de l'augmentation des mutilations sexuelles chez les femmes," *La Presse*, 7 May 1994, H9.

12. Collette Guillaumin, "Pratique du pouvoir et idée de Nature," *Questions féministes* (1978), 28.

13. World Health Organization (Division of Family Health), *Chronique de l'OMS*, No. 20 (Geneva: WHO, 1981).

14. Regroupement des centres de santé des femmes du Québec, "Sans préjudice pour la santé des femmes," in *Les mutilations sexuelles: Le complot du silence* (Montréal: RCSFQ, 1996).

15. Belal and Blanchot, "L'excision entre crime et tradition," 54.

16. African immigration to Europe has been going on for much longer than to North America. In France, in 1982, the death following excision of a young girl from Mali and another in 1983 of a young girl from Ghana caused a scandal and aroused public opinion.

17. Erlich, *La femme blessée: Essai sur les FGM.*

18. Régie régionale de Montréal-centre, *Statistiques sur l'origine ethnique* (Montréal: RRMC, 1994). This figure seriously underestimates the number of Francophone immigrants from African countries because people who came to Quebec through Europe or the United States are counted as European or American immigrants.

19. K.H. Omer-Hasbi, "Female Genital Mutilation," *Treating the Female Patient* 7, no. 2 (1993), 12–13. African women who come to Canada to join their spouses often have only primary or partial secondary schooling.

20. Marian Shermarke, with the assistance of Marie-Claude Manga, *Report on Consultation on Female Genital Mutilation* (Montreal: Federal Interdepartmental Ad Hoc Working Group on Female Genital Mutilation, 1995). The FAH 2015 network has set its "horizon" at 2015 because girls born between 1985 and 1995 will be adult women in 2015 (between twenty and thirty years old). It took close to fifteen years (1984–1995) to sensitize the world to issues of FGM. The network is dedicated to seeing that our daughters and our granddaughters do not have to go through what our grandmothers, our mothers and we ourselves have experienced. These young women must be able to live without violence, without poverty and without excision. Since 1995, we have been fighting to have FGM definitively abolished, and we hope to see concrete results in the decade 2005–2015.

21. "Parents ontariens accusés d'avoir fait excisé leur fille," *La Presse*, 15 February 2002.

22. See, for example, Conseil du statut de la femme, *Les mutilations génitales: Une pratique qui doit disparaître* (Québec: Gouvernement du Québec, 1995); Canadian Advisory Council on the Status of Women, *Female Genital Mutilation: A Bibliography* (Ottawa: CACSW, 1994); M. Drapeau and H. Wolde-Giorghis, *Les mutilations sexuelles: Une atteinte illicite à l'intégrité de la personne* (Québec: Commission des droits de la personne du Québec, 1994). This document was adopted during the 388th session of the Commission, as Resolution COM-388-6.1.5; B.L. Calder, Y.R. Brown and D.I. Rae, "Female Circumcision/Genital Mutilation: Culturally Sensitive Care," *Health Care for Women International* (1993), 227–238; S. Daya, "Un nouveau problème de santé: La mutilation génitale de la femme," in C. Desjardins, ed., *La relation médecin-patiente: Au carrefour de la multi-ethnicité,* Report of the Department of Obstetrics and Gynaecology Symposium (Montréal: Université de Montréal, 1995), and "Editorial: Mutilation génitale de la femme mettre fin à une coutume néfaste," *Journal de la Société des gynécologues et obstétriciens du Canada* (April 1995), 319–321; M. Maldonado and L. Bouchard, "Nouveau problème de santé au Canada: la mutilation génitale," *l'Omnipraticien* (March 1995), 13–15 ; and Aoua Bocar LY-Tall, "Marcher pour éliminaer les muti-

lations génitales-féminines (MGF): Une forme extrême de violence faite aux femmes," *Recherches féministes* 13, no. 1(2000); "Le passage des FGM de l'Afrique à l'Amérique du Nord" (paper presented at the Center for French and Francophone Studies, Colombia University, New York, January 31, 2000) and "Éradiquer les FGM: Un défi des Africaines à l'aube du IIIème Millénaire: Actions, stratégies et perspectives" (paper presented at the Conference on Rituals of Violence Against Women, Southern Ontario Francophone Women's Network/Solidarité 2000, Glendon College, York University, Toronto, September 24–25, 1999).

23. Research, Action, Information Network for the Bodily Integrity of Women, "Female Circumcision in the United States, A Declaration of Values," June 2, 1997.

24. In France, there is the Groupe femmes pour l'Abolition des mutilations sexuelles (GAMS), with a chapter in Belgium; in the Netherlands, the Foundation for Women's Health, Research and Development (FORWARD); in the United Kingdom, the London Black Women's Health Action Project (LBWHAP); and in Sweden, the National Association for Immigrant Women (RIFFI).

25. For example, see Canadian Advisory Council on the Status of Women, *Recommendations to the Government of Canada on Female Genital Mutilation* (Ottawa: CACSW, 1994), and "On exhorte le Gouvernement à empêcher la pratique des mutilations des organes génitaux des femmes au Canada," Press Release, March 8, 1994.

26. Drapeau and Wolde-Giorghis, *Les mutilations sexuelles*, 6.

27. World Health Organization, Division of Family Health, *Regional Action Plan for Elimination of Female Genital Mutilation* (Geneva: WHO, 1996).

CHAPTER 6

Body Talk:
Chronicles of Women's Experiences in Prison

Sylvie Frigon

ANY GIVEN SOCIETY produces and reproduces a specific corporal order, that is, an order of normative bodies. This order mediates the cultural and symbolic systems of that society at a specific historical moment and in a specific political context.[1] At the dawn of the twenty-first century, the *body*, both men's and women's, is increasingly becoming a central part of rethinking theory and practice in many disciplines, including sociology, psychology, medicine, anthropology, geography, history, law, psychiatry and criminology.

In this chapter, I explore the simultaneous construction of the body as a *site of control* and a *site of resistance*, as well as the notions of the *dangerous body* and the *body in danger*, in order to uncover how the (re)production of the "docile body" operates and, more specifically, how the docile body is constructed in criminological knowledge and practices.[2] My argument is built on the premise that, throughout history, criminology and law have probed, marked, measured and treated the "deviant body" in a variety of ways in the criminal justice system.[3] Moreover, the concern for the deviant body rests on the assumption that there is, in the corporal order, a "normal" body.[4] I also examine how confinement marks the body, how penal laws are imprinted onto it and how governance is achieved through it. In order to undertake this task, I use the body[5] as a pivotal concept whose parameters can help us to explore gendered practices of subjugation. The political anatomy of the body helps us to analyze how power within an institution can directly or indirectly take hold of the body, which is insured by practices of subjugation and the *political technology of the body.*[6]

This chapter is divided into three sections. The first establishes the foundations for the emergence of the body in criminology, particularly the emergence of the "wicked body" and the place of women's body in criminological knowledge and practices. In the second section, I examine the politics of confinement and how "dangerous bodies" are managed. As an example of this, I take a brief look at the intervention of an emergency response team at the Kingston Penitentiary for Women in Ontario, in April 1994, bringing into focus the politics of strip searching and segregation. The third section explores how women's bodies are marked by the experience of prison and how they use the marking as a form of resistance and survival. Through this analysis, I hope to show how the deviant female body and the (en)gendering of the deviant body are used to *govern* women's behaviour.

The Emergence of the Wicked Body:
The Interplay between Women's Bodies and Criminology

The question of the body is an important one in criminological and penal practices, but it has rarely been carefully theorized.[7] However, the links between the body and crime (that is, the body as a site of deviance, marginality and criminality) emerged well before the nineteenth century. These links can be traced back to the works of early philosophers. The corporal metaphor (the body-machine or the body-politic, for example) was indeed present in the writings of Aristotle, Plato, Montesquieu and Rousseau.[8] In the sixteenth and seventeenth centuries, for example, some characteristics of the body (whether they were too small or too big) were taken as explanations or signs of deviance and criminality. From the school of physiognomy and the development of typologies, phrenology and the "primitive stigma" came a science that located evilness, badness and wickedness in the brain.[9] In 1859, the Darwinian debate certainly contributed to the developing field known as criminal anthropology. In this historical context, Cesare Lombroso and G. Ferrero produced the anatomy of the criminal from which emerged an entire hierarchy of the criminal body.[10] Criminal women and prostitutes, more specifically, were placed at the bottom of the hierarchy as they were seen as being more atavistic and less developed.

We have seen in the work of Michel Foucault and others that historically the body of the condemned was supervised, controlled, tortured and even decapitated. The torture of Damien — a condemned man — is a graphic example of this control and extermination:

> On 2 March 1757 Damien the regicide was condemned to make the *amende honorable* before the main door of the Church of Paris, where he was to be taken and conveyed in a cart, wearing nothing but a shirt, holding a torch of burning wax weighing two pounds; then, in the said cart, to the Place de Grève, where, on a scaffold that will be erected there, the flesh will be torn from his breasts, arms, thighs and calves with red-hot pincers, his right hand, holding the knife with which he committed the said parricide, burnt with sulphur, and, on those places where the flesh will be torn away, poured molten lead, boiling oil, burning resin, wax and sulphur melted together and then his body drawn and quartered by four horses and his limbs and body consumed by fire, reduced to ashes and his ashes thrown to the winds.[11]

By the beginning of the nineteenth century, punishment-as-spectacle[12] was replaced when the transition of the *macropolitics of the spectacle* into a *micro-physics of power* occurred. Torture was eliminated and, according to Foucault, "the gloomy festival of punishment was dying out"; capital punishment, which appeared to be less barbaric in its method and confinement, became a more humanitarian form of punishment. Indeed, punishment became "a less immediately physical kind" of act demanding a certain "discretion in the art of inflicting pain." Again, according to Foucault, "the body as the major target of penal repression disappeared."[13] Instead, it came to serve as an instrument of its own punishment, where limits on its mobility and rights replaced physical torture:

> The body, according to this penalty, is caught up in a system of constraints and privations, obligations and prohibitions. Physical pain, the pain of the body itself, is no longer the constituent element of the penalty. From being an art of unbearable sensations punishment has become an economy of suspended rights.[14]

As a result, "a whole army of technicians took over from the executioner, who had been the immediate anatomist of pain: warders, doctors, chaplains, psychiatrists, educationalists" reassured prisoners that the body and the spectacle of pain were not the ultimate objects of their punitive action.[15] In this new form of non-corporal penalty, these specialists focused on different elements of the body. The modern rituals of execution (for example, lethal injection) attest to this double process: the disappearance of the spectacle and the elimination of the prisoner's pain.[16] Nonetheless, certain modern elements of punishment involve the body itself: rationing of food, sexual deprivation, loss of freedom, corporal punishment, solitary confinement, strip searching, body cavity searching and segregation, to name a few. Yet even in this "internal economy of the penalty" there is still a trace of "torture." That is, the body remains central to the penalty: "It is always the body that is at issue — the body and its forces, their utility and their docility, their distribution and their submission."[17]

According to Foucault, we must understand punishment as a complex social function and as a political tactic in which the body is invested, trained, marked and tortured, even if the torture is not physical or immediately apparent. Furthermore, the body becomes both *productive* and *subjected.* This is, for Foucault, the culminating point of the normalization of disciplinary punishment. In fact, bodies are "malleable under [such] power."[18] How is this normalization of disciplinary punishment being projected onto women's bodies, then? On this, Foucault and others have remained silent, for which they have been criticized. Feminist scholars have made valuable contributions that redefine, reshape and engender the practice of normalizing discipline and how it affects women.[19]

Women's Bodies in Criminological Knowledge and Practice

Cesare Lombroso — a noted physical anthropologist, and often presented as the father of positivistic criminology of the late 1800s — measured, observed and classified the female body. He developed a typology of female criminality based on Darwinian and degeneracy theories which were current in the second half of the nineteenth century. According to David Horn, in Lombroso's criminology, "The body of the 'female offender' was constituted as a particular kind of text: an index of present and potential risks to the larger social organism."[20] For Lombroso, the female criminal was much more terrible because her deviance was twofold: she had transgressed the law and, more importantly, she had transgressed her role as woman, wife and mother. In fact, she was viewed as a "monster."[21]

In this tradition, traits of degeneracy were attributed to women's bodies. Therefore, the biological constitution of a female criminal was viewed as pathological, a view which helped to develop typologies of offenders (for both men and women) as well as philosophies of intervention in penal institutions for women. According to Russell Dobash and his co-authors, Henry

Maudsley appears to be the first nineteenth-century British doctor to identify the "normal functionings of women's bodies as a cause of insanity and
deviance, arguing that normal menstruation, pregnancy and lactation could
form part of a pathological condition."[22] Maudsley concluded that sexual
deviations in women were the product of the "irritation of the ovaries or
uterus — a disease by which the chaste and modest woman is transformed
into a raging fury of lust."[23] In 1890, Havelock Ellis argued that women
found guilty of infanticide were "endowed with excessive down in their
faces, that female thieves went grey more quickly, were uglier, and exhibit-
ed more signs of degeneracy (especially of the sexual organs) than ordinary
women."[24] Maudsley, like Ellis, links women's crimes to the corruption of
their physical virtues:

> [T]o what a depth of degradation woman sometimes sinks ... she com-
> pletely loses all sense of shame, modesty, self-respect, and gentleness, all
> her womanliness, and becomes violent, cruel, outrageously blasphemous,
> and impudently immodest; in fact, a sort of fiend with all the vices of
> woman in an exaggerated form, and with none of her virtues.[25]

The general tendency in the literature produced by religious ministers,
concerned philanthropists, doctors and later psychologists of the day was to
present "bad" women as "mad." In fact, an entire generation of authors produced works on the mental illness of women that bore traces of misogyny.[26]
Early twentieth-century views of female crime were also drawn from the
"eugenics" movement, which provided a fertile ground for the birth of the
"degenerate woman." The female offenders, of course, were the antithesis of
the ideal woman. To achieve this ideal, women had to regulate their bodies
and minds and fit into the role of mother and wife:

> The analysis of women was particularly important in these efforts since
> women in their role as mothers were seen as the biological and social
> source of degeneracy, and patriarchal assumptions about the true nature
> of women led to attempts to identify and classify those who deviated
> from this norm.[27]

This concept of female criminals as physically and psychologically depraved
still influences how they are perceived and treated in the criminal justice
system and, indeed, in prison today.[28]

Even more importantly, however, is that "what emerged from
Lombroso's studies was less the (hoped for) transparent pathology of the
female offender than the barely legible *potential* dangerousness of the normal woman."[29] As a result, all women could justifiably be watched and

controlled. According to David Horn:

> Of particular importance, however, was the lengthy discussion of the "normal" woman that opened the book and that in many ways provided its framework. The normal woman, a figure that had no real counterpart in Lombroso's studies of male criminality, was ostensibly constructed as a background against which the female offender might become distinct, visible, and legible ... the portrait of the normal woman contributed substantially to locating all women with the domain of the social expert.[30]

This is what can be referred to as the symbolic function of the deviant body, which led to the idea that all women are suspect and therefore potential targets for surveillance, control and "risk management."

This concept of women's bodies as potentially deviant is translated into the politics of incarceration. The prison is a very good example of how the body is positioned, marked and controlled in a penal-related environment. And as we shall see, women's bodies are sites and targets for surveillance in the ideology and politics of confinement.

The Politics of Confinement: Governing Women's Bodies

I hope to demonstrate that the body is still central in the ideology of incarceration. In order to more fully explain this, I use two important concepts: (1) the body as a surface onto which social and penal norms are inscribed, and (2) the body as a site of lived experience.[31] In these concepts, the body can be understood as a hinge, that is, as a pivotal point. In this section, I attempt to describe how various devices of power are used to control bodies. How does confinement work to change the body? How is the body invested? How does confinement (en)gender deviant female bodies? How is the body simultaneously *dangerous* and *in danger*? How is the body simultaneously a *site of control* and a *site of resistance*?

However, before looking at how imprisoned women's bodies are marked by their experience in the penal system, it is necessary to understand their situations in Canadian prisons today.

Canadian Women in Custody

Women in custody are, as two authors have put it, "a social inconvenience" and "too few to count."[32] In 1990, provincially sentenced women (two years or less) represented 7 percent of the Canadian prison population; federally sentenced women (two years or more) represented 4 percent of the entire federally sentenced population. In the same year, 305 women were incarcerated for federal sentences compared with 13,234 men.[33] Until 1996, the Kingston Prison for Women (P4W) was the only penitentiary for women in Canada compared with more than forty institutions for men (with some federal–provincial exchange of services that permitted women to "do their time" in provincial institutions near their families).[34] In September 1995, 619 women were serving a federal sentence. More than half (322) were in detention and the others were in surveillance in their communities. Forty-two percent of the women were at the Prison for Women in Kingston, and half of the women serving time in the Prairies were Aboriginal women.[35] Between 1990 (the year that the Canadian task force on federally sentenced women was created and which fundamentally reconfigured female imprisonment in the 1990s) and 2001, the number of federally sentenced women increased by more than 75 percent: from 210 to 370.[36]

Until very recently, then, the existence of only one penitentiary for women created several difficulties, including a lack of programming, insufficient penal classification (all women, no matter their offence, were housed in a maximum-security setting) and geographical dislocation (many were far from their communities and children). This is quite alarming given that two-thirds of all the women were mothers and 70 percent of these mothers were the sole providers for their children. This differs sharply from incarcerated men who generally have a partner taking care of their children when they are inside. Another alarming issue is the rate of suicides. According to non-official sources, between 1977 and 1991, a dozen women (of which eight were Aborignal) killed themselves.[37] (Self-mutilation and self-injurious behaviour[38] are discussed below.) The plight of Aboriginal women at P4W has raised many issues concerning their treatment and overrepresentation in the wider prison system and the systemic racism they face in the criminal justice system.[39]

In 1990, the Task Force on Federally Sentenced Women recommended the closure of the Kingston Prison for Women and the construction of five new regional facilities (in addition to the existing prison in British Columbia).[40] The closure of P4W had been recommended since it first opened in 1934. Over the years, more than a dozen commissions, committees and inquiries have identified the institution's serious limitations in the resources it provides to its prisoners.[41] Much less attention, however, has been paid to provincially sentenced women, even though they constitute the vast majority of incarcerated women in Canada.[42]

In order to bring this group of women into sharper focus in my research, I interviewed twenty-five provincially sentenced women serving time in Maison Tanguay in Montreal.[43] These women were of different ages and backgrounds: they were mothers, single, heterosexual, homosexual, lower and middle class, from different ethnic origins and serving a variety of sentences for a variety of offences — short to longer periods of incarceration, multiple incarcerations, first time offenders, repeat offenders, at the beginning or at the end of their prison term. Through these women's voices, I try to uncover the daily negotiations they use to cope, survive and even resist the subjugation of prison culture. This approach is rooted in the guiding principles of "standpoint feminism,"[44] incorporating the women's personal perspectives and their experiences of how incarceration marked their bodies. Women's experiences of their bodies in prison demonstrate the processes and techniques involved in "governing the prisoner"[45] through the body. Women's bodies in prison are marked and alienated; they are victimized and mutilated. The feminist sociology of the body also provides the framework and theoretical underpinning for this research. Together with Natalie Beausoleil's work on makeup and appearance, this chapter confirms "that while *limited by structural forces of domination*, women are actively 'negotiating the body.'"[46]

I now turn to the violence the incarcerated women at P4W experienced during a raid on their cells the night of April 27 and the strip searching of their bodies that was carried out by the Institutional Emergency Response Team (IERT). The IERT were called in as a response to a hostile confrontation between a group of prisoners and prison staff that took place in the Segregation Unit earlier that week. Hostilities had been brewing for a while over issues of a poorly managed unit. In order to reconstruct the women's experiences of this event, I refer to the 1995 broadcast of *the fifth estate* and to the *Report of the Commission of Inquiry into Certain Events at the Prison for Women in Kingston*, prepared by the Honourable Louise Arbour.

The Politics of Confinement: Managing the Dangerous Body

The intervention by the IERT at P4W did not become a public debate until the broadcast of *the fifth estate* on February 21, 1995, which showed the IERT in action on the night of the raid. Male officers stormed into the women's cells where everything was quiet and calm. Some women were, in fact, asleep and the majority did not offer any resistance when they were woken up. The images that follow are troubling. The women were stripped naked by masked and shielded officers wearing black combat suits. The women were restrained; their naked bodies surrounded by the men. The images are almost pornographic. The broadcast of the event provoked an inquiry, which resulted in the publication of the *Report of the Commission of Inquiry into Certain Events at the Prison for Women in King*ston in 1996.[47]

Violating Dangerous Bodies

This episode began on the evening of Friday, April 22, 1994, when a brief but violent physical confrontation took place between six prisoners of the Segregation Unit at the Prison for Women and a number of the correctional staff. The reason for the outbreak revolved around issues concerning the operation of a living unit, which was to be

> in accordance with explicit legal or policy requirements. The failure to provide the inmates with what they were entitled to while in segregation, if not intentionally punitive, could only be perceived as such by the inmates. This produced an escalation of anger and confrontation.

When the women were "restrained," they were returned to the Segregation Unit, and criminal charges were laid against them by the prison administration. On Tuesday, April 26, correctional staff demonstrated outside the prison, protesting the "dangerous" working conditions. That evening, Correctional Supervisor Warnell prepared a memorandum in which he recommended that the IERT be called in:

> Given the fragile psyche of the Officers at the institution at this time, I strongly recommend that an IERT cell extraction team be brought in and all inmates in the dissociation side be taken from their cells, strip searched and placed in stripped cells. I do not feel that our Officers should have to continue to suffer this type of abuse when we have the means to put a stop to it. Otherwise, I fear that we will have more staff requesting stress leaves and a diminished credibility toward management.

According to Warnell, the intervention was seen as a safe method to re-establish order. In his memo he gave another (less legitimate) reason for calling in the IERT:

> *Due to the poor mood of the institution* which was set by the incidents of the weekend past, and which was aggravated by the picket this afternoon, administration decided to call in the Emergency Response Cell Extraction Team ... (emphasis added).

The IERT intervention, then, was not justified by the actual seriousness of the situation but by the incapacity of the administration to re-establish order.

An IERT is made up of a group of volunteer Correctional Services staff members and is usually deployed in male prisons. The P4W deployment was the first to occur in a women's prison. The team's dress and equipment are designed to intimidate:

> The dress consists of a black combat suit and associated protective gear — shin pads, safety boots, slash-proof vest, elbow pads, protective gloves, gas mask with an eye shield, and a protective helmet. The weapons carried by IERT members include batons, mace cans, and at least one plastic shield per team.

A standard IERT cell extraction proceeds as follows:

> A team (in this case eight men, plus one co-ordinator) marches into the area in formation (as part of the intimidation technique) and approaches the cell of the inmate who is to be extracted. The plastic shield is banged against the cell, producing a very loud and frightening noise. The inmate is told to lie face down on the floor and warned that if the order is not obeyed, mace will be used. If the inmate complies, the cell door is opened and members of the team enter the cell and assume an "on guard" stance with batons and mace around the inmate. Restraint equipment — usually handcuffs and leg irons — is applied to the inmate. The inmate's clothing is cut off, and the inmate's body is visually inspected … If the cell is to be stripped, the inmate is taken from the cell and made to walk backwards — which is thought to be safer, both for the IERT and the inmate. The cell is then stripped. The naked inmate is then returned to the cell … The IERT's activities are videotaped.

As for strip searches, the law stipulates:

> Men may not strip search women. The only exception is where the delay in locating women to conduct the search would be dangerous to human life or safety, or might result in the loss of evidence.
>
> No one can apply restraints to an inmate as punishment, or participate in any cruel, inhumane or degrading treatment or punishment of an inmate.

The video shown of *the fifth estate* begins when the IERT is already in Joey Twins's cell and she is being submitted to a strip search. She obeys. She is being taken out of her cell and "while she is still being held in the corner, a paper gown is brought to Ms. Twins and tied around her neck. The effect is something like that of a bib. The paper gown neither covers her, nor provides warmth." Upon her return to her cell, a body belt is applied in order to restrain her.

The last inmate to be strip searched was Brenda Morrison. In response to their order for her to kneel and remove her clothing, she asked questions about what would happen if she did not remove them. The questions were not answered (which is part of the procedure). Rather, restraints were applied over her clothing, at which point she offered to take off her clothes. She was told to lie face down. She did not immediately do so and they forced her to the ground. Three IERT members held her down, ripped and then cut her shirt open at the back while the female correctional officer cut off her pants. Brenda Morrison's testimony at the inquiry identified the fact that men were strip searching women, commenting that it was almost a spectacle as even construction workers were allowed to watch the strip search:

> I was pacing back and forth in my cell, and I was trying to decide if I should take my clothes off or just leave them on. I came to the conclusion that I won't take off my clothes for men because — I'm sorry I tried my best to ... Because I know it is in [the] law that you are not supposed to take your clothes off for any man ... When I was on the ground, on the cement, I did look on the side and I seen ... two construction workers standing in front ... watching me.[48]

The women were not given any level of control over their bodies, and their different demands were denied:

> Throughout the strip searches, there is a fairly constant level of talking ... Other requests for tampax, medication, eye glasses, are called out ... Some called out that they were being raped ... Some expressed their fear at the memory of previous sexual assaults. Consistent with IERT training, questions and requests were not answered.

The institutional physician, Dr. Mary Pearson, who was there for the first portion of the intervention, was devastated to see that women were naked in front of men. She was asked to leave the unit so she would not interfere. At the inquiry, one of the IERT members testified that one of the women was flirting with him. Dr. Pearson, who knew the inmate for some time, testified on the her behalf:

> The inmate was in fact in a dissociative state, speaking in a girlish voice, possibly reliving a childhood episode of sexual abuse ... this very emotionally fragile inmate was exhibiting signs of having lost all contact with reality ... The many references to menstrual periods, tampax and rape is consistent with the fact that they were experiencing the events as having a significant sexual aspect.

For many of the women, this brutal intervention "had the effect of re-victimizing" them, especially those "who had traumatic experiences in their past at the hands of men." Inmate Shea filed a complaint in which she testified, "I have been sexually abused all my life and this brought back those terrible times. I never been so humiliated in my life for six men to be allowed to do this to me." In her final *Report*, Justice Arbour condemned the strip search and argued that it reflected systemic problems in women's corrections. She suggested a series of remedies that included the appointment of the first Deputy Commissioner for Women for Correctional Services of Canada who would be responsible for issues facing women offenders, strategic planning and policy initiatives.

Segregating Dangerous Bodies

The six women who were involved in the confrontation with the prison staff spent seven to nine months in segregation. Their prolonged segregation was unjustified, according to Justice Arbour:

> Correctional Service proceeded on the basis that the women would continue to be segregated until their charges were disposed of, notwithstanding the fact that outstanding criminal charges per se would not constitute a reason for continued segregation under the *Corrections and Conditional Release Act.*

The law distinguishes between administrative and disciplinary (punitive) segregation. An inmate may be placed in administrative segregation "only on the basis that her presence in the general population is a threat to security of the penitentiary, the safety of anyone including herself, or the investigation of a criminal charge" and only if there are no reasonable alternatives. An inmate may be placed in disciplinary segregation only as punishment after conviction of an institutional offence and there are limits to its duration. Also segregation conditions must be respected:

> The Segregation Unit must be visited every day by the Warden, or by a senior manager designated by the Warden in Standing Orders accessible to inmates. Inmates are entitled to access to counsel, daily exercise, and to conditions of confinement set out below.

As the above quote suggests, the appropriate conditions of confinement were not met. Warden Cassidy visited the Segregation Unit twice between April and September. Furthermore,

> [a]ccording to the Segregation Unit visitor's log, from April 22, 1994 until January 19, 1995 ... the Unit Manager visited 43 times. During the same period, there were 101 weekdays and 77 weekend days on which there were no visits by any senior manager ...

Other breaches were also noted: reduced access to legal counsel, to daily exercise and to hygienic products (toilet paper, vaginal cream) and the failure to maintain a clean unit. Moreover, the addition of a heavy metal meshed plate across the open bars created a massive visual obstruction and constant camera surveillance increased the claustrophobia experienced by the women.

Research has proven that negative ramifications can result from long-term isolation. According to a report produced by the medical team at the Prison, the following symptoms were observed among the segregated women: perceptual distortions; auditory and visual hallucinations; flash-backs; increased sensitivity and startle response; emotional distress due to extreme boredom and monotony; anxiety, particularly associated with leaving the cell or segregated area; generalized emotional lability at times; fear that they were "going crazy" or "losing their minds" because of limited interaction with others.

In the particular instance of the IERT raid on P4W, the "dangerous body" was punished and managed in response to a situation the administration perceived as threatening and which it was ill-equipped to manage. These women were once again put in a position of victimization and hopelessness, and the incident revealed the systemic problems that exist in the correctional system for women. Had it not been for the broadcast of *the fifth estate* and the subsequent *Report,* would we have ever known the full story? Would the women have had a chance to voice their experiences? Even though their experience is on record, what has happened to these women? Has it really changed anything inside the system? The closing of P4W and the opening of the new regional facilities, despite their shortcomings, might prevent a repetition of similar events.

While I have tried here to capture women's experiences during which the body was used as a site of control, what do incarcerated women experience on a daily basis?

Humiliation and Marking as Forms of Control

When they first arrive at the prison, incoming inmates experience the first of the "degradation ceremonies" that are intended to weaken their sense of identity and humiliate them.[49] As Monique Hamelin notes, women (as well as men) are stripped of their identity as subjects and the mechanisms by which this is achieved include humiliating tactics such as having to undress in front of strangers and taking their shower with a disinfectant.[50] When interviewing Ève at Maison Tanguay, she recalled that she felt she was treated as though she were a "leper."

Many of the women interviewed described the humiliation they were subjected to during strip searches and body cavity searches, which can occur at the intake process and throughout their entire stay in the prison. Many see it as breach of their intimacy and, as Ève points out, of their dignity: "Lift your breasts, spread your legs, lift your hair, open your mouth, lift your tongue ... I hate it; it's humiliating." Nikita says, "Being naked is humiliating for me because I am fat; it's very difficult." For Isabelle, the search is the most humiliating part of leaving prison to go to court: "You get undressed and you remove a sanitary napkin; you put it in a tissue; they give you another one and they watch all the time you do this. There really has to be blood in the sanitary napkin." Similarly, in a study conducted with women at Fleury-Mérogis in Paris, Gisèle Ginsberg recounts the women's feelings of humiliation when they had to reveal their bloody sanitary napkins during body cavity searches.[51] And even though the Ombudsman of Quebec (the Protecteur du citoyen) considers body searches to always be humiliating, the strip searches continue.[52]

Strip searches and body cavity searches devalue a woman's body and contribute to her loss of status and identity. Women no longer see themselves as women and are often surprised at their own reflections. Louise told me, "Sometimes I look at myself in the mirror and I find myself looking frightful." As Marie Gagnon explains, women begin to lose self-definition:

> I look at myself in the mirror. I am not the same person. Now, my eyes are hard, dark; my cheeks are rounder ... I am heavier but I look thinner. Progressively, I become a hermit. I have the colour of the prison painted on my skin. I am pale. My hair is dry and dull ...[53]

The marking of the body also results in a woman's intense sense of alienation and even the disappearance of her body. The senses are disrupted through "sensorial confinement," as expressed by Gayle Horii, an ex-prisoner of Kingston's Prison for Women:

> Grey days and black nights are the colours of precisioned function — the colours of punishment ... The fragrance of flowers, of incense, of jasmine tea, the scent of your lover's skin — all are displaced with the odour of disinfectant, of mould, of foul-smelling water and stale food, of dusty paper and institutional soap which permeates your nostrils. The only sequence is dislocation.[54]

Markings of sexuality may also alienate, as was the case in Fleury-Mérogis in Paris until 1984, when lesbian women were segregated in a special "tomboy unit."[55] Pregnancy too can be a marker. The bodies of pregnant incarcerated women are perceived as being inferior to law-abiding bodies:

> The body of the imprisoned woman, however, is not only inferior in relation to that of the "normal body" but also in relation to the conceptualization of the "good" woman. A positivistic, scientific view of the body denotes "criminal" bodies as ontologically inferior to "law" abiding bodies. Under such an ideologically position, pregnant imprisoned women possess bodies that reflect a qualitative and quantitative multiplication of levels of inferiority by virtue of their criminal "abnormality" or "atavism" and feminine inferiority.[56]

Women do not feel as though they are real women and legitimate mothers-to-be. Often, they feel they are treated as inferior and suspect.

The Mutilated Body

> Bodies talk and become mediums of a text, of a story ... codes, laws, norms and social ideals are embodied in the bodies.[57]

Women's bodies are mutilated through illness and the victimization they experience, not only in prison but also in their lifestyles before their incarcerations. Once inside, health problems often reappear. For example, it is not uncommon for women to come to prison with sleeping and eating disorders, medical and dental problems, social isolation, gynecological infections and even HIV and AIDS, which are linked to prostitution and addiction and often tied to their poverty and marginalization. Various psychosomatic illnesses are tied to the stress of trials, incarceration, children, partners and money. These illnesses include insomnia, hypertension, headaches, skin rashes, hair loss, vertigo, vision problems, anorexia and bulimia.[58] For women who share a cell with only one toilet, chronic constipation problems often occur. The loss of intimacy and the loss of control over their lives, their bodies and their health tend to produce a sick, mutilated body. According to *Creating Choices*, some imprisoned women feel as though they have lost the control over their own bodies, which is exacerbated by their inability to access medical advice and medication.[59]

However, we should note that for some women, incarceration becomes a time when they can reconstruct themselves, both physically and mentally. They eat three meals a day, sleep, receive medical attention and are protected from the abuse outside (that is, domestic violence or violence on the street). Many women in prison have come from abusive backgrounds. According to *Creating Choices*, between 60–90 percent of federally sentenced women have been abused at one time in their lives or even throughout their entire lives (sexual abuse, incest, domestic violence). For some, this abuse is linked to racism, sexism and economic marginalization. For many, the prison system reproduces and perpetuates this violence. This institutionalized violence highlights how *victimization* might be linked to the process of *criminalization*.[60] For some women, criminal behaviour might become a survival strategy.[61] As a way of coping with the "pains of imprisonment," women may choose to mark themselves through self-injury or self-mutilation. These acts not only communicate pain, distress and powerlessness, they also express resistance.

Self-mutilation as Resistance

The body functions as a tool of struggle, survival and resistance in prison. Different strategies that involve the body and body image are used to achieve this. These include makeup and clothes, tattoos, body piercing, overeating or not eating. They also include self-mutilation.

Self-mutilation[62] occurs at a higher rate in women's prisons than in men's prisons. Men, in general, direct their anger at others while women turn it onto themselves.[63] A 1979 study in Ontario found that 86 percent of provincially sentenced women had mutilated themselves.[64] In 1990, Jan Heney conducted interviews with forty-four federally sentenced women and found that 59 percent had mutilated themselves and 92 percent had cut their veins or slashed themselves as a way of inflicting self-injury; others hit their heads and burned themselves.[65] More recent research has shown that the rate of women's self-mutilation continues to be higher than that of men and that rates of provincially sentenced women were higher than those of federally sentenced women.[66]

For certain women, mutilating their bodies is a way of reclaiming them and is sometimes used as a strategy to exercise control. They decide when to slash, where to slash, when to stop and how far they go, all of which contrasts with their experiences as powerless victims of abuse. Although destructive, self-mutilation is a way that some women can regain a sense of power. According to Heney, self-mutilation may be a survival strategy, and Shoshana Pollack considers it a strategy that can separate oneself from the body, a way to dissociate the body from the spirit that is suffering.[67] One Aboriginal inmate expressed it this way:

> It is no wonder that so many of us cut our throats, lacerate our bodies, hang ourselves. It is no wonder that we need to identify our pain onto our

physical bodies because our whole lives have been filled with incredible pain and traumatizing experiences — psychic pain, physical pain, spiritual pain.[68]

The frustration women experience as a result of their confinement may also pave the way to their self-mutilation and produce, in return, a sense of relief. When I interviewed Sara, Ève and Lyne, they explained it to me this way:[69]

> I remember how they cut my temporary absence because my papers were badly done. The system had "fucked up." I worked so hard for this to happen, to get there, and they tell me this before Christmas. My son tells me, "I thought you were my Christmas gift?" I went crazy. I went to my cell. I had to do something, I had rage inside of me. It had to come out. There was too much pain inside and I cut myself open for the first time. It felt like "whoosh," like a "release," as if I had released the tension inside of me. It scared me because it felt like such a good "release." (Sara)

> I was in my cell, my razor was still there. It was the razor day. I took my razor and I cut myself open … (Lyne)

> I did it with a can of pop … I was angry with my mother because my mother does not love me. (Ève)

Through the process of self-injury, women can use the lacerations to recount the painful moments in their lives. Each laceration tells a story of isolation, desperation and loneliness that is related to being separated from their children, grieving the death of a mother or being in prison at Christmas. When women feel powerless, when they become alienated from their bodies, they need to feel "alive" and often this is achieved through self-mutilation. However, many women have found other strategies to help them feel "alive" and reconstruct a sense of self, which can help them to resist the reality of prison.

The Art of Survival

Through art and creativity, women unmask the link between their oppression and their bodies. In workshops, women create masks, drawings, sculptures, pottery and poetry. Prison Arts Foundation encourages the personal development of convicted offenders through their involvement in arts. For example, women prisoners from the Joliette facility in Quebec, with the support of the institution and the Correctional Services of Canada, created a comic book to help demystify the issues of HIV and AIDS. Published in 2000 and entitled *From Darkness to Light*, the comic book illustrates the potential of personal growth and recovery through expression.

At the conference Women's Resistance: From Victimization to Criminalization held in Ottawa in the Fall of 2001, this creativity was also celebrated. Dvora Newmark, an interdisciplinary artist, presented a workshop entitled "How Creative Arts Affect the Process of Healing and Transfer into Political Acts"; Faith Nolan, a composer and guitarist, informed her audience about the process of healing through music; and Edith Regier and Pat Aylesworth of Crossing Communities Art Project: Art as Reparative Justice[70] presented innovative ways to resist the "pains of imprisonment." Through art, the women's sufferings, desires, alienation and pleasures that mark their bodies[71] are mediated through their creative works and become a constructive way to survive.

*

Women's bodies are marked, alienated, victimized and mutilated while they are in prison. But women also use their bodies as a form of resistance. To the body as a *site of control* is juxtaposed the body as *a site of resistance*. Often, it is only through their bodies that women's struggles to survive incarceration can express themselves. Through their voices and the chronicles of their experiences, they can be heard and understood as active subjects rather than as passive victims.

NOTES

1. Marc Préjean, *Sexes et pouvoir: La construction sociale des corps et des émotions* (Montréal: Les Presses de l'Université de Montréal, 1994); Sylvie Frigon and Michèle Kérisit, eds., *Du corps des femmes: Contrôles, surveillances et résistance* (Ottawa: Les Presses de l'Université d'Ottawa, 2000).

2. My interest in the construction of the body stems from different sources: (1) while writing my PhD thesis at the Institute of Criminology, University of Cambridge, UK, the issue emerged in my analysis of the development of feminist criminology, especially in the chapter "A Gallery of Portraits: Women and the Embodiment of Difference, Deviance and Resistance"; (2) the discourses of women who kill their violent partners in Canada, France and Belgium that emerged in my research, which touched on the transformation of their own identity and their own body; (3) when I visited Argentina in 1994 I was struck by how differently we relate to our bodies

and realized more acutely that the world is mediated through our bodies and that this is culturally specific; (4) co-editing with M. Kérisit the book *Du corps des femmes: Contrôles, surveillances et résistance*; (5) researching the social regulation of women's bodies in prison.

3. For a historical overview, see P. Conrad and J. W. Schneider, *Deviance and Medicalization: From Badness to Madness*, 2d ed. (St. Louis: Mosby, 1992). Consider the past practices of witch-burning, frontal lobotomies, electric shock therapy and castration and the present practices of electronic monitoring, chemical treatment through pharmacology and racial profiling.

4. Jennifer Terry and Jacqueline Urla, eds., *Deviant Bodies: Critical Perspectives on Difference in Science and Popular Culture* (Bloomington: Indiana University Press, 1995).

5. I refer to the "body" in the singular form as I am referring to a pivotal concept, but it should be noted that this singular form is meant to cover many different bodies.

6. The "political technology of the body" is a term used by Michel Foucault to mean how the body is used to achieve a state of submission and docility. See Michel Foucault, *Surveiller et punir: La naissance de la prison* (Paris: Gallimard, 1975); or Michel Foucault, *Discipline and Punish: The Birth of the Prison*, trans. Alan Sheridan (New York: Vintage Books, 1979).

7. For notable exceptions, see Foucault, *Discipline and Punish;* Clarice Feinman, *The Criminalization of a Woman's Body* (New York: The Haworth Press, 1992), which discusses the criminalization of motherhood (abortion, pregnancy, surrogate motherhood and maternity); Jean-Michel Labadie, "Corps et crime: De Lavater (1775) à Lombroso (1876)," in Christian Debuyst, Françoise Digneffe, Jean-Michel Labadie and Alvaro Pires, eds., *Histoire des savoirs sur le crime & la peine*, Vol. 1, *Des savoirs diffus à la notion de criminel-né* (Québec: Les Presses de l'Université de Montréal, Les Presses de l'Université d'Ottawa, DeBoeck Université, 1995) on the history of the emergence of the body in criminology; Sylvie Frigon, "A Gallery of Portraits: Women and the Embodiment of Difference, Deviance and Criminality," in Thomas O'Reily-Fleming, ed., *Post-Critical Criminology* (Scarborough: Prentice-Hall, 1996) for a genealogy of the representations of women as embodying deviance and criminality; Frigon and Kérisit, eds., *Du corps des femmes* on the construction of deviant female bodies in various disciplines, including history, sociology, criminology, social work, psychiatry; and Sylvie Frigon, *Femmes et enfermement: Le marquage du corps et l'automutilation* (Montréal: Les Presse de l'Université de Montréal, 2001) on the control and resistance of women through their bodies in a prison setting.

8. See Michel Porret, *Le corps violenté: Du geste à la parole* (Genève: Librairie Drosz S.A., 1998) for a discussion of these early conceptualizations of the body.

9. F. Gall, *Anatomie et physionomie du système nerveux en général et du cerveau en particulier avec des observations sur la possibilité de reconnaître plusieurs dispositions intellectuelles de l'homme et des animaux par la configuration de leurs têtes* (1810), the second edition was published in 3 vols. as *Sur les fonctions du cerveau et sur celles de chacune de ses parties* (Paris: J.B. Baillière, 1825); Bénédict Auguste Morel, *Traité des dégénérescences, physiques, intellectuelles et morales, de l'espèce humaine* (Paris: J.B. Baillière, 1857); Labadie, "Corps et crime: De Lavater (1775) à Lombroso (1876)."

10. Cesare Lombroso and G. Ferrero, *La femme criminelle et la prostituée* (1895; reprint, Grenoble: Éditions Jérôme Million, 1991).

11. Foucault, *Discipline and Punish*, 3. This description echoes the burning of witches. On this, see Sylvie Frigon, "Femmes, hérésies et contrôle social: Des sages-femmes et au-delà," *The Canadian Journal of Women and the Law/Revue femmes et droit* 7, no. 1 (1994), 133–155; Frigon, "A Gallery of Portraits."

12. See, for example, Richard van Dülmen, *Theatre of Horror: Crime and Punishment in Early Modern Germany* (Cambridge, UK: Polity Press, 1990).

13. Foucault, *Discipline and Punish*, 8.

14. Ibid., 11.

15. Ibid.

16. This age of sobriety in punishment and execution is sometimes breached. The media attention around the execution of Karla Fay Tucker in Texas on February 3, 1998, is a case in point.

17. Foucault, *Discipline and Punish*, 25.

18. Elizabeth Grosz, "Le corps et les connaissances: Le féminisme et la crise de la raison," *Sociologies et sociétés* 24, no. 1 (1992), 47–66.

19. See, for example, Sandra Lee Bartky, *Femininity and Domination* (New York: Routledge, 1990); Susan Bordo, *Unbearable Weight: Feminism, Western Culture and the Body* (Berkeley: University of California Press, 1993); Judith Butler, *Bodies that Matter: On the Discursive Limits of "Sex"* (New York: Routledge, 1993); Natalie Beausoleil, "Makeup in Everyday Life: An Inquiry into the Practices of Urban American Women of Diverse Backgrounds," in Nicole Sault, ed., *Many Mirrors: Body Image and Social Relations* (New Brunswick, NJ: Rutgers University Press, 1994); and Frigon and Kérisit, eds., *Du corps des femmes*. More specifically, in the field of criminology, see Gisèle Ginsberg, *Des prisons et des femmes* (Paris: Éditions Ramsay, 1992); Karlene Faith, *Unruly Women: The Politics of Confinement and Resistance* (Vancouver: Press Gang, 1993); Adrian Howe, *Punish and Critique: Towards a Feminist Analysis of Penalty* (London: Routledge, 1994); Frigon, "Femmes, hérésies et contrôle social"; Frigon, "A Gallery of Portraits"; Sylvie Frigon, "Une radioscopie des événements survenus à la Prison des femmes: La construction d'un *corps dangereux* et d'un *corps en danger*," *Canadian Woman Studies/les cahiers de la femme* 19, nos. 1/2 (1999), 154–160; Sylvie Frigon, "Corps, féminité et dangerosité : de la production de 'corps dociles' en criminologie," in Frigon and Kérisit, eds., *Du corps des femmes*, 127–164.

20. David Horn, "This Norm which Is Not One: Reading the Female Body in Lombroso's Anthropology," in Terry and Urla, eds., *Deviant Bodies*, 109.

21. Lombroso and Ferrero, *La femme criminelle et la prostituée*, 152.

22. Russell P. Dobash, R. Emerson Dobash and Sue Gutteridge, *The Imprisonment of Women* (Oxford: Basil Blackwell, 1986), 113–114; Henry Maudsley, "Review of Female Life in Prison," *Journal of Mental Science* 9 (1863), 69–87.

23. Maudsley as quoted in Dobash, Dobash and Gutteridge, *The Imprisonment of Women*, 114.

24. Havelock Ellis, *The Criminal* (London: Scott, 1891). See also Lucia Zedner, "Women, Crime and Penal Responses: A Historical Account," in M. Tonry, ed., *Crime and Justice: A Review of Research* (Chicago: University of Chicago Press, 1991), 337.

25. Maudsley as quoted in Dobash, Dobash and Gutteridge, *The Imprisonment of Women*, 113.

26. See, for example, Carol Groneman, "Nymphomania: The Historical Construction of Female Sexuality," in Terry and Urla, eds., *Deviant Bodies*, 219–250. More generally, see Jane Ussher, *Women's Madness: Misogyny or Mental Illness?* (Amherst: The University of Massachusetts Press, 1991).

27. Dobash, Dobash and Gutteridge, *The Imprisonment of Women*, 111.

28. Elsewhere, I have discussed the social control of women's bodies through witch-burning, the legal relevance of the pre-menstrual syndrome and the battered woman syndrome. See Frigon, "Femmes, hérésies et contrôle social"; "A Gallery of Portraits"; "Femmes et enfermement: Le marquage du corps et l'automutilation," *Criminologie* 34, no. 2 (2001), 31–56; *La Création de choix pour les femmes incarcerées: Sur les traces du groupe d'études sur les femmes purgeant une peine fédérale et de ses conséquences* (Montréal: Les Presses de l'Université de Montréal, 2002); and Frigon and Kérisit, eds., *Du corps des femmes*;

29. Horn, "This Norm which Is Not One,"109. Italics in original.

30. Ibid. 115.

31. Grozs, "Le corps et les connaissances."

32. See L. Berzins and Renée Colette Carrière, "Les femmes en prison: Un inconvénient social!" *Santé mentale au Québec* 4, no. 2, (1979), 87–103; E. Adelberg and C. Currie, *Too Few to Count: Canadian Women in Conflict with the Law* (Vancouver: Press Gang, 1987).

33. See Correctional Services Canada, *Creating Choices: The Report of the Task Force on Federally Sentenced Women* (Ottawa: Minister of Supply and Services, 1990), 1.

34. See Faith, *Unruly Women*, 138.

35. Louise Arbour, *Commission of Inquiry into Certain Events at the Prison for Women in Kingston* (Ottawa: Public Works and Government Services Canada, 1996).

36. Danielle Laberge, "Women's Criminality, Criminal Women, Criminalized Women? Questions in and for a Feminist Perspective," *Journal of Human Justice* 2, no. 2 (1991), 37–56, has rightly pointed out that it can be misleading to rely solely on percentage increases given the relatively small absolute numbers of offenders referred to. For example, a 100 percent increase may reflect an increase of five to ten inmates.

37. See Faith, *Unruly Women*, 139.

38. For a discussion of self-injurious behaviour of Aboriginal women, see Colleen Anne Dell, "Correctional Service of Canada Ideology and 'Violent' Aboriginal Female Offenders" (PhD diss., Carleton University, 2001).

39. Mylène Jaccoud, "Les femmes autochtones et la justice pénale," *Criminologie* 25, no. 1 (1992), 65–85; Patricia Monture-Angus, "Aboriginal Women and Correctional

Practice: Reflections on the Task Force on Federally Sentenced Women," in Kelly Hannah-Moffat and Margaret Shaw, eds., *An Ideal Prison? Critical Essays on Women's Imprisonment in Canada* (Halifax: Fernwood Publishing, 2001), 52–60.

40. Correctional Services Canada, *Creating Choices*. The new regional facilities are Okimaw Ohci Healing Lodge for Native women located in Maple Creek, Saskatchewan; Nova Institution in Truro, Nova Scotia; Edmonton Institution for Women in Edmonton, Alberta; Grand Valley Institution in Kitchener, Ontario; and Joliette Institution in Quebec.

41. As early as 1938, a Royal Commission recommended the closure of P4W. For a history of *Creating Choices*, see Hannah-Moffat and Shaw, eds., *An Ideal Prison?*

42. For example, between April and December 1996, when Maison Tanguay (a provincial prison in Montreal) still housed federally sentenced women, there were 2,031 admissions. Despite the absence of this federal population, the number of women being incarcerated in this institution has not decreased.

43. I would like to thank all the women who agreed to speak with me; Aline White, counsellor at Maison Tanguay in Montreal for all her help in conducting this research; and Brigitte Lavigne, my assistant who participated in all stages of the research.

44. See Sandra Harding, *The Science Question in Feminism* (Ithaca: Cornell University Press, 1986); Sandra Harding, ed., *Feminism and Methodology* (Bloomington: Indiana University Press, 1987); Sandra Harding, *Whose Science? Whose Knowledge?* (Ithaca: Cornell University Press, 1991); Dorothy Smith, *The Everyday World as Problematic: A Feminist Sociology* (Boston: Northeastern University Press, 1987).

45. Kelly Hannah-Moffat, *Punishment in Disguise: Penal Governance and Federal Imprisonment of Women in Canada* (Toronto: University of Toronto Press, 2001).

46. Sue Fisher and Kathy Davis, eds., *Negotiating at the Margins: The Gendered Discourses of Power and Resistance* (New Brunswick, NJ: Rutgers University Press, 1993), cited in Beausoleil, *Makeup in Everyday Life*, 37. Emphasis added.

47. Louise Arbour, *Report of the Commission of Inquiry into Certain Events at the Prison for Women in Kingston* (Ottawa: Public Works and Government Services Canada, 1996). All extracts and quotes in this section are taken from this *Report*, unless otherwise noted. Extracts and references can be found on pages 56, 58, 66–68, 72, 73, 75, 76, 87, 88, 130, 135, 137–138, 140 and 153.

48. Arbour, *Commission of Inquiry ...*, 75. For her personal account, see Brenda Morrison, "A Time to Heal," *Elm Street* (March 1997), 112–118.

49. H.Garfinkel, "Conditions of Successful Degradation Ceremonies," *The American Journal of Sociology* 61, no. 5 (1956), 420–424.

50. Monique Hamelin, *Femmes et prison* (Montréal: Éditions du Méridien, 1989), 60.

51. Gisèle Ginsberg, *Des prisons et des femmes* (Paris: Éditions Ramsay, 1992), 148.

52. Protecteur du citoyen, *Le respect des droits des personnes incarcérées* (Québec, 1985).

53. Marie Gagnon, *Bienvenue dans mon cauchemar* (Montréal: VLB Editeurs, 1997), 112. My translation.

54. Gayle Horii, "The Art in/of Survival," *Journal of Prisoners on Prisons* 5, no. 2 (1994), 6, 7.

55. Ginsberg, *Des prisons et des femmes*, 156. My translation.

56. Lisa Finateri, "The Paradox of Pregnancy in Prison: Resistance, Control, and the Body," *Canadian Woman Studies/les cahiers de la femme* 19, nos. 1/2 (1999), 136–144.

57. Grosz, "Le corps et les connaissances," 55. My translation.

58. Ginsberg, *Des prisons et des femmes*, 118.

59. Correctional Services of Canada, *Creating Choices*.

60. See Faith, *Unruly Women*. On the issue of institutionalized violence, see a special issue on women in prison in different countries produced by the *Journal of Prisoners on Prisons* 5, no. 2 (1994). It is interesting to note the Canadian Association of Elizabeth Fry Societies and the Canadian Association of Sexual Assault Centres organized the conference Women's Resistance: From Victimization to Criminalization held in Ottawa, October 1–3, 2001.

61. See Sylvie Frigon, *L'homicide conjugal au féminine d'hier et aujourd'hui* (Montréal: Les Éditions du remue-ménage, 2003).

62. For a more in-depth discussion of the self-mutilation of women in prison, see Frigon, "Femmes et enfermement: Le marquage du corps et l'automutilation."

63. This is well documented, for example, by Faith, *Unruly Women*, and Kathleen Kendall, *Evaluation des services thérapeutiques offerts à la Prison des femmes* (Ottawa: Service Correctionnel du Canada, 1993).

64. Robert Robertson Ross and Hugh Bryan McKay, *Self-Mutilation* (Toronto: Lexington Books, 1979) in Faith, *Unruly Women*, 243.

65. Jan Heney, *Report on Self-Injurious Behaviour in the Kingston Prison for Women* (Ottawa: Correctional Services of Canada, 1990).

66. Marc Daigle, Mylène Alarie and Patrick Lefebvre, "La problématique suicidaire chez les femmes incarcérées," *Forum* 11, no. 3 (1999), 41–45.

67. Heney, *Report on Self-Injurious Behaviour in the Kingston Prison for Women*; Shoshana Pollak, "Opening the Window on a Very Dark Day: A Program Evaluation of the Peer Support Team at the Kingston Prison for Women" (MA thesis, Carleton University, 1993).

68. Ms. Cree, "Entrenched Social Catastrophe," *Journal of Prisoners on Prisons* 5, no. 2 (1994), 45–48.

69. Translations from the French are mine.

70. The Crossing Communities Art Project is a partnership between the Winnipeg Arts Community and the Elizabeth Fry Society. It is an art studio mentorship program designed to enable women in conflict with the law access to the arts community and to establish a forum for visual communication. This presentation presents the project as a cultural method of "visual listening" that dialogues between women in conflict with the law and the arts community. This visual dialogue opens up a space in which "reparation" can be enacted to heal the epistemic violence in our societies'

correctional system. Women's Resistance Conference, Workshop Presentation Summaries, Ottawa, 2001.

71. See, for example, the sculptures created by Gayle Horii in the *Journal of Prisoners on Prisons* 5, no. 2 (1994), which use the body as a medium to address women's oppression.

CHAPTER 7

Feminist Bioethics and Empirical Research:
The Abortion and FTT Debates

Michelle A. Mullen

WHAT IS A FEMINIST BIOETHICS? What is empirical research in bioethics and what does it measure? What does it mean to undertake empirical bioethics research from a feminist orientation? This chapter examines some answers to these questions. Drawing from my research on the use of electively aborted fetal tissue for medical treatment (FTT), I will attempt to describe the architecture required to bridge feminist scholarship and the burgeoning field of bioethics. My intent is to demonstrate the possibility of a richer discourse on bioethics that is grounded in feminist ethics research. There are two central points to this analysis: (1) the dialectic by which feminist ethics informs bioethics and the sorts of questions and answers that it generates, and (2) the way in which empirical research informs and challenges both bioethics and feminist thought. The analysis uses descriptions of bioethics, feminist bioethics and empirical research, with particular attention paid to the problems and importance of method, using FTT as an example.

A Feminist Bioethics?

The term feminist bioethics suggests a variety of ethics analyses that have arisen under the rubric of feminist scholarship. There is no single cohesive ethical theory within feminism, and approaches range from liberal to socialist to radical feminist theories. Yet each of these approaches shares certain assumptions. Susan Sherwin argues one of the central assumptions this way: women and certain minorities are subject to systematic discrimination and disadvantage within our culture, and the elimination of this discrimination, including the elimination of patriarchy, is required if we are to have a truly just society.[1] This concern with the (mal)distribution of power and opportunity within society is central to a feminist bioethics as it seeks to evaluate the ethical and human effects of the new healthcare practices and how these, in turn, affect marginalized groups.

A feminist bioethics is further concerned with issues of context, narrative and "voice" — who gets to tell the story? The paradigm acknowledges that the experiential dimensions of moral decision-making take account not only of isolated and legalistic principles but also of the extended relationships between the players. Thus, decisions about personal healthcare are not confined to the immediate context but influence relationships (both enabling and oppressive) with families and children and influence obligations within the community. More recently, Sherwin has developed the notion of a "relational autonomy" to describe the complex terrain in which "autonomy" (self-governance) operates.[2] Her description constitutes, in part, a response to the "principlism" that has dominated North American bioethics discourse for more than a quarter of a century,[3] and, in particular, its preoccupation with the choices of "autonomous" persons understood as narrowly self-interested.

Sherwin's understanding recognizes the importance of personal autonomy and how it is shaped, limited and modified by various relationships. Fundamentally, this account considers both macro relationships (including systematic vulnerability on identifiable characteristics such as gender, age, ability/disability, socio-economic status, sexual orientation and so on) and micro relationships (with families, partners, peers, for example). In particular, this formulation offers a perspective by which to examine critical claims about (healthcare) practices which are seen as "free choices." Put simply, we need to consider issues including age, gender and economic need when deciding how "free" these choices truly are. A relational autonomy perspective requires us to ask more and different questions about healthcare and ethics. Who can inform our discourse about these issues?

The question of voice is central both to feminist scholarship and to the burgeoning interest in "narrative" ethics. Narrative ethics is a rubric of approaches ranging from structural literary criticism to postmodern decon-

structionism. At its core, narrative ethics distinguishes itself from the trap-
pings of impartial philosophical systems of ethics and asks "whether, either
in conjunction with, or instead of the aforementioned elements, *narratives*
might not play a central role in the moral life."[4] The subjects of research in
a narrative ethics are transformed into participants. Their stories, under-
standings, questions, needs and moral suasion are made central to the
discourse. The "problems" of technologies and healthcare practices, and the
"answers," cannot be discerned without the voices of those most directly
involved (and often those who are most vulnerable) being brought clearly
and loudly into the fray. Not all narrative ethics are feminist, but it is not
possible to imagine a feminist bioethics that does not take into account
narratives.

What, then, constitutes method in bioethics research undertaken with
a feminist orientation? From an empirical basis, a knowledge of practices is
required by both practitioners and those intimately practised upon, that is,
the patients in the healthcare system, their families and others enmeshed in
the intricate connections that are so much a part of individual human lives.
The practices under scrutiny encompass not only medical diagnostic, prog-
nostic and treatment "facts" but also the values and meanings embedded in
these and who or what is privileged or marginalized. This provides the foundation for empirical feminist bioethics research.

Empirical Research in Bioethics

Empirical research in bioethics assumes varied roles. These include descriptions of the attitudes, behaviours, experiences, beliefs and values of key
players in the healthcare context and the refutation or substantiation of
claims about healthcare practices as constructed within the extant literature
of both providers and bioethics pundits. Sometimes, it compels the subversion of hegemonic depictions and the reframing of the discourse. The
methods used are similarly varied. Two principal domains are quantitative
(quasi-statistical) methods and qualitative methods.

Quantitative methods include survey and questionnaire methodologies, as well as analysis of healthcare records, prospectively or retrospec-
tively. The analysis might examine an individual's beliefs (Likert scales, that
is, numeric scales indicating level of agreement/disagreement with a posited statement, are common), her or his preference for type of healthcare
provider and healthcare practices and her or his personal values. It might
examine the validity of a technology or healthcare practice. I consider an

example of this when I look at the mainstream debate over the use of electively aborted fetal tissue (FTT) for treatment. It is crucial to appreciate that
such research reflects a descriptive ethics, telling us what people do or
believe (or at least what they tell us they do or believe). In short, if it works,
it describes *what is*. It does not tell us about *what ought* to be, as does a
normative ethics. Nonetheless, it sometimes proves an effective tool to
inform or subvert a mainstream armchair discourse. For the feminist
bioethicist, it also reveals which voices and whose experiences and values are
counted in the hegemonic discourse — and whose are not.

Qualitative methods are receiving increasing levels of attention and
reflect a broad range of ontological and epistemological assumptions.[5] These
include positivist (that there is a "real" reality) and post-positivist (a reality
that is statistically apprehensible) frameworks. A post-positivist framework
is accomplished by experimental or quasi-experimental means whereby
qualitative data may be viewed numerically under good conditions (sufficient numbers of respondents per question, for example).

These frameworks are clearly distinguished from critical theory and
constructivist approaches. Ontologically, critical theories assert that historical "realities" are shaped by social, cultural, political and gender (among
other) values over time, while constructivism is concerned with relativism.
These foundations have implications for epistemology (subjectivist in both
instances, with value-mediated findings from critical and created findings
from constructivist perspectives). Methodology in both frameworks is
dialogic.

Why the fuss about method? That method *matters* is central to feminist scholarship and to a feminist bioethics. Wittingly or unwittingly, the
choice of method in research determines assumptions about knowledge,
privilege, ethics and use of the findings. Positivist and post-positivist
approaches assert an apprehensible reality (at least statistically); "objective"
observers analyze this and report findings as value-neutral. Hence, the ethics
of such research is *extrinsic*[6] (for example, professional codes and research
ethics committees) and the voice is that of the dispassionate scientific
observer. By contrast, critical and constructivist approaches assert that realities are created over time by means of hegemonic forces. Further, ethics are
intrinsic to the enterprise: a critical approach entails explicitly defined values (the minimalist feminism described above is one example) and a
constructivism that is concerned with resituating the discourse in relation
to the participant's unique experience.

My ethics research engages an evolving and explicit critical foundation, which is based on the belief that there is a systematic vulnerability on characteristics like gender, age, ability/disability, socio-economic status, ethnicity and sexual orientation, and that there is an ethical requirement to document this vulnerability in empirical terms and to address it through a normative ethics approach. A commitment to issues of voice, power, relationships and authenticity is central to this. As I continue to work in the biomedical healthcare milieu, I frequently face the dichotomy inherent in quantitative and qualitative worldviews, and I must struggle with it in order to maintain credibility with my biomedical peers. Yet it seems that the choice of method ought to speak to the nature of the question that is in search of an answer. Thus, while I would seek out a good old-fashioned logico-positivist if I wanted to know about my liver enzymes, I would seek out a person with liver cancer if I needed to try and understand what it meant to live with that condition.

Similarly, while I applaud the efforts of "evidence-based clinical medicine" to generate the statistical information (which is necessary but insufficient to assess healthcare interventions), from a qualitative researcher's viewpoint I need only one eight-year-old child to ask why the emperor has no clothes on. There is no need to proceed to a randomly chosen sample of normally distributed children to determine how many would ask the same question. Thus, I continue to use quasi-statistical and qualitative methods without apology, depending on the nature of the question. The examples that follow demonstrate both the rationale behind and the results of such inquiry.

One Model of Inquiry:
The Case of Fetal Tissue Transplantation

The use of electively aborted human fetal tissue for transplantation and treatment (FTT) caused heated controversy in the 1990s. The unique biological properties of these cells — with their enormous potential for growth and differentiation; resistance to oxygen deprivation; ease of transplantation (by injection into the target organ); reduced capacity to evoke an immune response in the recipient (with tissue rejection the greatest biological impediment to success in transplantation); and their potentially large supply (approximately one hundred thousand elective first-trimester abortions are performed in Canada annually) — generated much scientific excitement.[7] Potential recipients of the tissues and their advocates were equally hopeful.

A host of debilitating or fatal conditions was believed to be amenable to FTT: Parkinson's disease, juvenile diabetes, leukemia, aplastic anemia, inherited metabolic storage disorders and radiation poisoning, among others.

Elective abortion was seen as the preferred source for these tissues, rather than spontaneous abortion or miscarriage, because aborted tissue would be free from contamination (from infectious agents or genetic anomalies). This caused a groundswell of protest from the anti-abortion faction, which asserted that FTT was complicit with an immoral act (abortion) and levied a series of other claims against the practice: that women would find abortion a more attractive option if they could donate tissue to benefit others; that unscrupulous doctors would offer donation as a positive incentive to abortion so that they would accrue material benefit from "harvesting" for FTT; and that more abortions were inevitable as a result of FTT. Those eager to proceed with FTT research countered with a series of procedures they claimed could be separated — or be morally insulated — from abortion decisions. Among these were alterations in the method or timing of abortion for FTT tissue collection and that a request for donation of tissues be made only after the woman had reached a firm decision to terminate her pregnancy. Pro-FTT avocates also called for the prohibition of the procedures commercialization. The discourse was reduced to a "Yes it can. No it can't" debate on the question of whether FTT and abortion could be separated.

Testing the Claims

Most of the claims about FTT and the practices it would engender, according to the anti-choice lobby, could be investigated empirically. With colleagues, I devised a physician questionnaire that would look at incentives for fetal tissue collection, at issues involved in obtaining consent for donation, at supply and demand issues and at regulation of the procedure.[8] Six hundred Ontario family doctors (FPs) and obstetrician/gynecologists were selected as the study population because these were the physicians who both counselled women about abortion decisions and performed abortions. Of these, 73 percent participated.

The physician participants were much in agreement with global statements about FTT : 84 percent agreed that using electively aborted tissue for FTT was morally justified; 75 percent agreed that there should be incentives to physicians to collect tissue at abortion; 90 percent agreed that decisions to terminate pregnancy and donate fetal tissue must be separate.

There was much less agreement about the details of the practice, however. Twenty percent of respondents agreed that the method or timing of abortion might be altered to improve "harvesting" (for example, delaying the procedure to select certain cell types or using dilatation and curettage rather than vacuum aspiration to collect unfragmented tissues); 11 percent stated that patients agreeing to donate could be given priority in scheduling the abortions. More than one-third (38 percent) agreed that consent to abortion suffices for the collection of tissues without specific consent from the woman; 35 percent agreed that women who choose abortion cede rights to make decisions about the use of their aborted fetuses. Alarmingly, 14 percent did not agree that a woman's safety must be foremost if method or timing of abortion were altered to facilitate tissue collection, and 11 percent were uncertain (25 percent total).

These findings speak to how FTT practices and the debate have evolved with very little attention being given to the prevalent attitudes towards women. As sole "suppliers" of fetal tissues, the interests, safety and stature of women ought to be central to the ethical concerns surrounding FTT. The quantitative data provided a first look at how FTT and the debate both reflect and shape the societal milieu, and form the basis for a shift in defining the ethical problems of FTT and for undertaking qualitative research that can explore the unique concerns of this debate. Qualitative research can place women — whose bodies are literally on the table for FTT — at the centre of the concerns.

The next phase of my research project sought to explore the complex issues that shape the interaction between healthcare providers and women seeking abortion services. Using a qualitative approach, I held open-ended interviews with twelve physicians identified in the survey and with twelve non-medical abortion counsellors. I approached the counsellors on the assumption that, as formal advocates for women and their health, they might voice a different orientation to FTT issues as they pertain to women's health and women's bodies. The interview questions focused on the counselling techniques used with women considering abortion; consent to FTT donation; women wishing to designate a recipient; the planning of pregnancy for FTT donation; and respect given to women undergoing abortion.

Physicians' Responses

Various themes emerged in the physicians' interviews: the dilemma of meeting perceived third-party obligations (those "needing" aborted fetal tissues);

using the "golden rule" (how would I want this dealt with if it were me/my daughter); and the importance of physicians maintaining control over these ethical issues (rather than having them externally regulated). Two themes are especially noteworthy, since they elicited strong commentary from more than half of the physicians interviewed.

First, physician participants made an important (in their estimation) distinction between a perceived difference in *medical* versus *psychosocial* abortions. One male gynecologist described it this way:

> I tell them that people are humans and humans are animals and animals look after their offspring pretty well, and humans do too. And it [the abortion] will bother them. I tell them that it will bother them the rest of their lives … I tell them that it's their decision, and they say, 'Well, would you advise me to have an abortion?' and I say that I wouldn't advise them to do anything. If you're healthy, you can have the baby … ninety-five to ninety-seven percent of abortions are abortions on demand, for no legitimate medical reason … for fetal abnormalities, that's a different problem … most of the abortions [done] on demand are unnecessary.

This distinction between "legitimate" and "non-legitimate" reasons for abortions needs to be challenged on normative grounds. Advances in management of pregnancy mean that abortions performed for the *physical* safety of a woman are very rare in our culture. As constructed by this gynecologist, medical abortions are those performed to avoid the birth of an infant with abnormalities, and this is to be distinguished from abortions performed for *psychosocial* reasons such as the ability to cope financially or emotionally with motherhood.

Clearly, however, both types of situations reflect the burdens of motherhood, the questions of available resources, issues of quality of life and individual values; in short, they reflect *a host of compelling social conditions*. It is equally plausible to regard abortion for reasons of fetal abnormalities as a lack of regard for persons with disabilities in our society, rather than a matter of medical necessity. If a minimal definition of justice requires that like cases be treated alike, then the values and needs of individual women ought to be equally acknowledged and enabled in both kinds of situations.

A second recurring theme in the physicians' responses focused on punitive attitudes towards women seeking abortions, especially repeat abortions. As one female gynecologist expressed it: "I think generally people should be forgiven for making a mistake or two, but if someone comes in and has six abortions and she's pregnant again, I would label her as a loser, but I wouldn't show her any less respect." This comment reflects both the *role* that some physicians assume ("to forgive") and the *attitudes* that are brought to bear (to label the woman a "loser" but still respect her). It is noteworthy that both the gynecologist cited here and above are self-described as "pro-choice" and perform abortions.

Similarly, the language used by physician participants revealed how they construct women who seek abortions. This construction tends to depict women as frail and in crisis and casts doubt on their capacity to make decisions. One male family physician said, "The usual patient being dealt with, whose coming for an abortion, is a person that's like a piece of crystal. She's usually very fragile at that time, and often depressed." Another male family physician described it this way: "I'm not even sure that the mother is capable of making that decision, a rational decision at that time." These statements, expressed in concerned tones, nonetheless manifest a construction of a fragile woman unable to make decisions and raises questions of how accurate or appropriate such a construction is.

When facing major health decisions, women may often be confronted with difficult and conflicting issues. Some may become fragile or uncertain in the decision process, while others approach their choices with a great deal of certainty. When women consider abortion, is the "concern" expressed here respectful, empowering, paternalistic or reflective of wider social configurations of women as weak? One tenet of bioethics assumes that adults seeking health services are capable and competent, unless there is evidence to the contrary. Is it the condition of pregnancy, or the seeking of abortion, that casts doubt on the ability of these women to make appropriate, ethical and authentic decisions?

Abortion Counsellors' Responses

Interviews undertaken with non-medical abortion counsellors proved to be a study in contrasts. These participants were recruited through the managers of free-standing abortion clinics; their professional occupations included nurses, psychologists, social workers and community workers. All were women. These counsellors were interviewed because they are the care providers directly engaged in detailed and ongoing discussions with women who are undecided about abortion and with women undergoing abortion. It was postulated that healthcare provides in this advocacy relationship and with an in-depth understanding of abortion-related issues might provide valuable insights into the contextual issues surrounding the donation of aborted fetal tissues.

Two key concerns emerged in these interviews. The first focused on the difficult choices women seeking abortion need to make and the complex and unique circumstances in which they make these decisions. For example, whereas a distinction between *medical* and *psychosocial* abortion emerged as a central theme in the physicians' interviews, this distinction was not made by any of the counsellors. Rather, the difficulty of decision-making was recognized and emphasized. As this social worker explains:

> I guess if I separate myself from it, I would have to say that it is from choice, that there maybe other issues that surround that choice for me … but I would rather be the agent of that choice … it brings in this concept of morality, and there isn't one worldview, and there isn't one philosophy. It differs throughout the world; it's very much a Western idea; it's not that translatable.

Here, the "legitimacy" of an individual woman's decision to terminate pregnancy is mandated to her and not left to the judgement of the care provider. In this counsellor's view, the pregnant woman is constructed as the *agent* of moral choice, and further, her agency cannot be bound by or limited to one worldview or moral perspective. This takes into account not only the social and contextual realities of a woman who is contemplating abortion but also recognizes her as the appropriate moral decision-maker.

"Respect for choice" necessarily includes those choices which others might not make nor be comfortable with, and it defines the context of counselling as non-directive and enabling. As one counsellor, who is trained as a psychologist, pointed out: "An interview process can be manipulated, I want to stress that clearly … [but] when I am sitting with a woman, we are partners. I will provide the information, but I will not direct decision-making at all. I will just lay [out all the options for] her." The perspective of this partnership that sees women as autonomous, capable and self-determining contrasts starkly with the gynecologist who described her role in "forgiving" women seeking abortion and who labelled those seeking more than one abortion as "losers."

A second key concern that emerged in the counsellors' interviews was that FTT might further entrench women's status of having no control over their reproduction, which could lead to the objectification and commercialization of women's reproductive capacity. Another counsellor, also trained in psychology, pointed out that abortion and FTT must be kept separate: "I think that the use of fetal tissue and a woman's decision to terminate a pregnancy are two separate issues. I think that her health, her safety, her state of mind should be first ... but I don't think that alternative planning [of abortion to collect tissue] is an okay thing, because the woman becomes this machine, this fetal tissue machine." In this care provider's view, the well-being of the client is foremost. The fear she expresses here is that the manipulation of the timing and the method of abortion to facilitate tissue collection could render the donor to nothing more than a "fetal tissue machine." The primacy of duty owed to the woman by care providers is subordinated to the needs or desires of third-party researchers, transplant surgeons and potential recipients of fetal tissue therapies.

Another counsellor sees this problem as reflecting the wider social attitude towards women: "With the whole issue, do you know what I see? Here we go again, women used as vessels. I see it as the same issue [it has] always [been]." The extent and ways in which the introduction of FTT practices may reinforce existing and instrumental social constructions of women demands our attention and critical examination. It deserves to be at the forefront of the ethical and policy debate about FTT.

The realm of language was also an important factor for the counsellors. In contrast to the *kinds* of language used by physicians to describe patients and their state of mind, the counsellors were concerned with the language used *about* women. One counsellor, also practising as a midwife, found the preoccupation with the words "success" and "failure" to describe pregnancy outcomes as problematic:

> I really take offense at a lot of the words that are used to describe women's processes. I think that we have to take success and failure out of the vocabulary, whatever the outcome, whether there's an abortion or a live baby or a baby that has died, or if you have a miscarriage, or if you have a baby who has a disability, it's all human experience ... if it's not in the context of failure, maybe people would be able to feel better about being able to accept life and death, that they are just part of the continuum.

For this care provider, who counsels and supports women through both abortions and full-term pregnancies, the issues are not about success or failure as defined by external parties but about the importance of validating women's experiences along the life continuum.

Another of the counsellors, who was also trained in psychology, attempted to give voice not to her judgements but to the experiences of women:

> Abortion is so difficult. In all the years I've counselled here, I've never met a woman who came in and said, "Well, this has absolutely no impact on

my life." Women have never said this, women always say, "Abortion is painful, I'm doing this because …" and they give you this long list of reasons why they cannot have a baby at this time. This comment hints at the many complex layers of issues that speak to a woman's experience of abortion decisions. The challenge in the discourse around FTT is to turn attention to the many voices of women, whose bodies are literally "on the table" if the technology is to proceed.

Non-medical abortion counsellors adopted a more nuanced view of abortion than their medical counterparts in cases where a woman had a designated recipient for FTT. Only one rejected the scenario outright, although all found it ethically worrying. The counsellor just cited above had this to say:

> Women make moral and ethical decisions based on their circumstances, women are not immoral or unethical. If that woman in her estimation needs to have that pregnancy [terminated] and [have] that abortion to give fetal tissue to her father with Parkinson's disease, then, that's not immoral. I don't see that there's a place to judge that. Women make moral and ethical decisions based on what's happening in their lives, and all the people that are dependent on women … those women help all the relationships they hold up and keep together … if she decides that's the most important thing to do … It gets back to saying, I can't see myself doing that, but…

In this comment, the nature of a woman's choice is acknowledged as a complex, contextual moral process. This process takes into account a woman's needs in relation to her connections and obligations to those closest to her: a private domain beyond the reach of external critics and controllers. Such a position echoes the relational ethics of care described at length by Carol Gilligan,[9] taking the realm of moral decision-making beyond closed issues into a realm that reflects the complex world of human experience. This recognition of the important meanings that reproductive decisions hold for women is in keeping with the observation made by several counsellors that women take pregnancy, their relationship to their fetus and abortion very seriously.

FTT: Revisiting the Mainstream Debate

The conflicts and concerns with the use of electively aborted fetal tissue have been quite narrowly defined within most of the published literature. Those who oppose FTT reject the practice a priori, on the grounds that the fetus is a distinct moral entity. In their view, the woman who chooses abortion morally abandons her fetus and this renders her unsuitable to provide consent on how the fetus is used. This also holds true for abortion providers, transplant teams and recipients, who are all seen to be complicit in the moral wrong. Further, the anti-FTT position is elaborated by claims that FTT will encourage women to end pregnancies thereby increasing the number of abortions performed and sending us down a slippery slope to practices such as infanticide.

Those who favour using electively aborted fetal tissues have responded to these claims by devising mechanisms to procedurally separate the act of abortion from any use of the tissues. This position is framed so that even if abortion is "wrong," it need not necessarily follow that using the aborted tissues is wrong, provided that we can construct a "moral insulation" between the two activities. These conventional approaches to FTT, devised by philosophers, lawyers and physicians, represent a very narrow focus: ethical concerns are measured in relation to the status of the fetus and society's obligations to "protect fetuses" from the uncontrolled practice of FTT. Few writers make any reference to how FTT affects women, their choices and, especially, their status and protection. The commentary provided by the physician participants in this study mirrors this dominant and conservative non-feminist ethics discourse.

The comments from the abortion counsellors offer an ethical perspective that is far more complex, contextual and relational than the dominant discourse. As advocates of women's health — a position of critical analysis — they do not necessarily reject any moral stature and respect owed to the fetus nor do they see that the links between abortion and donation of fetal tissue must always be prevented. Theirs is a perspective in which a woman's decisions around abortion cannot represent a moral monolith; rather, the soundness of her decision is judged in relation to how well it serves her personal life experiences and needs. While not nearly so "tidy" as approaches offered within the literature, these counsellors speak to the realities of human experience and morality. Such a perspective reflects a primary concern with the status of the woman rather than with the status of the fetus. The questions for these counsellors about the ethical meanings and impact of FTT are drawn in relation to the actual lives of actual women. They are questions of manipulation, power struggles, self-determination, burdens and reproductive autonomy. They suggest possibilities for redefining the FTT debate from a feminist perspective.

Recently, interest in FTT has begun to wane as the interest in using human stem cells taken from embryos in vitro has exploded. However, the interest in stem cells collected from electively aborted fetal tissue remains. In January 2002, the Canadian Institutes of Health Research completed recommendations for CIHR-funded researchers on the ethical use of stem cells derived from surplus human embryos that were created for the treatment of infertility from aborted fetal tissue.[10] Two of the recommendations require that research is permissible only when "the proposed research does not compromise the woman's decision on whether to continue her pregnancy" — a reiteration of the "moral insulation" approach — and when "there is free and informed consent from the pregnant woman."[11] How these recommendations will be embraced by the public and by policymakers remains to be seen. To date, there has been much vocal protest by the anti-abortion faction on the use of any CIHR plans to support stem cell research on cells derived from either surplus (IVF) human embryos or aborted fetuses. Promised legislation to regulate such research and clinical practice in Canada has not yet been passed by Parliament. The status, health and choices of women who face pregnancy decisions, clearly, remain peripheral to the debate.

Empirical research in feminist ethics has far to go in terms of influencing mainstream debate and public policy. Yet while there is resistance, incremental changes are evident in the multiple disciplines wishing to collaborate in research on the issues and in funding agencies wishing to support such work. Since I began my studies on FTT, I have been fortunate enough to work collaboratively in research that is examining the values and ethical dimensions of women's decisions around genetic testing for breast and ovarian cancer susceptibility,[12] and in research focusing on the emerging ethical issues around the provision of care to HIV-infected children.[13]

Empirical research in feminist ethics can enrich our discourse and has the potential to alter the landscape of our deliberations. As feminist bioethics poses challenges to algorithmic bioethics, so can empirical research urge reflexive examination of our critical postures. Susan Wolf has said of a feminist bioethics that

> change will not come easily or fast. Work on race, ethnicity, and gender was historically ignored in bioethics for deep structural reasons. That work is now held at arm's-length for similarly profound reasons. And if such work succeeds in bioethics, it will not be by merely creating satellite ethics ... Instead, it will be by catalyzing core upheaval and change.[14]

Empirical research in feminist bioethics holds the promise of displacing academic and ideological ruminations into the untidy world of lived experiences. It may not be able to tell us how many angels can dance on the head of a pin; it may, however, turn our attention to the authentic morality of human life, however marginalized, and sow the seeds for the core upheaval of change that a feminist bioethics requires.

NOTES

1. Susan Sherwin, "Feminist Ethics and the New Reproductive Technologies," in Christine Overall, ed., *The Future of Human Reproduction* (Toronto: The Women's Press, 1989), 259–271.

2. Susan Sherwin, "A Relational Approach to Autonomy in Health Care," in Susan Sherwin, ed., *The Politics of Women's Health: Exploring Agency and Autonomy* (Philadelphia: Temple University Press, 1998), 19–47.

3. The "Principles of Biomedical Ethics" as published by Tom Beauchamp and James Childress in 1979 include respect for persons, beneficence/non-maleficence and justice. Sometimes called the "Georgetown Mantra," these have been critiqued on a variety of claims in recent years. These include that the principles are narrow and legalistic; that there is no trump principle (the paradigm does not describe an overriding principle when duties conflict — for example, respect for autonomous choices versus beneficence); that they fail to take account of other important values; that they do not take account of systematic oppression, voice or narrative. Nonetheless, principlism remains a dominant paradigm in modern North American bioethics, even if, as Edwin Dubose and others observe, "the prevailing U.S. approach to the ethical problems raised by modern medicine is ailing. Principlism is the patient." See, for example, Edwin Dubose, Ronald Hamel and Laurence O'Connell, eds., *A Matter of Principles* (Valley Forge: Trinity Press International, 1994).

4. Nelson Hilda Lindemann, ed., "Introduction," in *Stories and Their Limits: Narrative Approaches to Bioethics* (New York: Routledge, 1997), vii–ix. Italics in original.

5. Egon Guba and Yovnna Lincoln, "Competing Paradigms in Qualitative Research," in Norman K. Denzin and Yvonna S. Lincoln, eds., *Handbook of Qualitative Research* (Thousand Oaks, CA: Sage Publications, 1994), 105–117.

6. See, for example, E. Diener and R. Crandall, *Ethics in Social and Behavioral Research* (Chicago: University of Chicago Press, 1978), and S. Bok, *Secrets: On the Ethics of Concealment and Revelation* (New York: Random House, 1982).

7. Michelle Mullen, *The Use of Human Embryos and Fetal Tissues: A Research Architecture* (Ottawa: Royal Commission on New Reproductive Technologies, 1992).

8. Michelle Mullen, John Ivan Williams and Frederick Hans Lowy, "Transplantation of Electively Aborted Human Fetal Tissue: Physicians' Attitudes," *Canadian Medical Association Journal* 151, no. 3 (1994), 325–330. The series of ethics studies

pertaining to FTT were undertaken for my PhD thesis, "Fetal Tissue Transplantation: Ethical Issues, Women's Health and Public Policy" (University of Toronto, 1995). All the quotations cited by participants are taken from the thesis. This work was supported by a doctoral fellowship awarded by the Social Sciences and Humanities Research Council of Canada.

9. Caroline Gilligan, *In a Different Voice: Psychological Theory and Women's Development* (Cambridge: Harvard University Press, 1982).

10. "Ethics in CIHR, Human Pluripotent Stem-Cell Research: Recommendations for CIHR-Funded Research." *Canadian Institutes of Health Research.* <http://www.cihr.ca/about_cihr/ethics/stem_cell?stem_cell_recommendations_e.shtml>. February 2002.

11. Ibid., item 4.2.

12. Michelle Mullen, Raluca Nedelcu, Joan Murphy, Barry Rosen and Donna Stewart, "Women's Decisions to Undergo Genetic Testing for Ovarian Cancer Susceptibility: Expanding the Boundaries of Autonomy, Relatedness, and Informed Decision-making" (paper presented at the Canadian Bioethics Society, Toronto, Ontario, October 30, 1999. Supported by the Women's Health Unit, the Toronto Hospital and Cancer Care Ontario).

13. Michelle Mullen, Lindy Samson, Diane Stevenson and Fanny Zegarra, "Paediatric HIV Infection: Human Experience, Values and Culture and the Possibilities of Medicine" (paper presented at the Canadian Bioethics Society, Edmonton, Alberta, October 30, 2000. Supported by the Ontario HIV Treatment Network).

14. Susan M. Wolf, "Erasing Difference: Race, Ethnicity and Gender in Bioethics," in Anne Donchin and Laura M. Purdy, eds., *Embodying Bioethics: Recent Feminist Advances* (Oxford, UK: Rowman and Littlefield, 1999), 65–81.

CHAPTER 8

Challenging Representations of the Female Victim in Contemporary Austrian Fiction

Agatha Schwartz

THE MUCH DISPUTED TOPIC of "woman as victim" versus "woman as perpetrator" and the related question of female aggression have been reconceptualized in the past few decades by authors coming from different disciplines and using various approaches. In the mid-1980s, German feminist psychoanalyst Margarete Mitscherlich wrote about women's aggressive tendencies and came to the conclusion that, by nature, women aren't any more peaceful than men. However, through their upbringing in a society that favours the image of the passive and docile female and that discourages girls from expressing aggressive tendencies outwardly, their aggression is turned inward and often manifests itself as masochism. Unlike psychotherapist Sigmund Freud who considered female masochism to be a "natural" part of the development of female sexuality, Mitscherlich considered female aggression to be a result of women's socialization: "On est en droit de penser que c'est leur position séculaire d'opprimées dans la société et dans la famille qui fait que tant de femmes ont des fantasmes masochistes" (It is justified to believe that women's secular position of the oppressed in society and family creates masochistic fantasies in many women).[1]

Some North American feminists, such as Naomi Wolf, confirmed Mitscherlich's findings. Wolf, arguing against what she calls "victim feminism," also sees women's socialization and not their nature as the reason for their generally less aggressive behaviour: "But the fact that women were relegated by force into creating a tradition of nurturing does not mean that women are themselves naturally better than men, or that they hold the patent on kindness, holistic thinking, or care for others."[2] Thinking along the same line, Claire Renzetti concludes that women's violent behaviour, unless used in a situation of self-defence, may often be underplayed because of the generally accepted social norm that "the woman who uses violence is inherently a 'bad' woman."[3]

Using the novels of two contemporary Austrian women writers — *Lust* by Elfriede Jelinek (published in 1989, English translation in 1992) and *Magdalena Sünderin* by Lilian Faschinger (published in 1995, English translation as *Magdalena the Sinner* in 1997) — I examine the theme of the woman as victim who becomes perpetrator. In both texts, this theme is embedded in a criticism of societal and patriarchal myths, which are deconstructed through their use of language. The two authors draw on different linguistic strategies in order to criticize and subvert representations of the feminine and gender roles, such as anti-pornography in Jelinek's case and humour in Faschinger's, with satire as a common denominator in both.

Elfriede Jelinek can, without exaggeration, be called one of the most controversial and productive writers in contemporary German-language literature. Born in 1946 in a small town in central Austria, she studied theatre, art history and music (specializing in the organ). She published her first poems in the 1960s when she was active in the student movement. Her first radio drama, in 1974, was declared the most successful radio drama of the year by *Die Presse*, one of Austria's most prominent newspapers. She has since published numerous other radio dramas as well as poetry, plays, novels, literary translations and essays, and has written movie scripts based on literary texts (the most well-known from Ingeborg Bachmann's novel *Malina)*. Jelinek has received several literary awards, among them the prestigious Heinrich-Böll-Preis in 1986 and the even more prestigious Georg-Büchner-Preis in 1998. Her works, which have been translated into several languages, are famous for their biting criticism of Austrian society, particularly the denial of its Nazi past. The condition of women in Austria has also been a continuous object of her scrutiny.

Lilian Faschinger was born in 1950 in southern Austria. She studied English and history, obtaining her doctorate in English literature in 1979 before lecturing in English at the University of Graz. She is an accomplished literary translator (of works by Gertrude Stein and Janet Frame, for example) and has been a freelance writer since 1992. She has published four novels, two volumes of short stories and two volumes of poetry; has written radio dramas and plays for the theatre; and has received several prizes and scholarships. She spent two terms as a writer-in-residence at Dickinson College and Dartmouth College in the U.S. She describes her books as "satirical and critical of society with a feminist touch."[4]

Jelinek's *Lust*

One critic writes of Elfriede Jelinek that "no contemporary woman writer has used literature in such a radical, consistent and thoughtful way as a medium and forum of critical consciousness."[5] And yet, despite the recognition this very deserving author has found in contemporary literary criticism, no other writer of her calibre has been subjected to so many scandals, attacks and misunderstandings. Critics and journalists targeted her novel *Lust* before and after its publication with an attention that far exceeded the appropriate and usual curiosity the media demonstrate towards a literary celebrity. In interviews, she was asked the most intimate questions about her personal life, such as "'What turns you on?' 'Do you watch porn videos?' 'Do you take notes while you have sex?'"[6] Jelinek is used to such provocations, having been called "a specialist in hatred,"[7] among other things, before. Ellen Risholm and Erin Crawley rightly observe that "a respected male author of the high culture variety would never be grilled in this manner."[8] They attribute this quasi-pornographic interest in the author to the disillusioned expectations that critics, particularly male critics, experienced after reading *Lust*. Not satisfied with the way Jelinek represents her female protagonist in the novel, the male gaze is turned towards the author herself.

Although the novel is not a linear narrative, there is a clearly discernible storyline the reader can follow. The scene is a small Austrian town, and the main protagonist, Hermann,[9] is the director of a paper factory. He and his wife, Gerti, have a young son. From the beginning of the story, it becomes evident that this seemingly idyllic setting is far from idyllic for the wife, whose marital life is reduced to forced intercourse with her husband. The following passage, which is found at the beginning of the novel, demonstrates Jelinek's style and the language she uses to describe this situation of continuous rape:

The woman hasn't the heart to refuse herself. She's defenceless. The Man is perpetually ready to go. Greedy for his pleasure. To pleasure himself. Lo, this happy day is there for the rich and the poor, but unfortunately the poor begrudge it the rich. The woman laughs nervously as the Man, still wearing his coat, deliberately exposes himself to her. And there it is, the thick-headed thick head and shaft of his member. The woman's laughter grows louder and she slaps herself on the mouth, startled. She's threatened with a beating. Her head is still full of music, Johann Sebastian Bach, expressing her feelings and those of others, music guaranteed to give pleasure, going round and round in circles on the record player, chasing its tail. The Man is chasing his tail too, or his tail is chasing and he is following. So it goes with men, ever onwards, their works ever greater but presently collapsing behind their backs. The trees in the forest are more stoutly and reliably upstanding. Calmly the Direktor chats about her cunt. How he will force it open in a moment. He seems intoxicated. His words totter and reel. He grips the woman's hip in his left hand and yanks her serviceable (easy to service her) clothing up over her head. She wriggles in his heavy-weight presence. He yells at her for wearing tights, which he long since forbade her to wear, stockings are more feminine and make better use of the available holes, if they don't indeed create new ones.[10]

Those readers who, after this "promising" start, would expect some pornographic pleasure to come out of the text, will be bitterly disappointed. The scenes in which Hermann brutally rapes his wife anally, orally and vaginally continue ad nauseam, and the language used to describe the sex organs seems to flow from an endless catalogue of invented terminology to describe the brutality eventually reaching a point where it becomes difficult to read on. The author plays with the reader's revulsion. About two-thirds of the way through the novel she inserts a little comment: "Still want to read on? And breed on? No? See."[11] The title, then, fails to fulfil its promise of lust and, at the same time, the pleasure of reading is challenged.

Originally, Jelinek's intention in *Lust* was to create a feminine language of the obscene, a feminine pornography, as a response to George Bataille's story from 1928, *Histoire de l'Oeil*.[12] Some elements in the text point in that direction: the protagonists are deprived of their individuality and function merely as body parts. Indeed, Jelinek had published an excerpt from the novel along with a short essay in a pro-pornography collection called *Frauen und Pornographie (Women and Pornography)*. However, she also contributed to a campaign that the German feminist magazine *Emma* had launched in 1988 for an anti-pornography law that aimed to reverse paragraph 184 of the German Basic Law,[13] which had legalized pornography in Germany in 1975.[14] It may, therefore, not come as a surprise that *Lust* turned out to be a piece of anti-pornography.

While working on the novel, Jelinek discovered that writing a feminine pornography was not possible, for the linguistic patterns or phrases that are used to describe erotic experiences are male-dominated. In Jelinek's mind, trying to write about female erotic experiences along the lines of Anaïs Nin or Erica Jong only reinforces the aesthetics of a masculine tradition of erotic writing. It is the male language of sexuality that has to be deconstructed first.[15] She does not only expose the language of sexuality as male-dominated but also exposes male–female relationships and sexual pleasure as male dominated: "In patriarchy it is still the case today that men and women don't enjoy [the same sexual pleasure] to the degree they would like to. I want to expose this relationship of power."[16] In a way, Allyson Fiddler is right when she uses Angela Carter's term "moral pornographer" to describe Jelinek's aesthetic and ethical point of view. A moral pornographer "might use pornography as a critique of current relations between the sexes."[17] Jelinek does precisely that, and she is very well aware of the effect her writing may have on the reader: "What I aim to achieve is that the reader no longer can roll around in lust, like a pig in its sty, but instead grows pale in the process of reading."[18] The anti-pornographic effect in *Lust* emerges, on the one hand, from the repetitive descriptions of marital rape and, on the other, from the way Jelinek lays bare the power relations that exist behind the sexual ones. In this process every illusion of pleasure is destroyed — as can be seen in the above passage.[19] All of which may explain the negative reaction by frustrated and challenged critics to such an "unfeminine" writing.

Through language, Jelinek exposes patriarchal violence and its discursive practices, which the female protagonist has to endure. Although it is by no means only Gerti who is the object of such violence (the author includes ecological and class issues as well as a criticism of the Catholic Church), she is ultimately the one who suffers the most from it. She is, therefore, definitely in the position of a victim. Although in *Lust* the absence of psychology in the development of the characters and their lack of self-identification as individuals[20] makes the connection to a possible extra-textual reality rather ambiguous, a close reading of the process of Gerti's victimization does suggest a very strong referentiality. In the example of *Lust*, referentiality refers to how Jelinek uses rape as a textual strategy which itself has a relationship to the external world, therefore the way rape is represented in the novel can help the reader to recognize patterns of abuse and victimization that occur in real life.

Sharon Lamb points out behavioural patterns that female victims of sexual abuse demonstrate: they often suffer from addictions and, for fear of being labelled, prefer to separate from other women who may suffer a similar fate. However, Lamb also stresses that female victims of sexual abuse are silenced for the sake of the acceptable image that society wants to maintain of them, namely, that of the weak and suffering victim whose agency and ability to heal are doubtful and taken away from her.[21] In Gerti's character we can recognize several of these patterns: she is an alcoholic who drinks more and more as the abuse goes on and on. Rather than a form of escapism, the drinking could be interpreted as a form of actively coping with the abuse, through "dissociation" or self-hypnosis. Gerti indeed displays some forms of active coping and resistance, however weak they may appear to be. During the rape, for example, she sometimes attempts to resist her husband's actions, only to be treated even more brutally by him:

> He bites the woman's breast, and her hands jerk forward. This only excites him more, and he hits her on the back of her head and tightens his grip on her hands, his enemies of old ... The woman is kissed. Spitting words of love are slobbered in her ear ... *Why is the woman turning her head aside?*[22]

Gerti endures her abuse alone and does not share her suffering with anyone else. The only other woman she has some contact with is a nosy neighbour who comes over for brief visits, but only out of self-interest — she is keen to secure her own husband's job at the paper factory. With her husband, however, Gerti's silence becomes a form of resistance, which transforms into a carnivalesque subversive laughter: "The woman is cloaked in the darkness of silence. But then she laughs, laughs till it seems she will never stop, to humiliate her husband."[23]

What may be Gerti's most evident gesture of resistance, however, is her affair with the student Michael, whom she meets during one of her escapades in the countryside. But Michael treats her in the very same way her husband treats her. The knight in shining armour she was hoping to find in the young man with the angelic name turns out to be just as brutal as Hermann. Yet, interestingly, Gerti experiences a sexual pleasure with Michael that she doesn't experience with her husband — an experience that could feed into the theory of female masochism. Mitscherlich explains masochism and masochistic fantasies in women, which inspired Freud to develop his theories about women desiring rape, in the following way: "La fonction de ce genre de fantasmes peut être de transformer des situations passives d'oppression en situations contrôlables, et le déplaisir en plaisir" (Such fantasies may have the function to transform passive situations of oppression into controllable situations and the lack of pleasure into pleasure).[24] Gerti's masochism, therefore, can be seen as a form of control over an unbearable situation from which she still has not found a way out, rather than an unconscious desire to feel pain.

In addition to manifesting masochistic tendencies, Gerti also displays a form of narcissism in her affair with Michael:

> The woman thinks — and in this she is as mightily astray as we are in the scraggy woods — that she cast a glorious net over the young man the day before. She clapped her frightful image upon him, and now he keeps the picture in a breast pocket, a dart of cloth, and is forever taking it out to look at it. Now it's time he came out from wherever he's hiding from her. Quietly thinking of him isn't enough for her. There's an incessant dull thud of lust in her.[25]

Mitscherlich explains that female narcissism, like maschosim, arises from a variety of cultural factors, once again going beyond Freud's rather simplistic view. She sees narcissism as a need for establishing a positive self-image, a compensation for the lack of social recognition and therefore a healthy expression of self-love, something she saw women desperately in need of when she was writing in the 1980s.[26] In Gerti's case, we can see a similar need to be fully recognized by another human being, an expectation that is brutally annihilated when Michael gang-rapes her with his friends at a ski resort where she had gone with him. Afterwards, Gerti goes alone to Michael's house, and it is here that the last blow to her hopes occurs when Hermann comes to fetch his sexual property. While Michael watches and presumably masturbates behind the window, her husband rapes her in the car.

This ultimate reinforcement of patriarchal power over a woman leads the reader to the last scene in the novel where Gerti strangles her only child and throws his body into the river. Violence comes full circle: the victim of one perpetrator after another, Gerti finally becomes a perpetrator herself. Sharon Lamb points out that it is more typical and more socially acceptable for a female than a male victim to become a perpetrator.[27] Thus, Gerti steps out of the female victim's framework and the expected behaviour.

This scene may, of course, be interpreted as violence being done by a weak and vulnerable woman against an even weaker and more vulnerable child. Yet it can also be seen as Gerti's ultimate gesture of resistance. She kills the male child who already exhibits the tyrannical characteristics of his father. Rather than a weak and innocent creature, the boy is portrayed as a future Herr-Mann, another representative of patriarchy and its all-pervasive violence. By murdering her son, Gerti, on a symbolic level, kills patriarchy and the possibility of its continuation. By doing so, she deconstructs the traditional role of the woman as the tacit and implicit reproductive and supportive force of patriarchy.

Faschinger's *Magdalena the Sinner*

The tone and atmosphere of Faschinger's *Magdalena the Sinner* is quite different from that found in *Lust*. The form of the narrative is a confession, which the reader is pulled into right from the first line: "And now you will listen to me, Reverend Father. Now it's your turn to lend me your ear, your Catholic priest's ear, fine-tuned to every gradation of cardinal and venial sin, which has been sympathetically turned to so many people in the past."[28] The humorous tone is evident immediately. However, a few lines later, the reader realizes the rather unusual situation in which this confession is taking place: it is not the expected location of the confessional in the church. Magdalena has abducted the priest and taken him to a forest, where she forces him to listen to her confession. Faschinger uses the priest as a passive listener and as the main narrator who tells the story of Magdalena's past, recounting it through her confession, and tells the story of the present through his own abduction. The abundant use of humour, irony and satire in Faschinger's writing prevents the reader from experiencing the horrifying effect Magdalena's confession initially has on the priest — the murder of her seven lovers.

Magdalena uses seven different methods to murder her seven lovers: drowning, burning, poisoning, stabbing, shooting, strangling and pushing off a cliff — all well-known in the repertoire of crime fiction. The number seven can be read, as has been pointed out repeatedly by critics, as an allusion to the seven deadly sins. Yet Faschinger plays with such biblical allusions, starting with the name of her protagonist, Magdalena, to deconstruct the biblical representation of the beautiful and sensuous woman as sinner. Magdalena is not only beautiful, but her seven murders can also be read as her attempt to find a relationship that would offer her long-term satisfaction without tying her down into a preconceived feminine role.

Indeed, Magdalena's initial flight from her native Austria on her motor-bike is not motivated by a need to flee the justice system; rather, she is fleeing from the family ties that are suffocating her. The life of a vagabond is more attractive to her than being a housewife or a career woman, choosing instead to reject these pre-existing and socially acceptable roles for contemporary women.[29] In each of her seven relationships, she searches for happiness, which none promise to provide. The seven relationships can be also read as prototypes of male–female relationships and as relationships that victimize women, from which Magdalena successfully escapes.[30]

She meets her first lover, the Frisian, in a catacomb in Italy. He is a melancholic whose only merit is that he is a good lover. All other practical matters are left to Magdalena who has to provide for both of them, and she does so by stealing and pickpocketing, disguising herself in a nun's costume (which can certainly be read as a satire of the Catholic Church). However, the Frisian's bouts of depression lead him to several suicide attempts and start to seriously affect his frequent and passionate lovemaking. Magdalena becomes afraid that she too will be drawn into a psychotic state herself and decides to drown him during a night swim in the Adriatic Sea. Here we could agree with Geoffrey C. Howes who writes that some murders are committed for therapeutic reasons, for example, Magdalena could have been choosing murder over her own madness.[31] But I would not call this murder and the other murders she commits therapeutic; I would call them "preventative murders": she murders before she falls into the position of victim or, as is the case in her other relationships, as a way of escaping from the position of victim.

She meets her next lover, Igor, a fiery Ukrainian, in Paris. The fire is not only a metaphor for their passionate love life but also represents the start and finish of the relationship. When Magdalena meets Igor in a café, he sets the newspaper he is reading on fire. His passion has a much less pleasant side, however. He is jealous and an alcoholic and becomes increasingly abusive towards Magdalena. At first he only insults her verbally, but those insults soon turn into physical injuries. When Magdalena meets her next lover, the Spanish dance teacher Pablo, she ends the abusive relationship with Igor by pouring vodka over his drunken body while he sleeps on the bed and setting him on fire. This time around, Magdalena has acted more out of self-defence, which could correspond to the findings about women committing violent crimes in intimate relationships.[32]

In her relationship with Pablo, it is Magdalena who experiences jealousy. Unlike Igor's jealousy, hers is not without grounds — Pablo is a Don Juan who sleeps with practically every woman he meets. When she meets the *clochard* from London, Jonathan Alistair Abercrombie, who lives in the basement of her Parisian apartment building, she decides to poison Pablo so she can escape with Jonathan to London.

This episode is probably the one which offers the reader the least-direct referentiality, for Jonathan turns out to be a living vampire. On a regular basis, he sucks out Magdalena's blood through her neck and with it her life force. This, of course, has an increasingly debilitating effect on her physical health. Once she is able to distance herself from her initial feelings of pleasure, Magdalena understands that living with a vampire is a question of life and death, and she chooses to stab Jonathan with a knife while he's having a shower. Magdalena definitely has the reader's sympathy — and that of the priest, who is listening to her confession — at this point in the story. The referentiality, then, lies in the metaphor of a woman who finds herself in a relationship that takes everything out of her and gives her nothing. In an interview, Elfriede Jelinek called the vampire "a metaphor for female existence,"[33] and Faschinger certainly uses it in this sense.

Magdalena's new partner, Michael, is a Romanian Jehovah's Witness. He pulls her into a well-defined role that fits his ideal of a woman based on the model of his mother. Magdalena has to wear his mother's clothes and he has no sexual relations with her. When she catches him *in flagrante delicto* with a homosexual lover, Magdalena shoots him on the spot. After this she has to flee London, in addition to the murder, some of Jonathan's fellow *clochards* suspect that she may be the one responsible for Jonathan's death.

She returns to the Continent where she meets a rich baron in a casino in Baden-Baden, Germany, and becomes his paid companion. In their sexual relationship, Magdalena acts out the baron's sado-masochistic fantasies, but in a role reversal of a sadistic situation: she plays the role of the dominatrix and he the masochist.[34] At the same time, she is having a "normal" and quite happy love affair with the baron's chauffeur, Clemens, who happens to be a fellow Austrian. But the baron finds out and seeks revenge: he sends the chauffeur back to Austria, cuts off Magdalena's salary and stops giving her expensive presents. During one of their S&M games, she strangles the baron and makes it look like suicide.

Before his departure, Clemens asks Magdalena to marry him. If she did so, however, she would have to go back with him to Austria, live in a shared household with his mother whom Magdalena would have to obey, look after the household and bear him six children, who would be brought up as decent Austrians. This, of course, is far from Magdalena's ideal of freedom, and, although heartbroken that Clemens is leaving, she ends the relationship with the excuse that she cannot abandon the old baron who needs to be looked after. But the real truth is that Magdalena cannot even consider the horror of the "perfect Austrian family," which she, in her confession to the priest, criticizes as hypocritical and as "the ideal background for the most terrible crimes."[35] Faschinger's biting criticism of Austrian society with its false moralities used to cover up violence and abuse shines through in Magdalena's words. This criticism is, of course, even stronger given the presence of the Catholic priest who, according to Howes, represents "petrified spirituality."[36]

In her seventh relationship, Magdalena is again forced into a predetermined role by her new lover, Karl. This time, she has to embody the "perfect" woman, which means she has to manifest the qualities which each of Karl's previous three wives had possessed: she must be attractive, a good cook, a talented singer and an athlete. These requirements are a biting satire of the superwoman ideal being imposed on contemporary women. She doesn't marry Karl, but lives with him in Bavaria. When the role of perfect female companion becomes too much for Magdalena to endure, she pushes Karl off a cliff, after which she returns to Austria with the desire to confess. After several unsuccessful attempts to find somebody who would listen to her story, she resorts to violence by abducting the priest in the middle of a mass and drives away with him on her motorcycle, taking him to the forest.

Faschinger plays with gender through the role reversal of the woman and the man: it is Magdalena who acts as the violent kidnapper (the police mistakenly search for a man) and the priest who is the victim; it is Magdalena who speaks and makes all decisions for the duration of the abduction, while the priest is reduced to a silent listener. In Faschinger's own words, she is playing with the fictional possibility of reducing the man "to a helpless wrap, which is what women are usually reduced to."[37] According to her, such a reduction of the man is necessary in order to make him understand what he and his sex normally do to women, and only through such an understanding is it possible for a somewhat normal and equal relationship to take place between the sexes. Unlike Jelinek, Faschinger leaves the reader with at least a sense of hope that positive male–female relationships are possible to attain. Magdalena escapes on her motorcycle after the priest — whom she has not only won over to her side during the confession but who is no longer capable of resisting her charms, which he abundantly enjoys during one of the nights they are together — is freed by the Austrian police, accompanied by his virgin sister Maria. The priest's last thoughts point in the direction of such hope: "Magdalena. She'd get by. And I would respect the confidence of the confessional. I would not betray her."[38]

*

What Magdalena achieves through her murders is the destruction of various stereotypical male–female relationships, which are manifestations of patriarchal power. She also inspires a sense of hope that real happiness and equality based on intersubjectivity[39] are possible, a hope that we do not find in Jelinek's *Lust*. According to Jelinek, given the omnipresence of violence and particularly gender-related violence, a utopia where positive expressions of sexuality and relationships can exist is not possible. Writing seems to be the only safe haven, but it cannot offer the hope, let alone the model, of a safe haven for others. Writing can cut through the lies and hypocrisies in society, but it cannot show a way towards healing. The circle of violence between men and women is therefore unending, and Jelinek's writing fails to offer cathartic relief.

Faschinger, in contrast, while operating along the same critical edge as Jelinek, subverts violence with the use of humour and satire. She pushes the power of laughter to its limits before turning it into disgust. The genre of the crime novel offers her a safe space to accomplish this. By introducing a female murderer at the beginning of the story, she prepares the reader to expect that violence will be committed both by and to a woman. She thus subverts the representation of the female victim as weak and helpless and, at the same time, secures the reader's support for Magdalena's actions. Jelinek, however, completely destroys any possible expectations. If Faschinger provokes her readers, Jelinek pushes their buttons beyond their limits. This is probably why Faschinger has not been subjected to the virulent attacks Jelinek has experienced.

Moreover, Faschinger's novel, as innovative and playful in its representational strategies as it may be, still profits from an already existing market of women's crime fiction in German-speaking countries, which has grown significantly since the 1990s.[40] Her protagonist, Magdalena, also acts in aggressive ways that are more acceptable for women. According to Patricia Pearson in her study of female violence, the "purpose and method" of women's aggression is different from men's: whereas men defend their property and their status, women defend human relationships.[41] Magdalena's murders can therefore be seen as acts to preserve her hope for the perfect relationship, whereas Jelinek's Gerti ultimately demonstrates "unfeminine" aggressive behaviour, one that falls in line with the "bad" woman in history and myth, such as Medea.

Jelinek's *Lust*, along with her other writings, is a unique literary phenomenon in Austrian women's writing. It may not offer therapeutic relief or hope and is certainly a much less pleasant reading than Faschinger's *Magdalena the Sinner*. What Jelinek offers, though, is a deep challenge to the aesthetics of representation deemed "suitable" for a woman writer, and this is what secures for her a notable place in Austrian literature and in German-language literature at large.

NOTES

1. Margarete Mitscherlich, *La femme pacifique: Étude psychanalytique de l'agressivité selon le sexe*, translated from the German by Sylvie Ponsard (Paris: Des femmes, 1988), 211. Translation my own.

2. Naomi Wolf, *Fire with Fire: The New Female Power and How It Will Change the Twenty-first Century* (Toronto: Random House of Canada, 1993), 148.

3. Claire Renzetti, "The Challenge of Feminism Posed by Women's Use of Violence in Intimate Relationships," in Sharon Lamb, ed., *New Versions of Victims: Feminists Struggle with the Concept* (New York: New York University Press, 1999), 49.

4. Lilian Faschinger, "Curriculum Vitae," submitted by the author on the occasion of her guest lecture at the international conference "Violence and Patriarchy: Perspectives for the New Millenium," organized by Fernando de Diego and Agatha Schwartz, University of Ottawa, October 18–21, 2001.

5. Matthias Luserke, "Ästhetik des Obszönen: Elfriede Jelineks *Lust* als Protokoll einer Mikroskopie des Patriarchats," (Aesthetics of the Obscene: Elfriede Jelinek's *Lust* as a Protocol of Patriarchy's Microscopy) *Text und Kritik* 117 (January 1993), 66. All quotations from the German sources in this essay were translated by Agatha Schwartz.

6. Quoted from Ellen Risholm and Erin Crawley, "*Lust* and Jelinek: Violating the Commonsensical," in Reinhold Grimm and Jost Hermand, eds., *High and Low*

Cultures: German Attempts at Mediation (Wisconsin: University of Wisconsin Press, 1994), 109.

7. Sigrid Löffler, "Spezialistin für den Hass: Eine Autorin, die keine Annäherung gestattet" (A Specialist in Hatred: An Author Who Does Not Allow for Any Closeness) *Die Zeit* 45 (11 November 1983), 23.

8. Risholm and Crawley, "*Lust* and Jelinek," 109.

9. Jelinek chose this name for the husband for a good reason. In German, the name Hermann derives from two words, both reflecting the power of patriarchy: "Herr" which means lord and master, and "Mann" which means man as well as husband.

10. Elfriede Jelinek, *Lust,* trans. Michael Hulse (London: Serpent's Tail, 1992), 15.

11. Ibid., 139.

12. See Allyson Fiddler, "Problems with Porn: Situating Elfriede Jelinek's *Lust,*" *German Life and Letters* 44, no. 5 (October 1991), 404–415.

13. The name for the German constitution.

14. See Beatrice Hannsen, "Elfriede Jelinek's Language of Violence," *New German Critique* 23 (1996), 92.

15. See Janet Blanken, "Elfriede Jelineks *Lust* als Beispiel eines postmodernen, feministischen Romans" (Elfriede Jelinek's *Lust* as an Example of a Postmodern Feminist Novel), *Neophilologus* 78, no. 4 (October 1994), 619.

16. Elfriede Jelinek, "Der Sinn des Obszönen," (The Meaning of the Obscene) in Claudia Gehrke, ed., *Frauen und Pornographie (Women and Pornography),* a special issue of *konkursbuch* (Tübingen, 1988), 102, quoted in Fiddler, "Problems with Porn," 412.

17. Angela Carter, *The Sadeian Woman* (New York: Pantheon Books, 1978), 19, quoted in Fiddler, "Problems with Porn," 413.

18. Interview with Birgit Lahann, *Stern* 37 (1988), quoted and translated by Hanssen, "Elfriede Jelinek's Language of Violence," 95.

19. See Günther A. Höfler, "Sexualität und Macht in Elfriede Jelineks Prosa" (Sexuality and Power in Elfriede Jelineks's Prose), *Modern Austrian Literature* 23, nos. 3/4 (1990), 106.

20. See Blanken, "Elfriede Jelineks *Lust,*" 615.

21. Sharon Lamb, "Constructing the Victim: Popular Images and Lasting Labels," in Lamb, ed., *New Versions of Victims*, 108–138.

22. Jelinek, *Lust,* 19. Emphasis added.

23. Ibid., 65. The subversive power of language has been recognized by many authors. On carnival and the subversive effect of laughter, see M.M. Bakhtin, *Rabelais and His World,* trans. Hélène Iswolsky (Bloomington: Indiana University Press, 1984). See also Henri Bergson, *Le rire: Essai sur la signification du comique* (Paris: Presses Universitaires de France, 1940).

24. Mitscherlich, *La femme pacifique*, 211. Translation my own.

25. See Gertrud Koch, "Sittengemälde aus einem röm.kath. Land: Zum Roman 'Lust,'" (A Portrait of Mores from a Roman-Catholic Country: About the Novel "Lust") in

Christa Gürtler, ed., *Gegen den schönen Schein: Texte zu Elfriede Jelinek* (Against the Beautiful Shine) (Frankfurt/Main: Verlag Neue Kritik, 1990), 150.

26. Mitscherlich, *La femme pacifique*, 207.

27. See Lamb, "Constructing the Victim," 127.

28. Lilian Faschinger, *Magdalena the Sinner*, trans. Shaun Whiteside (New York: Harper and Collins, 1997), 1.

29. See Geoffrey C. Howes, "Therapeutic Murder in Elfriede Czurda and Lilian Faschinger," *Modern Austrian Literature* 32 (1999), 83–84.

30. See Sigrid Schmid-Bortenschlager, "Violence and Women's Status as Victim: Changing the Role Model or Being Caught in a Trap?" in Fernando de Diego and Agatha Schwartz, eds., *Rethinking Violence and Patriarchy for the New Millennium: A German and Hispanic Perspective* (Ottawa: University of Ottawa Press, 2002), 113–120.

31. Howes, "Therapeutic Murder…," 84.

32. Renzetti, "The Challenge to Feminism…," 45.

33. Sigrid Berka, "Ein Gespräch mit Elfriede Jelinek" (A Conversation with Elfriede Jelinek), *Modern Austrian Literature* 26, no. 2 (1993), 134.

34. See Schmid-Bortenschlager, "Violence and Women's Status as Victim," 117.

35. Faschinger, *Magdalena the Sinner*, 226.

36. Howes, "Therapeutic Murder…," 84.

37. Gisela Roethke, "Lilian Faschinger im Gespräch" (Interview with Lilian Faschinger), *Modern Austrian Literature* 33, no. 1 (2000), 93.

38. Faschinger, *Magdalena the Sinner*, 276.

39. Jessica Benjamin defines intersubjectivity as follows: "The intersubjective mode acknowledges that the other person really exists in the here and now, not merely in the symbolic dimension." Jessica Benjamin, "A Desire of One's Own: Psychoanalytic Feminism and Intersubjective Space," in Theresa de Lauretis, ed, *Feminist Studies, Critical Studies* (Bloomington: Indiana University Press, 1986), 78–101.

40. For a reference on women's crime fictions and criticism on it, see Howes, "Therapeutic Murder…," 91–92.

41. Patricia Pearson, *When She Was Bad: Violent Women and the Myth of Innocence* (New York: Viking, 1997), 20, quoted, in Howes, "Therapeutic Murder…," 87.

III

SHAPING EQUITY FOR WOMEN IN PUBLIC SPACES

CHAPTER 9

Women in the Urban Landscape

Caroline Andrew

THE QUESTION IS NOT SO MUCH, Are there women in the Canadian urban landscape? Rather, the important questions are, Who are they? What are they doing? Why doesn't everyone see them? and, most importantly, What roles have they (and do they) play in the structuring and restructuring of this landscape?

The objective of this chapter is to look at gender as a constitutive element in the analysis of Canadian urban space. I first look at how this point has been studied before turning to a more empirical examination of the gender implications of some current issues in urban politics. Feminist urban research in Canada has a particularly interesting history; it has been an area in which the research has been very closely linked to political engagement and political practice, in both the sense of the research questions asked and the involvement of the researchers in urban practice.[1] Theory and practice have been closely intertwined; theory informing practice and practice informing theory.

In examining the role of gender in urban space, it is important to be sensitive both to the material reality of urban space and to representations or discourses created about this space. Material conditions frame and channel behaviours and so do representations. The importance of this double perspective is elegantly argued by Jacqueline Coutras in *Crise urbaine et espaces sexués* (*Urban Crisis and Engendered Spaces*).[2] Coutras examines residential patterns and gender relations and argues that the division of the public/private — and its concomitant association of women with the family, the home and residential neighbourhoods and of men with the labour market and the business and industrial areas of the city — is essential to our understanding the structuring of cities. That women are now permanently in the paid labour force has obviously marked our cities, but this structuring adds to, but does not replace, the earlier patterning. And interwoven as factors into this patterning are the discourses constructed around public/men and private/women and the ways that this constructs and reconstructs the ways in which we look at urban space, relate to it and act in it.

In addition, analysis needs to be sensitive to the interrelations of gender and class as it affects urban space. Add to this a sensitivity to race, ethnicity, language, age, ability and sexual orientation and the complexity of the links to be made in understanding how gender plays into the structuring of urban space is clearly demonstrated.

This approach to relating discourse and material conditions is similar to that developed by Jane Jensen in her concept of "the universe of political discourse," or to Nancy Fraser who discusses "the politics of need interpretation."[3] My work is situated within a tradition of Canadian political economy that has incorporated both material reality and the representation of this reality.

The Urban Work of Women

A good deal of research has gone into conceptualizing relations between production and consumption and between production and reproduction as they relate to gender relations in urban space. Is the private home the space of reproduction, are urban services collective consumption, are the links between production and reproduction materialized as questions of transportation? Since the publication of Manuel Castels's *La question urbaine* (*The Urban Question*),[4] the evolution of the analysis has been from looking at these as distinct sectors to examining the relations between them to questioning the relevance of articulating them as separate sectors. A somewhat different way of thinking about these questions as they relate to gendered urban space is that suggested by Beth Moore Milroy and Susan Wismer in their triple conceptualization of women's work. Milroy and Wismer talk of traded work (or remunerated work in the labour market), domestic work and community work.[5] This allows us to think in terms of the role women have played in these different sectors but also to relate different forms of work to different urban spaces.

This rapid increase in the participation of women in the paid workforce over the past thirty years is a major factor in the current reshaping of the city. Suzanne Mackenzie's article, "Building Women, Building Cities," argues that there have been two periods in Canadian history where there have been, at the same time, a "women question" and an urban question and that, in fact, these two issues are interrelated. The solution found in the suburban city of the first period becomes a factor that complicates the finding of solutions in the crisis of the second period, in which women are attempting to combine paid employment with primary family responsibilities. As Mackenzie argues:

> Women are once again readjusting their use of space and time and breaking down the temporal and functional separation of home and work. Because many women work both at home and in the wage sector, they are organizing services at the interface ... Women are redesigning, or redesignating, homes and neighbourhoods: sharing houses with single parents, turning basements into workshops, or reoccupying and revitalizing inner cities.[6]

Women's entry into the paid labour force can be primarily understood in economic terms, as a manifestation of the growing inability of the one-wage earner to earn enough to support a family.

But there are also other factors at play. In a society such as our own where one's position in the paid-employment sector has become the primary definition of self, women's increasing engagement with paid labour manifests a desire for autonomy. The 1995 study by Francine Descarries and Christine Corbeil, based on interviews with 493 Montreal-based mothers with paid employment, revealed that 75 percent of these women would not give up their employment even if the economic well-being of their family could be guaranteed without this employment. The women felt that autonomy, a sense of self and significant social relations resulted from paid employment and that they wanted to keep these, just as they wanted to maintain their role as mothers.[7] Financial autonomy is obviously a primary but not a unique dimension in this evolution towards individualization,[8] egalitarianism or democratization.

At the same time, this drive for autonomy has to be understood within the confines of barriers based not only on gender but also on class, race and region. Women's entry into the paid labour force has been very uneven, with high concentrations of women in certain sectors and with a very limited presence in other areas. There are still very few women in the senior levels of private business, whereas clerical work continues to be very strongly female. Many authors[9] have argued that the effects of the private/public dichotomization of women and men plays itself out in the paid labour force with much of women's work still linked to the qualities of "caring," which they brought to their private roles as mothers and homemakers. The concentration of women in the fields of health, social services and education (particularly of young children) is seen to be a continuation of their private roles into the public sphere.

The movement of women, and particularly married women with children, into the paid labour market has not transformed the link between women and domestic work. Women still have the principal responsibility for children and for housework, and they are becoming increasingly responsible for the care of elderly parents or relatives. Men may spend somewhat more time doing household chores than previously, however, as Meg Luxton's classic analysis of domestic labour shows, the management and planning of domestic work continues to be largely a female responsibility.[10] Women may not be in the residential neighbourhoods throughout the day but they continue to be associated with the home and therefore the immediate neighbourhood.

Mentioning the neighbourhood brings us to Milroy and Wismer's third category of women's work, that of community work. To some extent, this can be seen as a category with ever-changing borders, which are dependent on the changing definitions of public and private, state and civil society, family and society. Even though childcare was at one time primarily the woman's responsibility within the family, there was always a large component of community work involved in her day as she often looked after other people's children through a variety of informal or shared arrangements. With more women in the paid workforce, some of the childcare has become a form of paid employment (largely for women). Nonetheless, working mothers are still involved in community work, partly through participating in boards of co-operative or non-profit daycares but also, and increasingly, through fundraising for daycare activities. This community work is not done entirely by women but, in my experience, the majority of it is.

Community work is both informal (checking on neighbours, raking leaves from a neighbour's lawn) and formal (bringing meals to seniors, volunteering at food banks). As Suzanne Mackenzie's earlier quotation suggests, it has involved establishing a range of services, many of which can be understood in terms of processes of urbanization which are very different from those that produced the modern city (separation of functions, distance between work and home, single-use sectors). Daycare centres, women's centres, transition houses, housing for women, services for immigrants — all of these help to hold together large urban centres and all require considerable community work in order to be created and to function effectively. Women do not do this community work alone, but they are very significant players.

Community work can also be seen in relation to women's desire for autonomy. Many of the services were created by women for women so as to create spaces for women to think of their own needs. Others were created by women thinking of their own autonomy. Transition houses, in this respect, support women's autonomy as do women's centres and housing for women. Daycare allows women to combine paid employment and motherhood. However, autonomy is not the only value underlying this community work; solidarity, connection and caring are also written into these spaces.

Discourses on Women and Cities

Women, therefore, are fully involved in all aspects of urban work — paid employment, domestic labour and community work. But this is not necessarily the perception we have of public life in cities. In order to better analyze this we must add to our description of material reality an understanding of our collective representations of women and cities.

Two very useful books in this area are Carolyn Strange's *Toronto's Girl Problem: The Perils and Pleasures of the City 1880–1930*[11] and Elizabeth Wilson's *The Sphinx in the City: Urban Life, the Control of Disorder, and Women*. In both cases, the authors look perceptively at how society has seen women in cities. The approach is therefore one that considers how "others" see women (the "others" may include women but it is not the same women as those being seen). In both cases, women were seen as representing forces of disorder and as problems that needed to be controlled. Elizabeth Wilson discusses urban planning measures that were put into place as ways to control the city, measures that saw women as representing one important dimension of urban disorder:

> Planners ... wished to eliminate not just dirt and disease, but slovenly housewives and rioting workers. The colonial imperative was close to the surface even in the imperial heartlands: the city was essentially for the white, male bourgeoisie; all others were there on sufferance.[12]

Wilson goes on to argue that Western civilization has been very ambivalent towards city life, both fearing it and desiring it. This ambivalence plays itself out in the ways women have been looked at in cities. Women have fared especially badly in Western visions of the metropolis because they have been seen as representing disorder. The fear stems from seeing the city as a realm of uncontrolled and chaotic sexual license; thus, the rigid control of women has been necessary to avert this danger. Urban planning, therefore, has been unsuccessful because its basic orientation has been to control the urban rather than celebrate it. It has attempted to impose order on disorder, and this disorder, according to Wilson, was strongly gendered.

Through applying techniques of control in urban planning, then, was one way of disciplining women. These techniques, in fact, can be seen in areas other than that of land-use planning. In *Toronto's Girl Problem*, Carolyn Strange deals with the "deployment of new regulatory, reformative, managerial, and medical techniques" put into place to control the moral problem of single women in the city. As Strange shows, it was not the type of work that single women were employed in (despite it being badly paid, precarious and in poor conditions) that preoccupied Toronto society, but what they were doing in their leisure time. "The relentless sexualization of working girls' behaviour is perhaps the most salient observation in this story," and the solutions included the medicalization of the single woman (psychiatric diagnosis of feeble-mindedness and moral degeneracy), the creation of delinquency (incarcerating "dissolute young women") and the preoccupation to promote wholesome leisure activities.[13]

What both Wilson and Strange demonstrate is how social fears about urbanization — the creation of heterogenous spaces where traditional social structures and hierarchies were seen as having less impact — were conflated with social views about what women would do once these traditional social structures and hierarchies had been loosened. Women on their own, women as autonomous human beings, were seen as one and the same — as morally corrupt and chaotic creatures of sexual depravity.

What both authors argue is not that these representations remain absolutely unchanging but that they remain as one overlay in our multilayered perception of cities and women. Toronto in the 1930s, and even more so in the early years of the twenty-first century, came to accept the presence of single women, but these early representations of single women as disorderly continue to be a part of the public discourse on urbanization and women. In fact, the uncontrolled city and the uncontrolled woman are images that coexist with others in forming views about public policy solutions.

However, this is only one representation of women that exists and that intersects with urban issues. There is also the image of woman qua mother who is associated with the private realm, with activities of consumption and with caring and compassion. This is the image of the happy woman within her private realm who is not associated with public life (or with public space) nor with the productive sphere. In this representation, the single-family home in suburbia becomes the physical expression of the woman, surrounded by a loving family and the full panoply of consumption goods.

That these two images of women as suburban "chatelaines" and as licentious city girls are almost diametrically opposite should not be surprising; they fit into the tradition of dichotomous thinking about and the characterization of women as either saints or prostitutes. What is important, then, is to see how these differing images coexist and interrelate within a particular construction of the interpretation of urban needs and within the formulation of urban policy.

Current Feminist Urban Policy Issues

Taking up the challenge to think about urban policy as celebrating the inclusion of women requires, first of all, a consideration of the actual state of Canadian cities. It is important to have the best possible sense of current trends in order to think intelligently about what should be done. The operative words to discuss current trends in Canadian cities are polarization, levelling down, privatization, decentralization, social heterogeneity[14] and dispersion and fragmentation. Cities are increasingly becoming places for the rich and the poor; employment for everyone is becoming increasingly like women's employment (casual, part-time, short-term, temporary); senior governments are giving over responsibilities to lower levels of governments, to non-governmental bodies, to the private sector; cities are becoming city-regions with low-density ex-urban development spreading across wider and wider spaces; transportation within these city-regions is dominated by networks of highways and by the private automobile; services continue to be developed for more and more specialized groups while at the same time funding cuts are fragmenting still further the provision of services.

Our present-day reality is somewhat more complex. The same trends towards polarization and levelling down continue as do pressures for more tax cuts and therefore cuts in services. At the same time, there is an increasing concern for social cohesion and for building social capital and a worry that reducing the public sector weakens social cohesion. The federal government seems to be thinking about urban policy and its role in urban policy, although no concrete results have emerged as of the writing of this essay. There has been no explicit gender dimension to these concerns about social capital and social cohesion and, indeed, one of the major federal themes, the concern for poor children, has been seen as an attempt to downplay gender.

So what are some of the current urban policy questions, and is gender being considered as part of the analysis and therefore part of the solution?

One of the first questions is the issue of homelessness, a situation on the increase in Canada.[15] Yet, despite data showing that "the proportion and absolute numbers of women, families and youth among the visibly homeless are growing," and that "destitution is becoming entrenched for more of them,"[16] the visibility of women within the homeless populations is relatively limited. The classic image of a homeless person is still that of the relatively elderly male. However, in terms of concrete services, there have been some resources allocated specifically for projects for homeless women, projects selected through local processes and funded in part through federal funds. Women are not totally absent but they are certainly not sufficiently visible.

Municipal amalgamations are another major urban issue. A certain number of the largest cities, within the recent past, have been amalgamated so that at least a substantial portion of those cities' urbanized and urbanizing areas are within one political structure. What is and what will be the impact on women of such amalgamations? This question has been the most clearly debated in Quebec by the women's movement there, and feminists like Nicole Brais and Winnie Frohn have articulated the concerns of Quebec feminists. Over the past five years lively debates have focused on how women are being affected by regionalization and decentralization policies and by the Quebec program "Égalité pour décider," which provides grants to local groups for projects aimed at increasing the number of women in local and regional decision-making structures. The debates have pointed out some of the shortcomings; for example, the government missed an opportunity to advance the importance of gender equity in its discussions on amalgamations; the number of elected women will be reduced; elections may become more expensive as the size of wards greatly expands and this will discourage women more than men from voting; and amalgamations have been justified on the grounds of budget-cutting, which means service cuts that tend to be harmful to women. Even though these issues have been raised, however, the amalgamations in Quebec have proceeded with little or no explicit reference to gender.

What will the impact be on women? And, of course, on which women? There are clearly certain groups of women who are doing particularly badly in Canadian cities today. Single mothers are one such group, as are elderly women. Both of these groups are very vulnerable to the withdrawal of public funds and public services.

Public discourse in the late 1990s, as illustrated by the election of sharply right-wing provincial governments in Alberta and Ontario and of Reform Party MPs in the federal government, was replete with elements of backlash against "special interests" gaining "special privileges," that is, a backlash against all equity policies for racial minorities, gays and lesbians and women.[17] This backlash had a clearly anti-urban component, as large Canadian cities were seen to be the site of racial and sexual heterogeneity and the place where equity policies were demanded and created.

The current budget-cutting by all levels of government has increased the fragmented nature of service provision within cities. Certain services have disappeared because of budget cuts and others are have been altered because of changing pressures on services created by cuts elsewhere. There is still pressure for the creation of new services, particularly to specialized groups of the population (by age, ethnic group, language group or particular service requirements), but there are also counter-pressures arguing for the regrouping of services because of funding cuts. All of these create an ever increasingly fragmented service profile, with the concomitant increase in the numbers of people falling through the cracks. As women have fewer private resources and become more dependent on public services, they are particularly vulnerable to the fragmented-service environment.

Canadian cities have been particularly active regarding issues of urban safety initiatives and their links to women;[18] this policy area illustrates well the political tensions and ambiguous nature of urban policy responses in the early 2000s. In addition, it illustrates nicely the themes highlighted in this text — the need to consider both material reality and symbolic representations and the central importance of women's desire for autonomy along with society's resistance to autonomy.

Urban Safety

Women's urban safety is a particularly pertinent issue to study, all the more so in the Canadian context where there have been a number of interesting policy initiatives. As a policy area it illustrates the wide variety of practices and programs that impact on urban security — including planning, transportation, police, social services, housing, crime prevention, recreation services — and therefore the challenge of devising a co-ordinated strategy.

Analyses and descriptions of municipal initiatives in the area of women's urban safety exist for Toronto[19] and, to a lesser extent, for Montreal,[20] Vancouver,[21] Ottawa[22] and Quebec,[23] as well as in a number of other municipalities.[24] Toronto was certainly the early leader in terms of Canadian initiatives with the creation of METRAC (The Metro Action Committee on Violence Against Women) in 1984, the founding of Women Plan Toronto in 1985 and the formation of the Safe City Committee in 1989, but recently Montreal has been particularly active. Before looking in greater detail at the kind of local initiatives that have emerged, it is useful to put the question of women's safety into its material and discursive context.

The issue of personal security needs to be seen in the context of the modern city. Jane Jacobs's criticism of the segmented, single-use zoned city in *The Death and Life of Great American Cities*[25] is still pertinent today; it is the creation of cities with large areas that are unused by almost everyone for long periods of the day that sets the perception, and reality, of the unsafe city. It is therefore both material reality and the perception of that reality that, intimately interwoven, form the basis for public policy on issues of personal safety.

The question of perception is complex. We know, for instance, that most of the violence against women in urban areas is committed by males who are known by the women who suffer the violence. It is, so to speak, "private" violence and not "public" violence. Does focusing on the potential violence of strangers blur the responsibility of patriarchy for violence against women?

At the same time, one can also make the argument that addressing the issue of women's fears of the urban environment is a strategic way of raising the full range of questions about the unequal power of women, and of particular groups of women. It is clear, from a multitude of surveys,[26] that women feel much less safe than men do walking alone in their neighbourhoods after dark. And what is perhaps more significant is that many women who say they feel safe do so because they have self-imposed limits on their own activity, in terms of both time and space. Posing these questions is a concrete way of raising the more general question of women's equal access to urban space and to women's equal access to citizenship. It is not merely a minor question about convenience, it is fundamentally a question about the conditions of citizenship.

If citizenship implies the question of the conditions, the rights and responsibilities of belonging to a community, then the question of access to full participation is a central issue. And access must be defined, not only in conceptual terms, but also in very concrete ways, such as those raised by women's sense of security.

These questions can be raised in a way that link them to an understanding of unequal power relations in our society and therefore to the greater vulnerability of racial minorities, gays and lesbians, the young, the old, the handicapped. This approach makes the questions of unequal status and unequal access very concrete and visible. Pursuing questions of perceived security can also reinforce the argument that the people living in particular conditions are the real experts about those conditions.[27] Public policy should be constructed from the expertise of those living in cities and particularly from the experience of the most vulnerable groups. It is their understanding of how the city operates that should underwrite public policy.

Women's urban security also raises the question of equal access to urban citizenship. As the result of political protest or collective action, there have been changes to housing and housing projects, transportation systems, city centres, parks and improvements to services; long-term projects have focused on the prevention of violence against women; and educational and promotional projects have raised the visibility of the issue and publicized innovative community-based initiatives in a number of cities.

The innovative nature of these projects reinforces the importance of a gendered understanding of urban politics. The theme in one City of Toronto document is that the community has the expertise and that public policy should support this expertise, emphasizing that "[t]he stories in the document share a vision of community safety based on empowerment and action."[28] The same thrust can be seen in Quebec City where an advisory committee, Femmes et Ville, composed both of elected women and of women from the community, was set up. The committee conducted an extensive consultation across urban neighbourhoods and in the city to bring out the issues women felt strongly about. The major areas that emerged were housing, transportation, safety, recreation, neighbourhood quality of life and economic development. Based on these findings, the committee argued that women's grassroots involvement had led to their greater awareness of the important role municipal government can play in addressing their concerns. In Montreal, CAFSU (Comité d'action femmes et sécurité urbaine) has undertaken 101 separate activities, including safety audits, research studies, creating partnerships and doing planning centred on women's safety.

Nancy Fraser's analysis of the politics of needs interpretation helps us make sense of all these initiatives and demonstrates that political struggles take place between three kinds of discourses: expert, oppositional and "reprivatization."[29] Urban security is an important theme in each of these discourses. But urban security can be approached from very different political perspectives and therefore we must distinguish between concerns for safety that increase the policing and social control over urban space and those actions that increase the empowerment of women. This is crucial for thinking about women's urban security as a policy issue today.

In the current world where cities become "selling places"[30] (that is, selling themselves to attract tourist and investment dollars), urban security is a highly desirable commodity. For instance, Toronto's boast that it is "North America's most livable international city"[31] is based on the fundamental element that it is a safe city, which becomes an important part of selling the city to tourists and investors. Both tourism and the high-tech industry (two sectors all cities want to develop) are attracted to places that are seen as being secure; tourism because tourists do not want to get mugged on the streets and high tech because knowledge workers want to live in attractive, crime-free environments.

In this context, a wide variety of political interests consider urban security to be an important theme, each from different perspectives and each drawing on the three different discourses identified by Nancy Fraser. The expert discourses are particularly clear and numerous in the area of urban security. These discourses offer technologically sophisticated solutions, including emergency lights, security systems and so on, and they offer an industry of experts who can explain crime prevention through environmental design and crime prevention through social development. The expert discourses argue that the population does not know what the best solutions are for the problems they face; these are problems for experts to solve. The expert discourses do not see women as major actors in the question of urban security but see technology as crucial.

"Reprivatization" discourses are also prevalent. For Nancy Fraser, these are discourses that attempt to limit the issue and argue that public safety is not something that should be dealt with by the state. Civil society, the neighbourhood or the family should be responsible for issues of safety.

Oppositional discourses differ sharply from the other two. These discourses look at questions of urban security as a way of addressing unequal power and unequal resources. Women are not included as a unified or exclusionary group; rather, they are included as a way to emphasize concepts of vulnerability and as a way of initiating more inclusionary community development. Oppositional discourses argue that the solutions must come from the community and that the solutions must strengthen the community's ability to organize around these questions. Solutions are not technological, they are social and must be used to empower the community. Take the example of Femmes et Ville in Quebec City. This group went directly to the women living in specific neighbourhoods to find out what the most important issues are and how to address them. And in Toronto, organizations dealing with the most vulnerable groups of women require adequate resources to implement adequate solutions.

The urban security debates in Canadian cities include all three of these discourses and the policies that result reflect a variety of political tendencies. As stated earlier, Canadian cities have been, comparatively, more active than others on issues of urban safety. Does this illustrate the strength of the second wave of the women's movement? Does it illustrate the conservative or hierarchical nature of Canadian society, or the Canadian public's willingness to use the state for collectively agreed upon social goals? Does it illustrate the strength of the perception that women should be protected or does it illustrate the Canadian elite's fear of the urban masses, all the more now that these masses are portrayed as non-white? Or does it illustrate all of the above? Are recent initiatives in women's urban safety illustrations of the strength of reprivatization discourses, of expert discourses or of oppositional ones? The answer is that all three discourses are present and that each particular case must be examined to see who gains from the outcome, how it affects the material organization of the city and how it affects our perception of how the city operates and how we operate in the city.

*

These examples of urban safety illustrate how central gender relations are to questions of urban structure and urban policy at the beginning of the twenty-first century. Are these recent initiatives — for example, community-based services and better public transportation — merely examples of patchwork attempts to find ways that allow women to continue their triple day of paid work, domestic work and community work in an environment that is increasingly unsafe yet necessary for the continued profitable operation of our urban regions? Or are these initiatives part of the movement to create livable, women-friendly urban environments and part of the movement to challenge the unequal power relations that presently exist?

It is important that the role of gender in urban analysis is more widely understood. This chapter started by asking why the women in the Canadian urban landscape have not been visible to everyone. The answer is political, and it is also intellectual. Our future task is to analyze cities in such a way that celebrates the full complexity of urban life, and this can only be done when gender relations are central to that analysis.

NOTES

1. Caroline Andrew, Penny Gurstein, Fran Klodawsky, Beth Moore Milroy, Janet McClain, Linda Peake, Damaris Rose and Gerda Wekerle, *Canadian Women and Cities* (Ottawa: Canada Mortgage and Housing Corporation, 1994).

2. Jacqueline Coutras, *Crise urbaine et espaces sexués* (Paris: Armand Colin, 1996).

3. Jane Jenson, "Babies and the State," *Studies in Political Economy* 20 (1996), 9–46; Nancy Fraser, *Unruly Practices* (Minneapolis: University of Minnesota Press, 1989).

4. Manuel Castels, *La question urbaine* (Paris: Français Maspéro, 1972).

5. Beth Moore Milroy and Susan Wismer, "Communities, Work and Public-Private Sphere Models," *Gender, Place and Culture: A Journal of Feminist Geography* 1, no. 1 (1994), 71–90.

6. Suzanne Mackenzie, "Building Women: Building Cities: Toward Gender Sensitive Theory in the Environmental Disciplines," in Caroline Andrew and Beth Moore Milroy, *Life Spaces* (Vancouver: University of British Columbia Press, 1988), 23.

7. Francine Descarries and Christine Corbeil, *Famille et travail* (Montréal: Institut de recherche et d'études féministes, 1995).

8. Charles L. Jones, Lorna Marsden and Lorne Tepperman, *Lives of Their Own: The Individualization of Women's Lives* (Toronto: Oxford University Press, 1990).

9. See, for example, Pat Armstrong and Hugh Armstrong, *The Double Ghetto* (Toronto:

McClelland and Stewart, 1978); C. Baines, Patricia Evans and Shiela Naysmith, *Women's Caring* (Toronto: McClelland and Stewart, 1991).

10. Meg Luxton, *More than a Labour of Love* (Toronto: The Women's Press, 1980).

11. Carolyn Strange, *Toronto's Girl Problem: The Perils and Pleasures of the City, 1880–1930* (Toronto: University of Toronto Press, 1995).

12. Elizabeth Wilson, *The Sphinx in the City: Urban Life, the Control of Disorder, and Women* (Berkeley: University of California Press, 1981), 156.

13. Strange, *Toronto's Girl Problem*, 212–213.

14. For polarization, see Larry Browne and A.E. Olvet, *New Urban and Regional Geographies in Canada: 1986–1991 and Beyond* (Toronto: Centre for Urban and Community Studies, University of Toronto, 1995); for levelling down, see Pat Armstrong, "The Feminization of the Labour Force: Harmonizing Down in a Global Economy," in Isabella Bakker, *Rethinking Restructuring: Gender and Change in Canada* (Toronto: University of Toronto Press, 1996), 29–54; for privatization, see Paul Leduc Browne, *Love in a Cold War? The Voluntary Sector in the Age of Cuts* (Ottawa: Canadian Centre for Policy Alternatives, 1996); for decentralization, see Caroline Andrew, "Provincial-Municipal Relations," in James Lightbody, ed., *Canadian Metropolitics* (Toronto: Copp Clarke, 1995), 137–160; and for social heterogeneity, see Municipality of Metropolitan Toronto, *The Composition and Implications of Metropolitan Toronto's Ethnic, Racial and Linguistic Populations 1991* (Toronto: Access and Equity Centre, 1995).

15. Tracy Peressini and Lynn McDonald, "Urban Homelessness in Canada," in Trudi Bunting and Pierre Filion, *Canadian Cities in Transition* (Toronto: Oxford University Press, 2000), 525–543.

16. Sylvia Novac, Joyce Brown and Gloria Geller, *Women on the Rough Edge* (Ottawa: Canada Mortgage and Housing Corporation, 1999).

17. Steve Patten, "Preston Manning's Populism: Constructing the Common Space of the Common People," *Studies in Political Economy* 50 (1996), 95–132.

18. Organization for Economic Co-operation and Development, *Women in the City* (Paris: OECD, 1995).

19. See Gerda Wekerle, "Reframing Urban Sustainability," in Roger Keil, Gerda Wekerle and David Bell, eds., *Local Places in the Age of the Global City* (Montreal: Black Rose Books, 1996), 137–145; Carolyn Whitzman, "What Do You Want To Do? Pave Parks?" in Margrit Eichler, ed., *Change of Plans* (Toronto: Garamond Press, 1995), 89–110; Carolyn Whitzman, "How Women Got Lost in the Woods: A Case Study of Feminist Activism in High Park, 1989–1999" (paper presented at Canadian Association of Geographers Conference, Session on "Safe Places for Marginalized Groups," May 2001).

20. See Comité d'action femmes et sécurité urbaine, *Agir pour une ville sans peur* (Montréal: Ville de Montréal, 1994); CASFU, *Les prix Sécurité des femmes du CAFSU: Une première* (Montréal: CASFU, 1995); CASFU, *Agir ensemble pour la sécurité des femmes* (Montréal: CASFU, 2001); Anne Michaud, "L'aménagement sécuritaire du point de vue des femmes: L'expérience de la ville de Montréal," *Plan Canada* (May 1996), 23–24.

21. See Caroline Andrew, "Les femmes et le local: La construction des enjeux munici-paux dans l'ère de la globalisation," in Manon Tremblay and Caroline Andrew, eds., *Femmes et représentation politique* (Montréal: Éditions du remue-ménage, 1997), 179–196.

22. See Caroline Andrew, "Getting Women's Issues on the Municipal Agenda: Violence Against Women," in Judith Garber and Robyne Turner, eds., *Gender in Urban Research* (Thousand Oaks, CA: Sage Publications, 1995), 99–118.

23. See Winnie Frohn and Denise Piché, "Stratégies féministes sur la scène politique locale," in Tremblay and Andrew, eds., *Femmes et représentation politique*, 217–248; Ville de Québec, *Rapport de la Commission Consultative Femmes et Villes* (Québec: Service des Communications et des relations extérieures, 1995).

24. See Carolyn Whitzman, "The 'Voice of Women' in Canadian Local Government," in Caroline Andrew, Katherine Graham and Susan Phillips, eds., *Urban Affairs: Back on the Policy Agenda* (Montreal: McGill-Queen's University Press, 2002), 93–118; Caroline Andrew, "The Feminist City," in Henri Lustiger-Thaler, *Political Arrangements: Power and the City* (Montreal: Black Rose Books, 1982), 109–122.

25. Jane Jacobs, *The Death and Life of Great American Cities* (New York: Vintage Books, 1961).

26. Whitzman, "What Do You Want To Do? Pave Parks?"

27. Gerda Wekerle and Carolyn Whitzman, *Safe Cities: Guidelines for Planning, Design and Management* (New York: Van Nostrand Reinhold, 1995).

28. City of Toronto, *Lessons from Success Stories: Making Communities Safer* (Toronto: Planning and Development Department, 1996).

29. Fraser, *Unruly Practices*.

30. Gerry Kearns and Chris Philo, *Selling Places: The City as Cultural Capital* (Oxford: Pergamon Press, 1993).

31. Report of the Greater Toronto Area Task Force, *Greater Toronto* (Toronto: Queen's Printer for Ontario, 1996).

CHAPTER 10

Mission Impossible?
Employment and Education Equity
for Women Students and Professors
at the University of Ottawa

Christabelle Sethna & Donatille Mujawamariya

SINCE THE 1980S, feminist scholarship has documented how the "chilly climate" or, covert, systemic discriminatory practices, favours boys and prevents girls from attaining their academic potential at all educational levels.[1] However, recent research suggests that schools' girl-friendly reforms have penalized boys and privileged girls, mostly in literacy, math and science.[2] The "poor boys" argument that girls have succeeded at boys' expense in schools begs the question, Have girls' superior literacy skills and improved math and science scores in schools given women the edge in universities today?[3]

Comparative macrocosmic research on university women suggests that the answer is no.[4] Impressive microcosmic studies that chart the progress of women at individual institutions of higher learning over time also show the same results.[5] Despite the adoption of employment and education equity policies aimed at ameliorating the chilly climate at universities over the last two decades, women in academe continue to be caught in an "academic funnel." This term refers to the decrease in the proportion of women from undergraduate to graduate levels, from lecturer to assistant to associate to

Mission Impossible?
Employment and Education Equity for Women Students
and Professors at the University of Ottawa

full professor status and from part-time to full-time studies, especially in fields of study traditionally dominated by men. It is noted that the academic funnel is even more pronounced for minority women in academe.[6]

It may be helpful to evaluate in some detail the progress of women at one university to assess just how much of a putative advantage schoolgirls' scholastic skills has given them at an institution of higher education. We have chosen the University of Ottawa to serve as a valuable micro-level case study charting what post-secondary progress has been made by women.

As one of the mid-sized universities in Ontario, its location in Canada's capital, its service to the Franco-Ontarian community and its reputation as the nation's largest and oldest bilingual institution of higher learning make it unique. To further this uniqueness, the University has made the pledge in its Mission Statement not only to international co-operation, to the development of educational programs for the Ontario French-speaking population and to the maintenance of the highest quality of French and English research, but also to "continue to be a leader in the promotion of women in all aspects of university life."[7]

In this chapter, we evaluate the impact of the University's mission to promote female students and professors since the publication of its groundbreaking report, *Étude de la situation des professeures et des étudiantes à l'Université d'Ottawa* in 1988 (hereafter referred to as *Étude).*[8] Although the University has continued to amass its own statistics on female students and professors, it has not compiled them in any systematic fashion to assess their progress since the release of *Étude.* We will use University data to compare male–female student differentials that first appeared in *Étude* for the 1989–1990 to 2000–2001 periods regarding enrolment, program, hiring, rank and salary. We have located some data for this study in the University Archives and on the University's Web pages. Additional data have also been provided to us upon request by the Office of Institutional Research and Planning, Equity Program; the Office of Educational and Employment Equity; the Association of Part-Time Professors at the University of Ottawa; the Faculty of Graduate and Postdoctoral Studies; and the Office of the Secretary of the University.

Throughout our study we use two course disciplinary categories — the human sciences and the sciences — representing traditionally feminine and masculine fields of study, respectively. For the purposes of this case study, the former category encompasses the Faculties of Education and Social Sciences while the latter comprises the Faculties of Engineering, Science and Medicine. In total, these faculties represent nearly 50 percent of the student body at the University. This micro-level case study is the groundwork for a future macro-level research project in which we will compare the contemporary situation of women at the University of Ottawa with that of other Canadian universities.

Historical Background

The University of Ottawa began as a small Catholic college for boys in 1848, declaring itself a co-educational institution in 1958. It awarded its first bachelor's degree to a male student in 1872. It was not until 1919 that the University Senate approved the Bachelor of Arts program for the women's colleges affiliated with the University and that Bachelor of Arts degrees were conferred upon women. The number of women students rose overall after the end of the First World War then dipped. Although degrees in the traditional feminine fields of study — teaching, domestic science and nursing — were available, the proportion of women students climbed to only 20 percent in 1965, matching the national levels that had been attained in the mid-1920s. Indeed, the first women's residence on campus was completed only in 1966. After 1970, female enrolment swelled despite government cutbacks to education. Over the next decade, the majority of students were female.

The first lay female professor at the University was hired in 1932 to teach music. Nuns had already been teaching at the University's affiliated colleges and in the School of Nursing at the General Hospital. Well into the 1940s, certain faculties, like the Faculty of Arts, were opposed to women teaching regular courses. More women were hired to teach on campus after the University opened its School of Domestic Science in 1956. The increase in the female student population in the 1960s and 1970s combined with the explosion of second-wave feminist scholarship led to the hiring of more women as professors. Still, by the 1980s, only 22 percent of the professorate was female. The popularity of Women's Studies led the University to group together in 1981 existing courses about women and women's issues offered by various women faculty members. Just two years later, the University Senate approved an interdisciplinary degree program in Women's Studies, and in 1999, an Institute of Women's Studies was created. A Joint Chair in Women's Studies shared by the University of Ottawa and Carleton University was founded in 1985.[9]

Mission Impossible?
Employment and Education Equity for Women Students
and Professors at the University of Ottawa

The Equity Challenge

By the mid-1980s, comparative macro-level studies acknowledged that university women across Canada had gained some ground. Yet the bulk of female enrolment was at the undergraduate, part-time level. The proportion of women in graduate programs was substantially smaller than the proportion of men. When compared with male students, female degree-completion rates were lower and the length of time for degree completion was greater. The plight of female professors was even more disturbing. Women occupied less than one-fifth of all teaching positions across Canada. They were bottlenecked in the lower ranks of the profession where few attained job security or tenure. Regardless of rank or seniority, they were paid lower salaries than their male counterparts. Whether student or professor, most women were concentrated in the Faculties of Arts and Education.[10]

Calls for government-mandated affirmative action programs to force universities to improve conditions for women in academe coincided with the striking of a Royal Commission on Equality on Employment. Intended to address discrimination in the labour market, affirmative action usually encompasses a range of measures from advertising jobs in gender-neutral language to implementing hiring quotas. However, affirmative action continues to arouse the suspicion that employers will be forced to hire unqualified individuals to fulfill quota requirements at the expense of other more qualified candidates.

Canada's answer to affirmative action was "employment equity" as outlined in the Commission's 1984 report, *Equality in Employment*. The report established that (1) inequity was a systemic condition that intentionally or accidentally limited an individual's or a group's right to opportunities generally available; (2) four groups — Native peoples, visible minorities, persons with disabilities and women — were designated as disproportionately disadvantaged in society; (3) equity could not be based on the same treatment for all; and (4) government intervention was required to enforce employment equity policies.[11] The report was simultaneously criticized for not going far enough in implementing employment equity and praised for leaving behind the "nasty baggage" of affirmative action.[12]

The federal government took up the employment equity challenge by passing legislation to ensure the representation and advancement of these four groups in the workplace. Provincial governments followed suit with their own initiatives.[13] In response to an offer of provincial funding for equity programs in Ontario, the University of Ottawa engaged in a flurry of activity regarding employment and education equity. Although the University continues to use the terms "employment equity" and "education equity," we were unable to locate any official University definition for either term. Both employment and education equity have come to mean the removal of any arbitrary barriers as well as the implementation of support-ive measures to ensure an individual's full access to employment and educational opportunities. In institutions of learning, these measures may include the active recruitment of students, professors and staff from those groups designated as disadvantaged; pedagogical practices that encourage the participation of such groups; curricula that are built on diverse forms of knowledge; and formal and informal mechanisms such as special grants, bursaries and corridor programs.[14]

In 1985, the University adopted an Employment and Education Equity policy. An employment and education equity analyst was hired in 1986. Faced with the prospect of faculty retirements, the University devel-oped in that same year a Faculty Renewal Plan to increase the numbers of women and young scholars hired. As part of the plan, the University set an objective to achieve a similar male-female ratio of professors that exists among students within each faculty. In June 1987, the University of Ottawa Senate adopted its Mission Statement. An amended version was adopted in September 1991.[15]

An Employment and Education Equity Committee appointed at the same time by the Vice-Rector, Academic, Susan Mann Trofimenkoff, the first woman to sit on the Administrative Committee of the University, released its first report on women in administration in 1987, *Workforce Analysis of the Administrative Staff.* While it is not within the purview of this chapter to address the situation of women in administration, the report dis-played a distressing pattern of professional segregation by sex. Sixty-six percent of women who worked in administrative positions were clerks and secretaries. Nearly 22 percent were slotted into managerial positions. Only 12 percent were technicians. In the latter two categories, women occupied junior and middle management posts while men predominated in the mid-dle management and senior positions. The gap between the salaries earned by women and men was enormous. Women's average salary was 34 percent less than the average salary of men.[16]

A similar pattern was found in *Étude*, its second report. Published in French and in English, *Étude* painted an unflattering portrait of the

Mission Impossible?
Employment and Education Equity for Women Students
and Professors at the University of Ottawa

situation of female students and professors at the University. It showed that women constituted the majority of the undergraduate part-time and full-time student population. But male students were more numerous at the graduate level and were more likely than were women to be enrolled full time. Most female students continued to orient themselves towards traditionally feminine fields of study such as education as opposed to engineering. Although up 4 percent from the early 1980s, female professors continued to be in the minority — 19 percent — of the professorate. In a number of faculties, namely science and engineering, female professors were non-existent or accounted for less than 10 percent of the faculty. Eighty-one percent of lecturers were women. Female assistant, associate and full professors came in at 38, 16 and 6 percent, respectively, of the professorate. In contrast to the wage differentials in the first report, important salary gaps between male and female professors were also noted but the available statistics were not completely conclusive.

In the interests of facilitating employment and education equity for female students and professors on campus, *Étude* concluded with twenty recommendations. Those dealing with students were focused on promoting the enrolment of women at the graduate level and in masculine fields of study. Those dealing with professors spoke to the hiring, tenure and promotion of women scholars.[17] We would like to assess how far the University has come in regard to these recommendations.

The Enrolment of Female Students

Overall, the total number of female students enrolled has remained unchanged between the 1989–1990 to 2000–2001 period (fig. 1). However, the percentage of female students in the five faculties under investigation in this study — education, social sciences, engineering, science and medicine — has actually decreased from 54 percent in 1994 to 53 percent in 2001. It is unclear why we see a drop during this period.

The pattern of female student enrolment varies according to part-time and full-time status (fig. 2). In 2000–2001, women constituted 51 percent of full-time students and 58 percent of part-timers. Although there remains a large gap between the part-time enrolment figures for male and female students, women students have gained some ground as female part-time enrolment has dropped by 5 percent from 1994–1995 to 2000–2001. However, the percentage of the full-time enrolment of women has increased from 49 to only 51 percent over these five years.

Figure 1: **Percentage of Enrolment by Sex since 1994**

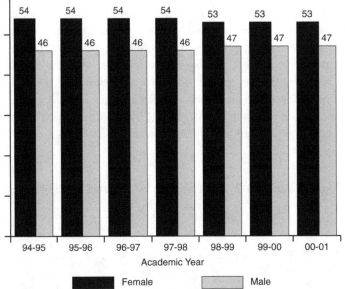

Figure 2: **Percentage of Enrolment by Sex and Status since 1994**

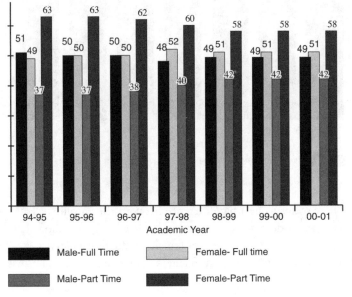

Mission Impossible?
Employment and Education Equity for Women Students
and Professors at the University of Ottawa

Unfortunately, any increase in full- and part-time female student enrolment does not appear as impressive when the two course disciplinary categories used in this study — the human sciences (Faculties of Education and Social Sciences) and the sciences (Faculties of Engineering, Science and Medicine) — are taken into consideration. It is tempting to conclude that the sciences are attracting more women students, given that female enrolment has jumped from 35 to 38 percent between 1994–1995 and 2000–2001 (fig. 3). Nevertheless, women students are still the majority in the human sciences. In effect, their percentage remains stagnant at 69–68 percent between 1994–1995 and 2000–2001. So does the percentage of men students in the traditionally feminine fields, at 31–32 percent for the same period.

Figure 3: **Percentage of Enrolment by Sex and Type of Faculty since 1994**

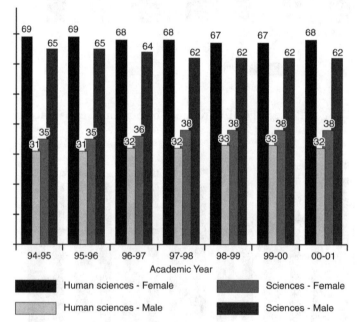

There seems to be a big difference between the enrolment patterns for graduate and undergraduate students. The data in figure 4 show that female undergraduates at 68 percent and female graduate students at 70 percent still predominate in the human sciences. The sciences remain a masculine domain, males comprising 62 percent and 63 percent of the student body at the undergraduate and graduate level, respectively.

Figure 4: **Percentage of Enrolment by Sex, Type of Faculty and Degree in 2000–2001**

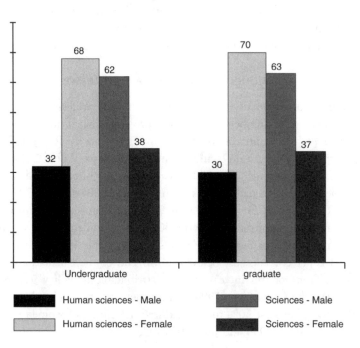

The diplomas conferred have the same profile as the data on enrolments. In the year 2000–2001, more women than men graduated except at the doctoral level (42.8 percent). This advantage is somewhat undermined, however, by the fact that the majority of women who graduated did so in traditionally feminine fields of study. Women who graduated in traditionally masculine fields of study remained a minority. To illustrate this discrepancy, we have chosen to contrast the numbers of diplomas conferred in the Faculty of Education and in the Faculty of Engineering. In the former, women represent 75.6 percent on average of diplomas conferred. In the later, women represent only 25.8 percent.

For example, in the Faculty of Education, doctoral degrees were awarded only to women. Yet more men (94.2 percent) than women (5.8 percent)

Mission Impossible?
Employment and Education Equity for Women Students
and Professors at the University of Ottawa

in the same faculty received Certificates of Technological Studies, reinforcing the pattern of male dominance in science and technology even in a traditionally feminine field. In contrast to the Faculty of Education, women graduates were far less numerous than were men graduates in the Faculty of Engineering. They are barely present at the bachelors level (26.5 percent). At the masters level, they are scarce in engineering management (7.1 percent) and non-existent in mechanical engineering. They are entirely absent at the doctoral level in both mechanical engineering and civil engineering.

Conditions for Female Professors

Étude's recommendations on the hiring of female professors were intended to increase their numbers.[18] The report projected that if the University continued to hire women according to its 1986 Faculty Renewal Plan, the percentage of women on faculty in the year 2000 would be 32. However, if the University decided that 100 percent of its new hirees should be women, the percentage of female professors in the year 2000 would be 39. Ten years after the release of *Étude,* there were 235 female professors, constituting 29 percent of the professorate. By the 2000–2001 academic year, the number of female professors had risen to 31.2 percent (table 1). The current figure of 31.2 percent falls just below the low end of the calculations made in *Étude.* Some of this increase can be attributable to Policy 94, the name given to the University's 1994 commitment to set a "global recruitment objective of at least 40% for the tenure-track hiring of women professors" between July 1, 1994 and June 30, 1997.[19]

Table 1: **Professors by Faculty, Rank and Sex in 2001 (Fall)**

Faculty	Full Professors		Associate Professors		Assistant Professors		Total	
	Male	Female	Male	Female	Male	Female	Male	Female
Administration	23	0	23	4	12	7	58	11 (15.9%)
Arts	55	22	51	30	19	18	125	70 (35.9%)
Common Law	9	6	8	5	4	5	21	16 (43.2%)
Droit Civil	15	2	2	3	0	3	17	8 (32.0%)
Education	8	6	6	12	5	7	19	25 (56.8%)
Engineering	46	1	12	5	24	3	82	9 (9.9%)
Health Sciences	5	7	10	18	5	19	20	44 (68.7%)
Medicine	44	6	13	7	8	7	65	20 (23.5%)
Science	42	3	25	5	13	4	80	12 (13.0%)
Social Sciences	37	18	27	13	12	10	76	41 (35.0%)
Total	**284**	**71**	**177**	**102**	**102**	**83**	**563**	**256 (31.2%)**

To increase the numbers of female professors hired, *Étude* recommended that the University reiterate its Faculty Renewal Plan objective to achieve a similar male–female ratio of professors to students within each faculty.[20] This laudable recommendation was, unfortunately, hampered by the fact that the University did not set a time limit on meeting this objective. Today, male student enrolment in the sciences remains consistently higher than female student enrolment at both undergraduate and graduate levels. Figure 5 shows that by the late 1990s, the ratio of male to female students in the human sciences was 32:68 percent. Among the male to female professors it was 64:36 percent. In the sciences the ratios were 62:38 and 85:15 percent, respectively. If we compare the current situation with the period just before the release of *Étude*, there has been obvious progress. Available statistics for the year 1987 indicate that in the Faculty of Arts 66 percent of students but 24 percent of professors were female. In the sciences, 41 percent of students as compared with 5 percent of professors were female.[21] Despite this progress, by 1997–1998 and 2000–2001 the numbers appear to have stagnated, quite possibly because of the end of the period of intense recruitment

Figure 5: **Percentage of Students and Professors by Sex and Type of Faculty in 1997-1998**

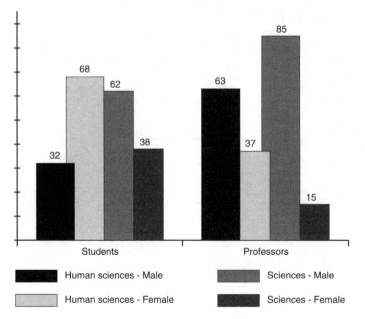

Mission Impossible?
Employment and Education Equity for Women Students
and Professors at the University of Ottawa

activity of female professors set out by Policy 94. As of 2000–2001, the ratio of male to female students in the human sciences was 32:68 percent; male to female professors was 61:39 percent. In the sciences, the ratios were 62:38 and 84:16 percent, respectively. To fulfill the University's official commitment to employment and educational equity, more effort towards equalizing the male–female ratio of professors to students is needed.

The Invisibility of Visible Minority, Aboriginal and Disabled Students and Professors

Étude did not deal with another important gap in the professor–student ratio. Although the University has legally had to adopt an employment and education equity policy that supports all the groups designated as disadvantaged by the Government of Canada, female and male Aboriginal professors, visible minority professors and professors with a disability are few in number. The University's limited data on professors who self-identify as visible minority according to its "Questionnaire d'auto-identification/Self-identification questionnaire," as Aboriginal or with a disability show that they are virtually non-existent. The largest numbers recorded appear in the Faculties of Administration and Engineering (table 2). It is possible that some of these professors do not wish to self-identify on the questionnaires to avoid any real or perceived negative consequences

Table 2: **Aboriginal, Visible Minority Professors and Professors with Disabilities in 1998–1999**

Faculty	Aboriginal Professors	Visible Minority Professors	Professors with Disabilities
Administration	0	10	0
Arts	***	3	3
Common Law	***	0	0
Droit Civil	0	0	0
Education	0	***	0
Engineering	0	8	0
Health Sciences	0	3	0
Medicine	0	***	0
Science	0	3	***
Social Sciences	0	***	0

***: Number too small to be expressed < 3

of such labelling. Because the University gives no indication at the moment of their sex or rank, it is impossible to draw any comparisons based on gender differentials.

The most recent statistics provided by the University show that 14.2 percent of students self-identify as a visible minority (table 3). However, this number may actually be higher because some students refuse to self-identify as a visible minority. Indeed, some students who did self-identify as such said they experienced prejudicial reactions from peers and professors.[22] Most of the students who have self-identified as a visible minority are registered in the Faculties of Administration, Science and Social Sciences.[23] However, there is no indication of the sex of the students, or whether they are enrolled in part-time or full-time programs, or whether they are at undergraduate and graduate levels or whether they are international students. According to 2000–2001 records, 5 percent of the University's total student population comes from more than 125 countries — among them, China, Saudi Arabia, India, Tunisia, Mexico, Cameroon and Somalia — whose citizens would most likely be classified as visible minorities in Canada.[24]

Table 3: **Profile of Students by Designated Groups and Faculty in 1996**

Faculty	Total Respondents		Aboriginal Persons		Visible Minorities		Persons with Disabilities	
	N	%	N	%	N	%	N	%
Administration	646	14.6	9	1.4	122	18.9	12	1.9
Arts	1011	22.8	18	1.6	89	8.8	44	4.4
Common Law	97	2.2	5	5.2	28	28.9	6	6.2
Droit Civil	115	2.6	5	4.4	12	10.4	***	***
Education	412	9.3	4	***	40	9.7	17	4.1
Engineering	280	6.3	***	***	77	27.5	7	2.5
Health Sciences	482	10.9	5	1.0	33	6.9	13	2.7
Medicine	52	1.2	0	0	10	19.2	0	0
Science	397	8.9	7	1.8	100	25.2	14	3.5
Social Sciences	945	21.3	20	2.1	119	12.6	40	4.2
Total	**4437**	**19.3**	**74**	**1.7**	**630**	**14.2**	**155**	**3.5**

***: Number too small to be expressed < 4

Mission Impossible?
Employment and Education Equity for Women Students
and Professors at the University of Ottawa

The disparity between the population of visible minority and Aboriginal professors/students and professors/students with a disability has been remarked upon even in larger academic institutions situated in bigger, more multicultural Canadian cities.[25] It remains a cause for concern, especially regarding tenure-stream faculty.[26] We suggest that the University could do more to respond to the query posed as early as 1992 in an issue paper on the teaching staff prepared for its Academic Planning Committee: "How can we ensure that the University's program in pursuit of gender parity be maintained, and expanded to include other designated groups, in an effort to ensure that target characteristics of the professorate reflect those of the student population?"[27]

Female Professors, Tenure and Rank

Additional recommendations in *Étude* concerning women professors referred specifically to tenure and promotion. When tenure-stream professors are judged to have successfully met the demands of teaching, research and service, they are awarded tenure and may also receive promotions in rank, from assistant to associate to full professor status. *Étude* recognized that female professors occupied the lowest ranks of the profession. When they became full professors, females were usually older than their male colleagues of the same rank but had less seniority and were less well-paid.

Current data show some progress. However, the majority of female professors are still concentrated at the lowest ranks of the profession; the higher the rank, the fewer female professors there are. Women at the rank of full professor rose from 6 percent in 1988 to 20 percent in 2000–2001. The percentage of female associate professors is now at 36 percent as opposed to 16 percent in 1988. In 1988, 38 percent of assistant professors were women. By the year 2000–2001, the number had risen to 44.8 percent. In fact, out of 185 assistant professors, 83 were women (see table 1). In the year 2000–2001, nearly 50 percent of lecturers were women (309 among 628), while 81 percent were in 1988.

In comparison to the situation in 1988, when there were few female professors at the University, five faculties — education, common law, civil law, arts and social sciences — can now be considered truly integrated by sex. Even the Faculty of Administration has female associate professors whereas this was not the case in 1988. It is, however, the only faculty as of this writing that does not have a female full professor. Today, four faculties as opposed to ten in 1988 remain predominantly masculine —

administration, engineering, sciences and medicine. Only one faculty, in 1988 and today, remains predominantly feminine — health sciences.

According to *Étude,* a faculty that is predominantly feminine is defined as one where 60 percent or more of the professors are women. A predominantly masculine faculty is one where 70 percent or more of the professors are male. A faculty considered integrated by sex has between 30 and 70 percent male professors and between 30 and 60 percent female professors.[28] Unfortunately, even in these definitions there exists a bias against women. The current data (see table 1) do not account for differences in the numbers of male and female professors in departments within each faculty. But they do reveal a slight numerical improvement when compared with the University in 1988. At that time, the University could be defined by *Étude* as a predominantly masculine workplace. Today, it can be defined as relatively integrated by sex. Overall, women now constitute 31.2 percent of professors at the University.

There has not been, however, a corresponding improvement in the salaries of female professors. Data reveal that female assistant professors in the Faculties of Administration and Arts earn less than their male colleagues despite their greater number of years of seniority at the same rank. Overall, salary differentials between female and male assistant professors are relatively small as women earn 99.7 percent of men's wages. But at the associate professor rank, the differentials increase. Women earn 93.5 percent of what men do, resulting in a salary that is, on the average, $5,000 less per year. Salary differentials are greater at the rank of full professor. Here women on the average make $6,000 less, or 93.9 percent annually of their male counterparts. Although the data do not allow confirmation that this wage differential is based on discrimination by sex, they do suggest that it is a valid possibility. It would be extremely useful to have access to more detailed records to appreciate the changes that have occurred since 1988, when the authors of *Étude* established that male professors earned, on the average, at least $10,000 more than female professors, regardless of rank.[29]

On a very positive note, there have been improved funding opportunities for newly hired female professors. The University's Regulation 94 has provided funds for female professors within the first three years of their hiring to work towards tenure. Regulation 94 provides successful applicants with money for second-language training in English or French or with course releases for a scholarly project or a career "interruption" due to pregnancy or heavy family responsibilities. However, funding peaked in

Mission Impossible?
Employment and Education Equity for Women Students
and Professors at the University of Ottawa

1995–1996 when $71,208 was distributed among thirty-three out of forty-six applicants but declined fairly steadily thereafter. By 2000–2001, only fourteen out of twenty-four applicants were funded with a total of $48,363.[30] This initiative needs to be more supported on a financial level. It also needs to be supported on an administrative level, as requests for funding under Regulation 94 must first have the permission of the professor's dean.

The Impossible Mission?

On the one hand, there have been positive developments at the University in regard to employment and education equity. Given that this University was originally slated to serve an exclusively male clientele, it is interesting to note that the student body is now composed of a majority of women. On the other hand, the data from the University show that despite some major improvements since the publication of *Étude* in 1988, female students and professors are mostly concentrated in the bottom strata of academia and constitute the majority in traditionally feminine fields of study. As this pattern is common to universities across Canada, it is clear that the University of Ottawa needs to do more in order to fulfill its Mission Statement to "continue to be a leader in the promotion of women in all aspects of university life."

This micro-level case study casts doubt on the long-term projection of the "poor boys" argument. If boys are being short-changed in schools, there does not appear to be a carry-over of male disadvantage into universities. Rather, it appears that any scholastic benefit girls receive in schools may gradually disappear as they continue with their university careers. Indeed, schools' girl-friendly reforms and universities' employment and education policies appear to have only mitigated, not eliminated, the academic funnel in which women in higher education are caught. More nuanced reflections on the "poor boys" argument have refused to essentialize boys and girls, invoking an interplay of race, class and sexuality to ascertain just which girls and which boys continue to succeed scholastically.[31] They conclude, for example, that schools remain unsafe places for many females, as well as for many non-white, gay, bisexual and transgender students.[32]

Chilly climate research in universities has gone a similar route. Before the implementation of equity policies, explanations for the funnel effect focused on overt systemic discrimination against women in academe.[33] After their implementation, the most persuasive explanations for the academic funnel centred on those covert, systemic discriminatory practices collectively known as the chilly climate. A great deal of this research focuses on the issue of violence against women on campus, ranging from graffiti to harassment to rape to murder, often occurring in opposition to feminism, feminist students and professors and to Women's Studies courses or content.[34] More recent accounts of relationship of the chilly climate to the groups designated as disadvantaged illustrate that universities operate on the basis of a hierarchical academic culture that promotes the experience, knowledge and values of the white able-bodied male as the norm. This culture generates "micro-inequities" that are often beyond the reach of equity legislation. They are so deeply embedded in university life that they are normalized in everyday interactions on campus.[35]

As Allison Young points out, employment and education equity are inextricably linked. She notes that without an equitable educational environment, it is impossible to attract a critical mass of qualified women, visible minority, Aboriginal and disabled students. Without qualified graduates from these designated groups, universities will not be able to hire diverse faculty members. A lack of diverse faculty will, in turn, work against students from the designated groups who seek role models and mentors.[36]

Recent accounts of the experiences of the micro-inequities students and professors who are women of colour face show just how precarious their toehold is in the academy. Female students of colour report that they are stigmatized as "affirmative action" candidates, have their qualifications called into question in departments that are primarily white and male, are silenced when they raise issues of race in the classroom and are unable to find mentors and supervisors.[37]

Female professors of colour are often hired specifically to develop and teach courses like anti-racism or Indigenous thought. But they report that student hostility over course content, condescension from colleagues, isolation within departments and a lack of support from administrators are daily occurrences. Many report difficulties in the tenure and promotion process, often because the mentoring, community organizing and publishing they do in support of their political beliefs are not valued academically by tenure and promotion committees. Women of colour on faculty uniformly attest to the contradictions between equity standards used to admit them versus those used to retain them such that they have begun to ask profound questions about the academy and its inadequate, selective understanding and application of the concept of equity itself. [38]

Mission Impossible?
Employment and Education Equity for Women Students
and Professors at the University of Ottawa

Ironically, the very groups that have been designated as disproportionately disadvantaged in Canadian society have experienced an even further drop in the academic temperature. Since the 1990s, drastic federal and provincial cuts to core university funding have forced universities to rely on the private sector for revenue. As a result, universities must now participate in a global economy that demands "faster turnover, higher productivity, lower costs and 24-hour accessibility" in an increasingly digitized working environment.[39] This corporatization of universities is occurring as the current Ontario government has repealed the province's equity legislation in the name of structural adjustment programs, which have widened the gap between rich and poor, eroded social safety nets and hardened societal attitudes towards the designated groups.[40]

While all Canadian universities face the challenges of corporatization, the University of Ottawa may be particularly vulnerable. It has been very successful in attracting private-sector funds for information technology research.[41] Indeed, as the City of Ottawa is the high-tech capital of Canada, the University has attempted to develop an established profile in this area.[42] Due to Ontario's 2003 double cohort, undergraduate applications to the University are also expected to rise by as much as 24 percent. The search for new faculty has, therefore, become a top priority as large numbers of professors are expected to retire between now and 2010.[43] Research critical of the corporatization of universities has shown that the process has the potential to exacerbate the chilly climate by reducing opportunities for universities to commit to employment and education equity. Notably, private-sector funding has raised serious concerns about the independence and integrity of university research. Most of the revenue is often channeled into traditionally masculine fields of study in order to facilitate research that contributes to a high-tech economy. Even the new federal funds for Canada Research Chairs has penalized traditionally feminine fields of study as only 20 percent of the chairs will be awarded to researchers in the human sciences.[44]

In addition, students have had to pay higher tuition fees, accept larger debt loads and work part-time while studying full-time. Those students from the designated groups who are also socio-economically disadvantaged have been unable to pay for the rising costs of education, especially at the graduate level. For instance, in 1992, households with the lowest income spent just over 11 percent of their disposable income on post-secondary tuition fees in 1992. By 1998, the number had jumped to just over 19 percent.[45]

Moreover, many professors have experienced greater fragmentation in their roles of teacher, researcher and administrator. But female professors typically report higher levels of occupational stress, more physical and psychological health problems, greater pressure to publish, more pedagogical demands and more conflict between career and family responsibilities. Some studies indicate that while the average work week for academics overall clocked in at 59 hours in the mid-1990s, female professors recorded an average of 64.5 hours per week by the end of the decade.[46]

*

Since the publication of *Étude,* the University has made great strides in improving female students' and professors' access to employment and education equity. Until 2002, the University funded a Women's Resource Centre that is now operated by one paid student and volunteers. It has also implemented a sexual harassment policy, opened a Pride Centre for the gay, lesbian and bisexual community on campus, appointed an Aboriginal Advisor and has adopted a policy statement on disability issues. These steps indicate that progress on equity for individuals belonging to the groups designated as disadvantaged has been made.[47] However, it is clear from this study, when it comes to the advancement of female students and professors, that progress has been uneven in many instances. As budget cuts, the search for research funding and the double cohort continue to place tremendous pressure on Ontario universities, it is imperative that the University of Ottawa resist compromising its stated commitment to women and to equity policies and practices. In the spirit of other wish lists compiled by university women intent on concrete institutional change in favour of equity,[48] we suggest that the University expand its Mission Statement to make employment and educational equity a key goal in the hiring of all professors, in the recruitment of all students and in the implementation of all policies.

Mission Impossible?
Employment and Education Equity for Women Students
and Professors at the University of Ottawa

NOTES

We would like to thank Diane Bélanger-Brisson, Michel Brabant, Hélène Carrière, Géraldine Cougnoux, Lisa Dillon, Camille Lafortune, Hélène Lacroix, Huguette Desmarais-Foisy, Pamela Ermuth and Yanne Le Corre for their invaluable assistance.

1. Roberta M. Hall and Bernice R. Sandler, *The Classroom Climate: A Chilly One for Women?* (Washington, DC: Association of American Colleges, 1982).

2. Christina Hoff Sommers, "The War Against the Boys," *The Atlantic Monthly* (May 2000), 59–74.

3. Dianne M. Hallman, "'If We're So Smart…': A Response to Trevor Gambell and Darryl Hunter," *Canadian Journal of Education* 25, no. 1 (2000), 62–67.

4. Mary Saunders, Margaret Therrien and Linda Williams, *Women in Universities: Survey of the Status of Female Faculty and Students at Canadian Universities* (Ottawa: Canadian Federation of University Women, November, 1992). See also Judy Stanley, Wendy Robbins, Rosemary Morgan, with the assistance of Andy Siggner, "Ivory Towers: Feminist Audits. Selected Indicators of the Status of Women in Universities in Canada and Further Equity Data, 2003" on the Canadian Federation for the Human Sciences and Social Sciences Web site: <http://www. fedcan.ca/english/policyandadvocacy/win/ publications.cfm>.

5. Constance Backhouse, "An Historical Perspective: Reflections on the Western Employment Equity Award," in The Chilly Collective, eds., *Breaking Anonymity: The Chilly Climate for Women Faculty* (Waterloo: Wilfrid Laurier University Press, 1995), 61–95.

6. Paula Caplan, *Lifting a Ton of Feathers: A Woman's Guide to Surviving in the Academic World* (Toronto: University of Toronto Press, 1993), 22.

7. "The Mission Statement of the University Of Ottawa." Retrieved from the University of Ottawa Web site: <http://www.uottawa.ca/sec-univ/eng/missione. html>. February 14, 2002.

8. Cécile Coderre et al., *Étude de la situation des professeures et des étudiantes à l'Université d'Ottawa* (Ottawa: University of Ottawa, August 1988).

9. *Université d'Ottawa: Un Héritage pour demain/University of Ottawa: A Tradition for Tomorrow* (Ottawa: University of Ottawa, 1990). See also Michelle Muir, "Producing Educated Women: Eveline Leblanc and the Universty of Ottawa" (paper presented at the Canadian Historical Association/La Société historique du Canada, University of Toronto, May 27–29, 2002).

10. Neil Guppy, Doug Balson and Susan Vellutini, "Women and Higher Education in Canadian Society," in Jane S. Gaskell and Arlene Tigar Mclaren, eds., *Women and Education: A Canadian Perspective* (Calgary: Detselig Enterprises Ltd., 1987), 171–192.

11. Abigail B. Bakan and Audrey Kobayashi, *Employment Equity Policy in Canada: An Interprovincial Comparison* (Ottawa: Status of Women Canada, March 2000), 13–14.

12. Carole Geller, "A Critique of the Abella Report," *Canadian Woman Studies/les cahiers de la femme* 6, no. 4 (1985), 20–22, and Lorna R. Marsden, "The Importance of Studying Affirmative Action," *Canadian Woman Studies/les cahiers de la femme* 6, no. 4 (1985), 13.

13. Bakan and Kobayashi, *Employment Equity Policy in Canada.*

14. Juanita Westmoreland-Traoré, "Educational Equity: 'No Turning Back,'" and Allison Young, "Linking Employment and Educational Equity," in Kay Armatage, ed., *Equity and How to Get It: Rescuing Graduate Studies* (Toronto: Inanna Publications and Education Inc., 1999), 38–61 and 62–78.

15. *Le Comité d'équité en matière d'emploi et d'éducation/Employment and Education Equity Committee: Sommaire du rapport/A Report Summary.* Supplement to *The University of Ottawa Gazette,* 17 May 1988, 7.

16. Cécile Coderre, Ida Deurloo, Susan Harris, Louise Pagé-Vain and Lise Martin, *Workforce Analysis of the Administrative Staff.* A Report Prepared for the Vice-Rector, Academic, by the Employment and Education Equity Committee, University of Ottawa, August, 1987. For a summary, see *Le Comité d'équité en matière d'emploi et d'éducation/Employment and Education Equity Committee: Sommaire du rapport /A Report Summary.* Supplement to the *University Of Ottawa Gazette,* 17 May 1988, 1–12.

17. *Étude.*

18. *Étude,* xv–xvi.

19. "Policy 94: Policy on the Pro-Active Recruitment of Women Professors." Retrieved from the University of Ottawa: <http:// www. uottawa.ca/sec-univ/eng/ reg94-a.html>. February 18, 2002.

20. *Étude,* xv.

21. Louise Crosby, "Report Gives University of Ottawa Mixed Marks on Role of Women," *Ottawa Citizen,* 8 December 1987, C15.

22. Gada Mahrouse, "Navigating Access: Managing the Ambiguity of 'Special Admissions'" (MA thesis, University of Ottawa, 2001).

23. "Profile of the University Of Ottawa Student Body: 1996 Self-Indentification Survey Report, August 1999." Retrieved from the University of Ottawa Web site: <http://www. uottawa.ca/service/equite/eng/report.html>. February 18, 2002.

24. "Healthy Numbers." Retrieved from the University of Ottawa Web site: < http:// www.uottawa.ca/services/hr/newweb/rfchiffre.html>. July 8, 2002.

25. Frances Henry, Carol Tator, Winston Mattis and Tim Rees, *The Colour of Democracy: Racism in Canadian Society* (Toronto: Harcourt Canada, 2000), 254.

26. Chandrakant P. Shah, "Actions Speak Louder than Words." Retrieved from the University of Toronto Department of Public Health Sciences Web site: <http://phs.med.utoronto.ca/faculty/shahcaut htm.> February 18, 2002.

27. Henry P. Edwards, Ronald Melchers and Raymond St-Jacques, "Issue Paper: The Teaching Staff" (University of Ottawa, October 1992), 10.

28. *Étude,* 8–9.

29. Ibid., 86.

Mission Impossible?
Employment and Education Equity for Women Students
and Professors at the University of Ottawa

30. Information provided by Hélène Carrière, Director, Organizational Development, Office of the Vice-Rector (Resources), University of Ottawa.

31. Jill Blackmore, "Achieving More in Education but Earning Less in Work: Girls, Boys and Gender Equity in Schooling," *Discourse: Studies in the Cultural Politics of Education* 22, no. 1 (2002), 125. Our thanks to June Larkin for this reference.

32. Lyndsay Moffatt, "Education for Gender Equity: Origins and Development," in Tara Goldstein and David Selby, eds., *Weaving Connections: Educating for Peace, Social and Environmental Justice* (Toronto: Sumach Press, 2000), 168–195.

33. Jill McCalla Vickers and June Adam, *But Can You Type? Canadian Universities and the Status of Women* (Canada: Clarke, Irwin and Co., 1977).

34. For example, see Anne Innis Dagg and Patricia J. Thompson, *MisEducation: Women and Canadian Universities* (Toronto: Ontario Institute for Studies in Education, 1988); Rachel L. Osborne, "The Continuum of Violence Against Women in Canadian Universities," *Women's Studies International Forum* 18, nos. 5/6 (1995), 637–646; Erica van Roosmalen and Susan A. McDaniel, "Sexual Harassment in Academia: A Hazard to Women's Health," *Women and Health* 28, no. 2 (1998), 33–54.

35. See Jacqueline Stalker and Susan Prentice, eds., *The Illusion of Inclusion: Women in Post-Secondary Education* (Halifax: Fernwood Publishing, 1998). For examples of these micro-inequities, see The York Stories Collective, ed., *York Stories: Women in Higher Education* (Toronto: Tsar Publications, 2000).

36. Allison Young, "Linking Employment and Educational Equity," in Armatage ed., *Equity and How to Get It*, 62–78.

37. Eric Margolis and Mary Romero, "'The Department is Very Male, Very White, Very Old, and Very Conservative': The Functioning of the Hidden Curriculum in Graduate Sociology Departments," *Harvard Educational Review* 68, no. 1 (Spring 1998), 1–32. See also "Undergraduate Voices" and "Graduate Voices" in The York Stories Collective, ed., *York Stories*, 17–43 and 44–93.

38. Rashmi Luther, Elizabeth Whitmore and Bernice Moreau, eds., *Seen But Not Heard: Aboriginal Women and Women of Colour in the Academy* (Ottawa: CRIAW, 2001), 87. See also, "Faculty Voices" in The York Stories Collective, ed., *York Stories*, 94–180; Enakshi Dua and Bonita Lawrence, "Challenging White Hegemony in University Classrooms: Whose Canada Is It?" *Atlantis* 24, no. 2 (Spring/Summer 2000), 105–122; Dolana Mogadime, "Black Women in Graduate Studies: Tranforming the Socialization Experience" and Njoki Nathani Wane, "Carving Out Critical Space: African-Canadian Women and the Academy," in Njoki Nathani Wane, Katerina Deliovsky and Erica Lawson, eds., *Back to the Drawing Board: African-Canadian Feminisms* (Toronto: Sumach Press, 2002), 129–157 and 175–196.

39. Heather Menzies with Janice Newson, "The Over-Extended Academic in the Global Corporate Economy." *CAUT Bulletin Online.* <http://www.caut.ca/english/bulleting/2001_jan/comments.asp>. February 11, 2002.

40. Westmoreland-Traoré, "Educational Equity: 'No Turning Back,'" 38–39.

41. "Research Perspectives, September 1999. Special Issue." Retrieved from the University of Ottawa Web site: < http://www.uottawa.ca/vr-recherche-research/perspectives/special/s3.html>. July 30, 2003.

42. Ann Dowsett Johnston, *The Maclean's Guide to Canadian Universities* (Toronto: Rogers Publishing, 2002), 114.

43. Tim Lougheed, "Double Cohort Crowd Comes Early," *University of Ottawa Gazette*, 8 March 2002, 2.

44. Canadian Association for University Teachers, "Canada Research Chairs," *CAUT Fact Sheet* #13 (Ottawa: CAUT, 2001).

45. Allison Young, "Linking Employment and Educational Equity," in Armatage, ed., *Equity and How to Get It*, 66–67; and Canadian Association for University Teachers, "Household Spending," *CAUT Fact Sheet* # 3 (Ottawa: CAUT, 2001).

46. Gail Kinman, *Pressure Points: A Survey into the Causes of Occupational Stress in UK Academic Related Staff* (London: Association of University Teachers, 1998). See also Sandra Acker, "Caring As Work for Women Educators," in Elizabeth Smyth, Sandra Acker, Paula Bourne and Alison Prentice, eds., *Challenging Professions: Historical and Contemporary Perspectives on Women's Professional Work* (Toronto: University of Toronto Press, 1999), 277–295; and Dianne M. Hallman, "Coming Up for Air: Feminism, a Pedagogy of the De/Pressed," *Resources for Feminist Research/Documentation sur la recherche féministe* 26, nos. 1/2 (1988), 109–116.

47. "Major Educational Equity Achievements at the University Of Ottawa." Retrieved from the University of Ottawa Web site: <http.www.uottawa.ca/services/equite/eng/achievements2.html>. February 18, 2002.

48. Constance Backhouse, "Reflections on Feminist Activism Within Two Distinct Universities: Timing and Location for Transformational Activities," *Resources for Feminist Research/Documentation sur la recherche féministe* 29, nos. 1/2 (2002), 118–119.

CHAPTER 11

The Community Owns You:
Experiences of Female Chiefs in Canada

Cora J. Voyageur

GOVERNMENT POLICY PREVENTED First Nations women from holding the office of chief prior to the *Indian Act* changes of 1951. A year later Elsie Knott, of Curve Lake, Ontario, broke through her band's leadership gender barrier by becoming Canada's first female chief. There has been a steady increase in the number of female chiefs across the country since Chief Knott was elected fifty years ago. About 15 percent, or ninety of more than six hundred chiefs in Canada, are women, according to the Assembly of First Nations (the national political organization representing First Nations in Canada). Even though women's leadership involvement in reserve politics has increased over the years, it is still slightly lower than the female representation of 18 percent in provincial and federal politics.[1] Although increasing in numbers, female chiefs are still viewed as an anomaly.

This chapter examines the experiences of First Nations female chiefs as they negotiate their multiple roles as women, mothers, administrators, mediators, liaisons, community representatives and decision-makers. I wanted to know who these women were and how they navigated the hierarchies of gender and race, and the sometimes-unkind world of reserve politics. Based on discussions with these women, I report on their demographic information, how they obtained leadership amid the peculiarities of reserve politics, how they maintain it and the costs and rewards of holding their positions. I also asked the women whether they believed being a woman made a difference in their experiences and in the expectations others had of them.

I felt I had stumbled upon a treasure when I began researching this unique topic. To my knowledge there has never been a comprehensive study that addresses, or has even begun to address, the issues and experiences of women chiefs in Canada. Literature searches uncovered few resources. An academic literature search produced no entries on contemporary First Nations women in community leadership. However, I did find Katherine Beaty Chiste's article, which profiles women's increased political activity through her analysis of the Native Women's Association of Canada (NWAC) challenge to the Assembly of First Nations' involvement in the Charlottetown Accord in 1992. She argues that First Nations women are organizing and becoming more politically involved in Canada and that First Nations women are calling for social and political change in their male-dominated communities.[2] This might explain the dramatic increase in women chiefs in Canada during the 1990s. Phil Fontaine, former grand chief of the Assembly of First Nations, stated that there were forty women chiefs in 1990.[3] As pointed out above, this number is now closer to ninety.

My literature search of leadership in the First Nations community showed a definite male bias. Joanne Fiske points out that First Nations women are subjugated by a patriarchal system set out by the state and adhered to and supported by male-dominated chiefs and councils. This assertion is supported by my research: I found that male-dominated reserve administrations generally did not allocate resources for "female issues" such as family violence, daycare and education.[4]

In her study of Indigenous political structures, Jennifer Arnott argues that Indigenous women must play a direct and indispensable role in any emerging forms of self-determination with the community. Women, she points out, have a lot to gain by participating in the community's political process and the community can gain from focusing more on social rather than on strictly economic issues.[5]

A search of the *Canadian Periodicals Index* produced a smattering of short biographical articles about individual women chiefs, which portrayed them as peculiarities and entirely out of the norm for First Nation leaders. Two separate articles in the regional magazine *The Saskatchewan Indian* discuss Mary-Ann Day Walker of the Okanese First Nation and Alpha Lafond of the Muskeg Lake First Nation.[6] In the 1998 article, it was reported that many Saskatchewan women were taking larger roles in Saskatchewan

Indian politics and that when Alpha Lafond was elected in 1960, she became the first woman chief in her Saskatchewan community, serving as chief for two years but remaining on council for twenty. Chief Day Walker was described as a long-serving Saskatchewan chief.[7] Chief Walker was more fully profiled in the 1989 article, at which time she was in her fifth term as chief of the Okanese First Nation near Fort Qu'Appelle, Saskatchewan. She attended Saskatchewan Indian Federated College and worked as a field worker for the Saskatchewan Indian Community College. As chief, she implemented band policies and oversaw road construction and the building of a water treatment plant.[8]

In *First Perspective,* the Assembly of First Nations newspaper, Ralph Seddon wrote a brief article on two women chiefs: a non-Aboriginal woman named Margo Horvorko, who was elected chief of the Washagamis First Nation in Ontario in 1995; and Yvonne Norwegian of Jean Marie River First Nation in the Northwest Territories who was reported to have married into that community. As chief, Margo Horvorko secured project money and developed programs for the community. Yvonne Norwegian was described as beginning her public life through participation in community events and membership on the community's education council.[9]

Chief Lorraine McRae of the Mnjikaning First Nation of the Chippewas was profiled in another *First Perspective* article. Again, like Alpha Lafond, McRae was the first female chief of her community in Ontario when she was elected in 1994. Before assuming the chief's role, she had worked in various capacities within the community. As chief, she was responsible for getting their profitable Casino Rama up and running, which benefits both the Mnjikaning and other First Nations communities in Ontario.[10]

In *Briarpatch,* Constance Deiter Buffalo wrote an article about Chief Florence Buffalo, the first female of the Samson Cree Nation in Alberta. Chief Buffalo was profiled as a progressive, educated and committed leader of the oil-rich central Alberta band of five thousand. Her social work background (she was a former welfare administrator with the band) was touted as one reason for her election win. It seems that former male chiefs were elected because of their business backgrounds. Deiter Buffalo writes, "The [election] suggests that members are more concerned with social issues than business."[11] Chief Buffalo was described as a committed member of the community who participated in many of its functions.

Chief Sharon Bowcott of the Tsawwassen Indian Band in British Columbia was the subject of Ted Laturnus's article in *BC Business.* His story outlined the political, social and racial issues faced by this hard-working woman. He also profiles the development of conflicts between the band and the neighbouring City of Delta over a residential expansion project of an eighty-six unit condominium development on the reserve. Laturnus discusses her dealings with the mayor and council and a citizens' group called the Canadian Foundation for Individual Rights and Equality (FIRE), which "actively oppose the treaty process. It's their opinion that Indians are a burden on white people."[12] Kim Baird, the current chief of the band, reported that the project did go ahead at great expense to the band; because they were unable to hook up water and sewage to Delta's existing system, they had to install new systems.[13]

In 1989, the feminist journal *Canadian Woman Studies/les cahiers de la femme* featured a three-page interview with Chief Nora Bothwell from the Alderville First Nation. The story documents the personal and professional struggles Bothwell experienced as the leader of the 250-member band in Ontario. She describes the long hours she worked and the amount of reading and studying she had do to keep abreast of the diverse issues confronting her community. She credited her university education with giving her many of the skills she needed to perform her job but also acknowledged the support and assistance she received from her family.[14]

Today, First Nations women are beginning to move out of their lower-level administrative positions in the community into leadership roles. In this chapter, I attempt to look deeper into these women's backgrounds, moving beyond the cursory descriptions provided in the articles identified above. I explore who the women are, how they got to their positions and what factors empowered them to improve their social and political standing in order to take on the most important role in their communities. This information is drawn from the preliminary findings in the first year of a three-year research project. I collected data from fifty-four women chiefs between February and July 2000 through face-to-face interviews, telephone interviews or questionnaires.[15] What follows is based on the results of their candid responses.

Demographic Profiles

The data show that the respondents vary in age, community affiliation, marital status and familial situations but that there are many similarities between them. Table 1 shows the demographic profile of the fifty-four women chiefs who participated in this research.

Table 1: **Respondents' Demographic Profile by Demographic Categories**

Respondents' Demographic Profile N=54			
Category	*Number*	*Percentage*	*Cumulative %*
AGE			
Younger	13	24	24
Middle	33	61	85
Older	8	15	100
Total	54	100	
BORN INTO BAND			
Yes	43	80	80
No	11	20	20
Total	54	100	
MARITAL STATUS			
Single	6	11	11
Married	34	63	74
Common Law	9	17	91
Other	5	9	100
Total	54	100	
PARENT			
Yes	50	93	93
No	4	7	100
Total	54	100	
PARENT WITH CHILDREN AT HOME			
Yes	37	74	74
No	13	26	100
Total	50	100	
GRANDPARENT			
Yes	29	54	54
No	25	46	100
Total	54	100	

Source: Voyageur, *Female Chiefs Study, 2000.*

The women range in age from thirty to seventy-two years of age. I separated the women into three age categories: younger (up to forty years of age); middle (between the ages of forty-one and fifty-five years); and older (fifty-six and above). The data show that 61 percent (the majority) of women are in the middle category, 24 percent in the younger category, and the remaining 15 percent in the older category. The most common age for respondents is forty-five.

Many women, by virtue of their age, are sandwiched between caring for their own children (or grandchildren in some cases) and caring for aging parents. The women are dedicated family members and responsible individuals who feel that they cannot let their family members down. In fact, most say that they were approached by community members to run for chief because they are so responsible, which means that they continue their roles as mothers, grandmothers, daughters, community workers and so on in addition to taking on the added responsibilities as chief.

Approximately 80 percent of the women were born into the community they now lead while close to 20 percent married into the community. The fact that many were born into rather than married into their community figures prominently in their relationship with their community. Being born into their community means that the women grew up under the watchful eye of their community members. Their behaviour and leadership potential would have been gauged over their lifetimes. If they were deemed suitable community leaders, they were approached to run for office by community members. I liken reserve communities to small towns where everybody knows everybody else, and people know each other's business. Gossip is an effective form of informal social control in this environment. Anybody familiar with reserves knows that community members have long memories. A person is judged by their actions. If you or any of your relatives exhibit the exuberance of youth, the community will never let you forget it. However, on a more positive note, the community can identify a particular woman as being a responsible individual and a good candidate for a leadership role.

Growing up in a community and being known by its residents can be advantageous to a person with political aspirations. The recognition a woman receives from being a member of a well-respected or wealthy family[16] can serve her well because she can rely on her family's reputation and community alliances to help her win support among community members for her political initiatives and when she runs for office. In addition, a woman raised in a community is likely have an opportunity to work at various jobs where her commitment and performance can be assessed. This assessment can either support or hinder her later bid for political office. The women who married into the community and have become chiefs are actually leaders of their spouses' bands. These women too rely on the reputations of their families and their families' links with their communities. These associations can translate into support when they run for office.

One of the women who married into the community is non-Aboriginal.[17] This case is highly unusual; reserve communities are often socially closed and those born outside the community are not always accepted. One can assume that if a non-Aboriginal woman ran for office and the other contenders were from the community then the non-Aboriginal woman would have to have more support than the other candidates. In addition, non-Aboriginal women do not integrate well into the reserve setting. In some cases, Aboriginal women view them scornfully and see them as "stealing our men."[18] In this case, however, the non-Aboriginal woman overcame these obstacles and gained enough acceptance and support to win the election. She said at first she was reluctant to run but was asked repeatedly by community members who treat her reasonably well. She also reported that she is treated very well by the community Elders. This good relationship means a great deal to her and she feels comfortable going to them for advice. This respondent overcame the obstacles of race and worked hard to obtain support for her initiatives.

Most respondents have spouses: 80 percent are cohabiting, 63 percent are married and 17 percent are living in common law. These women said they rely heavily on their spouses for support. However, as with most cohabiting women and employed women, the domestic responsibilities rest solely with them. Only one of forty-three cohabiting respondents reported that she did not have domestic responsibilities. Balancing the demands of home, family and job is overwhelming for most of them. As one commented:

> It's different when you are a man. You have a wife. She is there to cook and clean. A man comes home, he puts down his briefcase, and his wife brings him some tea. He gets to relax. Even if he is unmarried, he generally has a mother or sisters who "take care of him." That would be the day when my brother would come over and clean my house because I had been at meetings all week!

Some women spoke with embarrassment of having to hire someone to clean their house. They feel as though they are not fulfilling their role as caretaker for their family, which suggests that the women think they should do it all.

Women with children living at home have a great deal of trouble juggling all that is expected of them. One chief I was interviewing said that she had just finished an all-day meeting with government officials and then had to stop at the grocery store to pick something up for dinner. She had been so busy that she had not had time for grocery shopping and the fridge was empty. She asked, "Who else is there to do it?"

A small percentage of respondents are single and are more likely to be younger and less likely to have children. Single chiefs have fewer domestic responsibilities than those with spouses and children and can more easily concentrate on work. But they also note that this lack of other responsibilities causes them to be consumed by their role as chief. They have to make a conscious effort to "get away from work" because there are always so many issues that need their attention.

Almost all the respondents are mothers (93 percent) with between one and eight children. The largest number of respondents have two children. Sixty-nine percent of the mothers still have children living at home with them. More than half (54 percent) are grandmothers with between one and thirty-five grandchildren, and some are great-grandmothers. Fifteen percent of grandmothers have grandchildren living with them. This means that many of them have to deal with the same childcare issues as their younger colleagues. This is not too unusual since having grandchildren living with grandparents, on either a long-term or short-term basis, is a fairly common situation in the First Nations community.[19]

Since chiefs travel as much as they do, they must find somebody to take care of their children, and it is important for the women to have a consistent and reliable person to do this. For the women with spouses, the spouses are the most likely person to take care of children when they are away on business. When spouses are unavailable, most of the women rely on relatives to help take care of their children. The reserve community differs from most urban centres because it contains an extended family network. Since most communities are small, the home of a relative who can care for the children is generally within walking distance of the mother's home and of the school, or the school bus provides transportation. For women living in urban areas, transporting children to and from school can pose a problem for those caring for their children.

This demographic profile shows that the female chiefs are fairly similar in their age, community affiliation and domestic situations. The majority are middle-aged women who were born into the community they now lead; the majority are married; all but one maintains a household; and most are responsible for caring for children, and in some cases, grandchildren. Their concerns of juggling work, home and family are similar to any other working mother. However, their positions place them in situations that are not usually experienced by most working mothers or by mainstream female politicians.

Obtaining Leadership

The reasons the women ran for chief were similar. The largest group stated that they felt that there needed to be "new blood" in leadership. "Leaders become complacent after a while and sometimes lose touch with the people who put them in office" stated one respondent. Another commented, "I knew I could do a better job than the guy who was our chief." Leadership in the reserve community can be held by one person over a series of elections or can be passed between a few people in the community.

Often, Elders, family or other band members mount campaigns to encourage the women to run. The women said they were honoured to be asked to run for chief but they had to determine whether they had enough support to win before agreeing to do so. A combination of support from family, encouragement, experience with community administration and a desire to make the reserve setting better for all members convinced them to throw their hats into the ring. "I was encouraged by others to run and they said they would support me," said one respondent. Another said that she ran to "carry on a family tradition."

The first campaign was a shock for many of the women, who confessed that they were unaware of how nasty an election campaign could be. There is a lot at stake — power, prestige, status and income. The winner has the power to make decisions that can affect the community forever; her victory will raise her status and give her the opportunity to deal directly with the community as well as with government and industry. The prestige of being a chief gives her membership into such exclusive circles as the Assembly of First Nations. What this person thinks can have an effect on local, provincial/territorial and federal politicians. Finally, the chief has the opportunity to earn a steady income. In many reserve communities, unemployment is relatively high. For example, Statistics Canada reports that the on-reserve labour force participation rate is only 56 percent, which is 10 percent lower than the Canadian labour force participation rate.[20]

The majority of women (61 percent) were elected the first time they ran. This success rate could be a result of name recognition, a desire for new leadership or the women's reputation of having a strong work ethic. Name recognition often comes from being a member of a politically involved family; it also comes from serving as a band councillor or from working in positions within the community. Many of the women said community members knew them for their past job performances. They had been effective and efficient community administrators and agency workers, which instilled confidence in their constituents.

The women experienced many of the peculiarities found in reserve elections but not often found in the mainstream electoral system. For example, a candidate with the biggest family can win an election because family members are expected to vote for relatives running for office. Voting for relatives is less likely to occur in mainstream politics since family members can be more dispersed and therefore less likely to live in the particular riding of the relative running for office. As with any election, it is always better to be on the winning side than on the losing side. Being on the winning side comes with the potential for political favour. The chief and council have the power to allocate scarce resources on the reserve.

There are usually a few families on the reserve that vie for leadership. One family may have a series of election wins or the leadership might seesaw between two or three families. This is not unlike federal politics in Canada. The Liberals and the Progressive Conservatives can alternate political leadership between them or one party can have a series of election wins. Most of the women come from politically involved families on the reserve. (This is discussed more fully below.)

Another oddity of reserve politics experienced by some of the women was that, as incoming chiefs, they could not depend on the outgoing chiefs and council to brief them and their new council members on pending band business or on current issues. Defeated chiefs are sometimes bitter over losing the election and will not orient the newcomers to office. This situation is less likely to happen in mainstream politics where the outgoing administration is expected to help the incoming government learn about policies, issues and other business. In mainstream politics there is a transition period between administrations where a few wrinkles are expected, but in reserve politics there is sometimes a complete breakdown of communication between the new and old government.

To further exacerbate their unfamiliarity, some new chiefs change the band administrators when they come into office. This often happens when the incoming chief is suspicious of the employees' loyalties; that is, the "old" employees might have an allegiance to the former chief. When this happens, the incoming chief and council[21] are at a disadvantage because then there are too few employees who can familiarize them with current policies, protocols and issues. If there is a lack of continuity with band business, current negotiations with industry or government could be temporarily halted.

Anyone familiar with band elections knows that the results can cause great divisions in the community. However, in the small reserve community it can also cause fissures within a family. Rarely in mainstream politics do you have siblings or other close relatives vying for the same seat in an election, but this is a regular occurrence in band elections where family members sometimes run against each other. I raised this situation with one chief and she said that this does cause problems for voters. Siblings can have the same attributes that make a good leader — the same upbringing, the same family connections and the same community support. She said to alleviate this problem, family members should decide who in their family[22] will run for office. This would ensure that the vote would not be split between family members. As the saying goes, "politics makes strange bedfellows."

Another unique electoral situation posed itself in one community when a band election saw a woman pitted against her husband for the chief's office. She won. She said that things were very cool around her house for a while after the election. "My husband felt rejected by the community, but he also felt too embarrassed about losing to me — a woman. He got teased." The above illustrations show that reserve politics create some unusual situations not normally found in mainstream politics.

People who live in the small community see each other almost every day. The winners must sometimes work or have constant contact with failed candidates, the failed candidate's relatives or those who supported other candidates. One woman said the former chief is now on her council and that he is "a royal pain." She pointed out that he opposes everything she tries to do. "It's like he is throwing up obstacles in front of me. He is supposed to try to help me but instead he tries to make things harder. He's undermining me." The situation can be tense, but many take the attitude that somebody had to lose, that this time they won, but next time they might not. One is reminded of the temporary nature of the position these women hold. They could potentially be out of job at the next election, which could be held within two years of taking office.

Maintaining Leadership

The women were able to maintain their leadership by using the formal and informal training they received. Their formal education ranges from Grade 9 to graduate university degrees, with the majority having completed Grade 12 (66 percent). The younger chiefs have higher levels of education than the older chiefs, and a number of chiefs have law degrees. Slightly more than half the women (56 percent) have some form of post-secondary education or training in business administration, political science, community development and law. Although the formal training provides them with the fundamentals to do the job, slightly less than half (47 percent) feel their academic training has prepared them for their role. As some pointed out, "Sometimes you just have to go with your gut."

Many noted that formal academic credentials earned in mainstream society did not necessarily ensure their success and support in the community. As one women put it, "The credentials are more for the outside world. 'Non-Indians' seem to respect you more if you have an education." Some feel, as many educated Indigenous people do, that they had to prove themselves all over again to the community. They had to win the trust of their detractors, and prove that they had not "sold out" to mainstream society but that their hearts and minds were still in the community.

However, a more significant factor in their political preparation came from the informal training they received during their socialization process; that is, what they learned from their families when they were growing up. They say they learned a great deal from being present when others (relatives and close friends of the family) were involved in and spoke of politics, strategies, government policies and band concerns. The majority of the women (77 percent) come from families that are politically involved. This includes primary male relations such as fathers, brothers, uncles and grandfathers — 56 percent of whom have been chiefs and 21 percent of whom have been band councillors. However, 11 percent of the women from politically active families have mothers, grandmother or aunts who are actively involved in politics.

Many of the women have been influenced by these politically involved family members. The women witnessed the respect these family members garnered in their communities, and commented that these relations taught them to keep themselves aware of what was going on in the government and in the community. Information and knowledge were seen as good things, and they were taught to file information away for a later date, because it might come in handy. They said they learned the "ins and outs" of politics at an early age, which acculturated and socialized them into the political realm of reserve politics. Many agreed that they were being groomed, however unknowingly at the time, for their present positions.

In addition, before becoming chiefs, 50 percent of the women were politically involved with a variety of organizations, ranging from Native women's associations, trade unions, student organizations, professional associations and Native Friendship Centres. Many commented that being involved with these organizations educated them on the idiosyncrasies of politics, taught them to deal with personalities and how to deal with others' personal agendas, and how to allocate scarce resources. These early political experiences were not seen entirely as "trial by ordeal," since many said that through these experiences they got to "know themselves," "trust their own judgement" and "live with their choices." Many gained confidence knowing that "they could live through the battle and come out on the other side," which taught them that because battles take up a lot of energy they had to "choose their battles wisely."

Sixty percent of the women were active on band councils as well. This made them aware of issues, agencies and protocol before taking on the leadership role as chief. Many mentioned that serving as a band councillor was a good "stepping stone" to the chief's position. The length of time they served on council ranged from one year to twenty-three years. The personal experience, education and training gained from these experiences have helped them to be effective chiefs, since chiefs often deal with many of the same issues.

For most chiefs, a longer term in office gives them more time to better familiarize themselves with the job and issues. Longer terms also allow them to give the community members better results. "When terms are short, you spend the first year getting to know the job and the second year trying to make things happen. The next thing you know, it's time for another election." Another respondent remarked, "With shorter terms, the leadership is on a continuous learning curve. This makes it difficult for new leaders because they need transition time to learn the ropes but many must 'hit the ground running.'"

Once in a leadership position, open dialogue with their community members becomes crucial. "Transparency is the name of the game," stated one chief. She said she "ran an open-door operation," which is the only way to maintain support. "If the community members think you are hiding something from them, look out!" While in office, most women seek support and advice from their community Elders, who hold a lot of respect and political clout on reserves.

The community has many issues that require attention, and the key to successfully addressing them is long-term and short-term planning. Long-term goals take planning and resources, while short-term goals can be realized more quickly and the community can see quicker results. For example, building a new school or nursing station takes time and commitment of capital. However, after-school or recreation programs can be more easily set up. They say their persistence and lobbying for funds sometimes pays off. This tenacity has allowed some communities to launch much-needed community programs and services such as providing a fire hall and a fire truck. The devolution policy incorporated by Indian Affairs and Northern Development has grossly underfunded program delivery monies to the reserve, which has stood in the way of some of their community initiatives.[23]

Does Being a Women Make a Difference?

Slightly more than half the respondents (51 percent) were the first woman to take this leadership role in their community. Others were the fourth female chief elected by the community. I asked whether they believed that gender was an issue for the voter. A majority said that they do not think the fact that they are female has much if anything to do with them being elected. As one chief pointed out, "I think they simply chose the person they thought would do the best job, [and] that person just happened to be a woman." However, another woman commented that she thought that some men in the community probably did not vote for her because she is female: "There are those male chauvinists in our community just like there are in every community. Too bad for them — I'm now the chief."

When I asked whether the community expected different issues to be addressed by female chiefs than by male chiefs, most women said yes. A slight majority (53 percent) said that different things are expected from them than are expected from men. They feel they are expected to be more motherly, gentler and more humanitarian in their policies and decision-making. While they are expected to deal with major issues such as high unemployment and housing shortages, they are also expected to deal with social issues such as family violence, education, social services and community healing.

The women chiefs emphasized a need to heal the community. They expressed deep concern over the legacy left by residential schools and believe that many people have fallen prey to alcohol and drug abuse. They were also concerned about the exchange of one vice for another, pointing to the phenomenon occurring in the community where drinking or using drugs is being replaced by gambling, video lottery machines or bingo. These activities detract parents from taking care of their children and their other responsibilities. The chiefs emphasized the need for a healthy community where children are well cared for by their parents and other social problems are under control. Although economic development is needed, it all depends on having healthy people to take on and maintain the jobs.

Seventy-one percent said they thought being a woman did play a role in their experiences; 27 percent said that being a woman did not make a difference; and the remaining 2 percent did not know whether their gender made a difference. Some of the younger chiefs said they felt they had two strikes against them when dealing with individuals outside the community because they are young and are women. One woman recalled that when she was at a chiefs' meeting and she made a suggestion, "everyone stopped and listened to what I had to say and then the discussion carried on like I hadn't said a word. A little while later, a male chief suggested exactly the same thing I had and he was acknowledged. They reacted like his suggestion was the most brilliant thing they had ever heard."

Those who feel that gender plays a role in their experiences are sometimes dismissed by people outside their community because they are women. Industry representatives are particularly disrespectful of them as women. One said "she had to play hard ball with an industry representative to let him know that she had some power of her own." Some spoke of being treated disrespectfully by Indian Affairs representatives when they first became chiefs. This treatment is consistent with the paternalistic attitude of some government workers but is said to have improved over time. Another chief commented, "I think they are starting to realized that we as Indians are gaining authority in legislation, policy and in the courts. We are now being asked our opinion and not just being told what to do by the department."

Perhaps the most startling finding in the research is that many women have feared for their physical safety since taking office. Many have been intimidated both overtly and covertly, reporting experiences of verbal abuse and threats of physical violence. One chief was almost run her down when she was walking along a road on her reserve; one had her home vandalized; and yet another reported that a note telling her to "back off" and a bullet were left on her doorstep. They have also been threatened more openly at meetings. Recalled one respondent, "Some of these men on council get so mad when you do not go along with them. Sometimes they bang on the table. I was pretty scared when this big hulking man was looking down at me trying to get me to change my mind. I didn't change it."

Coping Mechanisms

The women have developed a number of coping mechanisms to help them deal with all the pressures placed upon them. They learn very early on that they cannot personally do everything that needs to be done and realize the importance of having technical and emotional support. A support network of trusted friends, colleagues and family members is crucial. Trusted friends and family members who have served as chiefs are valued advisors, and Elders provide spiritual support. Many cited their spirituality as a source of strength during their low times. Some rely on traditional ceremonies while others attended organized church services. All said they pray for guidance.

They also surround themselves with trusted, loyal and competent workers, and delegate as much work as they can to council members and band administrators. The chiefs are not afraid to seek expertise in areas where it is needed, but will give specific portfolios to band councillors so they can develop expertise in a particular area and, at the same time, free the chief of those responsibilities.

It is critical, the women agree, to take time for their families and for themselves. This sometimes means taking time away from the community, since members have no qualms about coming to the chief's house if they need something or stopping the chief on the street to talk about issues or concerns.

Costs and Rewards

The women spoke honestly about their election experiences and the huge price they pay for their decision to enter reserve politics. Their choice to seek office hit some of them where it hurt them the most — with their family. Some say their children are bullied and taunted at school after the election. One respondent said that she was called at her hotel room when she was away on band business and told by the anonymous caller that her "old man was running around." Another commented, "If it is a close race it seems that all the stops get pulled out. Anything becomes fair game — family, children, your indiscretions as a teenager, something your cousin did — anything. When I think about it now it seems pretty pathetic but it was hurtful at the time."

Many of the women have problems dealing with media attention because it is sometimes probing and generally negative. Many are reluctant to speak with media people because, as one woman put it, as a First Nations person "I am often shown in a bad light. I'm shocked at some of the things I read in the paper because they are practically the opposite of what I said." Negative press is a taxing experience.

Nor is there much job security. "We do administration much like the Chief Executive Officer of a large company," reported one woman. "We make a fraction of what they make. If you listen to the Canadian Alliance you'd think we live like millionaires. We place ourselves in a precarious situation by taking this job. We have no job security, no pension and no benefits."

Many dislike the amount of travelling required to do the job effectively. Being away from their children and families is difficult for them because it disrupts their family life. It is not uncommon to hear them say, "My family complains that I don't spend any time with them anymore." Not only do they have less time with their families but they also have very little time for themselves. Their absence also causes complaints from the community. It is a Catch 22 situation, because chiefs must be out of the community and away from their families to meet with government and industry officials with whom they are planning development projects that will benefit the community. They also need to attend regional, tribal and national chiefs' assemblies to discuss common issues.

The job is not all bad, though. As mentioned earlier, the position does involve some pomp and circumstance. As leader, the women meet dignitaries, industry leaders and high-ranking government officials. They gain status by serving in the most prestigious position in the community and their decisions greatly influence and shape their community. The women liked being in a position of helping the community and trying to make things "get better for everyone." Many like the challenge of building a dynamic community and being part of new initiatives. As one woman put it, "It is a thrill to see something completed that started as an idea." Another woman said, "I have always been a doer. I like taking action and getting things done." Overall, the women have undergone many positive personal and professional changes since they became chiefs. On a personal level, they have learned more about themselves, improved their self-confidence and gained greater trust in their own judgement. On a professional level, they have come to know more about political and community issues and have a deeper appreciation for the challenging work that leadership entails.

*

I would like to thank the women chiefs who participated in my study. Their responses were honest, open and candid and made the writing of this chapter possible. Being a chief can be compared with being the mayor of a small town. But there is one significant difference. When you are a chief, you are expected to be universally available to your band members. As one chief expressed it, "The community owns you. There is no professional distance between you as leader and the band members who elected you. If they need something, they come to your house. I don't think that happens with a mayor."

NOTES

An earlier version of this chapter appeared in *Canadian Research Institute for the Advancement of Women 25th Anniversary Issue: Women and Leadership* (2002), 205–224. I would like to acknowledge my funding sponsors: the University of Calgary, the Canadian Research Institute for the Advancement of Women (CRIAW) and the Social Sciences and Humanities Research Council.

1. Jane Arscott and Linda Trimble, "In the Presence of Women: Representation and Political Power," in Jane Arscott and Linda Trimble, eds., *In the Presence of Women: Representation in Canadian Governments* (Toronto: Harcourt Brace, 1997), 1–17.
2. Katherine Beaty Chiste, "Aboriginal Women and Self-Government: Challenging Leviathan," *American Indian Culture and Research Journal* 18, no. 3 (1994), 19–43.

3. Linda Richardson, "Fontaine Urges Gender Equality: Native Women Must Fight for Freedom, National Leader Says," *Calgary Herald*, 30 November 1998, A9.

4. Joane Fiske, "Political Status of Native Indian Women: Contradictory Implications of Canadian State Policy," *American Indian Culture and Research Journal* 19, no. 2 (1995), 1–30.

5. Jennifer Arnott, "Re-Emerging Indigenous Structures and the Reassertion of the Integral Role of Women," in Arscott and Trimble, eds., *In the Presence of Women*, 64–81.

6. "Indian Women: Chief Mary-Ann Day Walker," *Saskatchewan Indian* 19, no. 2 (1989), 12; "Women Taking Over a Larger Role in Politics," *Saskatchewan Indian* 28, no. 2 (1989), 13.

7. "Women Taking Over a Larger Role in Politics."

8. "Indian Women: Chief Mary-Ann Day Walker."

9. Ralph Seddon, "Female Chiefs Recognized for Service Above and Beyond the Call," *First Perspective* 6, no. 2 (1997), 23.

10. B.B. Hobson, "First Woman Chief of Chippewas Gambles on the Future," *First Perspective* 6, no. 2 (1997), 35.

11. Constance Deiter Buffalo, "Florence Buffalo: The People's Chief," *Briarpatch* 25, no. 9 (1996), 2.

12. Ted Laturnus, "In your Face: When Tsawwassen Indian Chief Sharon Bowcott Wants Something, She Doesn't Let Diplomacy Get in Her Way," *BC Business* 25, no. 2 (1997), 3.

13. Kim Baird, personal communication with author, July 22, 2003.

14. "The Life of a Chief: An Interview with Nora Bothwell," *Canadian Woman Studies/les cahiers de la femme* 10, nos. 2/3 (1989), 33–35.

15. I used a semi-structured interview format that sought a variety of information about the women and their experiences. Approximately half the participants completed self-administered questionnaires that they completed and returned. The questionnaire included information in nine categories including demographic information; preparation for political life; role as chief; experiences as chief; community support; gender; family responsibilities; and views on other women chiefs.

16. The woman could potentially carry the stigma of belonging to a disreputable family, but generally those families are less likely to be involved with and successful in local politics. However, it is the "individual" themselves who must create a strong track record irrespective of familial ties.

17. Prior to 1985 and the passage of Bill C-31, the *Indian Act* allowed non-Aboriginal women to become an Indian legally. So, theoretically, there are non-Aboriginal women — women who are non-Indian at birth — who gained status through marriage and have become chiefs. This situation has caused quite a lot of controversy as was witnessed in a northern Alberta community in the late 1980s when a Métis woman who married into the reserve was elected chief.

18. There is resentment felt by some Indian women towards Indian men who marry non-Indian women similar to the feelings of women in the Black community or

other visible minority cultures whose men choose not to marry them but to marry someone from outside the culture.

19. Grandchildren sometimes live with grandparents to keep them company and to "look after" the grandparents. Grandparents sometimes provide short-term child-care and provide a stable environment for grandchildren when parents are having difficulties in their personal lives, are leading busy lives or away from home a lot.

20. Indian and Northern Affairs Canada, *Aboriginal Labour Force Characteristics from the 1996 Census*, Catalogue No. R21152000 (Ottawa: First Nations and Northern Statistics Corporate Information Branch, 2001), 2.

21. Councillors generally have staggered terms to help retain continuity after an election. However, this is not always the case.

22. Many reserves elections experience family-block voting. This means that people vote for their family members.

23. The devolution policy transferred the administration of programs to the reserves but did not provide the funding required to operate them.

IV

THE

INTERSECTION OF

GENDER, CLASS,

LANGUAGE AND

ETHNICITY IN

CYBERSPACE

CHAPTER 12

How Wired Are Canadian Women?
The Intersection of Gender, Class and Language in Information Technologies

Ann B. Denis and Michèle Ollivier

IN BOTH THE POPULAR PRESS and academic circles, increasing numbers of social analysts argue that we are witnessing the emergence of a new type of society, in which knowledge and information are becoming a major source of economic power and loose networks are replacing rigid hierarchies.[1] Analysts of the knowledge-based society, or information age, contend that knowledge, especially of a scientific and technical nature, has displaced raw resources and cheap energy as the driving force of economic change. In a globalized world shaped by stiff competition and rapid technological innovation, the ability to produce and use knowledge in different contexts is seen as a key to the economic success of individuals, corporations and nations alike. Analysts of the network society argue that we're moving away from a "little box society"[2] of well-defined social roles towards horizontal societies composed of weakly bounded and overlapping networks of equals.

The new information and communication technologies play a major role in these processes: first as a means of access to information, and second as a means of creating and maintaining ties, both strong and weak, with family, friends, acquaintances and colleagues. At least in principle, the Internet gives access to unlimited sources of information. It also provides the technical means for maintaining relationships across geographical boundaries. In spite of widely divergent stakes in the development of the new technologies, private corporations, governments, public institutions and progressive community groups unanimously claim that access to the new technologies is essential to meaningful participation in the knowledge-based, networked society.

This rhetoric of access to technology goes hand in hand with concerns about new sources of social inequality based on differential access to information and networks. In his trilogy on the information age, Manuel Castells[3] foresees the emergence of worldwide class divisions, which will place upper classes of highly educated, technologically savvy and mobile professionals living in megacities around the globe in oppositon to lower classes excluded from education and technology, most of whom live in the less economically developed South but also in disadvantaged areas of industrialized countries.

Fuelling these concerns, sociologists working in different fields and using diverse methodologies show that high socio-economic status is associated with wide-ranging social networks and broad cultural repertoires.[4] People with higher levels of income and education generally report knowing more people in a greater number of social categories. They also report wider knowledge of the arts and culture. Broad cultural resources serve as a "conversational lubricant," which facilitates access to wider social networks,[5] in turn increasing access to information about personal and professional opportunities.[6] Access to the full range of the new technologies, to broad cultural repertoires and to wide-ranging social networks are then mutually reinforcing sources of power: technology gives access to diverse cultural resources, which facilitate interaction with others in enlarged social networks. These networks provide diverse sources of information, which in turn increase one's ability to act strategically in different situations. Castells cautions against a Web "populated by two essentially distinct populations, the *interacting and the interacted*,"[7] the first using the medium's full capacity, the latter limited to a "restricted number of prepackaged choices."[8]

How do women fare in the knowledge-based, networked society? What kinds of information are especially useful to them, given the subordinate positions that they continue to occupy in many fields? How do women use networks to maintain ties with family members and friends? How do they use networks at work to gain information and create alliances? Do women's personal and professional networks differ from men's in terms of their breadth and strength? How do women use the Internet to access information and networks? What happens to gender inequality in the supposedly "horizontal" society? While current work on the knowledge-based and networked society provides a few insights on these issues, a full analysis of the implications of these changes from the point of view of women remains to be done.

In this chapter, we explore some of these issues. We are using data from the latest Canadian General Social Survey (GSS), Cycle 14, which in 2000 questioned a random sample of adult Canadians (fifteen years of age and older) about their access to and use of new information and communication technologies.[9] The limited available research on Canada indicates that these issues are not gender-neutral.[10] We first compare the access to and use of the Internet by women and men. We then focus exclusively on women, considering the effect of the intersection of socio-economic status and language on their Internet access and use. In the final section we reflect on our results within the broad framework of women and technology in a knowledge-based society, and we argue that a new conceptual framework is needed, one which starts from women's experience, rather than considering that women are deficient if their patterns of use do not conform to those of men. Although primarily based on our analysis of the GSS data, we situate our analysis in the context of other scholars' research and also draw on some findings from an exploratory study we carried out in the spring of 2000 with senior high-school students in four francophone schools in different regions of Ontario.[11]

Women and the Internet: The Gender Gap in Access and Use

The Gender Gap in Access

One of the first surveys of Internet use, undertaken by the Graphics, Visualization & Usability Center (GVU) in 1994, showed that women made up only about 5 percent of Internet users.[12] This widely publicized survey fuelled interest in issues surrounding women's access to and use of the new information and communication technologies. Since then, the gender gap in access has narrowed considerably and, in some recent studies, practically disappeared.[13]

Our analysis of the GSS data shows that in Canada small but persistent gender differences in access remain (see table 1). Throughout this cycle of questions, men systematically report a higher level of access than women do. Thus, 65 percent of men but only 60 percent of women have access to

Table 1: **Computer and Internet Access and Use by Sex**

| | Men | | Women | |
	%	N	%	N
Computer Ownership & **Internet Access**				
Access to a computer				
at home, work or school	64.5	7082	59.9	8408
Own a computer at home	54.2	5959	48.5	6824
Internet access at home	39.9	4381	33.1	4649
Internet Use				
Used the Internet:				
over past 12 months	52.3	5757	45.1	6352
Length of time has used Internet:				
less than 12 months	19.5	1113	27.1	1702
1–3 years	46.2	2628	50.1	3154
over 4 years	34.2	1944	22.8	1435
Intensity of Use				
Hours of Internet use at home, past week				
less than 2 hours	26.6	989	35.0	1259
3–7 hours	34.0	1263	31.6	1137
more than 7 hours	33.1	1230	22.7	815
not used during past week	6.2	232	10.7	384
Hours of Internet use at work, past week				
less than 2 hours	35.6	745	44.0	858
3–7 hours	29.1	611	24.5	477
more than 7 hours	26.4	553	17.6	34
not used during past week	9.0	188	13.9	270
Knowledge of how to use computers				
excellent	14.7	1124	8.0	736
v. good, good	46.4	3534	52.9	4896
average, poor	39.0	2971	39.0	3615

a computer, whether at home, at work, at school or elsewhere. Rather fewer of either sex have a computer at home (54 percent of the men and 49 percent of the women) and fewer still live in a household with Internet access (40 percent and 33 percent, respectively). Men are more likely than women to have used both a computer (63 percent versus 59 percent) and the Internet (52 percent versus 45 percent) during the past twelve months.[14] Men are also likely to have been earlier users of the Internet: over a third of the men and less than a quarter of the women have used the Internet for four years or more, while 20 percent of the men and 27 percent of the women have used it for less than a year. All of these differences are statistically significant: women's access to both computers and the Internet is less than men's.

Where does the gender gap in access come from? A recent American study using multivariate techniques of analysis suggests that the gender gap in access is to a large extent due to socio-economic factors.[15] Using data collected in 1996, 1998 and 1999 in the United States, this study shows that gender has no effect on Internet access when income and education are taken into account. In other words, the main reason that explains women's lower access to the Internet is their lower levels of income, rather than their technophobia or lack of interest.

Our own analyses of the GSS show a more complex picture (see table 2). When household income is taken into account, differences between women and men almost disappear and, in fact, in all but the lowest income category, women's use is slightly above men's.[16] When we take education into account, however, both among those with no post-secondary education and among those who have studied beyond high school, men were significantly more likely than women to have used the Internet during the past twelve months. Note that we refer to whether respondents have used the Internet over the past twelve months, not to whether or not they have access at home, at work or elsewhere. It is interesting that, although the GSS survey includes a question about access to *a computer* outside the home, there is none about access to *the Internet*.

All who had used a computer at some point were asked in the GSS survey to evaluate their computer competence, relative to others of their age (see table 1). While more men (14.7 percent) than women (8 percent) consider that they have excellent knowledge of how to use a computer, differences are small for the other response categories, with more women saying their knowledge is very good or good. Aside from the top response

Table 2: Internet Access and Use by Sex
Controlling for Income and Education

	Men		Women	
	%	N	%	N
Internet access at home by sex				
controlling for household income				
less than $20,000	18.3	186	13.5	269
$20–39,999	27.1	517	26.1	623
$40–59,999	39.7	724	40.0	769
$60,000 and more	62.6	1781	63.4	1494
Internet access at home by sex				
controlling for level of education				
primary and secondary	24.9	1182	19.7	1215
post-secondary	51.9	3169	44.0	3394
Used Internet over past 12 months				
by sex controlling for household income				
less than $20,000	30.7	311	26.7	533
$20–39,999	40.8	780	42.3	1009
$40–59,999	55.9	1021	57.3	1105
$60,000 and more	75.4	2143	77.2	1819
Used Internet over past 12 months				
by sex controlling for level of education				
primary and secondary	32.6	1547	24.8	1536
post-secondary	68.3	4172	61.8	4770

category of "excellent," women do not overall feel less competent compared to men. Turning to data which is not included in table 1, of the relatively few people interviewed in the GSS study who would be interested in using a computer, but have not done so, either within the past year or ever, there were modest gender differences in the major obstacle identified: a larger proportion of women than men mentioned cost (44 percent versus 40 percent) or not having access to a computer (10 percent versus 7 percent), while a larger proportion of men mentioned a lack of time (18 percent versus 15 percent), and not needing to use a computer (10 percent versus 7 percent) and equal proportions of men and women (16 percent) mentioned a lack of knowledge.

These results suggest that reducing the remaining gender gap in access would best be achieved with policies designed to improve women's economic situation and educational opportunities. In this sense, we do not share Bruce Bimbet's interpretation that the gender gap in Internet access "is not the product of gender-specific factors,"[17] since women's disadvantaged economic position results from gender-specific processes in the home and in the labour market. Moreover, our results do not suggest that women are more prone than men to technophobia.

The Gender Gap in Intensity of Use

While the gender gap in access has decreased, differences in the intensity remain important. Studies in Canada and the United States consistently find that men spend more time on-line than women. Men are overrepresented among moderate and heavy users while women are more likely to be light users.[18] Using multivariate techniques of data analysis, Bimbet found that the gender gap in time spent on the Internet remains relatively large, even when income and education are taken into account.[19]

Our own analyses of the GSS are consistent with these findings. Both at home and at work a higher proportion of women than men are light users, spending less than two hours during the week on the Internet, and a higher proportion of men were heavy users (see table 1). Our recent study of Internet use among young people suggested similar conclusions. Even among high-school students, young women spend less time on-line compared to boys.[20] Internet use at school, however, does not differ by gender, probably because Internet use in high school is highly structured within class time, and in post-secondary education, by course assignments.

The persistent gender gap in intensity of use suggests that access to the Internet and the intensity of its use are different issues. Whereas gender differences in access appear to be almost entirely reducible to income differences, the same conclusion does not apply to the gender gap in intensity of use. As argued by Paul DiMaggio and his co-authors, "[T]here is evidence that measures of access reflect resource control, whereas measures of intensity of use are driven more by demand."[21] The specific nature of women's "demand" remains to be explored.

Women and the Internet:
The Intersection of Socio-economic Status and Language

Internet Use and Socio-economic Status

Measures of socio-economic status and class are strongly correlated with Internet access and use.[22] American and Canadian multivariate analyses consistently find that access to and use of computers and the Internet are heavily (and independently) influenced by factors like income, education and occupation.[23] A higher level of education is associated with a higher rate of Internet use. Household income also has a strong influence on the likelihood of owning a computer and having Internet access at home. People with computers at home tend to use the Internet more, and in more varied ways than those who access them in other settings such as work, public libraries, schools or friend's houses.[24] Socio-economic differences in Internet access and use have weakened over time, with an increase in Internet use among those with low and middle incomes, but they nevertheless remain strong in Canada and the United States.[25]

The analysis we reported in the previous section of the continuing effects of gender on access when education was taken into account also demonstrated the very substantial effects of education, an important indicator of socio-economic status. Continuing our analysis of the effects of socio-economic status, we first confirmed the effect of education in the GSS data on patterns of differential access to and use of both computers and the Internet for men and women combined. We then focused our attention on women only (see table 3). Regardless of the specific variable considered, women with post-secondary education were about *twice* as likely as those with less education to have access to or to have used either a computer or the Internet. Turning to household income, computer and Internet access and use by women increased in a linear fashion from those whose annual household income was less than $20,000 to the highest category, those whose household income was greater than $60,000, typically with a gap of about 50 percentage points between the percentage in the lowest and the highest income bracket. Thus, 38 percent of the lowest income category and 92 percent of the highest one had access to a computer, while the percentages with an Internet connection at home ranged from 14 percent to 63 percent.

Table 3: Computer and Internet Access and Use among Women: The Influence of Education, Income and Language

| | LEVEL OF EDUCATION | | HOUSEHOLD INCOME | | | LANGUAGE SPOKEN AT HOME | |
	Post-sec. %	No post-sec. %	$60,000+ %	< $20,000$ %	English %	French %	Non-official/Multiple %
Computer & Internet Access & Use							
Access comp. work, home, school	78.3	37.7	91.9	38.1	63.3	53.2	47.5
Own computer at home	62.0	31.9	80.3	24.9	51.0	40.2	45.9
Internet access at home	44.0	19.7	63.4	13.5	35.6	23.7	32.0
Used Internet past 12 months	61.8	24.8	77.2	26.7	48.9	36.6	33.4
Intensity of Use							
Internet use at home, past week							
less than 2 hours	40.3	35.5	47.5	19.8	39.3	48.1	22.2
3–7 hours	35.3	35.9	35.9	36.0	36.0	31.1	36.4
more than 7 hours	24.4	28.7	25.2	44.2	24.7	20.8	41.3
Internet use at work, past week							
less than 2 hours	50.5	54.8	52.1	43.6	50.3	57.8	44.0
3–7 hours	28.5	28.1	28.8	28.2	28.4	27.4	32.1
more than 7 hours	21.0	17.2	19.1	28.2	21.3	14.8	23.8

Among women who *had* Internet access, the intensity of use, whether at home or at work, was affected much less by level of education or by household income. In fact, more of those with lower household incomes were high users at home (44 percent of the lowest income group as against 25 percent of the highest income group). Almost half the women in the top income category used the Internet two hours a week or less at home, in contrast to only 20 percent of the women in the lowest income group. This led us to wonder whether they were all using the Internet to do similar things. More research would be needed to explore whether the types of use also differ by income or education, a direction which follows from our proposal in the final section of this chapter that Internet use be analyzed as an aspect of cultural consumption.

Internet Use and Language

Studies of Internet use among francophones and anglophones show a persistent language gap in both Internet access and use in Canada[26] and in Quebec.[27] Compared with francophones, anglophones are more likely to have Internet access and they spend more time on-line. A recent study of Internet use in Quebec[28] shows, for example, that only 38 percent of respondents whose mother tongue is French had used the Internet in the week before the survey compared with 49 percent of those whose mother tongue is not French. Similarly, studies of Internet use among women's groups in Canada[29] and in Quebec[30] show that francophone women's groups are less likely to use the Internet than groups in anglophone Canada. Barriers cited by francophone women include inadequate financial resources, the scarcity of relevant French content, lack of time and training, as well as the absence of a critical mass of connected individuals and groups with whom to exchange information.

For our own analysis, we distinguished households where English is the main language spoken at home, households where French is the main language used, and those where the main language is neither of the official languages combined with those in which there are multiple main languages.[31] Comparing anglophones and francophones, the English speakers systematically have a greater access to computers and the Internet, with women speaking non-official or multiple languages occupying a middle ground between the two with regard to computer ownership and Internet access at home (see table 3). Francophones are more likely than anglophones to be light users at home and at work while anglophones are more likely to be heavy users. Compared with francophones and anglophones, women speaking multiple or non-official languages are overrepresented among heavy users both at home and at work.

Internet Use and the Intersection of Income and Language

Finally, we examined the effect of the intersection of language and income on Internet access and use during the past year. We wanted to see whether differences in Internet access and use between anglophone and francophone women disappear when household income is taken into account, as we found above when comparing women and men. The GSS data show that anglophones report higher levels of income compared with francophones: only 15 percent of the anglophones but 21 percent of the francophones have household incomes below $20,000, while 38 percent of the anglophones and only 25 percent of the francophones have a household income over $60,000.

Language and income level both significantly affect Internet access and use (see table 4): access and use increase as income increases, and at each income level, anglophones are more likely to have Internet access at home and to have used the Internet over the past twelve months. This suggests that the language gap in computer access and Internet use cannot be accounted for by income differences between the two groups. When we compared anglophones and francophones at similar income levels, the former remain more likely than the latter to own a computer and to have used the Internet over the past twelve months.

Women, the Internet and
the Knowledge-based, Networked Society

Should the gender gap in access and intensity of use be a source of concern for feminist researchers and activists? And, among women, should the class and language variations be of concern? Feminist perspectives on these issues have often been framed within a "women and technology" perspective, which emphasizes women's exclusion from the culture and practice of technology. This perspective generally rests on two interrelated assumptions. A first assumption is that access to, and more intensive use of, technology is inherently a "good thing" or, alternatively, that it is neutral, "simply a set of skills to be acquired."[32] Sharing the optimism and utopianism of early perspectives on the Internet, feminist analyses of the digital divide often continue to assume that the Internet brings desirable social outcomes such

Table 4: Internet Access and Use among Women: The Effect of Language Controlling for Household Income

	English only %	N	French only %	N	Non-official/Multiple %	N
% with Internet access at home by language controlling for household income						
less than $20,000	15.6	302	9.8	73	24.2	80
$20–39,999	28.3	819	19.9	206	31.7	113
$40–59,999	42.5	1125	31.8	272	39.7	96
$60,000 and more	65.2	2649	52.6	449	62.7	173
% having used the Internet over the past 12 months by language controlling for household income						
less than $20,000	29.9	579	22.3	166	30.0	99
$20–39,999	45.0	1305	33.5	346	38.0	136
$40–59,999	60.2	1596	47.7	1033	49.4	120
$60,000 and more	78.7	3197	67.1	572	67.5	187

as connectedness to others, better access to information and greater social participation. Underlying this argument is the belief that "people can convert Internet access into other valued goods, services and life outcomes."[33]

For example, in her insightful analysis of the knowledge-based economy and society, Heather Menzies equates intensity of use with social integration: "Although men and women reported almost equal degrees of usage in the 1–10 hour per month range, heavier use showed a dramatic divergence, with men constituting over 70 percent of more intense use — use associated with *meaningful participation*."[34] How one defines and measures meaningful participation, however, is not very clear.

A second and related assumption of the women and technology perspective is that women's lower access to and less intensive use of technology is a *problem* resulting from *barriers* such as lack of time, low financial resources and cultural conceptions of technology as masculine. This perspective too often leads to the adoption of a "deficit model"[35] of women and technology, in which women and girls are perceived as "somehow deficient and as needing to 'catch up' with men and boys by gaining access to this set of technical skills."[36] Women's more recent and less intensive use of the Internet is thus taken as an indication of their technological backwardness, which excludes them from full participation in the knowledge-based economy and society.

There is no question that economic, social and cultural barriers limit women's opportunities not only in the field of technology but also in many other aspects of their personal and professional lives. As argued above, lack of financial resources is largely responsible for women's lower rate of access to the Internet. Similarly, several feminist scholars associate women's less intensive use of the Internet with a lack of control over their time, which is too often "most legitimately allocated to the service of others both in the home and at work."[37] For example, Cynthia Fuchs Epstein argues that women (and other disadvantaged groups) face more rules and cultural prohibitions about using time in a way which allows "delegation, flexibility, and retreat from certain family obligations."[38] As well, women's relation to technology is influenced by pervasive cultural schemas which define men and their activities as high-skilled and technical while considering women as non-technical. In a qualitative study of women in computer courses, Flis Henwood argues that the gendered conception of technology has major consequences for women's ability to succeed in the field of computer science. She shows that, while women often succeed better than their male counterparts, they consistently underestimate their own ability and, more importantly, their expertise fails to be recognized by others.[39]

As in other aspects of their lives, women's lower economic resources and lack of control over their time, along with powerful cultural representations which define them as non-technical, undoubtedly represent serious limitations on their ability to access and use the Internet. Nor do we question that access to and use of the Internet can provide positive outcomes to individuals and communities. Given the scarcity of research on this question, it is probably prudent to assume that women's lower rate of access to and use of the Internet is a source of concern which must be addressed in research and public policy.

What we find problematic in this perspective, however, is the untested assumptions on which it rests and the broad generalizations to which it leads. For example, one can question whether intensity of use is necessarily a good thing leading to more *meaningful participation* in the new economy and society. Until we have a better idea of what people actually do on-line and off-line, this assumption is unwarranted and might simply reflect our tendency to take masculine behaviour as the norm and women's activities as a deviation. Is spending ten hours a day on chat lines or randomly surfing the net more *meaningful* than reading a book? Perhaps it is, but this needs to be demonstrated through careful argumentation rather than be assumed. We need to question the blanket assumption that each and every type of use of the new technology is equally beneficial to everyone involved. Research on these issues overwhelmingly indicates that technology, in and of itself, does not create positive outcomes.[40] Rather, the Internet tends to complement or reinforce existing activities. In a study of how people create and maintain networks on-line and off-line, Barry Wellman and his co-authors conclude that people's patterns of interaction on-line supplement "their face-to-face and telephone communication, without increasing or decreasing it."[41] Some research also suggests that positive outcomes disproportionately accrue to the already advantaged. Paul Attewell and Juan Battle, for example, show that, while access to a home computer is associated with students' math and reading grades, the benefits are greater for boys, whites and the economically advantaged.[42] The Internet thus provides advantages, but in a way that is unequal and that generally reflects existing patterns of advantage rather than radically altering them.

The deficit model of women and technology as articulated by feminists may thus inadvertently contribute to the reproduction of a binary conception of the world in which women are defined as deficient and technologically backward, and in which the Internet is seen as a threatening and unsafe space for them.[43] Men are depicted as having power and agency, whereas women are seen as powerless and victimized.[44] Masculine behaviour is taken as the norm and women's behaviour as a deviation. Because it rests on untested assumptions and leads to sweeping generalizations, this perspective may reinforce rather than challenge the very power structure that perpetuates women's exclusion from technology.

What can feminist research do to overcome the limitations of the deficit model of women and technology? We suggest three directions. First, we need more nuanced analyses of the various ways in which the Internet is used in everyday life. We cannot just assume that the Internet, with its extremely diverse uses and applications in the contexts of leisure, learning and work (both paid and unpaid), always leads to positive outcomes. Creating Web pages using html language, on the one hand, and surfing the Web looking for pornography or for Céline Dion's home page, on the other, involve different levels of skills and different orientations towards the medium. Increasingly, studies suggest that the "Internet is a very coarse unit of analysis. Interpreting what people do online requires analysis of various patterns of usage with regard to various applications."[45] We need to understand how women use the Internet in ways that change, accommodate or reproduce relations of power in various areas of their lives.

Second, research would benefit from shifting its focus away from the Internet as technology towards an understanding of the Internet as culture. As argued by DiMaggio and his co-authors, the Internet integrates both different *modalities of communication* (two-way interaction, group discussions, broadcasting and so on) and different *types of content* (text, video, audio).[46] The Internet has a cultural dimension, since it is shaped by people's cultural preferences — the types of music they prefer, the genres of books and magazines they read, the information they seek, as well as by how they relate to family and friends. Our study of how young Franco-Ontarians use the new technologies, for example, shows that the Web sites visited by girls and boys largely mirror gender differences in the quantity and types of books and magazines read by youth and adults.[47] Women and girls generally read more than boys and men, and a greater percentage of girls say that books are more interesting and useful for schoolwork compared with on-line resources. Men and boys, on-line and off-line, are more likely than women and girls to seek information related to sports, computers and politics. Should girls' preference for books over the Internet for leisure and schoolwork be considered a deficiency? Maybe it should, but the answer to this question needs to be built on careful arguments that are based on more detailed information about the meaning of these activities. Otherwise, our analyses simply reproduce binary assumptions about women's technological backwardness and about the lower value of their activities.

Finally, we need a better understanding of women's positions in the relations of power associated with the knowledge-based, networked society. If the new economy is based on access to diverse sources of information and on the ability to span wide networks, we need to know more about how women and men access information as well as how they create and maintain networks at home and at work and for what purposes. In order to understand whether the new technologies are beneficial or detrimental to women, we need to start from the point of view of their lives in the new economy. Analysts of the Internet often distinguish between two types of applications: one which gives access to networks (e-mail, chat rooms, electronic forums) and the other which mainly provides access to information (Web sites).[48] The second type is most useful for the acquisition of cultural or informational capital (access to information), while the first contributes to the creation of social capital (ties to others which provide emotional support and instrumental benefits). We need to understand how women use the new technologies in ways which increase their overall levels of cultural and social capital and, most importantly, how their uses of these technologies increase and/or constrain their power to make choices that enhance their lives in the new society.

NOTES

We wish to acknowledge with thanks the research assistance of Vickie Coghlan and the financial support of the Faculty of Social Sciences, University of Ottawa.

1. Barry Wellman and Keith Hampton, "Living Networked On and Offline," *Contemporary Sociology* 28, no. 6 (1999), 648–655; Manuel Castells, *The Information Age: Economy, Society and Culture,* Vol. 1, *The Rise of the Network Society* (Cambridge, MA: Blackwell Publishers, 1996).

2. Wellman and Hampton, "Living Networked On and Offline," 648.

3. Castells, *The Rise of the Network Society.*

4. Richard A. Peterson, "Understanding Audience Segmentation: From Elite and Mass to Omnivore and Univore," *Poetics* 21 (1992), 243–258; Bonnie Erickson, "Culture, Class, and Connections," *American Journal of Sociology* 102 (1996) 217–235.

5. Paul DiMaggio, "Cultural Capital and School Success: The Impact of Status Culture Participation on the Grades of U.S. High School Students," *American Sociological Review* 47 (1982), 189–201.

6. Mark Granovetter, *Getting a Job: A Study of Contacts and Careers* (Chicago: University of Chicago Press, 1995).

7. Castells, *The Rise of the Network Society*, 371. Italics in the original.

8. Cited in Paul DiMaggio, Eszter Hargittai, W. Russell Neuman and John P. Robinson, "Social Implications of the Internet," *Annual Review of Sociology* 27 (2001), 327.

9. Statistics Canada initiated the General Social Survey in 1985. The GSS is performed on a regular basis and it has two main objectives: to gather data on social trends in order to monitor changes in Canadian society over time; and to provide information on specific policy issues of current or emerging interest.

10. For recent Canadian feminist perspectives on women and the Internet see Melanie Stewart Millar, *Cracking the Gender Code: Who Rules the Wired World?* (Toronto: Second Story Press, 1998; now available from Sumach Press, Toronto); Barbara Crow and Graham Longford, "Digital Restructuring: Gender, Class and Citizenship in the Information Society in Canada," *Citizenship Studies* 4, no. 2 (2000), 207–230; Ellen Balka and R.K. Smith, eds., *Women, Work and Computerization: Charting a Course to the Future* (Norwell, MA: Kluwer, 2000); Leslie Regan Shade, *Gender and Community in the Social Construction of the Internet* (New York: Peter Lang, 2002).

11. Ann Denis and Michèle Ollivier, "Nouvelles technologies d'information et de communication: Accès et usages chez les jeunes francophones en Ontario," *Francophonies d'Amérique* 12 (2001), 37–49.

12. "GVU's WWW User Survey." *GVU (Graphics, Visualization & Usability Center)*. Georgia Institute of Technology. <http://www.gvu.gatech.edu/user surbeys/surbey-01-1994>. June 19, 2003.

13. For a review of recent Canadian and American studies, see Eric Fong, Barry Wellman, Melissa Kew and Rima Wilkes, "Correlates of the Digital Divide: Individual, Household and Spatial Variation." Barry Wellman's Home Page. <www.chass.utoronto.ca/~wellman/publications/index.html>, June 19, 2003.

14. In order to avoid having tables that are too extensive, certain percentages are discussed in the text but are not included in the tables. The information presented in this sentence is one such case.

15. Bruce Bimbet, "Measuring the Gender Gap on the Internet," *Social Science Quarterly* 81, no. 3 (2000), 868–876.

16. Both household and individual income are, however, questions with high non-response rates, so that on household income, we have information for less than two-thirds of the total sample. The pattern of non-response is higher for non-users compared with users as well as for females compared with males.

17. Bimbet, "Measuring the Gender Gap on the Internet," 868.

18. Fong et al., "Correlates of the Digital Divide."

19. Bimbet, "Measuring the Gender Gap on the Internet."

20. Denis and Ollivier, "Nouvelles techonologie ..."

21. DiMaggio et al., "Social Implications of the Internet," 311.

22. Fong et al., "Correlates of the Digital Divide."

23. Reza Nakhaie and Robert M. Pike, "Social Origins, Social Statuses and Home Computer Access and Use," *Canadian Journal of Sociology* 25, no. 2 (1999), 427–450; Bimbet, "Measuring the Gender Gap on the Internet."

24. Fong et al., "Correlates of the Digital Divide"; Christian-Marie Pons, Jacques Piette, Luc Giroux et Florence Millerans, *Les jeunes Québécois et Internet* (Québec: MinistPre de la Culture et des Communications du Gouvernement du Québec, 1999). Available on-line at http://www.gouv.qc.ca/culture/indexf.htm>.

25. Fong et al., "Correlates of the Digital Divide."

26. Ibid.

27. Centre francophone d'informatisation des organisations (CEFRIO), "NETendances – Années 2000" (2001). Retrieved from <www.infometre.cefrio.qc.ca/fiches/fiche 281.asp>. February 2003.

28. Ibid.

29. Leslie Regan Shade, *Report on the Use of the Internet in Canadian Women's Organizations* (Ottawa: Status of Women Canada, 1996); Michèle Ollivier and Ann Denis, *Les femmes francophones en situation minoritaire au Canada et les technologies d'information et de communication* (Ottawa: Fédération nationale des femmes canadiennes françaises and Industry Canada, 2002).

30. Nina Duque, *Recherche sur les impacts des nouvelles technologies d'information et de communication (NTIC) dans les groupes de femmes du Québec: difficultés et potentiel* (Montréal: Relais-Femmes, 1998).

31. For reasons of confidentiality, the GSS micro data file produced by Statistics Canada for public use only distinguishes these three categories. Such a breakdown does not lend itself to a refined examination of language variables. We would like to thank Kathryn Stevenson of Statistics Canada for her assistance, which allowed us to do special runs using more refined language distinctions. Since these results — for English (with or without a second main language) and for French (with or without a second main language) — were similar to those for English only and French only respectively, we have chosen to report the latter here, since this allowed us to use the same data base (the publicly available sample drawn from the GSS) throughout our analysis.

32. Flis Henwood, "From the Woman Question in Technology to the Technology Question in Feminism," *The European Journal of Women's Studies* 7 (2000), 210.

33. DiMaggio et al., "Social Implications of the Internet," 312.

34. Heather Menzies, *Women and the Knowledge-Based Economy and Society Workshop* (Ottawa: Status of Women Canada, 1998). Retrieved from <http://www.swc-cfc.gc.ca/publish/kbes-e.html>. February 2003.

35. Henwood, "From the Woman Question in Technology..."

36. Ibid., 210.

37. Gillian Youngs, "The Political Economy of Time in the Internet Era: Feminist Perspectives and Challenges," *Information, Communication and Society* 4, no. 1 (2001), 14.

38. Cynthia Fuchs Epstein, "Border Crossings: The Constraints of Time Norms in the Transgression of Gender and Professional Roles," Working Paper Series on Symbolic Boundaries 1. University of Virginia. <http://www.people.virginia.edu/~bb3v/symbound/wps/>. February 2003.

39. Henwood, "From the Woman Question in Technology ..."

40. DiMaggio et al., "Social Implications of the Internet."

41. Barry Wellman, Anabel Quan Haase, James Witte and Keith Hampton, "Does the Internet Increase, Decrease, or Supplement Social Capital? Social Networks, Participation, and Community Commitment," *American Behavioral Scientist* 45, no. 3 (2001), 437–456.

42. Paul Attewell and Juan Battle, "Home Computers and School Performance," *The Information Society* 15, no. 1 (1999), 1–10.

43. The following quote from Menzies illustrates this point. Barriers to women's participation in the new technologies, she argues, "include an overall social environment on the net that is *inhospitable* or *chilly* toward women, a lack of appropriate training and relevant content — good, *safe* women's discussion groups as well as data — and *outright sexual harassment* and prolific *pornography*." Menzies, *Women and the Knowledge-Based Economy and Society Workshop*. Our emphasis.

44. Chandra Mohanty makes a similar argument with regard to presentations of Third World women in Western feminist scholarship, which too often gloss over the complexities and heterogeneities of their lives to uniformly depict them as backward, illiterate, traditional, victimized and powerless. See Chandra Tapalde Mohanty, "Under Western Eyes: Feminist Scholarship and Colonial Discourses," in Anne McClintock, Aamir Mufti and Ella Sohat, eds., *Dangerous Liaisons: Gender, Nation, and Postcolonial Perspectives* (Minneapolis: University of Minnesota Press, 1997), 255–277.

45. B. Anderson and K. Tracey, "Digital Living: The Impact (or Otherwise) of the Internet on Everyday Life," *American Behavioral Scientist* 45, no. 3 (2001), 456–475.

46. DiMaggio et al., "Social Implications of the Internet."

47. Denis and Ollivier, "Nouvelles technologies..."

48. Michèle Ollivier, "Femmes, francophonie et nouvelles technologies d'information et de communication: Entre citoyenneté et consommation," in Andrea Martinez and Michèle Ollivier, *La tension tradition-modernité* (Ottawa: Presses de l'Université d'Ottawa, 2001), 69–84; Wellman et al., "Does the Internet Increase, Decrease, or Supplement Social Capital?"

CHAPTER 13

The Rise of Aboriginal Women's Global Connectivity on the World Wide Web

Andrea Martinez & Elizabeth Turcotte

WITHOUT ANY DOUBT, the Internet has played a critical role in the development of a "global sense of proximity," regardless of the time, space and geography that separate continents, countries and cultures. However, this tribal connectivity is not inclusive when around the world social stratification has created a vertical hierarchy of those who "have" and those who "do not have" access to the World Wide Web. In cyberspace, just as in the conventional media, discrimination and inequalities that are inherent to the larger social context shape agendas and communication practices. Beyond the philanthropic promises of information and communication technologies (ICTs), the American "free-flow of information" doctrine continues to reinforce the old patterns of cultural domination, appropriately described by Herbert Schiller[1] as a marketing system for the dissemination of alien values and stereotypes.

Moreover, the so-called new era of information and communication takes place within a general framework of *commodification*,[2] which is shaped by global media conglomerates whose objectives are to expand the production, distribution, exchange and consumption of marketable goods, services and information within and across nations. As a result, managerial interests that are broadened to include institutional and cultural areas such as public education and broadcasting tend to sweep aside citizenship alternatives to corporate power and electronic consumerism. In the last five years there has been an explosion of writing concerning the impact of the Internet technologies, most of it directed at business and the global market.[3]

Still, as Manuel Castells notes, information technology has quickly become an "indispensable tool for the effective implementation of ... networking as a dynamic, self-expanding form of organisation of human activity. This prevailing, networking logic transforms all domains of social and economic life."[4] Indeed, networking is not just about business, though, as people with at least some information about "power-knowledge" can use the Web to develop networks of advocacy for far-ranging issues and concerns. David Kim Juniper reaches similar conclusions, stressing the particular ability of the Internet to unite diverse groups into "powerful, transnational collectives"[5] whose decentralized operations, based on coordination rather than control, contribute to the rise of a global civil society.

Aboriginal women in North, Central and South America are one of the groups of people creating new kinds of electronic grassroots communication. It is hard, however, to find specific statistics to indicate with any accuracy the current and future trends concerning "women's internet use in developing countries ... The standard indicators are not disaggregated by sex, and the available data are not very reliable or comparable. However, it is clear that the numbers are small and the distribution limited."[6] Despite these small numbers, research still suggests that ICT is making gradual inroads into developing women's worlds.[7] But neither their empowerment as social subjects nor their contribution as active producers of meaning via the Web has been taken into serious consideration. The scientific literature often underscores the ways in which they are naming and reframing histories of oppression that transcend geographical as well as linguistic boundaries.

As the Internet expands possibilities for strong identity formation and coalition building, Aboriginal women are emboldened to voice complaints and raise questions about important issues such as racism, colonialism and imperialism, which were formerly ignored in mainstream feminist discourse.[8] However, connecting these issues simultaneously brings to the fore the existing imbalances in the world marketplace and the existing rigid social structures endemic in many Latin American countries which deserve renewed attention in order to make the notion of a shared global community more meaningful. Based on a substantial literature review, this chapter examines some of the contributions that Aboriginal women of the Americas have made to opening democratic spaces of political action. It also selectively explores a number of Aboriginal women Web sites in order to better understand the role the Internet plays in their ability to weave a new *rhizomatic*[9] gender-based fabric of struggle against invisibility, poverty, devaluation and daily violence. The sociohistorical conjuncture (that is, the unequal treatment and the exclusion rooted in colonization and patriarchy) and the multifaceted characteristics of Aboriginal women's emerging social movements provide the framework for the critical discussion.

The Sociohistorical Conjuncture

All over the world, most Aboriginal Peoples still do not have rights to their own territories. In Canada, the *Indian Act* — legislated in 1876 to determine who was entitled to be registered as an "Indian" — destroyed local economies by preventing the sale of produce off-reserve and by making it necessary for Aboriginals on-reserve to mortgage reserve lands in order to finance the purchase of farm implements with which to develop an agricultural economic base. In Central and South America, traditional livelihood and economic activities like hunting, food gathering and harvesting have become extremely difficult as large landowners and transnational mining companies deprive Indigenous peoples of their lands. Military force has frequently been used to impose an economic growth model based on the exploitation of cheap labour. As a result, most Aboriginal peoples remain confined to what UN General Secretary Boutros-Boutros-Ghali has termed *the margins of national and international life.*

Even the domestic agenda is daunting, with survival and racial and gender discrimination topping the list. Poverty and illiteracy are major obstacles inhibiting Internet access; most Aboriginal families do not have access to the Internet because they lack the financial resources to buy the technology and the technical skills to use it. Some efforts have been made to overcome these barriers through the establishment of various community networking projects, and especially projects directed at women's networking organizations. One of the main catalysts of Aboriginal women's political action to resist discrimination, transform gender domination and gain international visibility has been the establishment of the Indigenous Women of the Americas (IWA), a broad coalition of various autonomous women's organizations that was formed in 1996. With representatives from sixteen countries, IWA aims "to promote common understanding and goodwill between Indigenous women of the continent."[10]

Engaged in a long-term process of co-operation, IWA has become a strong Aboriginal voice in political, social and educational institutions. Sheila Genaille,[11] president of the Métis National Council of Women and co-chair of the IWA's Canadian Committee, notes that the Internet has provided an invaluable resource for networking among Indigenous women's groups and has enabled them to share ideas and experiences. Some of the issues discussed on-line include education; land rights and Aboriginal territory; preservation and transmission of Aboriginal languages, cultures and traditions; crafts and farm product marketing; reinforcement and autonomy of women's organizations; the exodus of Aboriginal youth to cities; and preservation of Aboriginal knowledge in the health field.

However, even once material conditions are created to provide computers, literacy and language still remain significant barriers. In the United States, the Native American Distance Education Community Web is attempting to address these material conditions by "gathering, cataloguing and distributing high performance computing programs, tools, and resources from the National Computational Science Alliance for utilization by Native American serving schools, colleges and universities."[12] Likely such a project will benefit young Aboriginal women as well as men attending educational institutions. Ironically, the latest data on Internet use collected by the American government excluded American Aboriginals. The government's report, *A Nation Online: How Americans Are Expanding Their Use of the Internet*, "is essential reading for it observes American's digital divide and serves as a primary reference point for federal decision makers attempting to expand digital opportunity to underserved communities."[13] As Kade Twist of the Digital Divide Network points out, the exclusion of data related to American Aboriginal peoples leaves the report unable to "provide a current measurement of the progress of information technology deployment efforts in America's most underserved geographic regions — Indian Country."[14] Though the absence of reliable statistics in the U.S. render the American Indigenous population invisible, Aboriginal and non-Aboriginal initiatives seek to address the digital divide even in Western developed nations.

Anyone "surfing the Net" cannot help but recognize the plethora of Web sites posted by Aboriginal groups across the Americas that are designed to promote cultural, political and economic activities and information sharing. Many of these sites aim to strengthen an Aboriginal culture destroyed by European contact with Indigenous peoples. Of the two thousand Aboriginal peoples who existed before Columbus arrived, only five hundred remain today.[15] Their proportion of the entire population varies depending on the country they live in. For example in Canada, Aboriginals represent only 3 percent of the total population, while in Latin American countries like Guatemala and Bolivia, Aboriginals constitute 66 and 71 percent of the total population, respectively. "There are 40 million indigenous people in the part of the Americas that stretches from Mexico to Cape Horn in Chile, with 59 percent of the women living in rural areas," notes Maria Elena Hurtado, adding, "four fifths of illiterate peasants are women of indigenous origin."[16]

However, these estimates of Indigenous peoples must be read with caution since different countries use different criteria for taking census counts of Aboriginal populations, particularly for persons of both Aboriginal and European heritage. In Latin American countries these census counts exclude mestizos, while in Canada an even more complex and fragmented Aboriginal identity has been constructed by state officials to count status Indians, non-status Indians, Métis and Inuit. Access to the Internet has the potential to challenge colonial impositions of imposed degrees of whiteness that fragment Aboriginal identity and representations of culture.

Indeed, the mission statements of many Aboriginal sites expressly emphasizes that part of their mandate or objective is to promote and strengthen Aboriginal identity. For example, the Confederation of Indigenous Nationalities of Ecuador (CONAIE) has led the Indigenous peoples of Ecuador from relative isolation to a more central position within Ecuadorian society. "CONAIE is the representative body that guarantees indigenous people the political voice that has too long been denied them, and that expresses their needs and goals within a rapidly changing world."[17] In tangible terms, however, such organizations rely on internal allies that are not always inclusive and reflective of Aboriginal women's experiences and needs.

Historically, the degree to which Aboriginal women held positions of authority in the family, clan and nation varied widely across geographic location and Indigenous tribal connections. Yet most Indigenous nations strongly believe that European colonization led to a "long and systematic devolution of the Aboriginal women's inherent rights."[18] In Canada, section 12(1)(b) of the *Indian Act* stripped Aboriginal women of their status rights upon marriage to a non-status Aboriginal or non-Aboriginal man. As a result, many Aboriginal women, along with their children and grandchildren, were dispossessed of their inherent rights. It was illegal for them to own, reside or be buried on "Indian lands," and they were denied any monetary benefits resulting from treaties. Although Bill C-31 was passed in 1985 to amend the *Indian Act* in order to eliminate the historical gender-based discrimination against Aboriginal women, "the current regime has a de facto form of a one-quarter blood rule, thus causing more Aboriginal people to lose or not qualify for Status Rights than the Indian Act."[19] Intermarriage between registered Indians and others over two successive generations has resulted in descendants who are not entitled at law to be status Indians. The struggle to reclaim respect for their own cultures and to promote Aboriginal women's identity in the larger society is reflected on these Internet sites as well as on those of larger Aboriginal projects.

The Canadian-based First Nation Information Project, for example, has a vision to "create an on-line atmosphere connecting the Aboriginal community with each other and sharing the aboriginal experience with those who desire this experience."[20] These themes of identity and collective voice are also echoed on the pages of Web sites devoted exclusively to Aboriginal women who are challenging interlocking hegemonic systems within Indigenous culture and within white culture. According to John Tomlinson, culture may be defined "as all these mundane practices that directly contribute to people's ongoing 'life-narratives.'"[21] That is not to say that the same mundane practices that contribute to these life-narratives are identical across gender, households, communities or countries. How these cultures reach across geography is one aspect of globalization. Fashion, labour, economics and ecology connect diverse peoples in one part of the world with those in another, but whose culture is being transmitted?

To what extent do these global cultural transmissions reach down into the lives of millions of people without access to marketing materials and the Internet? In other words, does the global community, or the connectivity that modern technology has provided across oceans and continents, really matter to those living in rural, remote or poorer areas of the globe? Are there vertical (or hierarchical) structures of accessibility that render notions of globalization a mute point to certain cultures? Moreover, whose local mundane life-worlds become culturally meaningful on a global scale? Can people with access to the Internet create transforming connections across global communities and how does "culture" remain intact or viable as a means of creating identification with that culture?

These are some of the challenges facing Aboriginal women as they attempt global connectivity via the Internet as a way to develop a strong voice for their political, social and economic agendas. Yet, at the same time, there is no single Aboriginal culture. Part of the struggle is to create horizontal connections and support networks to build greater awareness of these many and varied cultural identities. How then have Aboriginal women started to carve out a cyber-niche within the scheme of globalization?

Aboriginal Women's Networking

Many Aboriginal women's Internet sites are posted by individual, free-standing organizations and can be accessed through the links of a larger sites which are, in turn, hosted by an umbrella Aboriginal organization or by a mainstream information service provider.[22] The great variety of Web sites is owing not only to the different cultures from which they originate but also to the diversity of messages and services they offer. Although some Aboriginal women's sites clearly state that their intention is to empower Aboriginal women and create networks of education and knowledge, any person of any culture can access the information on these sites, and it is clear that information dissemination to non-Aboriginal people is a definite benefit. In other words, some sites may only offer membership to Aboriginal women but will simultaneously offer education to non-Aboriginal people about Indigenous women's issues and concerns.

The Institute for the Advancement of Aboriginal Women,[23] based in Western Canada, is a non-profit organization dedicated to promoting, improving and advancing the interests of Aboriginal women. It also promotes the unique contributions of Aboriginal women to both Indigenous women and those women in the larger society. For example, as a way of reclaiming the derogatory term "squaw," which they recognize as evolving out of Europeans' inability to pronounce the Indigenous word e*squao*,[24] the IAAW instituted the Esquao Award to honour deserving women who have made a difference in the Aboriginal women's community. In this way they promote the positive meaning of the word and educate women on issues of language and colonization. The site also posts local, regional and national conferences and special events and hosts links to other First Nations, Aboriginal and Indigenous Women's sites, as well as links to government, justice, media, culture, rights, education and business sites.

The American-based Native Web has a resource database that provides a number of links to other Aboriginal organizations, many of them specifically related to Aboriginal women's issues and concerns.[25] A large Canadian clearinghouse, the Turtle Island Native Network,[26] also provides links to dozens of organizations across Canada and the United States and in the Third World. There is also a page devoted to First Nation, Aboriginal and Métis women with links to historical articles and biographies of famous Indigenous women, current personalities and political issues.

Many Web sites not only promote cultural identity and respect for Aboriginal women but also address wider sustainable development objectives that are shared by both women and men of Indigenous cultures. The Indigenous Women's Environmental Network, for example, emerged from concerns around biodiversity issues. This network is "an ad hoc group of Aboriginal Women in Saskatchewan (Canada) who are concerned about environmental issues and the impact that mega projects have on Indigenous people."[27] Its Web site, which allows the group to disseminate information across the world, was made possible through the sponsorship of the American Indian Heritage Foundation in Washington, DC, demonstrating the international collaboration among Indigenous organizations to work collectively on matters of shared concern. This is another example of how larger and better-financed organizations act as service providers for smaller organizations to facilitate their ideas and worldview. As Steve Cisler points out, "One of the strongest reasons for having a presence on the Internet is to provide information from a viewpoint that may not have found a voice in the mainstream media."[28]

Other Web sites combine information, advocacy and economics. For example, the site of the Niagara Chapter of Native Women notes that its members "first came together for the purpose of organising political activities and supporting one another in an urban environment."[29] Its site is devoted to education, childcare and crafts. Browsers can view cornhusk dolls, jewellery, fabric items and sweetgrass and sage, which they can order on-line. The Upper Island Women of Native Ancestry,[30] based in British Columbia, sales raffle tickets on its Web site for handmade Native-designed quilts. Sales from the raffle raise funds for an academic scholarship for off-reserve students. Another Canadian site, ImagiNATION Cards, sells art cards and posters with Aboriginal messages that honour the earth.[31]

Using the Web to sell Native women's crafts is part of the economic structure of women's co-operatives in Latin America. In Guatemala, the Centro de Communicadoras Mayas[32] has a site where browsers can book workshops with a woman's co-operative to learn how to make videos or view and purchase handicrafts produced by women in rural co-opera-tives. The sales are handled directly by the women themselves. A few of these sites provide information about the success of their craft sales or about the number of people who have "visited" their sites, however small these numbers may be. An umbrella organization like Turtle Island Native Network, however, which provides links to many of these smaller organiza-tions, boasts twenty thousand to thirty thousand "hits" a day and more than six million hits a year.

Major Barriers and Challenges

Despite evidence that Aboriginal women in North, Central and South America have developed Internet networks to inform, involve and inter-weave their issues and identities in the global context, they still face many barriers in accessing and using Internet technology.

Lack of Infrastructure and Accessibility

One of the primary problems for large numbers of Aboriginal women is the lack of a technical infrastructure that support Internet resources in their communities. As one United Nations representative has written, "In a world where 80 percent of Internet users live in the richest nations and half the people on the planet have never made a telephone call, bridging the 'digital divide' will be an immense task."[33] South America's phone penetra-tion remains relatively low, in spite of variations from country to country. Despite great growth in Internet hosts during the last decade in the Latin American commercial sector, access to electronic communication by the majority of citizens and community groups is still limited. Key deterrents vary across the region — from monopoly ownership over telecommunica-tions infrastructure development by the state or a few transnational companies to basic infrastructure deficits, such as a national shortage of phone lines, service set up and operation costs and prohibitive tariffs for small businesses and community organizations.

The "digital divide" between the information rich and the information poor countries was a focus of the G8 summit in Okinawa, Japan, in August 2000. At that time, a Digital Opportunities Task Force (DOT Force) was established to work towards eliminating the divide in developing countries. "Moreover, the United Nations places access to information technology as the third most important issue facing women globally, after poverty and violence against women."[34] The digital divide, however, is not limited to developing countries. In the United States, "Native Americans (American Indians, Eskimos and Aleuts) rank far below the national average in their access to telephones, computers, and the Internet."[35] Rural Native American households, in particular, are lagging behind in connectivity. However, some Native Americans are gaining access to the Internet through the infrastructure available in school classrooms, from kindergarten to the twelfth grade. The propensity to seek out access in this way underscores the importance of making more community Internet centres available.

Native thunder.net has recognized the difficulties surrounding accessibility and has launched is own initiative to make the Web accessible to more American Indian Nations in both urban and rural areas. Its mission statement says, "With the emerging digital economy becoming a major driving force of our nation's economic well being, we must ensure that ALL Native Americans have the information tools and skills that are critical to their participation. Access to such tools is an important step to ensure that our economy grows strongly and that in the future no one is left behind." More importantly, the mission statement believes that "Nativethunder.net will become a major influence on the infrastructure development of the Tohono O'odham Nation."[36] Nativethunder.net, an Internet Service Provider (ISP) that is owned and operated by Native Americans, provides a diverse level of services and plans to offer low cost, local access to both rural and urban American Indian Nations, linking them to Native-focused businesses, artisans, educators and historians. In addition, Nativethunder.net is reaching out to schools to build its subscriber base, is establishing and supporting community access centres and community-based educational programs, as well as building strategic partnerships with other Indian Nations and technological alliances with major hardware and software manufacturers. This emphasis on public access is an important aspect that is needed to bring Internet opportunities to Aboriginal women and their communities across the Americas.

Social, Ethnic and Gender Inequities

The spread of community "free nets" such as the Association for Progressive Communications (APC), a global association of twenty-five non-profit computer networks, has established affordable, accessible, community-operated systems in many communities. But access for most people remains mediated by humanitarian groups or non-governmental organizations

(NGOs). To increase more direct access in communities, the APC implemented two community networking pilot projects in Latin America, in the mid-1990s, with the sponsorship of the International Development Research Centre (IDRC), a Canadian public agency. These projects, each of two years' duration, attempted to demonstrate the sustainability of telecentre facilities in marginalized urban neighbourhoods in Colombia and in Amazonian communities in Ecuador. The centres gave these communities greater access to computer networking and enhanced their ability to use and produce information to better meet their unique needs. The beneficiaries involved in these projects were three groups of Indigenous peoples in the Ecuadorian Amazon (the Sionas, Secoyas and Cofanes), and the low-income housing community groups in Santafé de Bogotá and Armenia of Colombia.

As primary providers of Internet access, two local APC nodes, Ecuanex and Colnodo, worked closely with local organizations whose mandates were to involve individuals in their communities' development. In partnership with a local NGO in the Ecuadorian Amazon, Ecuanex was expected to set up a telecommunications hub in Nueva Loja that would be linked with three to five computer-radio communications systems in Indigenous communities. In collaboration with Fedevivienda, a social housing umbrella organization in Columbia, Colnodo was expected to set up Neighbourhood Information Units where individuals and organizations could learn to use electronic communications in order to find relevant information and to participate in local community development.

Although APC telecentres represent an innovative approach to community network uses, results show that they generated conflicting dynamics among their executive members (NGOs, social organizations and grassroots communities). According to the project researcher, María Quintero, these conflicts seemed inextricably linked to the definition of priorities and the operational structures of each project participant.[37] Social participation in this regard goes beyond the idea of empowerment and democratization through a set of technologies; it points to a continual process of redistribution of social power connected to the larger economical, cultural and political context of the host societies.

In Colombia, popular grassroots movements have existed for a long time, and these movements have been linked to a well-established women's leadership that struggles against political repression and deterioration of family living conditions. Women have adopted collective survival strategies for the allocation of limited resources through informal networks of exchange and advocacy of community rights, thereby widening the symbolic context of the private domestic role into a public one. Consequently, women's participation as the project's telecentres' promoters received a positive community response: not only did the telecentres' team consist entirely of women, but the training process itself was driven by the specific realities of the women in charge of the Neighbourhood Information Units. In Ecuador, however, the Indigenous peoples involved in the project (the Sionas, Secoyas and Cofanes) did not have such organizational legacies to rely on, despite an emerging ethnic struggle of Aboriginal people fostered by the territorial expansion of oil and logging companies and the environmental effects of the irrational exploitation of natural resources.

Yet this consciousness-raising among Aboriginal women in Ecuador has not resulted in real advances in their living conditions. While Aboriginal men traditionally assume the leadership, women remain in subordinate positions and are reduced to working in the domestic and community realm. Furthermore, it is not surprising that, as a result of the women's participation in the pilot project, all the Aboriginal women chosen as the telecentres' promoters (seven out of a team of eighteen people) were close relatives (sisters and cousins) to the Indigenous community leaders. Consequently, failure to account for class issues and leadership structures meant an unequal distribution of the project's benefits and therefore obscured or silenced the experiences of women bound within patriarchal contexts. Far from reducing the gap between the information-rich and the information-poor, the project's restrictions on women weakened their ability to speak out publicly to their own people and to local government organizations and other state agencies. If access to new communication technologies is to be democratized, it will be necessary to ensure that gender, ethnicity, class, poverty, illiteracy and cultural inhibitions do not keep the technology out of Aboriginal women's reach.

More recently, APC and IDRC have been developing initiatives to improve marginalized women's access to the Internet. Many of these initiatives have a strong economic component as well. For example, the Internet Training for Brazilian Women's Network project was given CAN $10,000 for Rede Mulher de Educação (an NGO that promotes and facilitates the interconnection between women's groups throughout Brazil and abroad, constructing a network of services in popular feminist education). Ten women active in the Network in different areas of Brazil attended a sixteen-hour training session on ICTs and development. For these women, the Internet was seen as "a place to locate [themselves] in the world through the collective thought that transforms all human relationships and political action."[38] Another research program promotes using the Internet to strengthen communication among peasant women in Colombia. This project has earmarked CAN $11,525 to train fifteen women members of the Asociación de Veredas de La Calera and to "design and implement a strategic communication program that uses Internet resources and that is based on the daily lives of women in the Association."[39] These Internet tools are intended to help the Association's production and commercialization of handicraft and agricultural products, even though there is still the risk that the strategies focus on women as targets for economic integration and social processes of modernization.

In addition, the APC's Women's Networking Support Program (WNSP) — a network of over 100 women from thirty countries — provides training, participatory research, information facilitation and regional program support in order to respond to social, ethnic and gender inequities.[40] For example, the IDRC contributed CAN $242,200 towards Lessons Learned: Building Strong Internet-based Women's Networks, which was launched in September 1999 as an eighteen-month WNSP project. The WNSP has also helped to shape strategies for electronic networking, such as its "Gender and Information Technology" proposal made to the Fourth World Conference on Women in Beijing in September 1995, which has contributed to the ongoing implementation of Section J of the Beijing Platform for Action.

It is not impossible to imagine networks of Aboriginal feminists working together through Internet technology developing greater communications and reclaiming and restoring awareness of their respective issues and cultures. The Web already provides evidence of this type of global and decentralized networking through Aboriginal women's sites. The Indigenous Women's Network (IWN), founded in 1985, is one such collaborative effort founded to "support the self-determination of Indigenous women, families, communities and nations, in the Americas and Pacific basin." In 1997, this group partnered with Monsterbit Media to post live Internet broadcasts of the Indigenous Women's Network Third Biennial Gathering held in Texas.[41] The Global Women's Rights site posts resources, information and essays that support Indigenous women around the world, noting that "this site is dedicated to provide a forum for indigenous women to speak without the restrictions of borders through cyberspace on the issues concerning our survival."[42] Also politically oriented is the three-year-old World's Indigenous Women's Foundation, which was started by Native American author, professor and advocate Ardy Sixkiller Clarke. This site hosts the on-line journal "Smoke Signals" and schedules regular chat sessions. It also invites "men of goodwill, committed to the struggle of indigenous women ... to interact and collaborate with us in an effort to implement a global agenda for the rights of women of all ages throughout the world."[43]

Thus, although access to the Internet may be limited (and generalizations are difficult to make about the progress of Indigenous women's use of the Web), there is growing support across the Americas in favour of using information communication technology to generate collective voices for Indigenous women's rights and to disseminate information to non-Indigenous cultures about issues affecting them.

Both grassroots organizations (GROs) and grassroots support organizations (GRSOs) have been key players in the growth of the Third World independent sector and in the development of horizontal (that is, close to their constituencies) networking among women. As Julie Fisher points out:

> GROs are locally based groups that work to improve and develop their own communities through community wide or more specific memberships, such as women. Although many have been promoted by GRSOs, they have also become more active on their own. There are probably more than 200,000 of these in Asia, Africa, and Latin America. Faced with the deterioration of their environment and increasing impoverishment, both traditional and newly created GROs began organising networks among themselves.[44]

Intellectual Property Rights on Arts and Crafts

As Aboriginal women turn their knowledge of Internet technology to their economic advantage, the issues of ownership and potential exploitation of property come to the fore. A report about craft commercialization by Aboriginal women in Canada, co-ordinated by Angelina Pratt and Angela Laird of the Pauktuutit Inuit Women's Association (IWA), found that in 71 percent of the Aboriginal cultures represented in the sample, women were the primary producers of crafts. However, only 43 percent of respondents (90 percent were women) indicated that the sale of crafts was their only source of income. While Native artwork grows in popularity all over the world, very few Aboriginal women are taking advantage of the export market: most artisans rely on word-of-mouth for their business, operate as small business ventures and do not belong to any craft association or women's group. In looking at the major barriers faced by Aboriginal women artisans, Pratt and Laird cite start-up costs, lack of support networks and a lack of training, in addition to market saturation and family responsibilities. Although respondents were aware of the importance to protect their crafts by copyright, especially when they are original designs, only 12 percent have copyrighted their work. Many felt that they were unable to afford copyright because it requires financial resources to acquire and vigilance to enforce.[45]

As the Internet extends into most areas of the world without any international or even supra-jurisdictional control, the protection of intellectual property challenges regulatory policy interests and policy enforcement agencies. "Among Fourth World peoples," argues Harry Hillman Chartrand, "the oral tradition remains the dominant form of inter-generational and intra-generational transfer of knowledge. But can such knowledge be converted into property which will be recognized and respected by other cultures?"[46] At the moment, intellectual property rights are based on the concept of fixation in material form. No recognition is given to oral (ephemeral) tradition, even though it is essential for the preservation of Aboriginal cultural identity. Moreover, for Aboriginal peoples the issue of intellectual protection is based on a holistic concept of creation (intellectual property embodies the soul and spirit of a people) whereas to "the First World, intellectual property is a commercial commodity and the creator is the individual."[47] Indeed, add Pratt and Laird, many Native people

> feel that traditional designs cannot be the property of one individual or even any one Aboriginal group, which means that copyright and design protection laws, which by their very nature imply ownership by an individual or organization, are not effective for traditional Aboriginal designs.[48]

Based on the consensus that Aboriginal designs belong to all Aboriginal peoples, the World Intellectual Property Organization and the United Nations Economic and Social Council (UNESCO) created "Model Provisions for National Laws on the Protection of Expressions of Folklore against Illicit Exploitation and Other Prejudicial Actions" in 1985. Despite these guidelines for national governments to create legislation providing collective protection, and recommendation 3.6.7 of Canada's Royal Commission on Aboriginal Peoples[49] to ensure that "collective interests are adequately protected," Canada has not yet changed its legislation on the protection of intellectual property.

Meanwhile, the theft by non-Aboriginal people of Indigenous peoples' designs continues. In the absence of official legislation protecting Canadian Aboriginal crafts, Pratt and Laird highlight some solutions for artisans such as dating, signing and photographing works, developing their own "igloo trademark" that can be used on the sculptures produced by co-operatives, assigning serial numbers and doing limited editions. In the particular case of the Inuit, "etching a symbol on the bottom of their carvings even if the design has not officially being registered is another way of indicating that the design is not to be copied."[50]

Some discussions have been held concerning the use of information technology to digitally preserve Indigenous cultures. Representatives from Indigenous cultures across Canada and the United States, Australia, Brazil and Africa, along with academic experts in digital information research and technology, and representatives from cultural institutions and funding agencies met in Hawaii in the summer of 2001 to discuss technology, preservation and networking.

> The group learned that indigenous cultures hold varying perspectives about digital artifacts and networking. Indigenous cultures are rich, diverse, and precious. For those who seek and those who supply funding, technical assistance or other support the trusting role of each must be negotiated and sustained. They may find strength in collaborating; they may also find very marked differences in their perceptions, experiences and needs.[51]

These cultural differences, inevitably and inextricably, become entwined in the production of Web-based information and Web-page design in cyberspace.

The Issue of Language

"The issue of language dominance and the threat to linguistic diversity opens out to the broader issue of cultural imperialism: the idea that a global culture is in one way or another liable to be a hegemonic culture."[52] Because the vast majority of databases are created every year with English as the primary language, efforts have been concentrated on increasing Spanish and Portuguese information resources available through Web networks. Meanwhile, Native languages in cyberspace continue to be overshadowed by foreign (colonial) languages, regardless of the crucial role of the former to communicate among people at the grassroots level. Some believe that connecting Indigenous peoples to the Internet in the Northwest Territories may bring about "cultural assimilation and the continued erosion of Aboriginal languages." (Few of the nine Aboriginal languages spoken in the NWT are expected to survive this millennium.) Others like NWT journalist James Hrynyshyn consider that the Internet's "virtual communities" will help Aboriginal peoples maintain coherent group identities and resist assimilation into a larger society.

> Hrynyshyn believes that because the Internet can support an admixture of audio, video, and text, transcending the print medium, it is ideally suited to the oral story-telling traditions of the Aboriginal Community ... and ... predicts that Aboriginal cultures will "find it easy to identify themselves in the global culture linked by the net" and that the net will make it easier to "preserve artefacts of their culture" which will only make them stronger.[53]

It still remains to be seen whether adapting to technological change will keep alive the richness and diversity of Indigenous language and culture or perpetuate cultural dependency.

Among North American Aboriginal peoples, the preservation of Indigenous languages is a key issue to both Aboriginal women's and Aboriginal mainstream groups. While Latin American Web sites are commonly posted in English and Spanish, Canada's bilingualism is English and French. However, some innovative progress is being made. The Pauktuutit Inuit Women's Association's Web page is in both English and Inuktitut:

> It is Pauktuutit's belief that Inuit women have an integral role to play in the governing of our communities and our society. As Inuit women, we are the links to the past and links to the future. Inuit women are the vessels of culture, language, traditions, teaching and child rearing. These are the very important qualities to governing any society. Inuit women must take their rightful place as equals in the implementation of all self-governing arrangements and institutions.[54]

This language project is a work in progress but can be accessed through a special font downloaded from the Web site. Many problems were encountered in making this site operational in Inuktitut. The lack of compatible software and platforms between organizations; the absence of standardized keyboard mapping needed to get around a variety of dialects, each of which required a different font system; and finding ASCII coding for Inuktitut were among the major technical barriers.[55]

While the technology to develop software that can provide Web pages in Indigenous languages does exist and while the experience of the Inuit project could provide valuable lessons, these do not solve the problem of communication between Indigenous cultures. For instance, the Inuit and Cree languages are both syllabic but different, while the West Coast Haida have an alphabet language, making sharing of information in Indigenous languages across cultures very difficult.

Despite these obstacles, progress has been made in the development of language software. "Translation software, even to/from relatively obscure languages, is becoming easily available. However, more than translated material, original language content will go a long way to making IT relevant to local communities everywhere."[56] The Pauktuutit Inuit Women's Association Web page is one example, and another is the federal government's SchoolNet site, which hosts the First Peoples on SchoolNet Web pages. The section "Language Audio Samples" provides audio for nine different Aboriginal languages; one can hear someone speak in the language and, in some cases, simple English sentences can be translated into a specific Indigenous language.[57] The site also hosts language chat lines and mailing lists, development tools and provides links to language Web sites and language software. Thus, the barriers to accessibility created by an inability to translate the hegemonic languages into Indigenous languages are beginning to crumble. Networking and sharing of ideas must be an ongoing objective, however, in order to ameliorate English and Spanish as the dominant languages in the Americas.

*

This chapter provides evidence that information and communication technologies have been increasingly used by Aboriginal women in the Americas to promote cultural identity, informed advocacy and pride and respect for their Indigenous cultures. Although it is not our intent to make sweeping generalizations about the evidence presented here, the existing research so far suggests that one of the driving forces invigorating this social-oriented computer networking is the strength of women working with women from North to South as socio-political actors. Still, despite a growing number of Aboriginal stops on the information highway, access to computers and to low-cost service providers remain obstacles not only to poorer Latin American Indigenous peoples but also to poorer Aboriginal peoples in North America. European commissioner for development and humanitarian aid, Poul Nielson, says that "unequal access to ICT's among and within countries is a reflection of existing social and economic inequalities in both industrialised and developing countries. ICTs did not create inequality, but they may add to greater inequality unless we are conscious of their impact."[58]

Concerned non-profit organizations such as APC, government organizations like Canada's IDRC and even Aboriginal groups like Nativethunder.net are developing initiatives to push ICTs further into the poorer and rural communities across the Americas. Such projects also identify barriers that continue to prevent wider ICT use — for example, lack of financial resources and public access to computers, illiteracy and gender discrimination. For Aboriginal women, this situation is aggravated by their gender, economic poverty and ethnicity, often called the "triple burden." Even once basic infrastructure conditions are provided, the barrier of finding compatible software and platforms to meet their needs still exists. Although technology is developing programs for multilingual Web sites, these advances present a double-edged sword. Just as individual Indigenous Web sites may some day afford themselves of the potential to post Web sites in their own Indigenous language and thus reclaim this important cultural component, the multitude of Indigenous languages and dialects may be a greater barrier to inter-Indigenous collaboration and networking. In order to get their messages out to the global community and use the networking capabilities of the Internet to the fullest, Indigenous women of North, Central and South America still need to be bilingual (in their own language and in either Spanish or English) until such time that low-cost language conversion software allows women of one culture to translate into their own language the contents of other Aboriginal women's sites.

Engaging in alternative electronic networks represents a new trend in building a more democratic and empowered reality for Aboriginal women. However, the emergence of a global, network-based activism does not guarantee a better approach to transforming gender inequalities and redefining social and racial power distribution. "All the usual obstacles to mutual understanding and solidarity must still be faced by those involved in struggle."[59] In order to appreciate the "big picture," further feminist research into the significant factors of the digital divide that are stressed in this chapter — geography (urban versus rural), politics, economics, culture, language and literacy and gender — would be useful as would in-depth interviews with Aboriginal women actually using the Net.

NOTES

1. Kaarle Nordenstreng and Herbert I. Schiller, *Beyond National Sovereignty: International Communication in the 1990s* (Norwood, NJ: Ablex Publishing, 1993); Herbert Schiller, *Information Inequality: The Deepening Social Crisis in America* (New York: Routledge, 1996); George Gerbner, Hamid Mowlana and Herbert Schiller, eds., *Invisible Crisis: What Conglomerate Control of Media Means for America and the World* (Boulder, CO: Westview Press, 1996).

2. For a thorough analysis of this *commodification* process, see Vincent Mosco, *The Political Economy of Communication* (Thousand Oaks, CA: Sage Publications, 1996).

3. See, for example: Janice McLauglin, *Valuing Technology: Organizations, Culture and Change* (London: Routledge, 1999); Ray Broadus Browne and Marshall William Fishwick, *The Global Village: Dead or Alive?* (Bowling Green, OH: Bowling Green State University Popular Press, 1999); William A. Stahl, *God and the Chip: Religion and the Culture of Technology* (Waterlooo, ON: Published for the Canadian Corporation for Studies in Religion by Wilfrid Laurier University Press, 1999); David Shenk, *The End of Patience: Cautionary Notes on the Information Revolution* (Bloomington: University of Indiana Press, 1999); Naz Rassool, *Literacy for Sustainable Development in the Age of Information* (Clevedon, UK: Multilingual Maters, 1999); Zdenek Hanzlicek, "Effect of Information Technology on the Reproduction of the Dominant Class" (MA thesis, Carleton University, 1999); James Jeffrey, *Globalization, Information Technology and Development* (Basingstoke, UK: Macmillan, 1999); Brian Loader, *Cyberspace Divide: Equality, Agency and Policy in the Information Society* (London: Routledge 1998); Robert Waterman McChesney, Ellen Meiksins Wood and John Bellamy Foster, *Capitalism and the Information Age: The Political Economy of the Global Communication Revolution* (New York: Monthly Review Press, 1998); Manuel Castells, *The Information Age: Economy, Society and Culture*, Vol. 1, *The Rise of the Network Society* (Cambridge, MA: Blackwell Publishers, 1996); Manuel Castells, *The Information Age: Economy, Society and Culture*, Vol. 2, *The Power of Identity* (Malden, MA: Balckwell, 1997); David Homes, *Virtual Politics: Identity and Community in Cyberspace* (London, UK: Sage Publishers, 1997); Steven Johnson, *Interface Culture: How New Technology Transforms the Way We Create and Communicate* (San Francisco: Harper Edge, 1997); William J. Maertin, *The Global Information Society* (Aldershot, UK: Gower, 1995); David Lyon and Elia Zureik, *Computers, Surveillance and Privacy* (Minneapolis: University of Minnesota Press, 1996); Anthony Smith, *Software for the Self: Technology and Culture* (New York: Oxford University Press, 1996); William Wresch, *Disconnected: Haves and Have-nots in the Information Age* (New Brunswick, NJ: Rutgers University Press, 1996); Reginald Whitaker, *The End of Privacy: How Total Surveillance Is Becoming a Reality* (New York: New Press, 1999); Francis Fukuyama, *The Great Disruption: Human Nature and the Reconstitution of Social Order* (New York: Free Press, 1999); Andrew Calabrese and Jean-Claude Burgelaman, *Communication, Citizenship and Social Policy* (Lanham, MD: Rowman and Littlefield Publishers, 1999).

4. Manuel Castells, *The Information Age: Economy, Society and Culture*, Vol. 3, *End of Millennium* (Oxford: Blackwell Publishers, 1998), 336–337.

5. David Kim Juniper, "The Moccasin Telegraph Goes Digital: First Nations and the Political Usage of the Internet," in Sherry Devereux Ferguson and Leslie Regan Shade, eds., *Civic Discourse and Cultural Politics in Canada: A Cacophony of Voices* (Westport, CT: Ablex Publishing, 2002), 5.

6. Nancy Hafkin and Nancy Taggart, "Executive Summary," *Gender, Information Technology, and Developing Countries: An Analytic Study* (Washington, DC: Academy for Educational Development, June 2001), 1.

7. See, for example, the Web site *Development Gateway* at <http://www.development-gateway.org>, which provides links to a number of annotated articles concerning IT projects and developments specifically related to Indigenous communities in developing countries.

8. For a relevant feminist re-examination of the intersection of gender, class, racism and ethnicity, see Himani Bannerji, *Thinking Through: Essays on Feminism, Marxism and Antiracism* (Toronto: Women's Press, 1995); Patricia Hill Collins, *Black Feminist Thought: Knowledge, Consciousness and the Politics of Empowerment* (New York: Routledge, 2000); bell hooks, *From Margin to Centre* (Boston: South End Press, 1984); Rashmi Luther, Elizabeth Whitmore and Bernice Moreau, *Seen But Not Heard: Aboriginal Women and Women of Colour in the Academy* (Ottawa: Centre for Research in the Advancement of Women, 2001).

9. A metaphor drawn from Gilles Deleuze and Felix Guattari, *The Rhizome: A Thousand Plateaus* (Minneapolis: University of Minnesota Press, 1987), which refers to a horizontal and underground process of communication.

10. "Congress of Aboriginal Peoples." *Indigenous Women of the Americas.* <http://www.abo-peopoles.org/progams/iwa.html>. June 10, 2003.

11. Sheila Genaille, interview with Elizabeth Turcotte, Ottawa, Ontario, 6 November 2000. All subsequent references to Genaille's comments are from this interview.

12. Retrieved from the *Native American Distance Education Community Web.* <http://eot.ahpcc.unm.edu/community/>. June 10, 2003.

13. U.S. Department of Commerce, Economics and Statistics Administration, *A Nation Online: How Americans Are Expanding Their Use of the Internet* (Washington, DC: Department of Commerce, Economics and Statistics Administration, 2002).

14. Kade Twist, "A Nation Online, But Where Are the Indians?" *Digital Divide Network.*<http://www.digitaldividenetwork.org/content/stories/index.chn?key.215>. June 10, 2003.

15. Hélène Paré, *Aboriginal Women from Mexico, Central and South America* (Quebec City: CUSO, 1996), 7.

16. Maria Elena Hurtado, "Indigenous Women Suffer Double Discrimination." Retrieved from <http//yvwiiuusdivnohii.net/articles/indgart.htm>. June 10, 2003.

17. "Confederation of Indigenous Nationalities of Ecuador/Confederación de Nacionalidades Indigenas del Ecuador (CONAIE)." Retrieved from <http://www.conie.nativeweb.org/>. June 10, 2003.

18. Minister of Supply and Services, *Final Report of the Canadian Panel on Violence*

Against Women, "Extract of Chapter 15 on Aboriginal Women" (Ottawa: Minister of Supply and Services, 1993), 122.

19. Ibid.

20. "Home Page." *First Nation Information Project.* <http://www. johnco.com/firstnat>. June 10, 2003.

21. John Tomlinson, *Globalization and Culture* (Chicago: University of Chicago Press, 1999), 20.

22. See for example, *Sun Singer: Native Reference* at <http://www.sunsinger.org.refs/ canada/html>; *Native Web Resources,* which claims to prove a "cyber place for Earth's indigenous people," at <http://www.nativeweb.org>; and the *Aboriginal Multi-Media Society,* which offers an extensive list of links to dozens of Canadian Aboriginal newsletters, journals, articles and other information, at <http://ammsa.com/index.htm>.

23. "Home Page." *The Institute for the Advancement of Aboriginal Women.* <http://www. sites.netscape.net/iaw/homepage/iaaw.htm>. June 10, 2003.

24. The Algonkian word *esquao* — and its variants *esqua, squa, skwa, skwe* — means the totality of being female. Retrieved from the Web site <www.nativeweb.org/ pages/legal/squaw.html>. June 2003.

25. See <www.nativeweb.org>. It provides links to sites of such organizations as <http://www.nativecentres.org> and <http://www.honorearth.com>.

26. "News: Spotlight on First Nation, Aboriginal and Métis Women." *Turtle Island Native Network.* <http://www.turtleisland.org/front font.htm>. June 10, 2003.

27. "Home Page." *Indigenous Women's Environmental Network.* <http://www. indians.org/library/iwen.html>. June 10, 2003. This site does not allow browsers to have direct contact with the organization through e-mail but does include the area code and telephone number as well as the mailing address of one of its representatives.

28. Steve Cisler, "The Internet and Indigenous Groups." *Cultural Survival Quarterly* (1997). <http://www.cs.org/publications/CSQ/csqinternet.htm>. June 10, 2003.

29. "Home Page." *Niagara Chapter of Native Women.* <http:/www.ncnw.net/>. June 10, 2003.

30. *Upper Island Women of Native Ancestry.* <http://www.valleylinks.net/comunityser-vices/aboriginal/uiwna.shtml>.

31. *ImmagiNATION Cards.* <http://www.imaginationcards.ca>.

32. *Centro de Mujeres Communicadoras Mayas,* Venta de Productos Atesanales. <http://rds.org.gt/cmcm/coop2n.htm>.

33. Denis Gilhooly, "Deconstructing the Digital Divide," *Choices Magazine* (June 2001). Available on-line at <http://www.undp.org/dpa/choices>. June 10, 2003. Gilhooly is Senior Adviser to the United Nations Development Programme (UNDP) Administrator and Director of ICT for Development in UNDP.

34. Hafkin and Tagart, *Gender, Information Technology and Developing Countries,* 6.

35. "Fact Sheet: Native Americans Lacking Information Resources." *Nativethunder.net.* <http://nativethunder.net/about.htm>. June 10, 2003.

36. Ibid.

37. María Quintero, "Breves caracteristicas del Proceso. Informe de sistematización del Primer Año," in *Community Networking Pilot Projects in Latin America* (April 8, 1998). Electronic report submitted to the International Development Research Centre. Retrieved from <http://www.redecomunitarias.apc.org/research reports. html>. June 20, 2003.

38. PAN Projects: Equitable Access: Latin America, "Internet Training for Brazilian Women's Network." *IDRC*. <http://www.idrc.ca/pan/pr042404e.htm>. June 12, 2003. Further information can be found at <http://www.redemulher.org. br/ingles/projeto.htm#P5>.

39. PAN Projects: Equitable Access: Latin America: "Internet with Peasant Women Organization." *IDRC*. <http://www.idrc.ca/pan/pr04240_15_e.htm>. June 20, 2003.

40. "Women's Networking Support Programme" (1999). *Association for Progressive Communications*. <http://apcwojmen.org/>. June 12, 2003.

41. Andrea Thein, posting information about the broadcast of May 1997, on *Indigenous Women's Conference Broadcast Via the Internet*. <http://www.nativenet.uthscsa. edu/archiv/nl/9705/0065.html>. June 12, 2003.

42. "Home Page." *Global women's Rights*. <http://www.globalwomensrights.net>. June 20, 2003.

43. "Home Page." *World's Indigenous Women's Foundation*. <http://www.sixkiller. com/>. June 12, 2003.

44. Julie Fisher, "International Networking: The Role of Southern NGOs," in David L. Cooperrider and Jane E. Dutton, eds., *Organizational Dimensions of Global Change: No Limits to Cooperation* (Thousand Oaks, CA: Sage Publications, 1999), 213–214.

45. Angelina Pratt and Angela Laird, "Craft Commercialization and Intellectual Property Rights Among Aboriginal Women in Canada." A Report by the Indigenous Women of the Americas. (Ottawa, March 1997).

46. Harry Hillman Chartrand, "Intellectual Property in the Global Village." *Government Information in Canada/Information gouvernement au Canada* 1, no. 4.1 (1995). Retrieved from <http:.www.usask.ca/library/gic/v1n4/chartrand/html>. July 20, 2003.

4.7 Ibid.

48. Pratt and Laird, "Craft Commercialization and Intellectual Property Rights Among Aboriginal Women in Canada," 20.

49. *Canada's Royal Commission on Aboriginal Peoples*, Chapter 6, recommendation 3.6.7. Retrieved from <http://www.librauxus.com?RCAP/rcapdefault.htm>. June 12, 2003.

50. Pratt and Laired, "Craft Commercialization and Intellectual Property Rights Among Aboriginal Women in Canada," 20.

51. Daniel E. Atkins and Maurita Peterson Holland, guest editorial "Issues Regarding the Application of Information Technology in Indigenous Communities." *D-Lib Magazine* (March 2002). <http://www.dlib.org/>. June 12, 2003.

52. Tomlinson, *Globalization and Culture,* 79.

53. Barry Zellen "Surf's Up! NWT's Indigenous Communities Await a Tidal Wave of Electronic Information." *Cultural Survival Quarterly* (1997). Available from <http://www.cs.org/publications/csqinternet.html>. June 20, 2003.

54. "Home Page." *The Pauktuutit Inuit Women's Association.* <www.pauktuuit.n.ca>. June 20, 2003.

55. Pauktuutit Inuit Women's Association, "Inuit Women Connect: Telecommunications Report" from the 1997 Pauktuutit AGM, Ottawa.

56. Hafkin and Taggart, *Gender, Information Technology and Developing Countries,* 92.

57. "Language Audio Samples." *First Peoples on SchoolNet.* <http://www.schoolnet.ca/aboriginal>. June 20, 2003.

58. Poul Nielson, "Empowering the Poor: The Future for Information and Communication Technologies in Development." *ACP-EU Courrier* (May/June 2002). Available from <http://europa.eu.int/comm/development/publicat/courrier/index192en.html>. June 12, 2003.

59. Harry Cleaver, "The Zapatistas and the Electronic Fabric of Struggle" (1999). Retrieved from <http:/eco.utexas.edu/Homepages/Faculty/Cleaver>. June 20, 2003.

CHAPTER 14

The Gendering of a Communication Technology: The Short Life and Death of Audrey™

Leslie Regan Shade

THIS CHAPTER EXAMINES THE GENDERING of a recent communication technology — 3Com's Audrey™, an Internet appliance especially designed for women. Although released with great fanfare in October 2000, a mere five months later, in March 2001, 3Com announced "the end of life" for Audrey™. First, I describe Audrey™ via its promotional material and reviews, and situate it within an array of Internet appliances catering to the increasing domestication of the Internet. Then, I undertake an overview of the gender-technology dynamic as theorized in recent feminist literature with a specific focus on the gendering of digital technology, including Audrey™, as an exemplar of a new breed of domestic technology. Speculation as to Audrey's™ failure in the marketplace is followed by a brief survey of the "unintended consequences" of Audrey™, wherein a technology designed for women becomes appropriated by men in perhaps unforeseen ways.

Introducing Audrey™

In a 3Com press release, Audrey™ was described as

a breakthrough Internet appliance created for the kitchen, living room or "nerve center" of any home. Audrey, with one-touch access to email,

Internet channels, a household calendar, address book and Palm™
HotSync® technology, debuts as the first in 3Com's Ergo® line of
lifestyle-centered connected appliances.[1]

Internet appliances, a new addition to the panoply of consumer electronics,
are relatively inexpensive, single-purpose devices that typically feature a
browser and basic e-mail capabilities. International Data Corporation, a
telecom industry forecaster, released a study suggesting that by 2004 the
Internet appliance market would be worth U.S.$18 billion and encompass
90 million shipped units.[2] Internet appliances thus aim to position themselves as domestic appliances that will find a comfortable niche among an
array of other familiar appliances, such as the microwave oven, the toaster,
the pasta maker, the food processor, the bread maker and the cappuccino
machine. They are priced lower than standard PCs, although in the same
range as video game systems (between U.S.$200 and $600).

3Com's Audrey™ was introduced into the U.S. consumer market in
October 2000, with a suggested retail price of U.S.$499. According to Eric
Benhamou, chairperson and CEO of 3Com Corporation, "Audrey marks
3Com's entrance into a virtually untapped high-growth consumer market
and represents 3Com's strategic focus on providing radical simplicity to the
consumer."[3] 3Com is the company most famously known for its Palm Pilot,
the popular hand-held personal digital assistant that features a date book,
calculator, e-mail and wireless messaging application. Audrey™ was aimed
at early users, particularly family members who were already avid Palm
users. Synchronicity between 3Com products was possible as Palm users
could interact with Audrey™ "in order to share their daily schedules with
other family members."[4]

In a review of Audrey™, Jason Perlow described it as

fully self-contained ... in an 8-inch color touch-sensitive LCD
screen ... trapezoidal in shape and comes in a variety of neutral col-
ors, similar to those you would see on cappuccino machines, food
processors, blenders, and microwaves. It's patently obvious that
3Com intended Audrey for use in the kitchen or in other areas computers aren't normally designed for. The entire unit is constructed of
a strong plastic material, much like you'd see in a good kitchen
appliance. Audrey has a detachable wireless infrared keyboard that
slides onto the back of the unit for easy storage.[5]

With Audrey™, messages were meant to be composed by hand with a pen,
typed on the keyboard or spoken (no mouse was used). The operating system was the same as the Palm Pilot (the HotSync®), enabling users to

synchronize the Audrey™ date book and address list data with up to two Palm units using the built-in serial ports. It featured a built-in 56K modem for dial-up Internet access, allowing the user to access her/his personal Internet service provider (ISP) or link up automatically with AT&T's WorldNet, the proprietary ISP for Audrey™.

Market research (or, as the corporation termed it, "lifestyle research") conducted by 3Com revealed that "people want immediate access to specific information such as news, sports and weather,"[6] so Audrey™ came packaged with "preferred" Internet channels provided by 3Com providers (in other words, the content providers paid to be these "preferred" channels — a strategy similar to product placement in the film industry). These Internet channels scrolled across the bottom of the screen and included those provided by ABC (ABCNEWS.com for news), ESPN (ESPN.com for sports), CBS (MarketWatch.com for financial news) and Mr. Showbiz (entertainment and celebrity news). Up to six additional channels were available for selection, "from a growing list of lifestyle-oriented Internet content and e-commerce providers." Had Audrey™ taken off, other selected channels were to include Beauty.com, Drugstore.com, Wine.com, Food.com, Groceryworks.com, PurpleTie.com (a mobile dry cleaning and laundry service) and TVGrid.com (a source for television listings). To further encourage on-line shopping, credit card and shipping information would be kept "securely on file, allowing consumers to order Chinese take-out, purchase sunscreen for a weekend trip or buy a couple of CDs online at the turn of the dial."[7]

There is no doubt that 3Com was attempting to tap into the growing market of women on-line. A Pew Internet and American Life study released in 2000 revealed that women were the fastest growing on-line demographic, with older white and Asian-American women from a socio-economic range of middle to upper-middle class constituting the highest number. The most popular use of the Internet for women, the Pew study found, was e-mail, used as a way to keep up with distant family and friends and serving as an "isolation antidote." Women's most popular Web activities included looking for health or medical information, checking out job information, playing games on-line and hunting for religious or spiritual information. Men listed their favourite Web activities as looking for news and financial information, selling and buying stocks, looking for information about a product or service, participating in on-line auctions, looking for information about hobbies or interests, seeking out political information and checking sports and information.[8]

The Gender-Technology Dynamic

Feminist perspectives on technology have evolved over the last twenty years, but their insistence that social studies of technology instill a sense of the social consequences of technology has remained. Feminist theories and case studies of technologies have been preoccupied with ensuring women's equitable access to technological know-how in the workplace, in educational settings and in domestic contexts; with debunking the dominant masculinist mythos surrounding technology; and with the creation and practice of environmentally sound communities and technological methods.

As Cynthia Cockburn and Susan Ormrod argue, feminist historical analyses have underscored several conspicuous components missing from mainstream social studies of technology. Cockburn and Ormord point out that a focus on women can highlight the connections between production and consumption and between production and reproduction. It can also pinpoint the relevant social actors and the gendered assumptions in the design, diffusion and consumptive stages of a technology's life cycle. By bringing the "culture" of a technology into centre stage, "these studies show that technological change is quite capable of transforming detailed tasks and activities without changing the fundamental asymmetry and inequality of the relation between women and men."[9] Feminist analyses of technology, therefore, take an avowedly political stance through their concern with the implications of technologies for women, their work, reproduction and consumption, and in the wider sphere of the feminine domain: nutrition, horticulture, contraception, childbirth, the environment, and equitable educational and workplace sites.

Another significant body of research has looked at how communication technologies have been gendered both through their social uses — which have often been unintended — and their design.[10] The telephone is particularly illustrative here as demonstrated by Lana Rakow and Ann Moyal,[11] whose research has shown how women have used the telephone as a tool of community bonding and family "kin keeping." However, as Michelle Martin has demonstrated in a case study of the roll-out of telephone services in Canada, the original purpose of the telephone, as envisioned by Bell Canada, was as to meet the business needs of men.[12] The feminization of the telephone became apparent when women were first hired as operators, and then later when the telephone developed into more of a social culture. Telephone technology and design has since changed considerably in order to appeal to the female consumer, reflecting its status as an indispensable domestic artifact, through stylistic trends, including colours (from the plain black telephone to pale hues) to design (the Princess telephone and the cartoon-licensed phones) to technological innovations (push-button to portables).[13]

One of the focuses of feminist analyses has been on domestic technologies. These technologies, which were considered marginal or not subject to scholarly scrutiny, have become legitimate and vital venues for research, thanks to the pioneering work of Ruth Schwartz Cowan. In *More Work for Mother*, Cowan provides a history, not just of housework, but of household technologies. Through her concepts of work processes (wherein household work is inextricably linked to other household activities) and technological systems (wherein each household appliance is part of a system of implements), Cowan demonstrated how the rising industrialization of the nineteenth and twentieth centuries mediated the availability of tools necessary to fulfill domestic duties. She questioned how social and economic institutions affected the character and availability of the tools with which housework was done, and concluded that new tools and changing technologies created a rising expectation for American consumers. Ironically, the new tools and technologies also created "more work for mother" — between 1920 and 1960, women found that the new "labour-saving" devices multiplied their workloads. New technologies did not create more leisure time for mother, because "more" (in terms of cleanliness and a varied cuisine) was expected of her. As well, any semblance of the communality of household chores shifted to an individualized, suburbanized experience. For instance, laundry changed from practices such as neighbourhood "Blue Monday" sessions and the widespread availability of commercial services to individual home-appliance ownership. And the maintenance of many household technologies was simply not feasible unless there was someone at home full-time to operate them.[14]

The relations between gender, consumption and technology have been increasingly documented by several scholars, including Ruth Oldenziel, Cynthia Cockburn and Ruza Furst-Dilic, and Roger Horowitz and Arwen Mohun.[15] They have pointed out how, in many instances, technologies that exist in the women's sphere (such as domestic technologies) are oftentimes not considered "real" technologies. It is assumed that these "technologies of consumption," as Steven Lubar refers to them,[16] are to be consumed by women in a passive or prescribed fashion. Cynthia Cockburn remarks that technological designers are concerned with "designing the 'affordances,' what actions the machine can perform and the controls that activate them. They do their best to ensure that these are self-evident, 'speak for themselves,' encourage proper behavior, make disobedience or error impossible. The men have to imagine for this purpose the most unintelligent and catastrophe-prone woman."[17]

The gendering of computer system designs and feminist approaches towards these designs have also been the focus of a body of research and theory. Haraway has written that

> we must insist that high technology is for, among other things, the liberation of all women, and therefore usable by women for their self-defined purposes. Feminists must find ways to analyze and design technologies that effect the lives we all want without major dominations of race, sex, and class. Those goals will sometimes lead to insisting on small, decentralized, personally scaled technologies. Such technologies are not synonymous with soft, female, and easy.[18]

The late Margaret Benston was one of the first to consider how a feminist approach would differ from conventional design processes. For Benston, this involved a holistic look at technological systems and society, as well as a critical analysis of the various stakeholders involved in technological design and diffusion. Similar to feminist critics of science, Benston sought to demystify the masculinity underlying technological systems.[19] Joan Greenbaum and Suzanne Bodker have also analyzed the gender perspectives that underlie the systems development process, which typically ascribes male values (objectivity, impersonality, rationality, power) versus female values (subjectivity, personal feelings, emotions, love) towards "good system design."[20]

Lucy Suchman and Brigitte Jordan have argued that incorporation of the everyday work practices of the users of the technology is imperative in order to design appropriate technologies. In particular, a design that is sensitive to women's knowledge, concerns and work practices is necessary. For instance, women working in offices may have very different forms of organizational practices and routines that are either hindered or subverted by the technology they use.[21] The introduction of new communications technologies, can, in particular, exacerbate the tensions between management and the clerical sector, a majority of whom are women. It is very common for women office workers, as Ellen Bravo has illustrated, to have to cope with new computerized technology which they have not received prior support and consultation about nor received adequate training on.[22] Andrew Clement has examined how the introduction of computer systems in offices can disempower its female users when they are not consulted on the technology's use and purported applications for the office; and how women office workers "re-empowered" themselves through initiation of an action-oriented research project whose goals were to help office staff assess their needs and ultimately support their own use of computers.[23]

Eileen Green, Jenny Owen and Den Pain have also extended the principles of human-centered systems (HCS) to women who work in office situations, and they have asked "rather than reproducing existing class and gender divisions in the workplace, can human-centered approaches challenge taken for granted assumptions about the ways in which the 'technological' and 'social' or organizational domains are understood, during processes of systems development?"[24]

The Gendering of Audrey™

> We named it Audrey because we want to emphasize the personal nature of this appliance. We want you to think of her as a member of the family.
> — 3Com President Bruce Claflin[25]

How, then, was Audrey™ gendered? In her recent study of a community-based computer network in Amsterdam called the Digitale Stad (Digital City), Els Romms theorizes the concepts of user-representations, gender-script and domestication as entry points to describe its gendering through design.[26] I will use these concepts to tease out how Audrey™ was gendered.

When designers conceive a technology, they construct an "ideal" user for these technologies. Romms differentiates between explicit and implicit user-representations: explicit user-representations are those "in which statements are made of persons, of potential, embodied users or in which target groups are mentioned," whereas implicit user-representations refer to "neutral choices … that contain references to characteristics of users, which imply certain users and not others."[27] Technological scripts are defined "as the assumptions about the use context that are materialized in the technology, which pre-structure the use of technology … they attribute and delegate specific competencies, actions, and responsibilities to their envisioned users." When these scripts reveal gendered patterns, they become gender scripts, which "may emphasize or hide, and reinforce or diminish gender differences and gender inequalities."[28] Domestication refers to how technology is incorporated into the everyday patterns of the users and has been used by feminist scholars to study the ways in which users and families negotiate communication technologies within the household.[29]

Through its user-representations, technological scripts and overt normalization of domestication, 3Com conceived of Audrey™ in gendered terms. Consider its physical design. Computer design has developed over the years to reflect technological developments, from faster and smaller digitization mechanisms to wireless applications. With the exception of the Barbie computer and the Macintosh iMac computer (which comes in an array of funky colours), the design of the computer has been overtly masculine, although multimedia products are being increasingly designed for women, with ideas about femininity incorporated into the process.[30] However, the Audrey™ appliance can be seen as a particular instance where the technology (whose primary purpose is for e-mail and scheduling) has been developed as a specific female consumer item.

Judging by both its price and its promotional material (its gender scripts), Audrey™ was targeted and marketed expressly for upper- to middle-class women, and was featured in an array of designer kitchen colours — "ocean, meadow, sunshine, linen and slate." Advertisements featured Audrey™ as a new home appliance designed for women to keep up with their busy family lives. Indeed, 3Com hired anthropologists to study the "lifestyle habits" of families and found, not surprisingly, that "families are busy, and both their homes and their schedules are disorganized."[31] Audrey™ advertisements thus featured a date book ("keeps all your family's events in one place"), an address book, an e-mailer (letting one send "an e-mail in your own handwriting" and providing "instant access to e-mail"), and a Palm synchronizer ("keeps you on top of your family's busy schedule").

The marketing of Audrey™ as a domestic appliance was overtly described as "family friendly" and "a product easy enough for the whole family to use."[32] Ad copy further boasted that "Audrey has the taste for the latest information ... a flair for communication ... a gift for getting it done." One print ad, appearing in women's and lifestyle magazines like *Vanity Fair*, showed a refrigerator covered with a bevy of notes and photographs, birthday party invitations, soccer game schedules, prescriptions, magnets, notes ("Hi honey! Sorry I'm running late. Dinner is in the fridge, just pop it in the oven. I'll be back at 8"), shopping lists, recipes, postcards and children's paintings. The ad copy asked, "Audrey, anyone?" followed by the tagline, "Simple sets you free."[33] Another advertisement running on specialty cable channels showed a woman with her back to the camera and her face off-screen, looking for a soccer schedule over a cacophony of kids' voices and a dog barking. An off-screen female voice said, "Audrey, anyone?"[34]

According to 3Com's advertising copy, Audrey™ was designed as "the digital home assistant with style." Just as with the various designs the television set has assumed throughout the years to meld into the changing domestic décor,[35] the aesthetics of Audrey™ were carefully considered in relation to its alignment with other domestic appliances and its placement within various rooms in the home — kitchen, bedroom, family room. Audrey™ was a tool designed for the private, domestic sphere and was intentionally coded as female. Similar to other domestic technologies, it was designed with "affordances" and was promoted as a "labour-saving" device (think of the washing machine and dishwasher), a family organizer and communicator (e-mail replaces the telephone) and a leisure device (the Web-based channels, akin to television and radio soaps, perhaps).

Audrey™ Bites the Dust

The creation of gendered niche products is simply part and parcel of the crazy survival strategies of capitalism, and Audrey™ was no exception.[36] Why, then, despite the growing presence of women on-line and a fantastic surge in Web-based portals designed for women,[37] did Audrey™ cease to exist a mere five months after it was introduced into the marketplace? After all, it was even promoted by Oprah herself on her afternoon talk-show, publicity which targeted the right demographic of women.

One hypothesis I would advance here is that 3Com paid improper attention to the technology-gender dynamic.[38] According to 3Com's Website for Audrey™, the product was discontinued because "the market will take longer to develop than originally planned and require additional investment" and because of lower-than-anticipated sales. The end of 2000 witnessed what many analysts called a "dot.com meltdown," with e-commerce companies either drastically restructuring or going bankrupt. The business-to-consumer market declined precipitously, with lowered share prices, employee layoffs and stagnant on-line sales.[39] This slump, not unknown in the dizzying cycle of capitalist markets, was still, for many, a rude awakening in light of the ebullience of technological utopianism and market populism during the 1990s.[40]

One needs to ask whether women were responsible for the design or even consulted in the user-design process. Danielle Chabaud-Rychter argues that the design process of technological artefacts needs to involve a constant negotiation between the designers and the users of the products through usability trials.[41] Oftentimes, the marketing arm of the product generalizes the user, and in this case, it could be thought that "gender" was assumed to involve homogeneous characteristics. In her review of Audrey™, Alice Hill wrote that

> the set-up steps and all the various power cords and cables were carefully explained in a beautifully bound user manual that would look nice on a coffee table. Setting up Audrey was also a breeze. Sure, there were some over-the-top touches, like the little giggle when you powered up the unit, but the unit looked good in my kitchen next to the phone and answering machine.[42]

But, upon further interrogation, Hill became disenchanted with Audrey™. She found its design awkward: "The user interface was lifeless, while sending e-mail stooped over a kitchen counter was annoying at best, and surfing the Web on a slow and darkened touch screen was about as much fun as doing your taxes. Where was the need for that?"[43]

Was 3Com able to study how women use the Internet in their everyday life and how they become active users and negotiators of the technology? Studies on how women use e-mail and the Web show that they typically use it "instrumentally for activities which range from work, study, personal communication, seeking information, helping their children with homework, to buying and selling goods and services."[44] Audrey™ channels were limited to those with synergistic corporate relationships to 3Com, and the content of these focused on entertainment, sports, news and various e-commerce shopping activities. Perhaps the content of these could have been perceived by users as frivolous and not beneficial for their everyday needs; after all, if we are to believe the Pew report, women prefer to use the Web to access health, medical, religious, spiritual and job information.

The Resurrection of Audrey™

In an interesting twist, despite the "end of life" inflicted on it by 3Com, Audrey™ lives. Technological products often create unanticipated and surprising uses, and Audrey™ is no exception. A spontaneous community of

Audrey™ users thrives on the Internet, going beyond its proscribed tech-nological "affordances." Their goal: locating Audreys™, hacking Audreys™ and updating Audrey™ software. This virtual community is comprised of many Web sites, including Audrey Hacking (at www.audrey-hacking.com) and 3COM Audrey — The Unofficial Hack FAQ: Hosted by Chris Russo (www. 3rdmoon.com/crusso/audrey/). Some users have set up Audrey™ domain servers and others have configured its use as an MP3 player.[45] The curious thing is that, judging from the commentary from these Web sites, these avid Audrey™ users are all men who are tinkering with Audrey™ in their spare time.

In the meantime, other companies have started to promote gendered Internet appliances. For example, MailStation is a portable, cordless e-mail messaging unit that plugs into any household telephone outlet. Unlike Audrey™, MailStation only features e-mail, a date book and a spellcheck-er, and is priced considerably lower at U.S.$149. It is part of EarthLink, a national Internet Service Provider. Promotional materials on its Web site target housewives, as the on-line flash demo script is breathlessly read by a woman:

> What do I love about my MailStation? Let me tell you. I love getting mes-sages from my sister! I love that I can write her back while Emma's playing dressup! And I love that it's made staying in touch so absolutely simple. With my cordless MailStation model I can take it anywhere in my home and stay connected.[46]

Another communication technology designed with the female consumer in mind is the red "Ladyphone," developed by Samsung. The "Ladyphone" is a cellular telephone that is designed to be opened like a makeup compact, featuring "a biorhythm calculator, a fatness function that calculates a user's height-to-weight ratio, a calendar for keeping track of your menstrual cycle and a calorie-counting function. Enter an activity (cleaning, dishwashing, cooking, shopping) and the time spent, and the phone works out how many calories have been consumed."[47]

What is disturbing about these technologies is how they target, like many niche consumer products which include television genres, a stereo-typed vision of an upwardly mobile female commodified audience, which is what the commercial media system most wants to attract.[48] Absent from these technological designs (and their promotional material) is any awareness of the potential for women to use these communication tech-nologies to engage in the public sphere, contest political and social life and participate in civic engagement. Maria Bakardjieva and Richard Smith comment that what is needed is a "democratic counter-project for the shaping of the Internet as a communication medium," which is informed by an "emphatic understanding" of how ordinary users use the Internet in their everyday lives.[49]

Although these alternative technological designs will take time, women and gender must be incorporated into the design and use of technological products if change is to happen. This case study of Audrey™ reveals how benign technologies can become political entities, because their explicit and implicit user-representations, technological scripts and valorization of domestication continue to reify gendered roles and exclude women's politicized agency.

NOTES

Many thanks to Barbara Crow for her excellent commentary on drafts of this chapter.

1. 3Com Press Release, retrieved from <http://www.3com.com>. October 27, 2001. See also Jim Wagner, "3Com Unveils Audrey," *Internet News* (October 17, 2000). Available from <http://www.internetnews.com/bus-news/article/php/487011. html>.

2. Katherine Ohlson, "Will Net Appliances Edge Out PCs?" *PCWorld.Com* (June 18, 1998). Retrieved from <http://www.pcworld.com/news/article/0,aid,7056,00.asp>. July 3, 2003.

3. Bruce Meyerson, "Introducing Audrey: Charting Post-Palm Course, 3Com Unveils Internet Appliance," *ABCNews.com* (October 18, 2000). Retrieved from <http://www.abcnews.go.com/sections/tech/DailyNews/audrey001018.html>. January 5, 2003.

4. CNN.Com, "3Com Hopes 'Audrey' Will Rekindle Palm Magic," *CNN.com* (October 18, 200). Retrieved from <http://www.cnn.com/2000/TECH/computing/10/18/3com.audrey.reut>. January 5, 2003.

5. Jason Perlow, "Up Close and Personal with Audrey, 3Com's New Internet Appliance," *PalmPower* Magazine (November 2000). Retrieved from <http://www. palmpower.com/issues/issue200011/audrey 001.html>. July 3, 2003.

6. Technogadgets, "3Coms Audrey Brings the Net Home" (September/November 2000). Retrieved from <http://www.technogadgets.com/archives/September.Oct. Nov00/TG112800audrey.html>. January 5, 2003.

7. Ibid.

8. "Tracking Online Life: How Women Use the Internet to Cultivate Relationships with Family and Friends" (2000). *Pew Internet and American Life Project.* <http://www.pewinternet.org/ reports/toc.asp?Report=11>. July 3, 2003.

9. Cynthia Cockburn and Susan Ormrod, *Gender and Technology in the Making* (Thousand Oaks, CA: Sage Publications, 1993), 12–13.

10. See, for example, Leslie Regan Shade, *Gender and Community in the Social Construction of the Internet* (New York: Peter Lang, 2002).

11. Lana Rakow, *Gender on the Line: Women, the Telephone, and Community Life* (Urbana: University of Illinois Press, 1992), and Ann Moyal, "The Gendered Use of the Telephone: An Australian Case Study," *Media, Culture and Society* 14 (1992), 51–72.

12. Michelle Martin, *Hello Central? Gender, Culture, and Technology in the Formation of Telephone Systems* (Montreal: McGill-Queen's University Press, 1991).

13. Ellen Lupton, *Mechanical Brides: Women and Machines from Home to Office* (New York: Cooper-Hewitt National Museum of Design, Smithsonian Institute, and Princeton Architectural Press, 1993).

14. Ruth Schwartz Cowan, *More Work for Mother: The Ironies of Household Technology from the Open Hearth to the Microwave* (New York: Basic, 1983).

15. Ruth Oldenziel, *Making Technology Masculine: Men, Women and Modern Machines in America, 1870–1945* (Amsterdam: Amsterdam University Press, 1999); Cynthia Cockburn and Ruza Furst-Dilic, eds. *Bringing Technology Home: Gender and Technology in a Changing Europe* (Buckingham: Open University Press, 1994); and Roger Horowitz and Arwen Mohun, eds., *His and Hers: Gender, Consumption, and Technology* (Charlottesville: University Press of Virginia, 1998).

16. Steven Lubar, "Men/Women/Production/Consumption," in Horowitz and Mohun, eds., *His and Hers*, 7–37.

17. Cynthia Cockburn, "Domestic Technologies: Cinderella and the Engineers," *Women's Studies International Forum* 20 (1997), 361–371.

18. Donna Haraway, "Class, Race, Sex, Scientific Objects of Knowledge: A Socialist-feminist Perspective on the Social Construction of Productive Nature and Some Political Consequences," in Violet B. Haas and Carolyn Perrucci, eds., *Women in Scientific and Engineering Professions* (Ann Arbor: University of Michigan Press, 1984), 227.

19. Margaret Lowe Benston, "Feminism and Systems Design: Questions of Control," in *The Effects of Feminist Approaches on Research Methodologies* (Waterloo: Wilfrid Laurier University Press, 1989), 205–223.

20. Joan Greenbaum, "The Head and the Heart: Using Gender Analysis to Study the Social Construction of Computer Systems," *Computers and Society* 20 (June 1990), 9–17; Suzanne Bodker and Joan Greenbaum, "Design of Information Systems: Things Versus People," in Eileen Green, Jenny Owen and Den Pain, eds., *Gendered by Design: Information Technology and Office Systems* (Washington, DC: Taylor and Francis, 1993), 53–63.

21. Lucy Suchman and Brigitte Jordan, "Computerization and Women's Knowledge," in K. Tidjens, M. Jennings, I. Wagner and M. Weggellar, eds., *Women, Work, and Computerization: Forming New Alliances* (Amsterdam: Elsevier Science Publishers BV, 1989), 153–160.

22. Ellen Bravo, "The Hazards of Leaving Out the Users," in Douglas Schuler and Aki Namioka, eds., *Participatory Design: Principles and Practice* (Hillsdale, NJ: Lawrence Erlbaum Associates, 1993), 3–11.

23. Andrew Clement, "Computing at Work: Empowering Action by 'Low-Level' Users," *Communications of the ACM* 37 (January 1994), 53–63.

24. Eileen Green, Jenny Owen and Den Pain, *Gendered by Design: Information Technology and Office Systems* (Washington, DC: Taylor and Francis, 1993), 16.

25. Maria Godoy, "3Com Hopes Consumers Will Welcome 'Audrey' Home," *TechTV.com* (October 17, 2000). Retrieved from <http://www.techtv.com/news/computing/story/0,24195,3005889,00.html>. January 3, 2003.

26. Els Romms, *Gender Scripts and the Internet* (Enschede, The Netherlands: Twente University Press, 2002).

27. Ibid., 46.

28. Ibid., 15, 18.

29. See, for example, Ann Gray, *Video Playtime: The Gendering of a Leisure Technology* (New York: Routledge, 1992).

30. Hendrick Spilker and Knut. H. Sorenson, "A Room of One's Own or a Home for Sharing?" *New Media and Society* 2 (2000), 268–285.

31. Jennifer Couzin, "Too Cool for Christmas?" *The Industry Standard* (December 25, 2000). Retrieved from <http://www.thestandard.com/article/display/0,1151,20889,00.html>. July 3, 2003.

32. Todd Wasserman, "'Meet Audrey,' Says 3Com in TV Ads, Marking New Day for Web Devices," *Brandweek* 41 (November 27, 2000), 5.

33. Kate MacArthur, "3Com Refocuses on Brand in Wake of Its Palm Spinoff: Home Internet Strategy Starts with Audrey," *Advertising Age* (September 25, 2000), 233.

34. Wasserman, "'Meet Audrey,' Says 3Com in TV Ads, Marking New Day for Web Devices," 5.

35. Lynn Spigel, *Make Room for TV: Television and the Family Ideal in Postwar America* (Chicago: University of Chicago Press, 1992).

36. Consider the Gillette Company's Venus razor: it took four years, $300 million in development costs, and fifty patents in order to "revolutionize shaving and revitalize the company." Intense market research, including observing women shaving their legs, led to the Venus razor with its motto "Reveal the Goddess in You." See <http://www.gillettevenus.com/home.asp>.

37. Shade, *Gender and Community in the Social Construction of the Internet.*

38. I contacted 3Com to inquire about the design and marketing strategy for Audrey™, but they were unable to offer me any information.

39. "Internet Pioneers: We Have Lift-Off," *The Economist* (February 3–9, 2001), 69–72.

40. Thomas Frank, *One Market, Under God: Extreme Capitalism, Market Populism, and the End of Democratic Democracy* (New York: Doubleday, 2000).

41. Danielle Chabaud-Rychter, "Women Users in the Design Process of a Food Robot: Innovation in a French Domestic Appliance Company," in Cockburn and Furst-Dilic, eds., *Bringing Technology Home*, 77–93.

42. Alice Hill, "Jilted by 3Com's Audrey," *ZDNet News* (December 26, 2000). Retrieved from <http://www.zdnet.com>. January 5, 2003.

43. Alice Hill, "Why Internet Appliances Failed," *ZDNet News* (April 2, 2001). Retrieved from <http://zdnet.com.com/2100-11-529135.html>. January 5, 2003.

44. Supriya Singh, "Gender and the Use of the Internet at Home," *New Media and Society* 3 (2001), 397.

45. "For the Love of Audrey," *Telephony* (November 26, 2001), 26.

46. Retrieved from <http://www.earthlinknet/home/mailstation/models/ms150>. July 3, 2003.

47. "From Cell Phones to Self Phones," *The Economist* (January 24, 2002). Retrieved from <http://www.economist/com/business/displayStory.cfm?Story ID=954329>. January 5, 2003.

48. Eileen R. Meehan, "Gendering the Commodity Audience: Critical Media Research, Feminism, and Political Economy," in Eileen R. Meehan and Ellen Riordan, eds. *Sex and Money: Feminism and Political Economy in the Media* (Minneapolis: University of Minnesota Press, 2001), 209–222.

49. Maria Bakardjieva and Richard Smith, "The Internet in Everyday Life," *New Media and Society* 3 (2001), 67–83.

Contributors

CAROLINE ANDREW is a Professor of Political Science at the University of Ottawa. Her research interests include women and local politics, municipal politics and urban governance. Recent publications include *Urban Affairs: Back on the Policy Agenda* (co-edited with Katherine Graham and Susan Phillips, 2002); "The Shame of (Ignoring) the Cities," *Journal of Canadian Studies* (2000–2001); and "Municipal Restructuring, Urban Services and the Potential for the Creation of Transformative Political Spaces," in *Changing Canada* (2003). She is currently Dean of the Faculty of Social Sciences at the University of Ottawa.

SHARON ANNE COOK is a Professor in the Faculty of Education and also teaches in the Department of History at the University of Ottawa. She is the former director of the Anglophone Teacher Education Program and has taught history pedagogy in the program for fifteen years. She is a Canadian historian of women, education and moral movements. Along with Lorna R. McLean and Kate O'Rourke, she co-edited *Framing Our Past: Canadian Women's History in the Twentieth Century* (2001), which won the book prize from the Canadian Association of Educational Foundations in 2002.

ANN B. DENIS is a Professor in the Department of Sociology at the University of Ottawa. Her research interests focus on the intersection of gender, ethnicity/race and social class, women's paid and unpaid work, and the use of the Internet. Her publications include *Femmes de carrière. Carrières de femmes* (with C. Coderre and C. Andrew, 1999); "Rethinking Development from a Feminist Perspective" in *Advances in Gender Research* (2001); "Nouvelles technologies d'information et de communication: Accès et usage chez les jeunes filles et garçons francophones en Ontario" (with M. Ollivier) in *Revue Francophonies d'Amérique* (2002); "Women and Globalization in the Economic North and South" in *Global Shaping and Its Alternatives* (2003); and "A Gendered Analysis of the Impact on Women's Work of Changing State Policies in Barbados" in *Living at the Borderlines: Issues of Caribbean Sovereignty and Development* (2003).

SYLVIE FRIGON is a PhD graduate from the Institute of Criminology at the University of Cambridge, UK. Since 1993 she has been a Professor in the Department of Criminology at the University of Ottawa. In 1995 she founded the "Women Studies Series" at the University of Ottawa Press and was series editor until 2000. Her research areas include the reconfigurations of the carceral system for women in Canada, the health of women in prison, the construction of "violent" women in the media and in cinema, and the social and professional (re)integration of women in conflict with the law. She has co-edited with Michèle Kérisit a collection of essays entitled *Du corps des femmes: Contrôles, surveillances et résistances* (2000), and edited a special issue on women and confinement in Canada for the journal *Criminologie* entitled "Femmes, enfermemement au Canada : Une décennie de réformes" (2002). Her most recent book is *L'homicide conjugal au féminin : D'hier à aujourd'hui* (2003).

RUBY HEAP is Professor of History and Associate Dean at the Faculty of Graduate and Post-doctoral Studies. She teaches courses in Women's History and in the History of Education. She is the author of several articles and book chapters on the history of women's education and on the history of women's professions in Canada. She has co-edited, with Alison Prentice, thecollection *Gender and Education in Canada* (1991), which received the Founders' Prize of the Canadian History of Education Association. She is currently pursuing research on the history of women in engineering. She is the co-editor of a forthcoming collection on professional education in Canada, which will be published by the University of Ottawa Press.

AOUA BOCAR LY-TALL holds a doctorate in sociology from the University of Ottawa, where she is a Research Associate at the Institute of Women's Studies. She is founding president of the "Femmes Africaines, Horizon 2015" network. She is also a founding member of the Inter-African Committee on Traditional Practices Affecting the Health of Women and Children and served with this body as the first Secretary General of the Senegalese (national) Committee of the IAC (1984–1989). In this capacity, she partici-pated in the United Nations Conference on Women in Nairobi in 1985. She has received the 2000 Woman of Distinction Award for Voluntary, Community and Humanitarian Service from the YWCA Foundation of Montreal, and the Flambeau d'excellence in 2001 by the Groupe de reconnaissance communautaire.

ANDREA MARTINEZ is Director of the Institute of Women's Studies and an Associate Professor in the Department of Communication at the University of Ottawa, and is the co-ordinator of the Inter-American Training Network on Women and Development. She is the author of *Scientific Knowledge about Television Violence* (1992) and *How Do We Curb Violence in the Media?* (1995). More recently, she has written a number of articles on the issues of Aboriginal women, new technologies and globalization; cyberspace pornography; trafficking women and the impacts of Canadian immigration policies; and has co-edited with Michèle Ollivier *La tension tradition-modernité: Construits socioculturels de femmes autochtones, francophones et migrantes* (2001).

DONATILLE MUJAWAMARIYA, PhD, is an Associate Professor in the Faculty of Education at the University of Ottawa and a regular researcher with the Centre interuniversitaire sur la formation et la profession enseignante (CRIFPE). Her teaching and research inter-ests include teacher education, the pedagogy of teaching science, multicultural/anti-racist education and women in science. Her work has been published in a wide range of journals, including *Recherches féministes, Canadian Ethnic Studies Journal* and *Revue de Science de l'Éducation.* She edited the anthology *L'intégration des minorités visibles et ethnoculturelles dans la profession enseignante: Récits d'expériences, enjeux et perspectives* (2002), and is co-editor of *L'intégration des "minorités" et nouveaux espaces interculturels* (2003).

MICHELLE MULLEN, MHP, PhD, is Assistant Professor of Pediatrics in the Faculty of Medicine and of Women's Studies in the Faculty of Social Sciences at the University of Ottawa. She is also Consultant Bioethicist to the Children's Hospital of Eastern Ontario. Her current research interests traverse feminist bioethics and methods, public policy, genetics, pediatrics and women's health. She publishes across a broad range of scholarly venues, including commentary for the *American Journal of Bioethics*. She is a member and ethics designate of the Institutional Advisory Board of the Gender and Health Institute of the Canadian Institutes of Health Research.

MICHÈLE OLLIVIER, PhD, is Assistant Professor of Sociology at the University of Ottawa. She is co-founder of the PAR-L Research Network, a feminist electronic network of individuals and organizations interested in research and action on policy issues of concern to women in Canada. She has published articles and books on women's access to and use of information and communication technologies, popular music in Quebec, the transformation of tastes in contemporary societies, sociological theories of status and feminist research methodologies.

TINA O'TOOLE is a Post-doctoral Fellow at the English Department, National University of Ireland, Cork, where she is preparing a monograph on the New Woman of the 1890s. Between 1999 and 2002, she was project researcher on the HEA Women and Irish Society Project (www.ucc.ie/wisp), and in 2002, the Bank of Montreal Visiting Scholar in Women's Studies at the University of Ottawa, where she carried out comparative research at the Canadian Women's Movement Archives. Her research interests focus on Victorian and Edwardian feminist literature and activism, Irish women's/LGBT writing and the Irish Women's Movement 1970 to the present. She was a founding member of L.Inc in Cork (www.linc.ie).

AGATHA SCHWARTZ is Associate Professor of German at the Department of Modern Languages and Literature, University of Ottawa. Her specialization is turn-of-the-century Austrian and Hungarian literature and culture. She has published a number of articles on Robert Musil and on the women's movement and women authors of the period. More recently, she has researched contemporary literature from Austria and East Central Europe. She is the author of *Utopie, Utopismus und Dystopie in "Der Mann ohne Eigenschaften": Robert Musils utopisches Konzept aus geschlechtsspezifischer Sicht* (1996); co-editor with Marlene Kadar of "Women and Hungary: Reclaiming Images and Histories," Special Volume of *Hungarian Studies Review* (1999); and co-editor with Fernando de Diego of *Rethinking Violence and Patriarchy for the New Millennium* (2002).

CHRISTABELLE SETHNA is an Assistant Professor jointly appointed to the Institute of Women's Studies and the Faculty of Education at the University of Ottawa. She is a historian of education who researches in the history of sex education, birth control and population control. Her publications include "Wait Till Your Father Gets Home: Absent Fathers, Working Mothers and Delinquent Daughters in Ontario during World War II" in *Family Matters: Papers in Post-Confederation Canadian Family History* (1998); "The Cold War and the Sexual Chill: Freezing Girls Out of Sex Education," *Canadian Woman Studies/les cahiers de la femme* (1998); "High School Confidential: RCMP Surveillance of Secondary Student Activists" in *Whose National Security? Canadian State Surveillance and the Creation of Enemies* (2000); "The Social Purity Movement" in *The Oxford Companion to Canadian History* (forthcoming); and *The Facts of Life: Sex Education, Venereal Disease and the Moral Regulation of Children, 1900-1950* (forthcoming).

LESLIE REGAN SHADE, PhD, is an Associate Professor of Communication Studies at Concordia University. She was a Professor with the University of Ottawa's Department of Communication from 1998–2003. Her research and teaching interests focus on the social, policy and ethical aspects of information and communication technologies. Since 1993, she has written widely on gender and the Internet, with a focus on access issues, feminist uses of the Internet and the increasing corporatization of the Internet for women. Her work has been widely published in such journals as *The Information Society*, *Feminist Collections* and *The Canadian Journal of Communication*. Her book publications include *Gender and the Social Construction of the Internet* (2002), *Mediascapes: New Patterns in Canadian Communication* (co-edited with Paul Attallah, 2002), and *Civic Discourse in Canada: A Cacophony of Voices* (co-edited with Sherry Ferguson, 2002). She is currently working on a book about Internet policy and on a research project that looks at how youth are using the Internet.

MERYN STUART is a nurse historian who writes and teaches in the areas of the social history of nursing, healthcare and women as healthcare professionals at the University of Ottawa. She was the Associate Director of the Institute of Women's Studies from 2001–2003, managing its collaborative graduate program and facilitating interdisciplinary feminist research links. She was co-author of the *Nurses of all Nations: A History of the International Council of Nurses, 1899–1999* (1999) and is working on a book exploring the history of military nursing in the First World War.

CYNTHIA TOMAN, RN, PhD, is a historian and Assistant Professor with the University of Ottawa School of Nursing. She is consultant to the Canadian Museum of Civilization and Canadian War Museum for upcoming exhibits on nursing history. Her chapter in this collection is based on her doctoral thesis, "Officers and Ladies: Canadian Nursing Sisters, Women's Work, and the Second World War." Research interests include the history of nursing, medical technology, women's history and clinical research related to patient education and cardiovascular nursing.

ELIZABETH TURCOTTE is a PhD candidate in Women's History at Carleton University, Ottawa. Her research interests are communications theory, and the state and social construction of women's identity in nineteenth-century Canada. She has published two other articles on women's homespun production.

CORA VOYAGEUR, PhD, is a sociologist at the University of Calgary. Her research interests focus on politics, employment and economic development issues of Aboriginal women in Canada. She has conducted extensive community-initiated research with many First Nations and Aboriginal organizations and is currently completing research on female chiefs in Canada. During her academic career she has published twenty-five refereed academic journal articles and book chapters; written thirty technical reports; and been an invited speaker at more than forty conferences in Canada, the United States, Britain and Europe. She is a member of the Athabasca Chipewyan First Nation from Fort Chipewyan, Alberta.